BRUCE
Springsteen

The
Rolling Stone
Files

BRUCE
Springsteen

The
Rolling Stone
Files

The Ultimate Compendium
of Interviews, Articles, Facts
and Opinions
from the Files of ROLLING STONE

BY

THE EDITORS

OF

Rolling Stone

INTRODUCTION BY PARKE PUTERBAUGH

 HYPERION

NEW YORK

Portions previously published in ROLLING STONE magazine

Library of Congress Cataloging-in-Publication Data

Bruce Springsteen : the Rolling Stone files : the ultimate compendium of interviews,
    articles, facts, and opinions from the files of Rolling Stone / by the editors of Rolling
    Stone : with an introduction by Parke Puterbaugh.
        p.   cm.
      ISBN 0-7868-8153-4
      1. Springsteen, Bruce—Interviews.   2. Rock musicians—United States—Interviews.
    3. Springsteen, Bruce—Criticism and interpretation.   I. Rolling Stone (San Francisco,
    Calif.)
    ML420.S77A5   1996
    782.42166'092—dc20
    [B]   95-47362
              CIP
              MN

FIRST EDITION
10 9 8 7 6 5 4 3 2 1

Design by Robert Bull Design

'ENTS

FOREWORD

I T'S HARD TO BELIEVE there was a time when the name Bruce Springsteen was not known all over the world. The Springsteen exhibit at
the Rock and Roll Hall of Fame and Museum brings back those early
days, however. Alongside the Steel Mill poster and the original handwrit-
ten lyrics to "Jungleland," "Tenth Avenue Freeze-Out" and "Meeting
Across the River," there's an undated letter from Bruce to a Swedish fan.
"I didn't know people in Sweden knew my music," he wrote, thanking the
fan for her letter asking for lyrics to an unnamed song—probably one from
his first or second album. Mostly a Northeast club phenomenon at the time,
the New Jersey native began winning raves from ROLLING STONE as early
as 1973. Also that year, none other than Lester Bangs reviewed Springsteen's
debut, *Greetings From Asbury Park, N.J.*, for ROLLING STONE. Over the next
decade, as Springsteen's cult following exploded into worldwide Bossmania, ROLLING STONE was there every step of the way.

Bruce Springsteen: The ROLLING STONE *Files* compiles this wealth of editorial coverage from the pages of ROLLING STONE. Included are those very
first critiques and stories from 1973, as well as every concert and album review up to the mid-Nineties. Here, too, are the classic interviews with
Springsteen, as well as in-depth profiles by such Springsteen cognoscenti as
Dave Marsh. In addition, we've compiled Springsteen's numerous wins in
the annual ROLLING STONE readers and critics polls and included an assortment of Random Notes, news stories and interviews with E Street Band
members.

Former ROLLING STONE senior editor and longtime contributing editor Parke Puterbaugh has written an insightful overview of Springsteen's life,
career and work, from *Asbury Park* to "Dead Man Walkin'," the Oscar-
nominated title song to Tim Robbins' 1995 film. He also has compiled a
comprehensive Springsteen discography that includes albums, EPs, singles,
promotional and audiophile releases and Springsteen appearances on other
artists' LPs, anthologies and soundtracks.

A number of people helped to make *Bruce Springsteen: The* ROLLING
STONE *Files* possible. Kudos to Parke Puterbaugh and all the very talented
writers whose work appears here, as well as the endeavors of twenty-

something years' worth of Random Notes scribes. Many thanks to Shawn Dahl, Greg Emmanuel, Fred Woodward, Jann S. Wenner, Kent Brownridge and John Lagana at ROLLING STONE, and Laurie Abkemeier, Brian DeFiore, Bob Miller and Victor Weaver at Hyperion. Much appreciation also goes to Sarah Lazin, Marianne Burke, Jamie Chesler, Joe Tirella and Craig Inciardi. Most of all, thanks to Bruce Springsteen whose powerful music, evocative lyrics and amazing performances have made us all prisoners of rock & roll.

Holly George-Warren, Editor
Rolling Stone Press
April 1996

PARKE PUTERBAUGH

INTRODUCTION

THERE'S A PHOTOGRAPH of Bruce Springsteen taken in 1973 that triggers a flood of memories and cuts right to the heart of his appeal. It has run in ROLLING STONE several times, once as a two-page spread that served to introduce a lengthy mid-Eighties article about Springsteen's roots on the Jersey shore. The picture, shot by David Gahr, depicts a lean and hungry Springsteen standing on the sidewalk in Long Branch, New Jersey, a nondescript beach town that lies directly above Asbury Park. Everything except Springsteen himself appears rundown. Clumps of grass have broken through cracks in the pavement. The businesses that line the block look pretty beat, including The Turntable, a quaintly out-of-date record and stereo store. Nothing in the photo—telephone poles, parking meters, a pile of bikes parked outside a shop, a pole-mounted crown advertising some fly-by-night business—stands straight. The entire town appears to be listing, as if its economic and spiritual collapse is only a matter of time.

Amid this portrait of faded glory stands Springsteen. His hands are clasped to his chest, and his face is upturned in an expression of blissful contentment and homeboy pride. Happily surrounded by the beautiful-loser squalor of a boardwalk town that's seen better days, he looks like a man whose Converse-clad feet instinctively know their way around these streets. From his smile one intuits the conviction that there's a grimy beauty about these streets that, if nothing else, is real. You can almost feel the salt spray in the air, the heat of a summer's day at the shore, the cheap but alluring aromas of the not-too-distant boardwalk, and the way all these things worked to fire the imagination of Bruce Springsteen.

Over time, the home truths that Springsteen internalized and turned into songs would trigger a mass awakening in the rock & roll audience. He has given people the ears and eyes with which to apprehend their own surroundings—to recognize, to celebrate, to criticize and, most important, to understand. Springsteen is arguably the first credible rock & roll figure who didn't draw a divisive demographic line in the sand. Instead, his songs—

together with his rambling, spoken intros from the concert stage—endeavored to reconnect generations in the wake of the celebrated "gap" that was
such a fractious feature of the Sixties. Vivid recollections of hard times on
the home front, while not downplayed, were typically refracted through a
sympathetic and forgiving lens.

At the same time, Springsteen directly addressed and shaped the dreams
of an anxious generation feeling its way through turbulent, uncertain but
hopeful times. Broadly stated, his work can be seen as an ongoing commentary on the status of the American dream as an attainable reality. Over
the years, his outlook has passed from sky's-the-limit optimism ("Show a
little faith, there's magic in the night," he sang in "Thunder Road") to the
ominous onset of what he metaphorically termed "darkness on the edge of
town." In its later chapters, Springsteen's songwriting has taken on a more
personal and intimate tone; the darkness having lifted somewhat, he's tentatively identified his saving grace in the "human touch" of friends and family. For all of his hard-won happiness, however, Springsteen knows that none
of us (including himself) is ever really home free in the home of the free,
and his writing continues to zero in on an unfortunate truth: namely, that
darkness has become a constant and enduring feature of the psychological
landscape in latter-day American society. He remains a sobersided realist who
hasn't given up hope—a challenging combination that assures his continued relevance and longevity as a rock & roller.

Let us now rewind back to 1973, the year in which Springsteen's un-
troubled visage was caught gazing beatifically across the streets of his Jersey
Shore anti-paradise in the aforementioned photograph. That was the year
in which his second album, *The Wild, the Innocent & the E Street Shuffle,* was
released. In fact, it appears that he is wearing the same tank top-and-jeans
ensemble on the album's rear jacket photograph. With the evidence in the
grooves of this powerhouse album, it began dawning on critics and fans who
kept their ears to the ground that a new chapter in rock & roll was about
to be written. It can be argued that Springsteen almost single-handedly restored commitment to rock & roll lyrics, passion to rock & roll music and
visionary belief in the notion of rock & roll itself as a cultural phenomenon
capable of moving mountains.

It is impossible to emphasize enough just how bright a light Bruce
Springsteen shone during the doldrums of the early Seventies. At the time
he entered the picture, rock & roll was in a slump, burned out from years
of being under siege from the rock-hating establishment and undone by its
own bad habits. Excitement had given way to tedium as many key Sixties
acts had gone AWOL or died; for the most part, those who survived hadn't

yet found their footing in the new decade. Some never would. By the early Seventies, the blues-based rock that came out of England in the late Sixties via such bands as Cream had curdled into rank heavy metal a la Black Sabbath and the plebeian hard rock of Grand Funk and their ilk. At the same time, an emerging flock of singer/songwriters and country-rockers began performing in an earnest, low-key style that, however promising, didn't have much to do with rock & roll.

Into the breach stepped Bruce Springsteen, a born rock & roller who blended brains and volume, sweat and sensitivity. While the niche he filled seems obvious in hindsight, the talent he brought to his calling was extraordinary. And though his meteoric rise in the wake of *Born to Run*'s 1975 release made him appear to be something of an overnight success to readers of *Time* and *Newsweek,* nothing could be further from the truth. Springsteen's career had been a long time in the making when America's major news weeklies decided to plaster him on their covers during the same week in October 1975. As odd as it seems, Springsteen didn't make his first appearance on the cover of ROLLING STONE—which had been writing about him since the release of his 1973 debut album, *Greetings From Asbury Park, N.J.,* and didn't bite for the media feeding frenzy at mid-decade—until August 1978.

My own introduction to Springsteen began with the release of *Greetings From Asbury Park, N.J.* in January 1973. An English major at the University of North Carolina in Chapel Hill, I divided my time between classrooms, record stores and downtown watering holes, often with a rock journal spread out before me: *Creem, Crawdaddy, Melody Maker* and, of course, ROLLING STONE. In the beginning, Springsteen's share of press attention was completely out of proportion to his record sales. That's because Bruce Springsteen was a music writer's dream—a wordy lyric poet who played soulful rock & roll as if nothing else mattered. He was an original who nonetheless managed to evoke powerful associations with some of the biggest names in the rock pantheon, such as Bob Dylan, Elvis Presley, Otis Redding and Van Morrison. He provided continuity and renewal at a point when rock & roll was sorely in need of both.

My attention was certainly piqued by all the spilled ink. In a disenchanting period during which most of the excitement and fresh ideas were coming from overseas glam-rockers—e.g., David Bowie, Roxy Music and Mott the Hoople—all this talk about some guy from New Jersey who wrote more words than his songs could handle and who put on an amazing live show sounded intriguing. The early buzz pegged him as a "new Dylan." In fact, Springsteen was among a four-pack of would-be "new Dylans" that included Loudon Wainwright III, John Prine and Elliott Murphy. This comparison did a disservice both to the emerging artists and the "old Dylan," who was very much alive and well and didn't need replacing. But it also provided a useful reference point for rock fans trying to get a handle on this brainy new brood, whose roots helped anchor them in a rootless, amorphous decade.

Though *Greetings From Asbury Park, N.J.* appeared to come out of nowhere, it was actually the debut of an artist who had been making music for nearly ten years. Much of Springsteen's early history eventually seeped out in articles and interviews that have run in ROLLING STONE over the years. Certainly, his experiences as a struggling rocker on the Jersey shore provided grist for the character-filled songs on his first several albums. The litany of early band names will be familiar to those who closely follow Springsteen: the Rogues, the Castiles, Earth, Child, Steel Mill, Dr. Zoom and the Sonic Boom, the Bruce Springsteen Band. But the fact most worth noting about the young Bruce Springsteen is that from the beginning there was no question in his mind that he was destined to play rock & roll for a living.

His onstage battle cry—"I'm just a prisoner of rock & roll"—was a statement borne out in the plans he made from adolescence onward. In his very first profile in ROLLING STONE—"Bruce Springsteen: It's Sign Up a Genius Month," in April 1973—he admitted that he'd only briefly held one "real" job (as a gardener) and that he quickly aborted a halfhearted attempt at higher education. The would-be scholar bailed out of a New Jersey community college after the school's "nutty doctor" (his term for psychologist) told him that other students were complaining about his behavior. Said Springsteen, with dry, understated wit: "Well, I figured there was no use hanging around there, so I split."

A total bust as a student and wage slave, he was left with no alternative and nothing else in life he wanted to do but play music. Caught up in the feverish immediacy of rock & roll, the normally reticent Springsteen came alive. "Rock & roll was the only thing I ever liked about myself," he once said. It was his ticket out of a dead-end life in Freehold, the inland town where he grew up, and Asbury Park, the decrepit seaside "resort" where he lived after his parents moved to California in 1969. In return for the escape hatch it provided him, Springsteen vowed to hold up his end of the bargain. As he told journalist Robert Hilburn, "That's what rock & roll is—a promise, an oath. It's about being as true as you can at any particular moment."

As unlikely as it may seem, variety-show impresario Ed Sullivan played a key role in steering Springsteen onto his career path. It was Elvis Presley's overheated appearance on Sullivan's prime-time Sunday-night TV show in 1957 that motivated the awestruck youngster to ask for a guitar. But it was the Beatles' debut on the same show seven years later that inspired him to actually practice the instrument. Springsteen took it from there, much to the consternation of his father, who peppered the family's small house in Freehold with his nightly mantras: *"Turn down that goddamn guitar! Turn down that goddamn stereo!"* But Springsteen wouldn't be deterred or denied. Later on, his prolific work habits managed to test even his band mates' limits. Recollecting his days with Springsteen in the bands Child and Steel Mill, longtime E Street Band keyboardist Danny Federici told Robert Santelli in the fanzine *Backstreets:* "At the time, Bruce was incredibly energetic. He was writing an unbelievable amount of songs—five or ten a day. And they were epics. . . . The most amazing thing was that one night, say a Friday, we'd do a thirty-song set. The next night, Saturday, we'd do an entirely different thirty-song set—all written that week. We rehearsed every day."

In early 1972, Springsteen made the fateful decision to sign with manager/producers Mike Appel and Jimmy Cretecos. Prior to signing Springsteen, the duo made their biggest mark as a songwriting team who'd penned a 1971 Top Ten hit, "Doesn't Somebody Want to Be Wanted," for teenybopper faves the Partridge Family. At the time Appel and Cretecos entered his life, Springsteen was writing so compulsively that he had little time to think of anything else. The brash, take-charge Appel, a former marine, managed Springsteen as if he were a heavyweight prizefighter—the best in the business, at that. His cocky faith in Springsteen's talent wound up opening doors that hastened Springsteen's ascent and even, one could argue, sent it into orbit. But at what cost? Springsteen would later ponder that question during a protracted legal battle over the terms of the contracts that he recklessly and innocently signed with Appel and Cretecos' Laurel Canyon Ltd., including a critical one with Columbia Records (whose terms were grossly unfavorable to the artist) impetuously ratified by Springsteen on the hood of a car.

For several years, though, it was a productive match. Appel's first major coup was landing his client an audition with John Hammond Sr. A legendary executive and talent finder at Columbia Records, Hammond had scouted and signed such artists as Billie Holiday, Count Basie, Lester Young, Robert Johnson, Pete Seeger, Aretha Franklin and Bob Dylan. To that list, thanks to the persistence of Mike Appel, the name Bruce Springsteen was added in 1973. In setting up the audition, Appel goaded Hammond by saying, "You're the guy who discovered Bob Dylan, huh? Well, we want to find out if that was just luck or if you really have ears."

Springsteen informally auditioned for Hammond on May 2nd, 1972, in his Columbia Records office in New York. "So I'm sitting in the corner with my old beat-up guitar when all of a sudden Mike jumps up and starts hyping John Hammond," he told ROLLING STONE the following year. "I couldn't believe it. I had to start laughing. John Hammond told me later that he was ready to hate me. But he asked me to do a song, so I did 'It's Hard to Be a Saint in the City.' " So taken was Hammond by this budding bard from Jersey that he told ROLLING STONE, "He's much further along, much more developed than Bobby [Bob Dylan] was when he came to me."

Springsteen performed a dozen songs at his official audition, held a day later at CBS Studios. With Hammond announcing each take, Springsteen took turns accompanying himself on acoustic guitar and piano. No slouch on the keyboard, he struck an especially evocative mood with the stark chordings of "Jazz Musician." (Perusers of album-jacket credits will note that Springsteen played piano on "Spirit in the Night," one of his best-loved and most enduring songs.) Of the twelve songs performed at the Hammond audition, only five wound up on *Greetings From Asbury Park, N.J.,* recorded just a month or so later—an indication of his tremendous backlog and output as a songwriter. The still-unreleased Springsteen originals from that audition include: "Jazz Musician," "If I Was the Priest," "Arabian Nights," "Two Hearts in True Waltz Time," "Street Queen," "Southern Son" and "Cowboys of the Sea."

To this canon can be added a bottomless trove of demos recorded between 1972 and 1974 at 914 Sound Studios in Blauvelt, New York, under the aegis of Appel and Cretecos. Twenty-three of these lost originals would be released two decades later as *The Early Years,* a double CD issued in Europe on Early Records (and subsequently squelched by a Springsteen-launched lawsuit). Indeed, one could devote an entire book to all the Springsteen songs that *haven't* seen the light of day.

Greetings From Asbury Park, N.J. was reviewed in ROLLING STONE a half-year after its release by the redoubtable Lester Bangs, the savagely comic and charismatic rock journalist whose forte was album reviews. In retrospect, Bangs was off the mark in proclaiming Springsteen "a P.F. Sloan for 1973"—a disparaging reference to the topical, semi-obscure Sixties folk rocker who wrote "Eve of Destruction." Bangs paid homage to Springsteen's potential later in the review, however: "What makes Bruce totally unique and cosmically surfeiting is his words. Hot damn, what a passel o' verbiage!" And he presciently concluded: "Springsteen is a bold new talent with more than a mouthful to say. . . . Watch for him."

The album didn't make *Billboard*'s Top 200 Albums chart until it rode in on the formidable coattails of *Born to Run* in 1975. All the same, it served to ignite a slow-burning groundswell of support for Springsteen. How could a music fan reared and schooled on Dylan *not* appreciate the "Subterranean Homesick Blues"–style word-bath that filled *Greetings From Asbury Park, N.J.*'s nine songs? Springsteen cast some light on his mind-set at the time in an interview with Robert Hilburn: "I got a lot of things out in that first album. I let out an incredible amount at once—a million things in each song. They were written in half-hour, fifteen-minute blasts. I don't know where they came from. . . . Most of them were just jets, a real energy situation."

Though it's not a perfect record by any means, *Greetings* contains several of Springsteen's signature songs: notably "Blinded by the Light," "Growin' Up," "Spirit in the Night" and "It's Hard to Be a Saint in the City." In an inspired bit of packaging, the cover depicts the brightly colored vacationer's postcard that provides the album's title. Musically, *Greetings* was a rootsy stew that tipped its hat to Van Morrison, Dylan and the Band and was set to an R&B backbeat by way of Stax/Volt and Atlantic Records' soul clan. By contrast to his solo audition, this was a band album, featuring backup by a number of veteran musicians plucked from the Jersey Shore bar-band gauntlet: saxman Clarence Clemons, bassist Garry Tallent, keyboardist David Sancious and drummer Vini "Mad Dog" Lopez. Conspicuously absent, however, was Danny Federici, whose roots in Springsteen's music extend back the farthest, and who would become a cornerstone of his E Street Band by the time of his next record, *The Wild, the Innocent & the E Street Shuffle.*

The first show attributed to "Bruce Springsteen and the E Street Band" was performed in York, Pennsylvania, on November 12, 1972. During this time, Springsteen was busy cementing his reputation as a not-to-be-missed live performer. He continued to build a large fan base all over New Jersey and in Richmond, Virginia—an early outpost of Bruce-mania dating back to Steel Mill days—while venturing into some larger cities in early 1973. Everywhere he played, Springsteen garnered stellar reviews from breathless critics who withheld no superlatives. Some of the musicians he opened for during this stretch probably had a few choice words of their own, as he proved a tough—if not impossible—act to follow. (Just ask Canadian pop singer Anne Murray, whose manager insisted that Springsteen open a 1974 show in Central Park, only to watch 90 percent of the crowd leave after his set.)

Springsteen himself, with his managers' support and approval, routinely turned down opening-act offers, preferring to be the only act in a club or small hall to sharing the bill in a big one. The final straw for Springsteen was a thankless warm-up spot on an arena tour with the jazz-rock band Chicago, which commenced in the backwater military town of Fayetteville, North Carolina, on May 30, 1973. As a result of opening for others in cavernous environs, during which Springsteen's lengthy set was whittled down to a paltry half-hour, he swore off large arenas for three years, until his surging popularity with *Born to Run* left him with no plausible alternative. It was a risky move for a relative unknown, but one he passionately defended. "We didn't start selling records until we started playing smaller places," Springsteen noted in 1975. "It's a slow process, but I was *always* certain."

The door to greater recognition opened a little wider with the release of *The Wild, the Innocent & the E Street Shuffle,* which came out in November 1973. It was his second album in less than a year, a fact that did not go unnoticed by critics who increasingly honed in on his rising, uncontainable talent. "Springsteen is growing as a writer of music as well as of words," observed Ken Emerson in his ROLLING STONE review of the album. "The best of his new songs dart and swoop from tempo to tempo and from genre to genre, from hellbent-for-leather rock to luscious schmaltz to what is almost recitative. There is an occasional weak spot or an awkward transition, but for the most part it works spectacularly."

I personally rate *The Wild, the Innocent & the E Street Shuffle* as my all-time favorite Bruce Springsteen album. It's not that he hasn't subsequently written better songs or done more "important" work, and in a pinch I might also give the nod to *Tunnel of Love* or *Born to Run*. But for me it's the atmosphere of the album that will never be surpassed: the closely observed, carefree canvas it paints of a place and time when the fires of late adolescence and early adulthood still burned brightly. Despite the piling on of minute details—names, places and events—you didn't have to come from Asbury Park to appreciate the dreams and yearnings he salutes; anyplace in America would do for that. Ultimately, the album is more about a state of mind than the state of New Jersey, even though that was its undeniable place of origin. "The stuff I write is what I live with," he told ROLLING STONE in 1974. "The stories are all around me. I just put 'em down. They're all true. Even the names."

A wildly romantic album full of long songs that never seem to go on for *too* long, *The Wild, the Innocent & the E Street Shuffle* is the second in a trilogy of what I regard as Springsteen's "celebratory" albums. It is also, to this day, the most loose and unrestrained the E Street Band has ever been on record. Bach-trained, jazz-inclined keyboardist David Sancious and Clarence Clemons, blowing sax in a style that recalled King Curtis by way of James Brown's Famous Flames, played for all they were worth. There are only seven songs on the album; the shortest is the four-and-a-half-minute opening track, "The E Street Shuffle," while the longest is the album-closing "New York City Serenade," which runs for ten minutes. Between these bookends lie some of Springsteen's most memorable compositions: the gorgeous, evocative "4th of July, Asbury Park (Sandy)"; the ferocious, jazz-tinged R&B stomper "Kitty's Back"; and the rousing, anthemic "Rosalita (Come Out Tonight)," a suite-like song brimming with exuberance. In it, Springsteen, assuming the autobiographical role of an aspiring rock & roller, trumps his girlfriend's disapproving dad with the lines: "Your papa says he knows that I don't have any money / You tell him this is his last chance to get his daughter in a fine romance / 'Cause the record company, Rosie, just gave me a big advance!"

Dad might not have been all that impressed to learn that *The Wild, the Innocent & the E Street Shuffle* sold only 50,000 copies in its first year, once again failing to dent *Billboard*'s Top 200. Still, it's proven its mettle over the long haul, eventually attaining platinum certification (a million copies sold). Placing fifty-first on ROLLING STONE's annotated list of critics' Top 100 Albums of the Last Twenty Years (appearing in the August 27th, 1987 issue), it was accorded this accolade: "Springsteen proved himself a poet with this album and paved the way for his national breakout."

That national breakout came in 1975 with *Born to Run,* a creative milestone in rock's evolution. Not surprisingly, it wasn't an easy album to put together. The project consumed and exhausted all who worked on it—producers, engineers, musicians—as Springsteen reached for the stars. In his own words, speaking at length to John Rockwell in ROLLING STONE, the experience of making *Born to Run* was "a total wipeout. It was a devastating thing, the hardest thing I ever did." Sessions for the album ran from June 1974 to July 1975. Every song on it, whether long or short, was an epic, from "Born to Run" and "Thunder Road" to the lengthy side-closers "Backstreets" and "Jungleland." Densely layered in the grandly overdubbed rock-orchestral style of Sixties producer Phil Spector, *Born to Run* charged out of the gate with a desperate challenge in its opening track, "Thunder Road," whose protagonist begs: "We got one last chance to make it real / To trade in these wings on some wheels." And so begins an album that is intensely preoccupied with the notion of flight from boredom and entrapment to a promised land that has more to do with the journey than the arrival.

The album was given its due in an extraordinarily praiseworthy review by Greil Marcus, the latest in a nearly unanimous procession of heavyweight critics to offer benediction. "It is a magnificent album that pays off on every bet ever placed on him," wrote Marcus in ROLLING STONE. "And it should crack his future wide open." That it did. Just prior to its release, Springsteen played a now-legendary five-night stand at the Bottom Line, a 400-seat showcase club in Greenwich Village. Performing two sets a night, each lasting about two hours, Springsteen reached a collective audience of 5,000 during his stay. At least a thousand of them were Columbia Records staffers, as the label rallied support for *Born to Run* by exposing its promotional and publicity staffs to the phenomenon of Springsteen in concert.

I can truthfully claim that the first time I saw Bruce Springsteen was at the Bottom Line. That is not to say I saw him perform. As luck would have it, I made a late-summer visit to New York City that coincided with Springsteen's Bottom Line stand. One night I waited in line, to no avail, in hopes of lucking into a standing-room ticket to the early show. This is where I first saw Springsteen, who climbed out of a car and stood on the corner of West Fourth and Mercer Streets for a moment, not ten feet away, before entering the club to make rock & roll history. Dave Marsh, an early Springsteen booster, had this to say about Bruce and the band in a review of the Bottom Line shows for ROLLING STONE: "Springsteen is everything that has been claimed for him—a magical guitarist, singer, writer, rock & roll rejuvenator—but the E Street Band has nearly been lost in the shuffle. Which is ridiculous, because this group may very well be the great American rock & roll band."

The E Street Band's classic configuration was fixed by the time of the 1975 Bottom Line shows. The definitive E Street lineup consisted of keyboardists Danny Federici and Roy Bittan (the latter a recent addition), guitarist Steve Van Zandt (who defected from Southside Johnny and the Asbury Jukes), sax player Clarence Clemons, bassist Garry Tallent and drummer Max Weinberg (another new recruit). In concert the group gelled into a tight rock & roll machine that reacted intuitively to Springsteen's cues. From frantic frat-rock covers to quasi-orchestral epics, they could handle it all—and for long hours every night, with "the Boss" throwing them curve balls all the while.

The early show on the third night of the Bottom Line marathon was broadcast over New York's WNEW radio station. Tapes of this two-hour set have traded hands among collectors for years, and for good reason. What you hear is the take-no-prisoners assault of an artist and band playing as if their very lives depended on this one night's performance. Although that claim can be made for just about every show they've ever played, this night was truly exceptional. Dynamically, it ranged from Springsteen's riveting, intimate vocal on "Thunder Road," accompanied only by piano, to an extended volcano of a workout on "Kitty's Back." At the end of it all, the flustered, tongue-tied DJ couldn't even pronounce the band's name correctly: "Bruce Spring*street* and the E *Steen* Band," he babbled over the air.

"It was just overwhelming," drummer Max Weinberg told ROLLING STONE's David Fricke in a 1987 recollection. "My heart would begin to beat so fast. I would get so psyched up, the adrenalin would start to pump in the anticipation of playing. We hit the stage and blew the people back in their chairs."

Added Clarence Clemons: "We would have killed them if we'd stayed at the club any longer."

Another pivotal arrival in the Springsteen camp was Jon Landau. Formerly the editor of the ROLLING STONE record review section, Landau brought a fresh set of ears to the bogged-down, year-long Born to Run sessions. His listed role on the album was coproducer, a credit he shared with Springsteen and Mike Appel; in time, though, he would take over as Springsteen's manager. It all started with an oft-quoted remark made in Landau's review of a May 1974 concert for Boston's Real Paper: "I saw rock & roll future and its name is Bruce Springsteen." Manager Mike Appel couldn't have hoped for a more perfect P.R. statement if he'd written it himself. The scholarly, bespectacled Landau was temperamentally Appel's opposite. His enthusiastic endorsement carried great weight within the critical community precisely because he was not one to idly dash off superlatives. Springsteen had some kind words of his own for Landau, who quit his job at ROLLING STONE to coproduce Born to Run. "We needed an outside perspective," Springsteen told the magazine. "He got things on their feet again. Jon was a super-important figure."

The mid-Seventies were a period of highs and lows for Springsteen. One "high"—or low, depending on how you look at it—was his simultaneous appearance on the covers of Time and Newsweek in October 1975. It was a flukish occurrence largely plotted by Appel, who engineered a brilliant "no cover, no interview" strategy, stealthily pitting the two media giants against each other until both took the bait. Though it was an unprecedented feat for a recording artist with his modest commercial track record, Springsteen was decidedly ambivalent about the mainstream press attention, fearing the hype might destroy all the hard-won gains he'd made with his more deliberate, incremental approach. Fans who had been there from the beginning felt a little let down, too, worrying that they might lose their hero in the gears of the great American hype machine.

Bigger problems than that were brewing internally, however, as Springsteen and Appel squared off in court over the management contracts that had been signed years earlier. It ushered in two years of legal wrangling, during which Springsteen was barred from recording for ten months. In a sense, although he eventually emerged triumphant—having bargained for rights to the songs he'd written but never legally owned—Springsteen would never quite be the same. There would forever be a greater play of light and shadows in his music, and at least a few subsequent albums—*Darkness on the Edge of Town* and *Nebraska*—were engulfed in spectral bleakness. This might be an inevitable consequence of growin' up. But there's no question the lawsuits left their scars.

The legal imbroglio, documented in an investigative ROLLING STONE article by Dave McGee, began in May 1976, when Appel—whose influence on Springsteen was waning as the draconian terms of the now-expired managerial contracts became apparent to Bruce—sought through the New Jersey State Court to have a week's worth of concert revenues held in escrow until he could withdraw his management commission. Springsteen filed a massive suit against Appel on July 27th, 1976, charging fraud, undue influence and breach of trust. Appel responded two days later by seeking an injunction preventing Springsteen and Landau from recording, claiming that only Laurel Canyon Ltd.—Mike Appel and Jimmy Cretecos' management, publishing and production company—could authorize a producer. The injunction successfully kept Springsteen from recording at a time when his career was finally taking off. It also tied him up in court and diverted his attention from songwriting. "I have started countless numbers of songs which I have been unable to develop to their potential for lack of a proper recording opportunity," Springsteen told the court. "Many of these songs will never be finished."

All the while, Springsteen funneled songs to other artists. Fellow Jerseyites Southside Johnny and the Asbury Jukes were the principal beneficiaries, recording eight songs written or cowritten by Springsteen—nearly a full album's worth of material—on their first three albums, released between 1976 and 1978. (The real prime mover on the Southside recordings, though, was E Street guitarist Miami Steve Van Zandt, who brilliantly produced the albums and wrote many of the songs as well.) Others who benefited from Springsteen's overflow during this time frame included Patti Smith ("Because the Night"), Robert Gordon ("Fire") and Greg Kihn ("Rendezvous").

The tide began to turn when Springsteen retained a new legal team. In a telling piece of testimony delivered at a December 8th, 1977, deposition, Springsteen laid it all on the line: "[Appel's] interest in this action is strictly financial. My interest is my career, which up until now holds the promise of my being able to significantly contribute to, and possibly influence, a generation of music. No amount of money could compensate me if I were to lose this opportunity." In short, he was fighting for control of his songs and his right to make creative decisions on his own behalf. On May 28th, 1977, the two parties settled out of court. All contracts binding Springsteen to Laurel Canyon Ltd. were rescinded; Springsteen won control over his music publishing; and Columbia renegotiated Springsteen's contract directly with him on more favorable terms. Springsteen immediately began work on his fourth album, *Darkness on the Edge of Town*. A year later, in June 1978— nearly three years after *Born to Run*—one of rock's most eagerly anticipated albums was released.

I first saw Springsteen in concert sometime early in this mess, when he and the E Street Band undertook a swing through the South to put the impending "sue me, sue you blues" behind them. This was after the official Born to Run Tour, mind you. ROLLING STONE referred to the thirty-eight-date jaunt as "a strange tour, coming at a time when most major acts are planning Bicentennial blitzes of ballparks and festivals in all the largest cities." The date of March 28th, 1976, remains etched in my mind, as does the venue, Cameron Indoor Stadium at Duke University, in Durham, North Carolina. The concert remains historically notable for two reasons: the 6,000-seat basketball arena was the largest hall Springsteen had played to date (it now seems as intimate as a coffeehouse compared to the football stadiums he filled on the Born in the U.S.A. Tour), and this show reportedly marked the first time he performed every song from *Born to Run*. All I can remember is standing on a folding chair for three hours, blown backwards by a rock & roll force field.

Darkness on the Edge of Town was sparer sounding and more cleanly recorded than *Born to Run*. "I don't think I'll ever go back to the overdub method," Springsteen told Dave Marsh, adding that most of the album was recorded live in the studio. His lyric approach, too, was pared down, aiming at forceful directness rather than a blinding maze of images. And though it initially seemed a downcast record full of characters whose lives were slowly withering away, Springsteen passionately claimed its message was ultimately redemptive: "What it is, it's the characters' commitment," he explained to Dave Marsh. "In the face of all the betrayals, in the face of all the imperfections that surround you in whatever kind of life you lead, it's the characters' refusal to let go of their own humanity, to let go of their own belief in the other side." At the same time, he admitted that there was "a certain loss of innocence—more so than in the other albums."

Not surprisingly, given all the halted momentum and lost time, *Darkness on the Edge of Town* didn't sell as well as *Born to Run*. But the tone of the record may have had something to do with that, too. It was less exultant, with fewer rockers and a cramped aura of diminished expectations that seemed conspicuously out of step with the jovial mood of a nation caught up in a year-long Bicentennial bacchanal. On the road, however, Springsteen reverted to form. A willing prisoner only of rock & roll, he was otherwise a free man now, having been liberated from contractual tyranny, and the 118 shows on the *Darkness* tour rank among his most incendiary. Longtime ROLLING STONE masthead dwellers Paul Nelson and Dave Marsh tracked the tour, returning to file lengthy epistles during which each professed to be literally overwhelmed by the artist's energy and commitment.

Of Springsteen's tireless, selfless and plainly heroic concert efforts, Nelson was struck with this revelation in the middle of "Born to Run": "All of a sudden, I realize that we are making this glorious noise not for the pride of one man but for the power of rock & roll."

Without doubt, Springsteen has taken his responsibility to the audience more seriously than any other performer in rock history. As he put it in a backstage interview with Nelson, "There's just no room to compromise. . . . That's why every night we play a real long time, and we play *real hard*. I want to be able to go home and say I went all the way tonight—and then I went a little further." He concluded: "The whole idea is to deliver what money can't buy."

He also revealed something about his work habits in the same article, explaining why *Darkness on the Edge of Town* took a full year to make. "See, that's the funny thing," he said. "The album took a long time, but most of the songs were written real fast. It was just figuring out what to do with them."

Springsteen's next album—*The River,* released in August 1980—was his most complicated jigsaw puzzle yet, consuming a year and a half of recording sessions, plus "figuring out what to do with them." Throughout 1979, he conceived of a single LP with the working title *The Ties That Bind.* Not wholly satisfied, however, he changed gears in 1980 and decided to expand it into a double album—a twenty-song, four-sided masterpiece entitled *The River.* It was an album that exchanged the conceptual and thematic unity that had been a feature of his previous recordings for a mix of songs and styles that more closely mirrored the paradoxical ups and downs of real life. On the one hand, the album included some of his most lighthearted, upbeat material in years—fiercely playful party rockers like "Sherry Darling," "Ramrod" and "Cadillac Ranch." On the other, he delved into the emotional currents that run beneath the surface, summoning forth an emotional flood of thwarted desires and busted dreams in songs like "Stolen Car," "Independence Day" and "Point Blank."

With *The River,* Springsteen didn't so much resolve as accommodate life's inherent contradictions—which is a sort of answer in itself. As Springsteen told Dave Marsh in his book *Glory Days,* "In a funny way, I felt that I didn't have the center, so what I had to do was to get left and right, in hope that it would create some sort of center—or some sense of center." The album's back-and-forth trajectory is encapsulated in "Hungry Heart" (his first-ever Top Ten hit), sung in the first person by a down-at-the-heels character whose life moves onward "like a river that don't know where it's flowing." The album's episodic unfolding gave it an almost novelistic power. Springsteen relied heavily on metaphors—principally cars, streets and rivers—to describe people caught up in a fitful, unpredictable tide of movement, "going from nowhere to nowhere," as he once put it. Paul Nelson—heir to Landau's title as ROLLING STONE's record review editor—referred to *The River* as Springsteen's "summational record" and noted its use of "jump-cut juxtapositions of mood."

Recorded during the economic downturn of President Jimmy Carter's last year in office and during the "swing to the right" that would propel Ronald Reagan into office the month following its release, *The River* is a premonition of hard times to come, ending with the ominous "Wreck on the Highway." Referring to the sobering title track, Nelson observes: "In 'The River,' there are no idle thoughts about how nice true love might be. Instead, fate and the new Depression shoot the working-class hero and his high school sweetheart (Mary from 'Thunder Road'?) straight between the eyes."

Springsteen's double album consumed half a million dollars in recording costs. Somewhere in the vicinity of ninety songs were written, rehearsed, recorded and/or rejected along the way. Two of the latter—"Be True" and "Held Up Without a Gun"—turned up on the backs of singles, making them Springsteen's first non-LP B sides. *The River* retailed for a not-unreasonable $15.98 and became Springsteen's first album to reach Number One.

At some indiscernible point between *Darkness on the Edge of Town* and *The River,* the mainstream rock audience awoke to Bruce Springsteen. Not only did *The River* outchart its predecessors, but the accompanying 139-date tour saw ticket demand far exceed anything previously experienced. New York's Madison Square Garden was inundated with enough ticket requests for Springsteen to play the 18,000-seat arena for sixteen nights. So it went around the country. Springsteen had his own theory as to why this was true, telling ROLLING STONE's Fred Schruers: "The last tour . . . every single night in every town, the band played very hard. And people, I think they just remembered. They remembered, and this time everybody told their friends, 'You just gotta come down to the show.' "

Once again, Springsteen delivered. The shows were now running for three and a half hours, with an intermission, during which an average of thirty songs were played. It was a strange phenomenon: The more Springsteen sang about alienation, the more people turned out to listen. His marathon concert rituals became a way of overcoming alienation, of forging a larger sense of community, however fleetingly, in increasingly depressing, isolated times. One of the tour highlights was his six-night stand at New Jersey's Brendan Byrne Arena (a.k.a. the Meadowlands), whose construction had just been completed and which Springsteen inaugurated with a series of concerts that amounted to a hero's homecoming.

If it sometimes seemed as if Bruce Springsteen was almost too good to be true, one could find a few nits to pick with his performances on The River Tour. Parts of the show were sluggishly paced; for the first time, there were moments where I felt more restless than riveted at a Springsteen concert. His raps, often centering on strained adolescent relations with his father, occasionally rambled. ROLLING STONE's Christopher Connelly described one night's opening set at the Meadowlands as "curiously lackluster." Paul Nelson asked, in an otherwise rave-filled review of *The River:* "Will we never hear the spring and summer of 'Wild Billy's Circus Story,' '4th of July, Asbury Park (Sandy),' 'Thunder Road' and 'Born to Run' again? Must even the brightest days now be touched by autumnal tones and winter light? Bruce Springsteen isn't an old man yet. Isn't it odd that he's trying so hard to adopt the visions of one?" All of this was food for thought, though not exactly cause for concern.

By the time the tour drew to a close in September 1981, Springsteen had performed to more than a million people. Many a rocker has agonized about how to follow an act like that. Springsteen's answer—*Nebraska,* a haunting, lo-fi album of homemade demos—was surprising, to say the least. The album's review in ROLLING STONE elicited a tributary headline: "Springsteen Delivers His Bravest Record Yet." Steve Pond gave *Nebraska* four and a half stars, hailing it as "a violent, acid-etched portrait of a wounded America that fuels its machinery by consuming its people's dreams." (*Nebraska* was, incidentally, the first Springsteen record to be rated under the magazine's recently implemented "star" system, with five stars being the highest rating.)

The story of how *Nebraska* came to pass is an odd tale indeed. On January 3rd, 1982—less than four months after the end of The River Tour—Springsteen sang more than a dozen despairing, plain-spoken songs he'd recently written into a four-track tape recorder, envisioning his performances as nothing more than home demos. He later tried teaching them to the E

Street Band, but the songs wanted to remain plaintive and unadorned, refusing to yield to full-band arrangements. In the end Springsteen decided that those rough homemade demos could not be improved upon, and so they were released "as is." Putting them out presented technical problems, since he'd carried the tape (without a box) in his pocket for weeks. According to Springsteen, mastering *Nebraska* for LP was so problematic they considered issuing it in cassette form only.

Not surprisingly, *Nebraska* remains Springsteen's lowest-selling album—though, like all the others, it has sold more than a million copies and been certified platinum. Its harrowing character portraits and stark folk settings were not for everyone, and it allowed Springsteen to pull back the reins and reassert a bit more control over his career at a time when it was skyrocketing wildly. It also reflected the mood he was in. "I had a particular time when I felt pretty empty and very isolated, and I suppose that's where some of that record came from," he later reflected. Somewhat unsettlingly, in an interview with ROLLING STONE's Mikal Gilmore six years down the road, he revealed that in his own mind *Nebraska* had less to do with hard times in Reagan's America than many had supposed: "In a funny way, I always considered it my most personal record, because it felt to me, in its tone, the most what my childhood felt like."

If this sketch of Springsteen's life has thus far focused completely on his musical activities—songwriting, album-making and touring—that is because his existence had been almost obsessively dedicated to those things. He'd managed to keep his private life private and was always fairly stingy with interviews, which is one reason why there was never much in the way of extra-musical biography to report about him. All that would change after 1984, when the *Born in the U.S.A.* album and tour catapulted Springsteen to a level of fame few have ever known. Bruce Springsteen, Michael Jackson, Prince, Madonna—this was pop culture's reigning royalty in the 1980s, a decade in which the term *musician* often became interchangeable with (and indistinguishable from) *celebrity,* for better or worse. Springsteen at least came to the party well prepared. In short, he had a great album and a healthy attitude.

Unlike his earliest bout with the big time, Bruce decided that success wasn't necessarily something he was born to run *from*. "I was thirty-five, and I had a real solid sense of myself by that time," Springsteen told ROLLING STONE. "With *Born in the U.S.A.,* I had a chance to relive my 1975 experience when I was calm and completely prepared and went for it. It was like, 'Great. We're selling all those records? Dynamite.' "

Once again, however, assembling the album was grueling. Over half the lineup was recorded in May 1982, prior to the release of *Nebraska*. The rest was culled from sessions that stretched from mid-1982 to early 1984. Even when Springsteen thought the album complete, Landau advised him to add a unifying song and even gave him a list of requirements. Springsteen initially balked but returned three days later having written "Dancing in the Dark," the leadoff single that found him incorporating the then-popular synth-pop sound without unduly diluting his music. That was no small feat, although some purists' eyebrows were raised when the song was turned over to producer/studio whiz Arthur Baker to refashion into a twelve-inch dance remix.

As an album—twelve songs from roughly a hundred worked on over a period of two years—*Born in the U.S.A.* loomed larger than life, much like *Thriller* and *Purple Rain* from the same period. Springsteen seemed ready and willing to advance on all fronts, and if dance remixes and MTV videos were what it took, so be it. The E Street Band hit the road on June 29th, 1984, with a slightly amended lineup. Miami Steve Van Zandt left amicably to pursue a solo career. (Springsteen responded by penning an ode to their friendship, "Bobby Jean," for the album.) He was replaced by guitarist Nils Lofgren, a musician with whom he'd crossed paths even before there was an E Street Band. Patti Scialfa joined the group on vocals and percussion, breaking the E Street Band's gender barrier.

Along with most everything from *Born in the U.S.A.*, Springsteen worked full-band arrangements of songs from *Nebraska*, including "Atlantic City" and "Johnny 99," into the show. Surely, in terms of numbers and the excitement generated, it was the tour of the decade. The American leg of the Born in the U.S.A. Tour concluded in late January 1985 with two nights at Syracuse, New York's 39,000-seat Carrier Dome, the largest audiences of his career. Then he kicked off the European leg of the tour in June with an outdoor show in Ireland attended by 70,000 people. A few weeks before leaving for Europe, Springsteen the rootless roadrunner married actress/model Julianne Phillips.

In the Eighties, numbers—big numbers—were what it was all about, and Bruce obliged with his share of record-setters. *Born in the U.S.A.* has sold fifteen million copies in the States alone, making it Columbia Records' all-time best seller. The fifteen-month tour grossed $80 to $90 million, and the final four shows drew an astounding 330,000 people to the Los Angeles Memorial Coliseum. Springsteen's popularity even had political ramifications. Ronald Reagan—who was then bucking for a second term by peddling an ideological agenda that was the virtual antithesis of everything Springsteen stood for—dropped Springsteen's name into a speech at a September 1984 reelection rally in New Jersey. America's future, said Reagan, "rests in the message of hope, in the songs of a man that so many young Americans admire, New Jersey's own Bruce Springsteen. Helping you make these dreams come true is what this job of mine is all about."

Springsteen's retort, in a ROLLING STONE interview with Kurt Loder: "You see the Reagan reelection ads on TV—you know: 'It's morning in America.' And you say, well, it's not morning in Pittsburgh. It's not morning above 125th Street in New York. It's midnight, and there's a bad moon risin'. And that's why when Reagan mentioned my name in New Jersey, I felt it was another manipulation."

Another issue was the general misreading of the song "Born in the U.S.A." Far from being a flag-waving celebration of the red, white and blue, as some conservative jingoists made it out to be, the song was actually "an agonized, brutal modern-day blues" (Steve Pond's words) about the plight of a Vietnam vet who comes home from the war only to be greeted with indifference and derision. When Chrysler Motors chairman Lee Iacocca attempted to lease the song for an ad-campaign jingle, Springsteen turned him down cold.

Meanwhile, the hits just kept on coming. Seven songs from *Born in the U.S.A.*—more than half the album's contents—were bona-fide smashes in 1984 and '85. Springsteen entered the Top Ten more times in those two years than he had cracked the Top Hundred in the previous eleven. Just in case you happened to be crossing Antarctica via dog sled at the time, Springsteen's procession of singles comprised, in order: "Dancing in the Dark" (#2), "Cover Me" (#7), "Born in the U.S.A." (#9), "I'm On Fire" (#6), "Glory Days" (#5), "I'm Goin' Down" (#9) and "My Hometown" (#6). Moreover, every last one had some worthwhile non-LP B side to commend it, such as the sassy rockabilly wonder "Pink Cadillac" (my candidate for bossest Bruce B side), later a hit for Natalie Cole.

The album was, as its advance press made it out to be, more of a "fun" Springsteen album than any since the previous one that had *born* in its title. *Born in the U.S.A.* had its reflective moments, to be sure—such as the elegiac "My Hometown" and the angry, anthemic title cut—but overall the album exuded a winning, grin-and-bear-it kind of flavor that was most evident in numbers like "Glory Days" and "Working on the Highway." Springsteen's roomy landscape implicitly celebrated the indomitable American spirit of perseverance and rolling with the punches. It was just the sort of beat-driven tonic many folks needed to survive the spirit-sapping epoch of Reaganomics, wherein the rich got richer while the poor got trickled upon. In her five-star ROLLING STONE review, Debby Miller noted, "He may shove his broody characters out the door and send them cruising down the turnpike, but he gives them music they can pound on the dashboard to."

Having taken a year-long hiatus from rock journalism in mid-1984, I missed out on much of the *Born in the U.S.A.* hoopla. Oddly enough, I was engaged in a non-musical pursuit that Springsteen himself would no doubt have appreciated: researching a book about East Coast beaches with a fellow writer and Springsteen fan who'd likewise decided to cast fate to the wind and go beachcombing. And so we found ourselves standing on the boardwalk at Asbury Park one bright summer day around the time Springsteen and the E Street Band were working their way around the arenas of the Northeast. We found the town to be more dilapidated and down at the heels than we'd ever believed possible, even from all the lore that had circulated. As we wrote in our book's Springsteen-suffused essay on Asbury Park: "On a beautiful day in mid-August, all we saw were the boarded-up remnants of yesteryear. Only the stalwart Madam Marie still hangs her shingle." The beach looked inviting, though, if you could block the rest of the town from your frame of reference.

Although I didn't catch a single show on the Born in the U.S.A. Tour, I was inundated with songs from the album—lived with them every night for months in beach bars and clubs, where they made the perfect soundtrack for back-to-back American summers. Bruce Springsteen was a ubiquitous cultural presence during that time, from coast to coast, road house to White House. By the time the exhausted rocker disembarked from the road, he had performed fifteen months' worth of lengthy shows, refusing to quit each night until he and the E Street Band had completely worn out the audience. "We had a saying," Clarence Clemons told ROLLING STONE's David Fricke. " 'Are they still on their feet? Yeah, let's go back and get 'em. Can they still raise their hands? If they can, we haven't done our job.' "

Though he'd played in places so large that some sense of intimacy and community was necessarily lost between home plate and right field, Springsteen and company gave their usual 110 percent, with no loss of idealism. By the time of *Born in the U.S.A.,* he had truly become the most revered figure in rock & roll, and he didn't take the charge lightly, telling Kurt Loder: "I believe that the life of a rock & roll band will last as long as you look down into the audience and can see yourself, and your audience looks up at you and can see themselves—and as long as those reflections are human, realistic ones." Bucking the odds, he had managed to hang on to his integrity and regular-guy identity. And yet he was huge—a figure more meaningful to many than the president.

Born in the U.S.A. wasn't just an album and tour but a seismic event on the rock & roll timeline. Springsteen followed it with a career-encapsulating live box set. Springsteen's long-anticipated live album—fans had been clamoring for one since the Seventies—hit the stores in the fall of 1986, just in time for Christmas gift-giving. It turns out Springsteen had begun reviewing concert tapes just six weeks after tour's end, inaugurating a nine-month culling process. Some thirty shows in all, dating back to 1975, were scrutinized. The forty-song box set runs for close to three and a half hours—roughly the length of an average Springsteen concert.

Even off the road and out of the limelight, Springsteen remained a potent phenomenon. Lines formed at record stores in cities across the country when *Bruce Springsteen & the E Street Band Live/1975–85* went on sale, and the broadcast media sent camera crews out to document it. It wound up selling more than three million copies—an amazing number for a box set, though about 700,000 less than Columbia Records had pressed, creating the similarly amazing illusion that its sales were disappointing. (Only in the stilted world of corporate high finance could such a colossal figure be deemed "disappointing.") *Live/1975–85* was a treasure trove to longtime fans, though some felt there was a surfeit of *Born in the U.S.A.*–era material, relative to all the unreleased originals and cover versions from earlier tours for which hard-core fans hungered. "It's not enough," David Fricke half-jokingly complained in the opening line from his ROLLING STONE review.

Springsteen's fame continued to blitz the Eighties when ROLLING STONE's readers, participating in the magazine's 1986 Music Awards poll, voted him Artist of the Year for the third year in a row and the sixth time in nine years. In the accompanying article, writer Anthony DeCurtis posed an inevitable question: "Where does he go from here?" The answer was into a tunnel—*Tunnel of Love,* that is. Springsteen pulled back his musical focus into a more personal, smaller-scale framework, honing on one-on-one relationships rather than the larger rites of community that had been his preoccupation throughout *Born in the U.S.A.*'s long, exhilarating ride. "The way that you counteract the size [of stardom] is by becoming more intimate in your work," Springsteen told Steve Pond in a 1988 ROLLING STONE article. "I suppose that's why after I did *Born in the U.S.A.,* I made this intimate record . . . a record that was really sort of addressed to my core audience, my longtime fans."

Tunnel of Love was too intimate even for the E Street Band. Most of the parts were played by Springsteen at his home studio in New Jersey. E Street band members were used sparingly, and never all at once. Clarence Clemons blew not one note of saxophone on the record. Surely, something had come—or was coming—to an end. For the Tunnel of Love Express Tour, Springsteen took pains to alter the band's onstage configuration, moving them like chess pieces out of the spots they'd occupied for thirteen years. Tellingly, for those who would follow events in Springsteen's increasingly visible private life, Patti Scialfa was moved into Clemons' old spot, replacing him as Springsteen's onstage foil. A number of old favorites were dropped from the set as he endeavored to tell a different kind of story this time around. The tour steered clear of football stadiums; at least in the States, he played only indoor arenas.

As a record, *Tunnel of Love* came rather more easily to Springsteen than usual. It is his least labored, most natural-sounding record of the post–*Born to Run* era. The sessions occupied a few months, not a few years, and the album fell together without the ritual second-guessing and torturous refinements that typified past projects. He came up with the title *Tunnel of Love* after considering what he'd recorded, and then wrote the masterful title track around that phrase. Metaphorically and musically, it might just be his finest moment as a songwriter. Its lyrical premonitions leave a haunting aftertaste: "There's a room of shadows that gets so dark, brother / It's easy for two people to lose each other in this tunnel of love." Or try out these stark, summary lines, from the chorus to the angrily churning rocker "Spare Parts": "Spare parts / And broken hearts / Keep the world turnin' around."

For the first time, Springsteen gave an indication that his priorities were shifting. In concert, he went from shouting "I'm just a prisoner of rock & roll" to "I'm just a prisoner of *love*." Some unreconstructed Springsteen fanatics must have found it heretical when he told ROLLING STONE: "I guess I used to think that rock could save you. I don't believe it can anymore. It can do a lot. It's certainly done a lot for me. . . . But as you get older, you realize that it is not enough." Moreover, his interviews from this period revealed an increasingly political bent, as he began addressing himself to matters that, traditionally, rock & roll had provided an alternative to and distraction from. "The world is nothing but complex," Springsteen told Mikal Gilmore in a thoughtful, forthright interview in ROLLING STONE's twentieth anniversary issue, "and if you do not learn to interpret its complexities, you're going to be on the river without a paddle."

Such remarks presaged Springsteen's boldest political gesture yet: his joining Amnesty International's Human Rights Now! Tour in 1988. Prior to this, he had performed for several causes, including the anti-nuclear Musicians United for Safe Energy (MUSE) concerts in September 1979 and a pair of benefits for Vietnam vets in August 1981. The Amnesty International tour, however, represented an extended commitment to a six-week, fifteen-nation itinerary. Its September 2nd, 1988, kickoff at London's Wembley Stadium was preceded by the release of a four-song Springsteen EP, whose highlight was his recording of Bob Dylan's Sixties folk anthem "Chimes of Freedom."

The lineup of stars included Sting, Peter Gabriel, Tracy Chapman and Youssou N'Dour. The experience of touring with other artists for the first time in sixteen years inspired Springsteen to make his next record without the E Street Band. Overall, the years 1988 through 1991 were ones in which his personal life underwent changes that greatly affected his professional life and his relationship with his audience. His marriage to Julianne Phillips came to an end when she filed for divorce on August 30th, 1988, alleging irreconcilable differences, shortly before Springsteen joined the Amnesty International tour.

Their breakup had been preceded by his dalliance with Patti Scialfa on a hotel balcony in Rome during the Tunnel of Love Express Tour's European leg, shots of which were splashed across the pages of Britain's sleazy tabloid *The Sun*. The split with the E Street Band, announced in November 1989, was perceived as a disloyal move by longtime fans. The unkindest cut of all may have been Springsteen's relocation from New Jersey to Los Angeles, made official by his purchase in April 1990 of a four-and-a-half-acre, two-house estate in Beverly Hills that set him back $14 million. (He still retained his mansion in Jersey, however.) Almost all the news pertaining to him during this spell was of a personal nature. Springsteen and Scialfa had a son, Evan James, on July 25th, 1990; he was the first of three children. On June 8th, 1991, they got married.

A Bruce backlash ensued, as many former fans felt he'd abandoned his blue-collar roots. The extent of the disenchantment among his hard-core following could be gauged by the number of subscription cancellations to the excellent Springsteen fanzine *Backstreets*. Circulation dropped by two-thirds between its mid-Eighties peak and 1991. Certainly, a lot of the disgruntlement could be written off as pique by well-meaning but overly possessive fans who couldn't bear to watch him settle down and lead the quiet, private life to which he was entitled. And settle down he did, although there were some uncharacteristically messy moments as he made that passage. To be honest, there did seem to be some behavioral breaches in the romanticized ideals for which he'd stood for so many years. In a sense, though, it was almost endearingly reassuring to see him stumble a bit. It proved he was fallibly human after all. Who in his right mind could hold that against him? One headline from the time more or less said it all: MOST IDOLS WOULD HAVE BEGUN TO SHOW TARNISH MUCH SOONER.

One did have to wonder, however, just what was going through his mind as he retreated behind the walls of his Beverly Hills estate. This was the same Bruce Springsteen, after all, who in 1975 told *Melody Maker*'s Ray Coleman: "I throw out almost everything I ever own. I don't believe in collecting anything. The less you have to lose, the better you are, because the more chances you'll take. The more you got, the worse off you get." Did he not now feel a measure of the "cruel isolation" that had claimed Elvis Presley and against which he fought for so long with his approachable, anti-star persona? Just why did he need fourteen million dollars' worth of Beverly Hills real estate to buffer him from the world?

Springsteen offered thoughtful answers to such questions. In a 1992 interview, he told ROLLING STONE's James Henke: "Two of the best days of my life were the day I picked up the guitar and the day that I learned how to put it down." He expanded on his changes in attitude: "What happened was, all my rock & roll answers had fizzled out. . . . It's not your entire life. It never can be. And I realized my real life is waiting to be lived. All the love and the hope and the sorrow and sadness—that's all over there, waiting to be lived. . . . So I decided to work on it."

The longest break in time between Bruce Springsteen albums was the four and a half years that passed between *Tunnel of Love* and *Human Touch*. But *Human Touch,* the "main" album, was joined by a concomitant release— a more spontaneously assembled work that many critics actually preferred, entitled *Lucky Town.* Taken together, they represent Springsteen's most prolific outpouring, their collective twenty-four songs surpassing even *The River* in length. They also represented his first work without the E Street Band, for which reason they were subjected to more scrutiny than usual.

For the most part, the songs stood tall on their own terms, coming from a vantage point that was both tough-minded and mature. Taken together, they describe an emotional arc that passes from distrust and disenchantment to commitment and contentment. *Human Touch,* the more intensely produced and time-consuming album, underwent a lengthy, difficult gestation. By contrast, *Lucky Town* was written and recorded in three weeks.

Springsteen spoke more enthusiastically about the latter album: "I felt like that's where I am. This is who I am. This is what I have to say. These are the stories I have to tell. This is what's important in my life right now." He added: "I've been very, very happy, truly the happiest I've ever been in my whole life." Springsteen scribbled this brief comment about the song "Better Days," which ranks among his most moving lyrics, for the booklet that accompanied his 1995 *Greatest Hits* collection: "With a young son and about to get married (for the last time), I was feelin' like a happy guy who has his rough days, rather than vice versa."

Human Touch and *Lucky Town* entered the chart at Number Two and Number Three, respectively, upon their release in April 1992. Springsteen supported them with a fall tour for which he assembled a brand-new band that included five backup singers. The only E Street holdover was Roy Bittan. As if to lay to rest any lingering doubts about his popularity in New Jersey, the more than 200,000 tickets that went on sale for his shows at the Brendan Byrne Arena sold out in two and a half hours. Springsteen preceded the tour's kickoff with a November 11th performance on MTV's *Unplugged,* the novel Sunday-night concert series that found rock artists revisiting their repertoire in theoretically acoustic, or at least largely understated, settings. Undaunted by this formal premise, Springsteen brought ten accompanists, complete with electric guitars and amps, and gave a fully plugged-in preview of the tour to come. MTV conveniently scrawled an X over the "Un" in *Unplugged,* and Springsteen delivered nearly two hours' worth of material from the new albums, interspersed with familiar touchstones like "Thunder Road" and "Glory Days." Though it went unreleased in audio formats, *Bruce Springsteen in Concert/MTV Plugged* became his first concert video. For collectors, there was the added incentive of two previously unrecorded songs, one new ("Red Headed Woman," for wife Patti) and one old ("Light of Day," written for the 1987 movie of the same name).

The few years that have passed since the completion of the Human Touch Tour have been relatively quiet ones. In 1994, Springsteen contributed a somber song, "Streets of Philadelphia," to the soundtrack of the film *Philadelphia,* whose subject was AIDS. Its downbeat mood reflected not only the shrinking world inhabited by the film's lead character, played by Tom Hanks, but Springsteen's own mounting disenchantment with a society whose conscience ran a poor second to the bottom line. Apparently, he touched a nerve: "Streets of Philadelphia" became a Top Ten single (his first since "Tunnel of Love") and won four Grammys and an Academy Award. In much the same unadorned, plainspoken vein, Springsteen provided the title song for the Oscar-nominated 1995 *Dead Man Walking.*

Springsteen's *Greatest Hits* retrospective was released late in 1994, entering the charts at Number One. It included a previously unissued older song ("Murder Incorporated," from 1982) and three new ones that reunited him with the E Street Band. The tenor of those new tracks—mostly quiet songs that were barely accommodating of the E Streeters—made the much-touted reunion seem more like a forced coda than a new beginning. That impression was furthered by another short-lived reunion, this one at the massive, multi-artist stadium concert held on September 2, 1995, to celebrate the opening of the Rock and Roll Hall of Fame and Museum in Cleveland. A brief set by Springsteen and the E Street Band culminated in "Darkness on the Edge of Town"—a rather mordant selection, given the jubilant setting. But such appeared to be Springsteen's frame of mind at mid-decade.

He lent a hand to a kindred spirit, Joe Grushecky, on the latter's *American Babylon* album, which came out that fall. Grushecky is a veteran blood-and-guts rocker who wears his heart on his ragged sleeve, drawing upon hard times in his hometown of Pittsburgh for material. Springsteen's generous participation—he produced the album, played guitar and/or mandolin on eight songs and cowrote two of them—helped raise the deserving Grushecky's profile at a time when his career needed a boost. He furthered the gesture by performing with Grushecky and his band, the Houserockers, at several showcase gigs.

Springsteen closed the year by releasing *The Ghost of Tom Joad,* a haunted and cheerless album that found him inhabiting the lives of characters who drifted around the country without opportunity or hope. It was a landscape as bleak as (albeit better recorded than) that of *Nebraska.* One crucial difference: his perspective had shifted westward, as had his home base. Now his characters were immigrants and itinerants roaming the fields and valleys of the Far West for work. They are much like the downtrodden Okies who people John Steinbeck's novel *The Grapes of Wrath,* from which Springsteen borrowed and revived the character of Tom Joad.

Instead of the Joad family's naive belief in a better future, however, Springsteen sees only the dimming prospects of those who have necessarily shelved the American Dream for the far more pressing matter of survival. He tells their story without elaboration or adornment, presenting them in settings that amount to little more than recitatives with sparse accompaniment. The defeated, matter-of-fact tone of these songs ensured their unsuitability for airplay or big sales. It is simply too realistic a mirror to hold up to a nation that would rather deny the problems that plague and divide it. America will always choose an escapist cartoon over the black-and-white truth. When measured against the novelty aspects of the burgeoning alternative scene, *The Ghost of Tom Joad* seemed like an act of commercial suicide—and one of unflagging conviction, as well.

Springsteen supported the album with a solo acoustic tour of small halls during which he petitioned his audiences for quiet and prefaced his songs with thoughtful, lengthy introductions. It was a far cry from the celebratory, on-your-feet rock & roll marathons of the Born in the U.S.A. Tour, now a full decade in the past. Before, the triumphant communalism of a Bruce Springsteen concert would help people ward off hard times, if only for one long, raucous evening. Now he was offering no such reprieve. Without apology or concession, he stared into the heart of darkness.

It is, of course, anyone's guess as to where he'll go from here. His passage from rock star to family man, which calls to mind parallels with John Lennon's later years, leaves him free to act on his artistic impulses at will. Though the pace has slowed a bit, don't expect to see him pull a disappearing act. "I'm a lifetime musician," he has said. "I'm going to be playing music forever."

He is also the sort of musician whom, even if you've never made his acquaintance (and I haven't), can be considered a friend. If you've paid any attention whatsoever to rock & roll, he's probably someone whose music you've grown up with—laughed and cried to, played at parties, held onto for dear life. As an artist, he can be described—in words used by Joni Mitchell with reference to Prince—as "another one of those lifers. He's driven like an artist. His motivation is growth and experiment as opposed to formula and hits."

To put some kind of final word on this, I'm drawn back to a 1987 interview, during which Springsteen explained, "When I started in music, I thought, 'My job is pretty simple. My job is I search for the human things in myself, and I turn them into notes and words, and then in some fashion, I help people hold on to their own humanity'—if I'm doing my job right."

All I can add to that is "thanks for the ride—so far."

John Hammond, director of talent acquisition at Columbia Records, is recovering from a heart attack suffered following a Bruce Springsteen show at Max's Kansas City in New York. Hammond, in his late fifties, has suffered heart attacks on two previous occasions. He attributed the most recent attack to a heavy work schedule and weakness from a virus he picked up in Paris. His doctor, however, disagreed. He says it was due to Hammond's enthusiasm at the Springsteen show. Hammond recently signed Springsteen to the Columbia label.

STUART WERBIN

IT'S SIGN UP A GENIUS MONTH

IT'S MORE THAN a decade since John Hammond Sr. of Columbia Records signed Bob Dylan to a recording contract. Since then, Hammond has signed a number of other successes and, by his own admission, a number of "stiffs." Now he has signed Bruce Springsteen, 23, of Asbury Park, New Jersey, and Hammond says: "He's much further along, much more developed than Bobby was when he came to me."

Much about Springsteen reminds people of Dylan—the slept-in appearance, foggy manner, the twang, the lyrics and the phrasing of his songs. It seems only natural that Hammond should have signed him. But to Bruce ". . . it was just plain weird.

"I mean a couple of weeks ago I had just finished reading Dylan's biography and now I find myself sitting in Hammond's office with my beat-up guitar, and like the whole thing I've been reading about is about to happen to me. But what Mike was doing was even weirder."

Mike is Mike Appel, who with Jim Cretecos manages and produces Bruce. Appel and Cretecos' previous teamwork includes the creation of a couple of gold singles for the Partridge Family. For Springsteen, the managerial strategy is to ". . . start at the top and work down."

"Mike is a funny guy," said Bruce. "He's like a real hyper, and he gets into the whole thing like playing the role. So I'm sitting in the corner with my old beat-up guitar, when all of a sudden Mike jumps up and starts hyping John Hammond. I couldn't believe it. I had to start laughing. John Hammond told me later that he was ready to hate me. But he asked me to do a song, so I did 'It's Hard to Be a Saint in the City.' "

Despite the hype, Hammond signed him and Bruce moved from his free-wheelin' stage into phase two—exploitation. It worked like this:

A member of the press would get a phone call from the publicity department at Columbia and be told he would receive an advance copy of a record by a new artist (not unusual), and after he had a chance to listen to it, President Clive Davis would appreciate a call to get his reaction (highly unusual).

Meanwhile, visitors to the CBS Building encountered publicity personnel and suited executives alike greeting people with the question, "Hi . . . have you heard Bruce Springsteen yet?"

Bruce Springsteen is admittedly surprised by all the attention, but is showing no signs of stress. "Well, shit man, you know, what do I care, I'll do anything once. If it works it works. But I don't wanna be concerned with too much of what's going on with promotion. That don't seem so important to me, but it's important to Mike. I trust whatever he does. Anyway it never seemed like I had it that bad before," he laughed.

"I'll admit it seems a little weird the way these record company dudes operate. Seems like one dude says 'hey everybody's signing up geniuses this month. Genius is going to be good for business, we better lock one up fast.' But as I say, I'll do anything. I mean I have nothing else to do. I have nothing else to do at all."

Bruce was thirteen when his hometown cousin in Freehold, New Jersey, showed him how to make the same music on the guitar that the Beach Boys, the Shirelles, Gary "U.S." Bonds, the Chiffons and his other favorites were making on the radio. That was enough to alter his fantasy of becoming a baseball player to a fantasy of becoming a rock & roll star.

The new fantasy stuck, and long after his cousin had gone on to a nonmusical career at Freehold Raceway, Bruce continued to do nothing but play music.

"Well, actually, I did work as a gardener once, but that didn't last too long, even though I guess it was the only real job I ever had. I did go to college once, too: Ocean County Community College. But one day I got called into the nutty-doctor's office, and remember this was before a lot of people were getting weird. . . . The shrink asked me what was the matter. So I told him nothing could possibly be the matter getting to hang around a fine place like that campus. But then he told me that students had been complaining about me. That's what the dude said. Well, I figured there was no use hanging around there, so I split."

Bruce's musical career has not been interrupted since. A brief army physical cleared him of military duty, "for reasons of weirdness," and left him free to play bars and weddings, fronting for various groups, the most successful being a "Humble Pie–type band" called Steel Mill, which stayed together for a couple of years building a reputation in New Jersey, and the least successful being Dr. Zoom and the Sonic Boom, which featured everybody he knew who could play an instrument.

Dr. Zoom died after only a couple of booms, which left Bruce to form the (ten-piece) Bruce Springsteen Band, which was more successful, but not by much. At twenty-one, Bruce unplugged and set out on a solo acoustic career.

His present band of brilliant unknowns was put together here and there at bars Bruce was playing. And now, by his own account, they're living high off the hog. "When our band goes into a Holiday Inn, we step up in the world. The beds are nice. They got color TV. I love those places. When we go there we know we're gonna eat good and have a good time. I can't understand why those places get such a bum rap."

Bruce's only national exposure so far came via a live performance broadcast over fifty-three FM stations as part of the debut of the King Biscuit Flower Hour.

His recent week-long appearance at Max's Kansas City, however, created quite the scene in the Big Apple. The house was packed by the time he walked onstage each night. People were crammed on each other's laps. His sets ran close to an hour followed by an impatient demand for an encore, which, because of time, and because he was playing second bill to Biff Rose, he could not fulfill.

Onstage, he projected a dirty sexual energy that rivaled the best of the established stars with whom he has been compared (Robbie Robertson, Richie Havens, Van Morrison), coupled with a loose, cavalier attitude.

A number of distinguished guests not previously known to venture so far downtown showed up at Max's, including Mrs. Ted Kennedy. "Yeah, they told me Mrs. Kennedy was out there," Bruce said. "But I found that hard to believe. I mean, I had to ask myself, what would she be out there *for*?"

LESTER BANGS

GREETINGS FROM ASBURY PARK, N. J. ALBUM REVIEW

REMEMBER P.F. SLOAN? Sure you do. It was back when every folk rocker worth his harmonica holder was flushed with Dylan fever and seeing how many syllables he could cram into every involuted couplet. There was Tandyn Almer, of "Along Comes Mary" fame ("The psychodramas and the traumas hung on the scars of the stars in the bars and cars"—something like that), and David Blue had his own "Highway 61" too, but absolutely none of 'em could beat ol' P.F. He started out writing surf songs, but shook the world by the throat with his masterpieces "Eve of Destruction" and "Sins of a Family," and all his best material was just brimming with hate.

Boy howdy, the first thing the world needs is a P.F. Sloan for 1973, and you can start revving up yer adrenaline, kids, because he's here in the person of Bruce Springsteen. Old Bruce makes a point of letting us know that he's from one of the scuzziest, most useless and plain uninteresting sections of Jersey. He's been influenced a lot by the Band, his arrangements tend to take on a Van Morrison tinge every now and then, and he sort of catarrh-mumbles his ditties in a disgruntled mushmouth sorta like Robbie Robertson on Quaaludes with Dylan barfing down the back of his neck. It's a tuff combination, but it's only the beginning.

Because what makes Bruce totally unique and cosmically surfeiting is his words. Hot damn, what a passel o' verbiage! He's got more of them crammed into his album than any other record released this year, but it's all right because they all fit snug, it ain't like Harry Chapin tearing right-angle malapropisms out of his larynx. What's more, each and every one of 'em has at least one other one here that it rhymes with. Some of 'em can mean something socially or otherwise, but there's plenty of 'em that don't even pretend to, reveling in the joy of utter crass showoff talent run amuck and totally out of control:

"Madman drummers bummers and Indians in the summer with a teenage diplomat / In the dumps with the mumps as the adolescent pumps his way into his hat" begins the very first song, and after that things just keep getting more breathtakingly complicated. You might think it's some kinda throwback, but it's really bracing as hell because it's obvious that B.S. don't give a shit. He slingshoots his random rivets at you and you can catch as many as you want or let 'em all clatter right off the wall, which maybe's where they belong anyway. Bruce Springsteen is a bold new talent with more than a mouthful to say, and one look at the pic on the back will tell you he's got the glam to go places in this Gollywoodlawn world to boot. Watch for him; he's not the new John Prine.

KEN EMERSON

THE WILD, THE INNOCENT & THE E STREET SHUFFLE
ALBUM REVIEW

Springsteen Goes Gritty and Serious

REETINGS FROM ASBURY PARK, N.J., Bruce Springsteen's uproarious debut album, sounded like "Subterranean Homesick Blues" played at 78, a typical five-minute track bursting with more words than this review. Most of it didn't make much sense, but that was the point. Springsteen was rhyming and wailing for the sheer fun of it, and his manic exuberance more than canceled out his debts to Dylan, Van Morrison and the Band. *The Wild, the Innocent & the E Street Shuffle* takes itself more seriously. The songs are longer, more ambitious and more romantic; and yet, wonderfully, they lose little of *Greetings'* rollicking rush. Having released two fine albums in less than a year, Springsteen is obviously a considerable new talent.

Like *Greetings,* the new album is about the streets of New York and the tacky Jersey Shore, but the lyrics are no longer merely zany cutups. They're striking amalgams of romance and gritty realism: "And the boys from the casino dance with their shirts open like Latin lovers on the shore / Chasin' all those silly New York virgins by the score." The loveliness of the first line, the punk savvy of the second, and the humor of the ensemble add up to Springsteen's characteristic ambivalence and a complex appeal reminiscent of the Shangri-Las. In the midst of a raucous celebration of desire, "Rosalita (Come Out Tonight)," he can suddenly turn around and sing, "Some day we'll look back on this and think we all seem funny."

But none of this would matter if the music were humdrum—it isn't. The band, especially David L. Sancious on keyboards and Clarence Clemons on saxes, cook with power and precision, particularly on "Rosalita" and "Kitty's Back," the album's outstanding rockers. They're essentially an R&B outfit—funky-butt is Springsteen's musical *pied-à-terre*—but they can play anything thrown at them, be it jazz or "Highway 61 Revisited." Springsteen himself is an undistinguished but extremely versatile guitarist, which he needs to be to follow his own changes.

Springsteen is growing as a writer of music as well as of words. The best of his new songs dart and swoop from tempo to tempo and from genre to genre, from hell-bent-for-leather rock to luscious schmaltz to what is almost recitative. There is an occasional weak spot or an awkward transition, but for the most part it works spectacularly, and nowhere to more dramatic effect than on "Incident on 57th Street," the album's most stunning track, a virtual mini-opera about Johnny, a "romantic young boy" torn between Jane and the bright knives out on the street. Springsteen never resolves the conflict (if he ever does, his music will probably become less interesting). Instead he milks it for all it's worth, wrapping up all the song's movements and juxtapositions with his unabashedly melodramatic and loonily sotted Sloppy Joe voice.

PAT KNIGHT

BRUCE SPRINGSTEEN'S LONE STAR PROMENADE

THE BAND WALKED onstage with bowed heads and gathered around the grand piano. The keyboardist began trilling the solo introduction to "New York City Serenade," trying for a combination of Chopin and Brubeck. Eventually, Bruce Springsteen stepped up to his mike: a dark figure with low-slung acoustic guitar, black leather jacket, wispy beard, shades and asphalt-special sneakers. In a throaty whisper he intoned the opening lines:

> Billy, he's down by the railroad tracks, sitting low in the backseat of his
> Cadillac.
> Diamond Jackie, she's so intact as she falls so softly beneath him.
> Jackie's heels are stacked, Billy's got cleats on his boots
> Together, they're gonna boogaloo down Broadway . . .
> It's midnight in Manhattan, this is no time to get cute
> It's a mad dog's promenade

The serenade had begun and Bruce Springsteen implored the audience of 1,500 at Armadillo World Headquarters, in Austin, Texas, to "take my arm, walk with me, c'mon baby, move with me down Broadway!" Before the first number ended, the audience was giving Springsteen a standing ovation. Not bad when you consider most of those southern-fried kids had never heard of this city boy from the Jersey swamps.

Springsteen and his sidemen played Austin near the end of a four-city visit to the South. They rode the Amtrak rails south from New Jersey to Washington, D.C., and Houston, plus an overnight pleasure stop in New Orleans.

With two critically acclaimed albums (*Greetings From Asbury Park, N. J.* and *The Wild, the Innocent & the E Street Shuffle*) to his credit and a third in the works, Springsteen is just starting to tour nationally. Keyboardist Danny Federici explained, "We've done gigs around the Southeast and New England. Went to Chicago once. Single gigs to see what a tour might look like. We talked to some big names about opening tour shows for them, but, uh, some people won't play after us." He laughed. "They must think we're too strong to follow." It's the kind of problem any band leader would love to have—a band that's too good. The band members grew up in the same vicinity in Jersey. Except for a new drummer, the personnel has been roughly the same for five years. They're getting the same response on the road that the albums got from the critics: raves.

Springsteen—along with John Prine, Elliott Murphy, Loudon Wainwright III and Jackson Browne—has been touted as a "new Bob Dylan." He does share physical characteristics and a penchant for full-tilt rock & roll back-up bands and round-the-bend lyrics.

Springsteen is more bemused than annoyed by the comparisons. "Bob Dylan? I like the cat. The similarities are probably there somewhere. But we come from two totally different scenes, you gotta remember that." He stops and ponders something, then looks up with a grin, "Shit, man, I've been influenced by lots of people. Elvis was one of the first. Otis Redding, Sam Cooke, Wilson Pickett, the Beatles, Fats, Benny Goodman, a lot of jazz guys. You can hear them all in there if you want."

His music moves at a lightning pace, changing rhythm and shifting beats. One minute the horns are south of the border, two bars later you'd swear the Stax house band was in town. Most instrumental in driving the band is saxophonist Clarence Clemons. Clemons and Springsteen work off each other with practiced ease, Clemons' searing sax a counterpoint to Bruce's guitar. Federici and David Sancious cover keyboards with Ernest "Boom" Carter and Garry Tallent providing rhythm on drums and bass.

The songs themselves range from love songs to accounts of city life.

The realism of Springsteen's subject matter is no accident. He spent the last eight years doing street corner research after his parents moved out West when he was sixteen. Springsteen remained in New Jersey. Since then, the boardwalk of Asbury Park and the pavement of New York City have been his turf. "The stuff I write is what I live with. The stories are all around me. I just put 'em down. They're all true. Even the names, Big Balls Billy, Weak-kneed Willie, all of 'em."

After two nights at the Armadillo, Springsteen had the place wired. When the opening "Serenade" ended, he paused long enough to ditch his acoustic and grab a harp before kicking off "Spirit in the Night," an R&B elegy to teenage lust. The crowd began a foot-stomping love affair with the band that bloomed into several hours of fresh rock & roll—street punk Jersey style.

Springsteen left his own material occasionally to play a few favorites. Midway through the set he did a "Walking the Dog" so long and loud that Rufus Thomas would've been proud. When it came time for encores, oldies were Bruce's answer to a berserk crowd.

First came a tribute to the Fatman, "Let the Four Winds Blow." Austin has its share of rock & rollers, and it didn't take much prodding to get the chorus thrown back at the stage.

The nightcap was "Twist and Shout," and it got everybody off like a three-fingered shot of tequila. After umpteen go-rounds, Bruce collapsed to the floor clutching his chest. "My doctor told me not to play 'Twist and Shout' tonight. See, I eat a lot of cheeseburgers, got a lot of cholesterol around my heart. I don't think I can do it one more time." But he got up and did it at least one more time, leaving no bottoms unshook anywhere in the house. Springsteen could come back and play *anytime* as far as these people were concerned.

Backstage he slumped into a chair, visibly pleased with the show. "That set was it. Jesus, too much. For me, it's the music. Getting up there onstage, when it's coming down real tight and hard. When it works like tonight, it's great."

DAVE MARSH

A ROCK "STAR IS BORN" PERFORMANCE REVIEW

Bruce Springsteen and the E Street Band
The Bottom Line/New York City
August 13th–17th, 1975

NOT SINCE Elton John's initial Troubadour appearances has an artist leapt so visibly and rapidly from cult fanaticism to mass acceptance as at Bruce Springsteen's ten Bottom Line shows. Hundreds of fans lined the Village streets outside the 450-seat club each night, hoping for a shot at fifty standing-room spots. It was a time to hail from New Jersey with pride.

Springsteen is everything that has been claimed for him—a magical guitarist, singer, writer, rock & roll rejuvenator—but the E Street Band has nearly been lost in the shuffle. Which is ridiculous because this group may very well be the great American rock & roll band.

Like Springsteen, the E Street Band could cite a plethora of influences: Spector, Orbison, the Who, Van Morrison, Dylan and the Hawks, Booker T. and the MGs, any number of more obscure R&B and Sixties rock acts. The interpreted material describes the scope: "It's Gonna Work Out Fine," "Out of Limits," "When You Walk in the Room," the Crystals' "Then He Kissed Me." "Kitty's Back" is the best blues-based instrumental since the Butterfield Blues Band of *East-West* days.

The songs invariably build from a whisper to a scream, not only because Springsteen's composing focuses so often on dynamics, but also vocally and emotionally. When Springsteen slips into one of his sly tales of life in the Jersey bar bands all of them matured in, drummer Mighty Max Weinberg and bassist Garry Tallent key their comping to his every expression and gesture; it sounds natural but it's about as spontaneous as Pearl Harbor. Saxman Clarence Clemons and guitarist Miami Steve Van Zandt are perfect foils for these stories, the ominous cool of Clemons playing off the strange, hipster frenzy of Van Zandt while Springsteen races back and forth like an unleashed puppy. They look tough and live up to their looks.

The recent addition of Miami Steve is the difference. Previously, when Springsteen had dropped his guitar to simply sing, the band was left with its focus on the keyboards. No great help since pianist Roy Bittan is inclined to overembellish everything and organist Danny Federici is too reticent to lead. Van Zandt plays perfect Steve Cropper soul licks and great rock leads; his slide playing on "The E Street Shuffle" had changed that song from an ordinary soul number to the focus of the show.

None of this is to obscure Springsteen's importance. Like only the greatest rock singers and writers and musicians, he has created a world of his own. Like Dylan and the Who's Peter Townshend, he has a galaxy of fully formed characters to work with. But while he is comparable to all of the greats, that may only be because he is the living culmination of twenty years of rock & roll tradition. His show is thematically organized but it's hard to pin down the theme: *American Quadrophenia,* perhaps. But Springsteen doesn't write rock opera; he lives it. And, as all those teenage tramps in skintight pants out there know, it's the only way to live.

JOHN ROCKWELL

NEW DYLAN FROM NEW JERSEY? IT MIGHT AS WELL BE SPRINGSTEEN

NEARLY THREE HOURS into the Friday late show during his recent stand at New York City's Bottom Line, Bruce Springsteen, singer, song-writer, guitarist and cause célèbre, staged a mock collapse into the arms of his sax player, Clarence Clemons.

"I don't think I can go on, Clarence," he croaked. "It's cholesterol on my heart. My doctor told me if I sang this song once more, he wouldn't be responsible. But I gotta do it, Clarence, I gotta."

With that, he hurled himself into a hoarsely exultant final chorus of "Twist and Shout."

It was pure corn, of course, but a perfect instance of the way Springsteen can launch into a bit of theatricalized melodrama, couch it in affectionate parody and wind up heightening his own overwhelmingly personal rock & roll impact.

The ten sold-out Bottom Line shows may have been carefully orchestrated to garner press quotes and industry attention, but that didn't make the enthusiasm any less genuine. There were block-long lines of people hoping to buy the fifty standing-room tickets sold for each show. Every performance saw a good 200 extra bodies crammed into a club that supposedly seats 400. Springsteen's entrances were greeted with standing ovations, and by the end of each set the crowd's mood was one of delirium.

Springsteen himself was happy about the New York dates. "It went pretty ideally," he said a few days after they were over and a few days before he headed out on the road for his first major national tour. "The band cruised through them shows like the finest machine there was. There's nothin'—nothin'—in the world to get you playing better than a gig like that. The band walked out of the Bottom Line twice as good as when they walked in."

Springsteen's problem has been that while he has won audience and critical acclaim wherever he's played, his first two records haven't sold all that well—as of the release of the third, *Born to Run*, about 120,000 for *Greetings From Asbury Park, N.J.* and 175,000 for *The Wild, the Innocent & the E Street Shuffle.* Here's a man who is twenty-six, has been playing in public for eleven years, has had a record contract for three and been hailed as yet another in the line of "new Dylans" for just as long—and he was still unknown to the bulk of the public. No matter how many critics call you the greatest thing since Elvis or Dylan, you aren't a superstar unless you sell millions of records. You aren't even ultimately a successful artist, especially when your artistry expresses itself in a popular idiom.

There are all sorts of possible explanations for why Springsteen hasn't made it big until now, and nearly all of them throw light on the nature of his talents. The first, which can be pretty much dismissed out of hand, is that he really isn't any good and that those who love him are the victims of in-crowd faddism, payola or localized mass hysteria.

No artist is universally admired; there are always some detractors. But in Springsteen's case there remains the special problem of aroused expectations. For the past year and a half, ever since ROLLING STONE reviewer John Landau called him the "rock & roll future" in Boston's *Real Paper,* the drumbeat of praise has mounted from the press. Maybe he is a critic's pet because he awakens aging writers' long-lost memories of when they and rock were young. One of the astonishing things about his music is the way he recycles stylistic bits and pieces from so many rock, pop, R&B and even Broadway artists of the past twenty years—from Elvis to Dylan to the Drifters to Van Morrison to Leonard Bernstein and his *West Side Story.* Maybe Springsteen is just a self-conscious master of pastiche and will leave a young, forward-looking audience cold. Perhaps, but most unlikely. Any original artist, in any field, is first perceived in terms of his influences. Springsteen has gone on to make an original statement that owes its depth to that very past.

Another accusation is that he is an East Coast regional favorite. The trouble with both the "critic's darling" and "regional hero" theories is that audiences obviously love Springsteen as much as the critics do and that when he has ventured out of his immediate area (to Austin, for instance) the response has been just as loving. And now *Born to Run* seems to be catching on nationwide with a vengeance.

A rather more persuasive notion is that he is still growing musically. "You're dealing with a diamond in the rough," argued Mike Appel, the fast-talking ex-Marine who manages Springsteen. "It's been a gradual process. If you really want to know why Bruce Springsteen is better today, it's because he *is* better today."

Springsteen agreed. "Kids come up and say, 'Man, I seen you ten times and this time you were the best ever.' It's because there's a million things to do. I get good guys in the band and a good situation for growth. There's no moody stuff goin' on. If there is, it gets put into positive-type energy. And I'm finding out I can do more things, too."

According to his parents, Springsteen is a German name. He was born and raised in Freehold, New Jersey. When he was in his late teens, his parents moved to San Mateo, California; his father is a bus driver. Springsteen went to high school in Freehold and tried college briefly, but since the age of fifteen, his life has been focused on rock & roll. He's always been a leader, and during his teens he headed a series of bands with names like Child and Dr. Zoom and the Sonic Boom. He became a local bar favorite and even played as far afield as the Fillmore in San Francisco. He was also making regular runs into Manhattan, appearing as both a band leader and solo folkie in Greenwich Village clubs, learning his craft in the most basic and the most diverse way possible. In the spring of 1972 Appel became his manager and at about that time he began to concentrate on the deliberately poetic lyrics that characterize his work.

"I'd been reading that book [the Anthony Scaduto biography of Dylan] and read about how it all went down," said Springsteen, "and about John Hammond Sr. and stuff [Hammond signed Dylan to Columbia]. Then I went in and met Mike and he said he was takin' me in to see Hammond. I didn't get nervous. I figured nothin' would happen. It was amazing to me, reading that book and then I find myself sitting there in that office."

Hammond was impressed and got him to Clive Davis. In one of his last major signings for Columbia, Davis gave Springsteen a contract and pushed his first album hard.

But Columbia and even Appel thought of Springsteen as a solo, acoustic artist—the "new Dylan" hype was sincere but it was the pre-1965 Dylan everybody was thinking of. "I had to fight to get what band was on there," Springsteen said about his demand to have a band play behind him. "Mike didn't know what I was tryin' to do for at least a year after we were together."

The following year he began building his band in earnest, perfecting his stage show and redressing the balance between words and music in his songs. In conversation, he continually circles back to his musicians. Certainly the current E Street Band sounds better than anybody who has backed him since 1972, even with the departure of such a fine player as pianist David Sancious. Clemons is the key, with his gritty, evocative sax solos, but Miami Steve Van Zandt (a recent acquisition but a veteran of earlier Springsteen bands) is a welcome addition on guitar. Roy Bittan and Danny Federici do fine jobs on keyboards, and Garry Tallent (bass) and Max W. Weinberg (drums) provide a solid, lively, rhythmic underpinning. Words dominated the first album, but they don't any more.

"I never did separate the words and music all that much," Springsteen said. "The only time I did was when I was playin' by myself. The lyrics aren't as flashy now as on the first album. Then it was all a lot of images. I was writing about all the things that were happening around me. If it felt right, it was okay. Lately I've been trying to deal more with ideas—with concepts, with themes. The stuff I'm writin' now is closer to what I was writin' in the bars. I got pulled away then. I walked in off the street and was about to get a record deal. I wasn't about to argue."

Appel is thus correct in saying that the Springsteen whom people are wild about now is a different Springsteen from the word-fixated, electrified folkie people thought they heard on *Greetings From Asbury Park, N.J.* But although he has no doubt improved in the past eighteen months, he's been good for so long that there have to be more reasons to explain his delayed national recognition.

Some say that Columbia faltered in its support, backing off the second album after the disappointing response to the first. But there can be no doubt that the company is solidly behind *Born to Run.* Columbia bought 1,000 of the 4,000 seats for the Bottom Line dates—not only to proselytize the press, record dealers and radio personnel, but also to fire up its own employees for a maximum effort.

There has also been criticism of Appel, who can be arrogant, aggressive and belligerent, and of Springsteen himself, who takes a decisive role in managing his own career. Springsteen's insistence on doing two-hour-plus sets and his reluctance to defuse his impact in gigantic indoor arenas have meant that the time-honored methods of building a career through touring have been closed to him. He did a tour with Chicago a couple of years ago but hated it.

"The best part about the tour was the other band," he recalled. "But we had the problems of any opening act playing in 20,000-seat halls. They just won't listen to you. They can't hear, for one thing. They don't know how to listen, for another. Some groups just go out and plow through it. But I can't do it that way. And it showed—we played thirteen or fourteen gigs in them big halls and we sold no records. We didn't start sellin' records until we started playin' smaller places. It's a slow process. But I was *always* certain. I was just sure about what I was doin'."

Springsteen avidly defends Appel. "I think Mike is the greatest, number one. There never was a situation when he was guiding my career. I don't go out there to do half. Mike understands this. He ended up takin' the heat for a lot of decisions I made.

"I did other things. I painted houses. If you want your house green, I paint it green. But when I walk out onstage, I do what *I* want to do."

The real problem in his career so far has been the discrepancy between his live performances and his albums. And his own painful awareness of that threatened the momentum of his career for the past year. In early 1974 he toured wherever he could get dates, building up pockets of rabid followers. But from June 1974 to July 1975 he was hung up in the studio, struggling to come up with the album that everybody expected. His protracted work on that album not only interrupted his performing but left Columbia without a product to push. And careers are built on records; Springsteen, who shares with all great rock and rollers an almost cosmic ambition, knew that full well. "Bruce is determined before he dies to make the greatest rock & roll record ever made," was the way Landau put it.

Born to Run began with the title track. It was recorded last summer in Blauvelt, New York, site of the first two albums. Meant as Springsteen's bid for a commercial hit single, it took three-and-a-half months to finish and was four-and-a-half minutes long. Then things came to a standstill, however much Springsteen optimists like to talk about his "learning his way around a studio." From October until April, time was wasted unproductively in the studio or sitting about, working up the energy to try again.

The former producer of the MC5 and Livingston Taylor, Landau resigned as recordings editor of ROLLING STONE to coproduce the album. He moved the proceedings to the Record Plant in New York City and got things underway again.

"We needed an outside perspective," Springsteen willingly admitted. "Things had fallen down internally. He got things on their feet again. He was able to point out reasons why we weren't progressing. Nobody knew why; we were completely in the dark. Jon was a super-important figure. He came up with the idea, 'Let's make a rock & roll record.' His whole thing was to help me do things my way, but to make it easier."

Even so, things hardly sailed smoothly. Work was held up by rethinkings and outright indecision: Springsteen can explore all his options from performance to performance, but records are fixed forever, and you have to choose among options. As the summer went on, committed performance dates threatened to interrupt the sessions, and the final mixing was not finished until just before the Bottom Line dates.

"I was rehearsing the band in one studio, singing 'She's the One' in another and mixing 'Jungleland' in the third," Springsteen recalled the day before the Bottom Line stand began, sprawled on a blanket on the beach at Long Branch, New Jersey, where he's lived for the past year. "It was off the wall. I'm never gonna do that again." He made the key production decisions and chose a rich, Spectorian mix, full of overdubs and echo.

"When I had just made it, I hated it," he recalled. "I just couldn't listen to it. I went nuts or somethin'. It scared me off a little bit, maybe. I was puttin' down things I hadn't put down before; that's such a personal thing. You wonder how far, how much. I almost didn't put it out. But that was one of the few times I figured there must be something the matter with me, since everybody also said we should release it. I like it now.

"The experience of making a record was like a total wipeout. It was a devastating thing, the hardest thing I ever did."

Springsteen began his most ambitious tour yet on September 6th. It is scheduled to last most of the rest of the year with nearly all the dates in halls seating between 2,500 and 3,500. After that, there is talk of a European swing in January and considerations of how best to play large halls. "It's a problem," said Appel. "You can't stay in Avery Fisher Hall [which seats 2,836] for fourteen days. We're thinking of trying to block off part of a hall like Madison Square Garden, both acoustically and visually, so it would seat about 10,000."

And after that comes the awaited live album, Appel said. "We want it to be a two-and-a-half- to three-hour album, just like a concert. It will be two or three records—maybe a series of single records but probably one big set. When? It all depends. . . . "

What it all depends on, of course, is how well *Born to Run* is ultimately received. But by this time it seems just a matter of the degree of its success. Nobody this good, is the reasoning, can miss. The worries now are for the future.

Is Springsteen ready for fame? Can he handle the demands of rock stardom after a decade of hustling on the South Jersey shore? Will his writing, so closely tied to street life, still flourish with success?

"It's difficult," Springsteen mused on the beach. "It gets harder as it goes along. I guess it's because you got to fight your way through more and more of the bullshit. You have to go a little farther than you went the last time. Go a little deeper down into yourself. That's hard to do, because you gotta face emotions and stuff. I don't know—it's a bit scary."

Springsteen as superstar would find it hard to live the kind of life he's led up to now. It's been confining, but it's made him what he is. Even now, he finds it hard to live relaxedly in Long Branch. More friends than he ever knew he had invade his little green house a half block from the one that has his yellow Chevy with the brown flames on the hood parked out front. When he hangs out in clubs or walks down the beach hand in hand with his girlfriend, Karen Darvin, all sorts of people who look pretty much like himself stop and talk. It's a world he's raised to universality in his songs, but it's real, and one hopes he can function outside of it. Springsteen himself professes a street-punk confidence that ultimately makes you believe. "I don't know how important the settings are in the first place. It's the idea behind the settings. It could be New Jersey, it could be California, it could be Alaska. The images are like the coloring, not necessarily the picture. I can float any-where—uptown, downtown, anywhere. I want to do everything, I want to see everything, I want to go everywhere. I know what kind of situation it is. Inside, I got everything straight."

GREIL MARCUS

BORN TO RUN ALBUM REVIEW
Springsteen's Thousand and One American Nights

A S A DETERMINEDLY permanent resident of the West Coast, the furor Bruce Springsteen's live performances have kicked up in the East over the last couple of years left me feeling somewhat culturally deprived, not to mention a little suspicious. The legendary three-hour sets Springsteen and his E Street Band apparently rip out night after night in New York, Provincetown, Boston and even Austin have generated a great tumult and shouting; but, short of flying 3,000 miles to catch a show, there was no way for an outlander to discover what the fuss was all about.

Certainly, I couldn't find the reasons on Springsteen's first two albums, despite Columbia's "New Dylan" promotional campaign for the debut disc and the equally thoughtful "Street Poet" cover of the second. Both radiated self-consciousness, whereas the ballyhoo led one to hope for the grand egotism of historic rock & roll stars; both seemed at once flat and more than a little hysterical, full of sound and fury, and signifying, if not nothing, not much.

A bit guiltily, I found anything by Roxy Music far more satisfying. They could at least hit what they aimed for; while it was clear Springsteen was after bigger game, the records made me wonder if he knew what it was. Whether he did or not, with two "you gotta see him live" albums behind him, the question of whether Springsteen would ever make his mark on rock & roll—or hang onto the chance to do so—rested on that third LP, which was somehow "long awaited" before the ink was dry on the second. Very soon, he would have to come across, put up or shut up. It is the rock & roller's great shoot-out with himself: The kid with promise hits the dirt and the hero turns slowly, blows the smoke from his pistol, and goes on his way.

Or else, the kid and the hero go down together, twitching in the dust while the onlookers turn their heads and talk safely of what might have been. The end. Fade-out.

Springsteen's answer is *Born to Run*. It is a magnificent album that pays off on every bet ever placed on him—a '57 Chevy running on melted down

Crystals records that shuts down every claim that has been made. And it should crack his future wide open.

The song titles by themselves—"Thunder Road," "Night," "Backstreets," "Born to Run," "Jungleland"—suggest the extraordinary dramatic authority that is at the heart of Springsteen's new music. It is the drama that counts; the stories Springsteen is telling are nothing new, though no one has ever told them better or made them matter more. Their familiar romance is half their power: The promise and the threat of the night; the lure of the road; the quest for a chance worth taking and the lust to pay its price; girls glimpsed once at eighty miles an hour and never forgotten; the city streets as the last, permanent American frontier. We know the story: one thousand and one American nights, one long night of fear and love.

What is new is the majesty Springsteen and his band have brought to this story. Springsteen's singing, his words and the band's music have turned the dreams and failures two generations have dropped along the road into an epic—an epic that began when that car went over the cliff in *Rebel Without a Cause.* One feels that all it ever meant, all it ever had to say, is on this album, brought forth with a determination one would have thought was burnt out years ago. One feels that the music Springsteen has made from this long story has outstripped the story; that it is, in all its fire, a demand for something new.

In one sense, all this talk of epic comes down to sound. ROLLING STONE contributing editor Jon Landau, Mike Appel and Springsteen produced *Born to Run* in a style as close to mono as anyone can get these days; the result is a sound full of grandeur. For all it owes to Phil Spector, it can be compared only to the music of Bob Dylan and the Hawks made onstage in 1965 and '66. With that sound, Springsteen has achieved something very special. He has touched his world with glory, without glorifying anything: not the romance of escape, not the unbearable pathos of the street fight in "Jungleland," not the scared young lovers of "Backstreets" and not himself.

"Born to Run" is the motto that speaks for the album's tales, just as the guitar figure that runs through the title song—the finest compression of the rock & roll thrill since the opening riffs of "Layla"—speaks for its music. But "Born to Run" is uncomfortably close to another talisman of the lost kids that career across this record, a slogan Springsteen's motto inevitably suggests. It is an old tattoo: "Born to Lose." Springsteen's songs—filled with recurring images of people stranded, huddled, scared, crying, dying—take place in the space between "Born to Run" and "Born to Lose," as if to say, the only run worth making is the one that forces you to risk losing everything you have. Only by taking that risk can you hold on to the faith that

you have something left to lose. Springsteen's heroes and heroines face terror and survive it, face delight and die by its hand, and then watch as the
process is reversed, understanding finally that they are paying the price of
romanticizing their own fear.

> *One soft infested summer*
> *Me and Terry became friends*
> *Trying in vain to breathe*
> *The fire we was born in . . .*
> *Remember all the movies, Terry*
> *We'd go see*
> *Trying to learn to walk like the heroes*
> *We thought we had to be*
> *Well after all this time*
> *To find we're just like all the rest*
> *Stranded in the park*
> *And forced to confess to*
> *Hiding on the backstreets*
> *Hiding on the backstreets*
> *Where we swore forever friends. . . .*

Those are a few lines from "Backstreets," a song that begins with music
so stately, so heartbreaking, that it might be the prelude to a rock & roll version of *The Iliad*. Once the piano and organ have established the theme, the
entire band comes and plays the theme again. There is an overwhelming
sense of recognition: No, you've never heard anything like this before, but
you understand it instantly, because this music—or Springsteen crying,
singing wordlessly, moaning over the last guitar lines of "Born to Run," or
the astonishing chords that follow each verse of "Jungleland," or the opening of "Thunder Road"—is what rock & roll is supposed to sound like.

The songs, the best of them, are adventures in the dark, incidents of
wasted fury. Tales of kids born to run who lose anyway, the songs can, as
with "Backstreets," hit so hard and fast that it is almost impossible to sit
through them without weeping. And yet the music is exhilarating. You may
find yourself shaking your head in wonder, smiling through tears at the
beauty of it all. I'm not talking about lyrics; they're buried, as they should
be, hard to hear for the first dozen playings or so, coming out in bits and
pieces. To hear Springsteen sing the line "Hiding on the backstreets" is to
be captured by an image; the details can come later. Who needed to figure
out all the words to "Like a Rolling Stone" to understand it?

It is a measure of Springsteen's ability to make his music bleed that "Backstreets," which is about friendship and betrayal between a boy and a girl, is far more deathly than "Jungleland," which is about a gang war. The music isn't "better," nor is the singing—but it is more passionate, more deathly and, necessarily, more alive. That, if anything, might be the key to this music: As a ride through terror, it resolves itself finally as a ride into delight.

"Oh-o, come on, take my hand," Springsteen sings, "Riding out to case the promised land." And there, in a line, is *Born to Run.* You take what you find, but you never give up your demand for something better because you know, in your heart, that you deserve it. That contradiction is what keeps Springsteen's story, and the promised land's, alive. Springsteen took what he found and made something better himself. This album is it.

■ RANDOM NOTES (October 23, 1975)

Easy Street Shuffle: Bruce Springsteen, whose *Born to Run* album has already thundered to the top of *Record World*'s charts, is making believers out of audiences on his tour. He kicked things off in New Orleans by playing to a 2,400-seat sellout crowd who brought him back for two encores. Even after the lights went up the audience wouldn't let him go. So the wiry scion of the New Jersey swamps pulled Boz Scaggs out of the wings and together they finished with "Twist and Shout." Springsteen also sold out slightly larger halls in Austin and Houston, winning several standing ovations. He only half filled Dallas's 1,700-seat Convention Center, though. "They haven't got the word yet," said a spokesman for Springsteen's management. . . . Flo and Eddie have gotten the word. They postponed their six-day booking at L.A.'s Troubadour in October rather than face head-on competition with Bruce, who'll be playing the Roxy. Explained Howard Kaylan: "We'd rather see Bruce than play ourselves."

■ RANDOM NOTES (December 4, 1975)

For Bruce Springsteen, the meeting held all the tension and excitement of one of those encounters on the backstreets. And when he came face to face with Phil Spector, whose "wall of sound" he echoes in his *Born to Run* album, there was that five-second freeze-out as Spector fixed him with his notorious size-up stare. But then Phil offered his hand and said, "You're a very talented man." The ice was broken.

The scene was Hollywood's Gold Star Recording Studios, the place where Spector had cut some of his biggest hits. That night he was hoping to finish another, a Dion single-to-be. And after listening to a copy of *Born to Run* that a friend had brought him (his first reaction was, "I'm mildly interested, I'm hip to what the kid is doing"), he decided to invite Springsteen in to watch. Bruce, who had just finished his Roxy engagement, was only too happy to accept, and he arrived at 7:15 on the dot along with guitarist Miami Steve Van Zandt, who had once played behind Dion.

Over the next five hours Springsteen was the quiet, sheepish student/foil for Spector, who punctuated his work with good-natured barbs. "Okay, fellas," he announced to the musicians, "Bruce Spring*street* is here. He's on the cover of *Time* and he's born to run, so let's show him how to make a record." Then, inviting Bruce to watch him work from behind the control board, he said, "This record will make 'Born to Run' suck—let's play it again." On Springsteen's name: "How could a kid like you be a Wasp with such a Jewish name?" And as Springsteen was preparing to leave at 12:30: "If I were with you your records would be clear and better and you'd sell five times as many!"

Afterwards, a friend of Spector's said the meeting was like Sandy Koufax being introduced to Don Sutton. Spector corrected him: "It's more like Babe Ruth and Hank Aaron."

■ RANDOM NOTES (January 1, 1976)

Blunder road: Shortly before leaving the U.S. for a handful of Europe dates, Bruce Springsteen let it be known that he had had it up to his earring with Columbia's hype campaign. He told one reporter that the label's decision to hail him as the "future" of rock "was a very big mistake and I would like to strangle the guy who thought that up."

So Springsteen was not happy when he got to London's Hammersmith-Odeon theater and found that Columbia publicists had beat him there. He personally ripped off some of the "Finally the world is ready for Bruce Springsteen" posters that papered the lobby; he ordered that the boxes of "I have seen the future of rock 'n' roll at the Hammersmith-Odeon" buttons not be given out (*Born to Run* sneakers buttons were distributed instead).

Springsteen's pique seemed to carry over in his performance. He hardly moved around onstage; guitarist Miami Steve Van Zandt later said, "I've never seen him so subdued." But the typically reserved British audience could have been partly responsible too. After an enthusiastic greeting, they remained cool toward Springsteen until his high-energy finale and encores when they finally got up on their feet.

The next day critics also sniped at Springsteen's messiah build-up, though he got good reviews. Still, one British CBS executive thought Springsteen could have tried harder, saying, "We were disappointed."

SPRINGSTEEN TOUR: RUN SOUTH, YOUNG MAN

IT WAS ORIGINALLY conceived as a quick, one-month jaunt to battle boredom and frustration and to tighten up for the next album. But it's become a two-month, thirty-eight-date extravaganza that answers the question: "Whatever happened to Bruce Springsteen?"

The tour, which began March 25th, takes Springsteen into the South, parts of the Midwest and Pennsylvania. He will become the first hard-rock performer to headline the Grand Ole Opry House in Nashville, and he is booked at the U.S. Military Academy at West Point. "He's very popular here," said George Fink, president of West Point's Dialectic Society, which invited Springsteen. "They call him the second coming of Bob Dylan, and the way he sings . . . he sings things like they are."

It's a strange tour, coming at a time when most major acts are planning Bicentennial blitzes of ballparks and festivals in all the largest cities. But Springsteen had not planned a tour at all. Most of January was a break from a year on the road. At home in Atlantic Highlands, New Jersey, he began preparing for the followup to *Born to Run*. It would, he said, be a heavily lyrical album that he now expects to record in June at New York's Record Plant.

By late February he was reportedly entangled in a contractual fight with his manager, Mike Appel. Neither man would be specific about it. "It hasn't been ironed out," said Appel, "and I don't want to send out any misinformation." Springsteen got restless, and his band was bored. "It's a lot easier for me than the rest of the guys when we're not playing," said Springsteen. "I've got my piano at home, so I can write." But with the album slow in being written, Springsteen and his band decided on a solution: a tour.

To get ready, they began jamming at the Stone Pony, a bar in Asbury Park. On March 21st, a Sunday, Springsteen decided a full show was in order. Phone calls went out to friends, and by midnight the Stone Pony was packed with 300 people. The band's hour-long show included most of *Born to Run,* as well as a reworking of Eddie Floyd's "Raise Your Hand," which may well replace "Rosalita" as Springsteen's set-closer.

Three days later the band was back on the road. *Born to Run* has sold almost a million, but Springsteen's basically Spartan approach hasn't changed much. They travel in a Greyhound bus equipped with eight beds. And being on the cover of *Time* and *Newsweek* hasn't had much effect. The band's camaraderie remains impressive. And in Atlanta, when a DJ asked the question, "How does it feel to be compared to Bob Dylan?" Springsteen responded, "How does it feel to get a punch on the lip?"

At Duke University, in Durham, North Carolina, where Springsteen had never played, the audience seemed to know all the moves, cheering in anticipation when he went into the slow break at the end of "Spirit in the Night." The show was in a 6,000-seat basketball arena, the largest hall in which Springsteen appeared.

For the first time, the band played every song from *Born to Run* in one set, and at show's end, "Raise Your Hand" did its job: everybody stayed up through the three-song encore that ended with "Quarter to Three."

JIM PETERSEN

BRUCE SPRINGSTEEN'S E STREET SOFTBALLERS
Born to Hit and Run

AS THEIR COAST CITIES bus weaves through the streets of New Orleans' French Quarter, Bruce Springsteen tries to revive the flagging spirits of the E Street Rhythm Band, by night his backup band,
but by day a hot, barnstorming softball team. Springsteen's voice cuts through
the heavily hung-over air with shouts of "Okay, break in your mitts," and
the bus fills with the sound of fists slamming into leather pockets, while a
can of Glovolium is passed around. Before further rallying his team for the
day's game against the media heavies of New Orleans—a pickup team of
DJs and writers—Springsteen explains how the band got turned on to softball.

"The road crew challenged us to a game a few weeks ago," he recalls.
"We beat them 27-6. Everything sort of fell into place. So, the next day we
went out and dropped about $700 on equipment. Softball is our whole life
right now. That concert we played last night? That was just a pregame ceremony, like the 'Star-Spangled Banner.' "

In the back of the bus, guitarist Miami Steve Van Zandt is modeling the
uniform of the E Street Band: a white muscle shirt with blue trim, red pin-
striped shorts, a maroon velvet Big Apple hat and flip-up sunglasses with
maroon lenses. Asked if he's ever heard the expression "You throw like a
girl, you catch like a musician," Van Zandt replies, "We're serious—some
of us are so damaged we can hardly move onstage. If I jam my finger, I'll
just put it in a splint and play slide guitar all night. Pretend like I'm in a Southern boogie band."

As the bus approaches the field, the team gets ready. Saxophone
player/first baseman Clarence "Kahuna" Clemons covers his face with
BandAids; at appropriate moments in the game he'll rip them off and eat
the gauze, unnerving opposing players. The team practices cheers ranging
from the dive signal of a German U-boat to the death rattle of a late-night
golden oldies DJ.

Before a crowd of 500, the media team takes the field, one DJ hollering at the spectators, "Hey, let's hear it for the media; you know, the wonderful folks who brought you Bruce Springsteen." Nobody responds.

Miami Steve hits the first pitch into the swamp in deep left field for a home run. Then Springsteen steps to the plate and, after bowing in three directions, singles to right field. Organist Danny Federici starts to let a pitch go by, then has second thoughts and drives it into left. A smash by Rick "Mr. Ten Percent" Seguso, the road manager, brings in both runners.

The media recovers in their half of the inning, scoring five runs. On the first hit, Springsteen, at second base, makes a diving catch into a mud puddle. He twists his ankle, but continues to play, musing on "the thrill of victory, the agony of my feet."

By the fifth inning, as hangovers evaporate, the game gets serious. As Springsteen rounds third and tries to score on a long hit by Ten Percent, the catcher grabs him under one arm and holds him off the plate. Kahuna Clemons rounds third, picks up both the catcher and Springsteen and crosses the plate to score. At the top of the seventh, the media is declared victor by one run, while a check of the score card reveals the final tally is 9–9. Charges that the Columbia promotion department bribed the scorekeepers are investigated and proven false. The two teams settle for a tie.

Out in the stands, there are no encore calls, no matches held aloft, but one eleven-year-old potential Catfish gets next to Springsteen and asks him to autograph his glove. Suddenly, Bruce lights up and forgets all about the agony of his feet.

■ **RANDOM NOTES** (September 23, 1976)
Come blow my horn: Clarence Clemons, Bruce Springsteen's sax player, has a part in *New York, New York,* a Forties musical drama now being filmed in Los Angeles. He plays the best friend of saxophonist star Robert DeNiro and dresses in a boxy tan suit and—reluctantly—a pair of wing tips ("Every Sunday I had to get up and shine my father's wing tips for church. I've got a built-in prejudice against them"). He also plays the trumpet, which he hasn't mastered yet. So he's lip synching the notes.

Bruce Springsteen is a free man. After a ten-month forced hiatus from recording because of legal wrangling with former manager Mike Appel, Springsteen has returned to the studio to work on his fourth album.

The settlement came at 3:00 A.M. on May 28th in the office of Appel's attorney, Leonard Marks, who said his client received "substantial economic benefits . . . including a share of the profits from the first three Springsteen albums." Appel also received a five-year production deal from CBS and a cash settlement reportedly substantially less than $1 million.

Springsteen won control of his music publishing (past and future), master recordings, unused tapes and a concert film made in England in 1975. CBS sweetened the deal with a new recording contract.

Jon Landau (who produced Springsteen's *Born to Run* and was an issue in the legal battle) will produce the new album. Springsteen's guitarist, Miami Steve Van Zandt, said in a class at New York's New School that Springsteen has written "thirteen or fourteen really good, three- and four-minute songs with a sort of mid-Sixties, British-American rock feel to them and good strong melodies." The new album is expected to appear before the end of 1977.

DAVID McGEE

BRUCE SPRINGSTEEN CLAIMS THE FUTURE OF ROCK & ROLL

Believers and Betrayers: "A Textbook Example of a Naive Musician Learning the Meaning of Money"

A T 3:00 A.M. on May 28th, after ten months of legal battles and nearly two years after *Born to Run* had catapulted him to national celebrity, Bruce Springsteen and his former manager, Mike Appel, settled their differences and parted ways forever. The move finally enabled Springsteen to record a followup to *Born to Run* with Jon Landau, the producer of his choice. But despite pronouncements of satisfaction with the terms of the settlement, both sides paid dearly for the truce (Springsteen, especially, lost much valuable time). The case is a textbook example of a financially naive musician learning the meaning of money only upon success. And Springsteen's success is the only thing that separates him, in this regard, from countless other aspiring musicians.

Even though two key figures in the case, Springsteen and Landau, are close friends with various ROLLING STONE writers and editors (Landau himself is a contributing editor), details of the settlement are sketchy. Springsteen, Landau and Appel refuse to discuss the case; the only court document relating to the settlement is a single sheet of paper that says the matter has been resolved, and neither party can sue again. In addition, several thousand pages of depositions, which insiders say are both colorful and revealing, were suppressed by the parties involved and never entered the public record. A vow of silence may well have been part of the settlement, but even that no one will confirm.

Appel appears to have made out well; his attorney, Leonard Marks, calls the settlement "a complete victory for Appel." Marks says the settlement provides the former manager with "substantial economic benefits, including a share of the profits from the first three albums." Also included is a five-year deal between Laurel Canyon Productions, Appel's company, and CBS

Records, a third party to the litigation. "Substantial" reportedly means Appel will receive several hundred thousand dollars from Springsteen and CBS for relinquishing his interest in Springsteen.

Springsteen's chief concern, though, was not money but his freedom. His lawyer, Peter Parcher, says, "If Leonard Marks really says that he had a 'complete victory,' then it's just not so. I would suggest that the press observe who's producing Bruce's next LP; whether or not Laurel Canyon Music or Management has anything to do with it; and who now controls the entire catalog of previous songs."

Indeed, the three contracts (for publishing, recording and management) that bound Springsteen to Appel's Laurel Canyon Productions have been rescinded. His recording agreement with Columbia Records has been renegotiated, reportedly at a handsome rate (neither Columbia nor Springsteen would make the figures available), and Springsteen will now administer all of his publishing. Appel will continue to receive some proceeds from the records and publishing from Springsteen's first three albums, but he will not administer them. Such a major concession establishes a precedent for future artist–manager disputes, or at least those in which an artist is more interested in creative control than cash.

Springsteen paid a heavy price in lost time. He had planned to begin recording his fourth LP June 1st, 1976. Instead, he started exactly one year later. Springsteen also alleged in an affidavit sworn last December 8th that the delay hindered his songwriting: "Ever since the issuance of the court's preliminary injunction order, I have started countless numbers of songs which I have been unable to develop to their potential for lack of a proper recording opportunity . . . many of these songs will never be finished."

IN 1971 MIKE APPEL, who looks like a tough Paul McCartney, was a song and jingle writer for the Wes Farrell Organization. "Doesn't Somebody Want to Be Wanted," written with his partner Jim Cretecos, had been a big hit for the Partridge Family. He and Cretecos then made an outside move, producing the first album by Sir Lord Baltimore (described by a former Mercury A&R man as "a heavy-metal joke").

In 1971 Bruce Springsteen was playing clubs in Asbury Park, New Jersey. He knew nothing of Appel. He did know that his career was at a low ebb; in five years as a professional musician he'd never even made $5,000 in a year. Tinker West, a surfboard manufacturer who was Springsteen's manager at the time, suggested that Appel might be a port of entry into recordmaking. In the fall of 1971 Springsteen met with Appel, who was impressed but told Bruce to write some more songs and pay him another visit later. Springsteen decided to leave Asbury Park for California, hoping he might find his break there.

After about four months of travel and touring, Springsteen returned to Appel in March 1972 and signed with Appel's new management and production company, Laurel Canyon. For music publishing he signed with Sioux City Music, owned by Appel's partner, Cretecos. An audition with Columbia A&R man John Hammond, a subsequent Columbia Records contract and the first two LPs, both of which sold fewer than 200,000 copies, quickly followed the signings with Appel and Cretecos.

It's important to note here that money had never been one of Springsteen's priorities. Had his attitude about finances been different, he and Appel would probably never have had their contretemps. What Springsteen wanted, to the exclusion of almost everything else, was to make a great rock & roll record—and to find someone who believed in him without reservation. Appel was his man.

Mike Appel believed that Springsteen belonged in rock's pantheon alongside Dylan, Presley, the Stones and the Beatles. "When he sang," Appel said last year in a *Record World* interview, recalling their second meeting, "I couldn't believe what I heard. There was no doubt in my mind that this was a major, major talent find." A former associate confirms this: "He thought Bruce was the greatest, bar none. He also thought his way of dealing with the money was protecting Bruce. His plan was to set up proper books and run the business legitimately when everything broke for Bruce."

But before that happened, another believer appeared on the scene. Jon Landau bumped into Springsteen in early April 1974. The musician was reading an enlarged display copy of Landau's review of his *The Wild, the Innocent & the E Street Shuffle;* it filled a window at Charlies, a Cambridge bar where Springsteen was playing a benefit for a local friend. Landau introduced himself as the author, asked what Springsteen thought of the review, and the two became friends. Later that month, after seeing a Springsteen concert at the Harvard Square Theater, Landau wrote an impassioned review from which Columbia Records culled the now famous line, "I saw rock & roll future and its name is Bruce Springsteen," for its advertising campaign.

Landau and Springsteen continued to communicate by phone, and after the sessions for *Born to Run*—with Appel at the helm—had floundered for several months, Springsteen asked Landau to become involved. Landau left his job as records editor of ROLLING STONE, a position he had held for six years, and became coproducer. Soon Appel began to resent Landau, for logical reasons. Landau's influence over Springsteen was increasing, and he eventually replaced Appel as Springsteen's major personal and artistic confidant. In addition, it was clear to Appel that Landau was skeptical of his competence.

IN 1975 *Born to Run,* produced by Appel, Springsteen and Landau, made Springsteen a star. He appeared simultaneously on the covers of *Time* and *Newsweek.* But Appel's contracts were about to run out, and he suggested to Springsteen that they renegotiate. According to Leonard Marks: "When things started looking up, Appel offered to renegotiate the contracts with Springsteen—including giving him half the stock of all Laurel Canyon companies. Springsteen said he didn't want to deal with a written contract but wanted to work it out with Appel on a day-to-day basis with a verbal agreement based on trust. Appel had an audit done by Mason & Company and then sent Springsteen a letter saying that 'the books are open' and inviting another outside audit by Springsteen."

Springsteen, on Landau's advice, retained Mike Mayer of Mayer, Nussbaum and Katz, who also represented Landau's music business affairs, for the negotiations. Springsteen also had accountant Stephen Tenenbaum audit the money received and disbursed up to that point. Still, as late as March 1976, Springsteen remained confident of reconciliation with Appel.

The first legal blow was struck by Appel. In May 1976 he sought, through the New Jersey State Court, to attach funds from a week of Springsteen concerts in Red Bank, New Jersey. Appel wanted the money held in escrow until he could draw his management commission from Springsteen. He was denied by the court.

Then Springsteen and Landau, who were discussing the artist's fourth album, learned that Appel was planning to prevent Landau's involvement in that album. Springsteen filed a massive lawsuit on July 27th, 1976, as the result of both Appel's desire to block Landau as producer and Tenenbaum's independent accounting of Laurel Canyon's financial records. Tenenbaum reported in an August 9th affidavit that Appel "conducted Springsteen's business in a slipshod, wasteful and neglectful manner; that he failed to maintain adequate and complete books and records relating to Springsteen's activities; and that enormous amounts of expenses and cash disbursements are charged to Springsteen which are in large measure unsubstantiated." His conclusion: "My audit reveals a classic case of the unconscionable exploitation of an unsophisticated and unrepresented performer by his manager for the manager's primary economic benefit."

Leonard Marks replies: "When Springsteen's lawyers sent Tenenbaum in they gave him leeway to maximize any possible claims against Appel as a negotiating device. Later on, Springsteen's new lawyers saw that it was useless because it was so biased and full of holes that you could drive a truck through it. When the Tenenbaum audit was finished, they wouldn't even give us a copy until several months after the litigation started." (Springsteen lawyer Peter Parcher says, "As I recollect it, the Tenenbaum audit was being completed just as I came into the case. I sent Marks a copy of it after I saw it.")

The crucial charges in Springsteen's suit against Appel were fraud (representing himself as a knowledgeable and experienced businessman), undue influence and breach of trust. In the legal parlance of Springsteen's lawsuit, Appel, as an artist manager, had a "fiduciary" duty—a constant obligation, by the trust Springsteen placed in him, to act first and honorably in the best interests of his client.

But the Laurel Canyon management, according to claims made by Springsteen's lawyers in the lawsuit, formalized a massive conflict of interest that ran directly counter to that fiduciary obligation. The agreement provided that Appel's managerial responsibility was suspended in any of Appel's dealings with Laurel Canyon companies; it also denied Springsteen the right to retain any advisers other than Appel. In other words, in dealings with Appel's nonmanagement companies, Springsteen was on his own.

The recording agreement between Springsteen and Laurel Canyon gave Springsteen about eighteen cents per album sold; the agreement between Laurel Canyon and CBS gave Appel's firm a minimum royalty of forty cents per record. In addition, the CBS agreement itself was a boondoggle. It stated that Laurel Canyon would provide CBS with ten Springsteen albums; Laurel Canyon's production deal with Springsteen, however, called for only five LPs. Springsteen said he was never advised of his rights in these matters. He also said he had seen only one page of the CBS-Laurel Canyon agreement, which he signed, appropriately enough, on the hood of a car in a New Jersey parking lot.

Appel replied to Springsteen's suit two days later, July 29th, by seeking a permanent injunction in New York State Supreme Court barring Springsteen and Landau from entering the recording studio together. Only Laurel Canyon had the right to appoint a producer, Appel said in an affidavit, and that producer would be the "winning combination," as he put it, of himself and Springsteen. The threat of a permanent injunction had been underestimated by Springsteen's legal team. The case was assigned to Judge Arnold Fein, who has a reputation for taking the phrase "unique and exclusive" services in personal-management contracts at face value until otherwise demonstrated. Fein issued the injunction, and Appel suddenly gained the upper hand.

Appel had made Landau *the* issue in the case, charging in his affidavit that Landau saw in Springsteen "a potential gold mine," and that he had engaged in "a campaign to sabotage the relations between Springsteen and myself." Appel termed it "a classic example of bad faith and piracy." Consequently, Landau became the pivotal figure in the ensuing injunction battle. "The real issue appears to be whether Landau may act as the producer over the plaintiff's objection," wrote Fein in his decision granting the preliminary injunction. "Landau has no rights under these agreements."

Although CBS had been named as a defendant in Appel's state action, the company's policy of staying out of artist-manager disputes forced it into a neutral position during the early stages of the case. In an August 6th affidavit, Bruce Lundvall, president of CBS Records, said CBS intended to exercise its contractual right to Springsteen "without taking a position on the side of Mr. Springsteen or the plaintiff." As late as September 7th, CBS executive vice-president Walter Dean still characterized CBS as an "innocent third party."

When Fein upheld Appel's injunction at a second hearing on September 15th, Appel was clearly in a position to do just what CBS Records Group president Walter Yetnikoff says Appel told him he would: ". . . to fight and possibly destroy, through legal means, that which he had created, namely Springsteen's career."

By this time Springsteen knew he was "fighting for my life," as he told Judge Fein. Appel was not compelled to settle out of court; he was winning at every turn. Although Springsteen was no longer generating income for him, Appel had received a sizable royalty payment from CBS in May 1976—he could wait years, letting the suit run its course. And even if the issues at hand came to trial, they were so marginal that there would have to be another trial to finally settle the issues of the validity of the contracts.

In October Springsteen switched from Mayer, Nussbaum and Katz, primarily contract negotiators, to Peter Parcher, a highly skilled litigator and former law partner of Michael Tannen, who was retained at about the same time as a contract negotiator.

From the moment Parcher entered the case it began turning in Springsteen's favor. Earlier, Springsteen had given a deposition so damaging to his own case that Appel mailed portions of it to the press. For example, Leonard Marks asked Springsteen if Appel had not in fact computed his commission at 20 percent—rather than 50 percent—in all financial statements. Springsteen responded that Appel had, but did not explain that Appel had given him only one financial statement in their entire legal relationship. (Leonard

Marks explains: "Springsteen was constantly in the red for his first three albums. Financial statements were meaningless.")

But with the benefit of Parcher's advice, Springsteen's performance at deposition proceedings, according to insiders, was akin to his stage act. Colorfully and authoritatively, he parried each of Marks' allegations that Appel, not Springsteen, was the real architect of his success. If he was fighting for his life, he was adding to his battle all the considerable knowledge of stagecraft at his command. Friends said Bruce was proud of himself; he knew he was beating a fine attorney at his own game. As the record began to roll back, rumors of a settlement began circulating.

In his decision, Fein had left an opening for a trial to resolve the "underlying issue" in the case. Parcher took this to mean Appel's alleged breach of fiduciary duty—the issue on which Springsteen had filed his original federal complaint. On November 18th Parcher submitted an affidavit which in effect asked that the federal and state issues be linked into one trial. The affidavit was bolstered by affidavits from both Jim Cretecos, who noted he was considering suing Appel, and a former Appel employee, Robert Spitz. They alleged that Appel had reneged on promises he had made to Springsteen at the outset of their relationship. Moreover, Spitz claimed that "on numerous occasions Appel stated to me that he hoped Springsteen never became aware of those agreements. Appel also expressed to me on numerous occasions that he was aware that a court of law would find them unconscionable."

The key affidavit in the case was submitted by Springsteen himself on December 8th. First, he asked that he be allowed to record an album (for which CBS had agreed to advance recording costs), with Landau producing, and have it placed in the court's possession pending the outcome of the trial. Fein denied this request.

But Springsteen also detailed the potential damage the enforced absence from recording was doing to his career. Included in this account is a ringing defense of Landau, which was a forceful rebuttal to Appel's charge that he and Bruce were the "winning combination": "Landau has brought to the studio higher qualities which have given tremendous stride to my creative development. Specifically, with respect to the writing of musical compositions, I enter the studio with virtually millions of scattered ideas to which Landau, through his unique ability to communicate with me . . . has been able to provide the focus and direction necessary to shape my thoughts into finished musical compositions. Landau's ability to communicate with me stems from the simple fact that I trust him.

"[Appel's] interest in this action is strictly financial," Springsteen said in closing. "My interest is my career, which up until now holds the promise of my being able to significantly contribute to, and possibly influence, a generation of music. No amount of money could compensate me if I were to lose this opportunity."

On March 22nd, 1977, Springsteen won the motion to submit an amended answer to Appel's complaint. Thus, he was able to assert a fiduciary defense, join the issues in the federal and state cases and take the offensive once more. For the first time since the injunction was issued, Springsteen was in a position to win if the case came to trial. And at this point a settlement became imminent; a little over two months later the parties came to an agreement and the books were closed.

But Springsteen, in his own way, will have the last word. It's in a song which he sang on his last couple of tours. Though it's not necessarily about his relationship with Appel, it might as well be. Its crucial phrase, sung straight from a broken heart, is: "And when the promise was broken / I cashed in a few more dreams."

At the end of the song, there's a line that tells what might have been. It's so touching that you almost wish he and Mike Appel could still share it. "We were gonna take it all," he sings defiantly, "and throw it all away."

■ **RANDOM NOTES** (June 15, 1978)

Bruce Springsteen is back on the road to support his new album, *Darkness on the Edge of Town*. The tour, which started May 23rd in Buffalo, will last until mid-September. It's been two-and-a-half years since Springsteen's *Born to Run* was released, but the song he wrote with Patti Smith, "Because the Night," is a Top Forty single for her.

PAUL NELSON

SPRINGSTEEN FEVER

AT THE MUSIC HALL in Boston in late May, Bruce Springsteen begins a song in almost total darkness, a single blue spotlight faintly limning the singer during the quiet opening minutes of "Thunder Road." It's a magic moment, avoiding pretentiousness only because it works. Springsteen has carefully cultivated the Method actor's idiosyncratic timing, added a professional street character's sense of the dramatic, a dancer's knack for picaresque tableaux, and wrapped the whole package in explosive vulnerability and the practiced pose of a tender, punky hood. Thus the upcoming, split-second move from singular near-silence into vehement, resounding rock & roll as the band joins in—a strategy picked up from R&B groups and one which Springsteen will repeat all night—is a surprise only to the uninitiated, a delicious treat to the aficionado. The sound of the bass drum is so loud that the girl on my left literally clutches her heart.

Tonight has an air of expectancy—one may say even privilege. There's an intensity present, a premonition that this is where the best music in America might well be happening in the next few hours, and the hope that it may be true. It is. Between songs, Springsteen practically becomes a member of the audience. He prowls the edge of the stage, shaking hands and talking to those ecstatic fans who, by standing on their seats, can lean forward and touch him. He's an easy mark. After "Born to Run," when the crowd offers him a tremendous ovation, he subverts the applause by holding up his guitar as if it were some communal instrument of magic, something which he alone does not own. All of a sudden, I realize that we are making this glorious noise not for the pride of one man but for the power of rock & roll.

BACKSTAGE, Bruce Springsteen is so shy and unassuming you could mistake him for his own roadie. Since he's shaved his beard, few people seem to recognize him immediately, a fact that producer Jon Landau verifies by saying that, during the making of *Darkness on the Edge of Town*, Springsteen could walk the streets of New York City totally unnoticed.

Now, sipping a Pepsi and making everyone feel at home, he appears both eager to get people's reactions to the concert and LP and anxious to avoid drawn-out analytical questions about What It All Means. The notoriety of those *Time* and *Newsweek* cover stories about *Born to Run* still seems to haunt him somewhat, but like a tired, albeit polite, host who might secretly wish he could postpone *all* discussion until things cool out a bit, he's a model of professional and personal courtesy.

Springsteen and I first met in 1973, right before his first record, *Greetings From Asbury Park, N.J.,* came out. Tonight, I'm aware that this friendship gives me an edge—that instead of giving me a formal interview, he'd probably rather just talk—and I'm more than a little uneasy about it. When the tape recorder is turned on, both of us are careful not to cross a certain line. I'm glad to see him, but wish the circumstances were different. He seems to feel the same way.

Springsteen laughs when I ask him if it's true that he once said people riding in cars were his genre, and that he'd like to begin every song with the same line or image. And often seems to.

"Oh, yeah," he says. "During the record, I think Jon [Landau] said, 'What's all this about these cars?' I think we were doing 'Prove It All Night,' and it had a different first verse. But it [the car imagery] is just a general thing that forms the action in a particular way. The action is not the imagery, you know. The heart of the action is beneath all that stuff. There's a separate thing happening all the time. I sort of always saw it as the way certain people make certain kinds of movies."

Like detective movies and westerns?

"That's always how I saw the songs. They always had a sort of drive-in quality to them." Springsteen is animated now, smiling, punctuating his sentences with his hands. "Like I wasn't really going for—in a way, I was, aiming for the big Hollywood opening, but they really had more of a drive-in quality. Which is what I wanted because that's where I wanted to work. Plus I'd gotten into seeing movies. I saw *The Grapes of Wrath* on TV, which I used to turn off."

I shake my head in mock sorrow and horror. Springsteen breaks up.

"That's a terrible thing to say, but I always remember turning it off and turning on something that was in color. Then I realized it was a stupid thing to do because one night Jon and I watched it, and it opened up a whole particular world to me. It was very interesting, just a way to watch movies— just a way to observe things, period. Over the past year or two, I got into all the John Ford westerns and seeing just how he made his particular movies."

Sometimes Ford and other *auteur* directors remade the same movie with a slightly different emphasis, I suggest.

"Yeah, and that had a big influence on the way I approached my own work. I loved all those movies, you know. I just felt real close to that stuff."

So close, in fact, that he and Landau, while trying to come up with a name for the new album, jokingly flipped through the film-titles index of Andrew Sarris' classic text, *The American Cinema: Directors and Directions 1929–1968.* Springsteen's choice was *American Madness;* Landau's, *History Is Made at Night.*

Bruce Springsteen credits Jon Landau as being "a big help to me. He helped me see things—to see *into* things—and somehow it would come out in the songs. It's hard to explain. There's a certain little consciousness barrier that gets broken down. What happens in a funny sense is if you grow up in a particular house where the concept of art is twenty minutes in school every day that you *hate,* and there's no books, no music, there's nothing—well, until you bump into someone who grew up in a house that had a lot of books and different stuff, it's [difficult]. That's a problem for a lot of people—a lot of my friends. You just don't bump into [anyone who's] going to make you more able to use whatever brains you've got.

"That's why the importance of rock & roll was just incredible. It reached *down* into all those homes where there was no music or books or any kind of creative sense, and it infiltrated the whole thing. That's what happened in my house, you know."

A mutual friend told me that Springsteen had said that the songs on *Darkness on the Edge of Town* are about "people who are going from nowhere to nowhere." I wonder if this is correct.

"Yeah, that's what I always thought. That's why a lot of the action always takes place around cars. It's like everybody's always in transit. There's no settling down, no fixed action. You pick up the action, and then at some point—*pssst!*—the camera pans away, and whatever happened, that's what happened. The songs I write, they don't have particular beginnings and they don't have endings. The camera focuses in and then out."

Springsteen says that he recorded thirty songs for the new LP and then made his final selection on the basis of "those I felt were the most important for me to get out. I wanted to put out stuff that I felt had the most substance and yet was still an album."

One of his best new songs is "The Promise," which remains unreleased. I ask why.

"Because too many people were interpreting it to be about the lawsuit. [Springsteen and former manager/producer Mike Appel sued each other, but settled out of court last summer.] I wrote it before there was a lawsuit. . . . I don't write songs about lawsuits."

We talk for a while about the inordinate amount of time it seems to take Springsteen to make a record. He's developed a keen sense of humor about this.

"The main thing is you owe your best. That's how I feel toward myself. I just couldn't understand why people would rush to get out an album by a particular date and then regret it afterward. I mean, a date is just a date, except to the machine kind of thing.

"I was at the Spectrum [in Philadelphia] the other night, and some kids ran backstage and said, 'Hey, that one was good, it was worth the wait,' and that makes it for me, you know. I've never had a kid come up to me and say, 'Hey, what were you *doing* all that time?' or, 'What took you so *long*? I don't get it!' That's how it rings true for me. That's the big important connection—you see what matters to the kids. They want to have the stuff, but if it's not the best you can do, it's not worth doing. Not for me, anyway."

What about "Factory"?

"I wrote that song in about half an hour. See, that's the funny thing—the album took a long time, but most of the songs were written real fast. It was just figuring out what to do with them. 'Factory'—that's like everybody's old man or something."

I mention that there are a couple of songs about fathers on *Darkness on the Edge of Town*. Springsteen looks thoughtful.

"Yeah," he says. "Yeah, there are. I wrote three songs that had to do with that, and one didn't get on. And that might have been the best one, but it just didn't fit. It's a song called 'Independence Day.' We've never played it, but it was a ballad, and we had too many slow songs. So . . . "

He leans forward. "But 'The Promise' and 'Independence Day.' Those were two that I got that'll definitely be on the next record. Which should be about another three years." We both laugh.

Many of the characters in the songs on Bruce Springsteen's new album appear to be trapped in a state of desperation so intense that they must either break through into something better (or at least into something ambiguous) or break down into madness, murder and worse. *Darkness on the Edge of Town* seems to be about the high cost of romantic obsession for adults, not teenagers ("Mister, I ain't a boy, no, I'm a man" instead of the wonderful but more sentimental " 'Cause tramps like us, baby we were born to run"), and while the LP offers hope, it's also Springsteen's blackest—though probably best—work.

Springsteen himself says: "My songs are all *action* songs. They're *action,* you know. All my songs are about people at that moment when they've got to do *something,* just do *something,* do *anything.* There's no halfway in most of the songs because I don't approach what I do in that way. There's just no room to compromise. I think, for most musicians, it has to be like life or death or else it's not worth it. That's why every night we play a real long time, and we play *real hard.* I want to be able to go home and say I went all the way tonight—and then I went a little further.

"My whole life, I was always around a lot of people whose lives consisted of just this compromising—they knew no other way. That's where rock & roll is important, because it said that there could be another way, you know. That's why I write the kind of songs I do, why they have a particular kind of immediacy. As you go along, I think you have to deal more directly with whatever's confronting you because that's the only way to get across.

"It's real hard to talk about the record because what I have invested in it—I'm not talking about money—what I have invested is *so much.* . . . "

It strikes me that *Darkness on the Edge of Town* is less urban than many of his albums, especially *The Wild, the Innocent & the E Street Shuffle.* Springsteen agrees.

"The stuff I always felt closest to was the small-town kind of stuff, because that's the way I grew up. And I thought about the things I liked best about the last record, what was the truest. Plus that's where I live—I don't live in New York. So when I wrote 'Racing in the Street,' that's like home. And 'Darkness on the Edge of Town.' 'The Promise' was, too. That's home stuff, you know.

"And the tone of the songs. The saxophone's a very urban instrument, and when Clarence plays it, it's got that warm, human kind of thing. On some of the songs, it collided with the texture or just the particular character of what was happening in a funny way. You can make it work—it worked on 'Born to Run' and it works on 'Prove It All Night'—but it's tricky. With the saxophone, there's *no* distance—that thing, it's right up to your *face.* But the guitar has always been a little cooler instrument, and the tone of the songs was a little cooler, so I played more guitar on this record than I did the last time. Whatever's functional, you know."

Backstage, Springsteen looks particularly boyish. Tired but pleased. He hooks a foot under the bottom rung of his chair and tilts it back and forth. Onstage, he's like an exuberant but dreamy montage of every rock & roll and film star whose picture ever graced your wall: Montgomery Clift, James Dean, Elvis Presley, Al Pacino, Robert DeNiro, et al. The collective resemblance is uncanny. Now that he's conquered rock & roll, can the movies be far behind? (Those close to him say he's thinking about it.) Bob Dylan figuratively replaced James Dean, and it's a better-than-ever bet that Bruce Springsteen could succeed both of them.

The interview is over, but I can't resist telling Springsteen that he seems to have as much loyalty to his fans as they do to him.

"You've got to have that," he says. "These people work all week and a lot of times wait in line for ten hours or some incredible amount of time. I mean, I go to shows—it's *hard* to go to a show. You can get *bonked* by somebody sitting next to you, or you don't know what's happening—it's totally disorienting. It's like you're stepping out there a little bit, you know.

"The kid, he's doing his bit. He's forking over his bucks, he's coming down. You've got to make sure he can come down, sit in his seat and not get blown up. That's your responsibility to the crowd, and that's the most important thing. That's much more important than anything.

"You can *never* take it for granted. I feel that very strongly. For the first four years, I had an attitude—I went into every place expecting it to be empty. So whoever was there was a big plus. I was glad they were there, and we played our best to whoever was there, *always*. You just don't lay back in this band, you know. That just doesn't happen. That's why people come down to see us—because something more is going to happen. Something—just somehow, someway.

"You've got to look into some of these people's faces. It's very important to have that contact because you get such a feeling. Sometimes after the show the kids'll wait out back, and that's the best part. It's like Christmas or something. They don't take it lightly, so you have no right to, either. It's something that I've never done and I never will do. I'll quit before I do that.

"The whole idea is to deliver what money can't buy. That's the idea of going out there. You don't go out there to deliver seven dollars and fifty cents worth of music. My whole thing is to go out there and deliver what they could not possibly buy. And if you do that, you've done whatever you could do."

BRUCE MANIA
LP and Tour Make Their Own Gravy

BRUCE SPRINGSTEEN'S *Darkness on the Edge of Town,* released by CBS on June 2nd, two years and nine months after *Born to Run,* almost immediately became a media event. For FM radio stations, the competition to be first to air it was intense. The Century Broadcasting group, with outlets in Los Angeles, San Francisco, St. Louis and Detroit, won the race, playing the album on the night of May 18th and into the morning of the 19th, until CBS sent telegrams to the stations ordering them to cease and desist. Over the next few weeks, WBAB, Long Island; WNEW, New York and WMMS, Cleveland, also played the album and were sent similar telegrams.

Springsteen, meanwhile, began his tour May 23rd in Buffalo. The fact that almost no one had heard the album yet didn't deter him from performing nine of its ten songs on opening night—and several of those songs, notably "Badlands" and "Adam Raised a Cain," earned standing ovations. The initial concert was a rare instance of rock pack journalism: reviewers and reporters from the *New York Times, Los Angeles Times,* the Field Newspaper Syndicate and *Newsweek* were all present. By the June 3rd show at Nassau Coliseum, Springsteen was performing only seven of the new songs and had reinstated several old songs into his show, which still runs nearly three hours including the inevitable multiple encores.

The tour will run until at least September 13th, after which Springsteen may tour in Europe. It marks a bit of a departure for Springsteen: He is playing arena-sized halls (8,500–15,000 seats) in ten of the seventy cities in which he's appearing. (The smallest halls he's playing seat about 2,600.)

Darkness entered *Record World*'s LP chart in the June 17th issue at twenty-six with a bullet; *Billboard* placed it at thirty-nine, bulleted. The single, "Prove It All Night," met with less-enthusiastic response from AM stations, but still did well enough (seventy-four, bullet) to earn *Record World*'s Chartmaker of the Week honors. This is somewhat less impressive than *Born to Run,* which debuted on *Record World*'s LP chart at ten with a bullet in 1975. But the competition is regarded as a bit stiffer this year. And the album did ship gold-plus—meaning more than 500,000 units.

DAVE MARSH

DARKNESS ON THE EDGE OF TOWN ALBUM REVIEW
The Boss' Triumphant Return

OCCASIONALLY, a record appears that changes fundamentally the way we hear rock & roll, the way it's recorded, the way it's played. Such records—Jimi Hendrix' *Are You Experienced,* Bob Dylan's "Like a Rolling Stone," Van Morrison's *Astral Weeks, Who's Next, The Band*—force response, both from the musical community and the audience. To me, these are the records justifiably called classics, and I have no doubt that Bruce Springsteen's *Darkness on the Edge of Town* will someday fit as naturally within that list as the Rolling Stones' "(I Can't Get No) Satisfaction" or Sly and the Family Stone's "Dance to the Music."

One ought to be wary of making such claims, but in this case, they're justified at every level. In the area of production, *Darkness on the Edge of Town* is nothing less than a breakthrough. Springsteen—with coproducer Jon Landau, engineer Jimmy Iovine and Charles Plotkin, who helped Iovine mix the LP—is the first artist to fuse the spacious clarity of Los Angeles record making and the raw density of English productions. That's the major reason why the result is so different from *Born to Run*'s Phil Spector wall of sound. On the earlier album, for instance, the individual instruments were deliberately obscured to create the sense of one huge instrument. Here, the same power is achieved more naturally. Most obviously, Max Weinberg's drumming has enormous size, a heartbeat with the same kind of space it occupies onstage (the only other place I've heard a bass drum sound this big).

Now that it can be heard, the E Street Band is clearly one of the finest rock & roll groups ever assembled. Weinberg, bassist Garry Tallent and guitarist Steve Van Zandt are a perfect rhythm section, capable of both power and groove. Pianist Roy Bittan is as virtuosic as on *Born to Run,* and saxophonist Clarence Clemons, though he has fewer solos, evokes more than ever the spirit of King Curtis. But the revelation is organist Danny Federici, who barely appeared on the last LP. Federici's style is utterly singular, focusing on wailing, trebly chords that sing (and in the marvelous solo at the end of "Racing in the Street," truly cry).

Yet the dominant instrumental focus of *Darkness on the Edge of Town* is Bruce Springsteen's guitar. Like his songwriting and singing, Springsteen's guitar playing gains much of its distinctiveness through pastiche. There are echoes of a dozen influences—Duane Eddy, Jimmy Page, Jeff Beck, Jimi Hendrix, Roy Buchanan, even Ennio Morricone's Sergio Leone soundtracks—but the synthesis is completely Springsteen's own. Sometimes Springsteen quotes a famous solo—Robbie Robertson's from the live version of "Just Like Tom Thumb's Blues" at the end of "Something in the Night," Jeff Beck's from "Heart Full of Soul" in the bridge of "Candy's Room"—and then shatters it into another dimension. In the end the most impressive guitar work of all is just his own: "Adam Raised a Cain" and "Streets of Fire" are things *no one*'s ever heard before.

Much the same can be said about Springsteen's singing. Certainly, Van Morrison and Bob Dylan are the inspirations for taking such extreme chances: bending and twisting syllables; making two key lines on "Streets of Fire" a wordless, throttled scream; the wailing and humming that precede and follow some of the record's most important lyrics. But more than ever, Springsteen's voice is personal, intimate and revealing, bigger and less elusive. It's the possibility hinted at on *Born to Run*'s "Backstreets" and in the postverbal wail at the end of "Jungleland." In fact, Springsteen picks up that moan at the beginning of "Something in the Night," on which he turns in the new album's most adventurous vocal.

One could say a great deal about the construction of this LP. The programming alone is impressive: each side is a discrete progression of similar lyrical and musical themes, and the whole is a more universal version of the same picture. Ideas, characters and phrases jump from song to song like threads in a tapestry, and everything's one long interrelationship. But all of these elements—the production, the playing, even the programming—are designed to focus our attention on what Springsteen has to tell us about the last three years of his life.

In a way, this album might take as its text two lines from Jackson Browne: "Nothing survives—/But the way we live our lives." But where Browne is content to know this, Springsteen explores it: *Darkness on the Edge of Town* is about the kind of life that deserves survival. Despite its title, it is a complete *rejection* of despair. Bruce Springsteen says this over and over again, more bluntly and clearly than anyone could have imagined. There isn't a single song on this record in which his yearning for a perfect existence, a life lived to the hilt, doesn't play a central role.

Springsteen also realizes the terrible price one pays for living at half-speed. In "Racing in the Street," the album's most beautiful ballad, Springsteen separates humanity into two classes: "Some guys they just give up living / And start dying little by little, piece by piece / Some guys come home from work and wash up / And go racin' in the street." But there's nothing smug about it, because Springsteen knows that the line separating the living dead from the walking wounded is a fine and bitter one. In the song's final verse, he describes with genuine love a person of the first sort, someone whose eyes "hate for just being born." In "Factory," he depicts the most numbing sort of life with a compassion that's nearly religious. And in "Adam Raised a Cain," the son who rejected his father's world comes to understand their relationship as "the dark heart of a dream"—a dream become nightmarish, but a vision of something better nonetheless.

There are those who will say that "Adam Raised a Cain" is full of hate, but I don't believe it. The only hate I hear on this LP is embodied in a single song, "Streets of Fire," where Springsteen describes how it feels to be trapped by lies. And even here, he has the maturity to hate the lie, not the liar.

Throughout the new album, Springsteen's lyrics are a departure from his early work, almost its opposite, in fact: dense and compact, not scattershot. And if the scenes are the same—the highways, bars, cars and toil—they also represent facets of life that rock & roll has too often ignored or, what's worse, romanticized. *Darkness on the Edge of Town* faces everyday life whole, daring to see if something greater can be made of it. This is naive perhaps, but also courageous. Who else but a brave innocent could believe so boldly in a promised land, or write a song that not only quotes Martha and the Vandellas' "Dancing in the Street" but paraphrases the Beach Boys' "Don't Worry Baby"?

Bruce Springsteen has a tendency to inspire messianic regard in his fans—including this one. This isn't so much because he's regarded as a savior—though his influence has already been substantial—but because he fulfills the rock tradition in so many ways. Like Elvis Presley and Buddy Holly, Springsteen has the ability, and the zeal, to do it all. For many years, rock & roll has been splintered between the West Coast's monopoly on the genre's lyrical and pastoral characteristics and a British and Middle American stranglehold on toughness and raw power. Springsteen unites these aspects: he's the only artist I can think of who's simultaneously comparable to Jackson Browne *and* Pete Townshend. Just as the production of this record unifies certain technical trends, Springsteen's presentation makes rock itself whole again. This is true musically—he rocks as hard as a punk, but with the verbal grace of a singer/songwriter—and especially emotionally. If these songs are about experienced adulthood, they sacrifice none of rock & roll's adolescent innocence. Springsteen escapes the narrow dogmatism of both Old Wave and New, and the music's possibilities are once again limitless.

Four years ago, in a Cambridge bar, my friend Jon Landau and I watched Bruce Springsteen give a performance that changed some lives—my own included. About a similar night, Landau later wrote what was to become rock criticism's most famous sentence: "I saw rock & roll future and its name is Bruce Springsteen." With its usual cynicism, the world chose to think of this as a fanciful way of calling Springsteen the Next Big Thing.

I've never taken it that way. To me, these words, shamefully mistreated as they've been, have kept a different shape. What they've always said was that someday Bruce Springsteen would make rock & roll that would shake men's souls and make them question the direction of their lives. That would do, in short, all the marvelous things rock had always promised to do.

But *Born to Run* was not that music. It sounded instead like the end of an era, the climax of the first twenty years of this grand tradition, the apex of our collective adolescence. *Darkness on the Edge of Town* does not. It feels like the threshold of a new period in which we'll again have "lives on the line where dreams are found and lost." It poses once more the question that rock & roll's epiphanic moments always raise: Do you believe in magic?

And once again, the answer is yes. Absolutely.

DAVE MARSH

BRUCE SPRINGSTEEN RAISES CAIN
A True Believer Witnesses Mass Conversions, Rock & Roll Vandalism, a Rocket Upside the Head and a Visit With God

ONE OF BRUCE SPRINGSTEEN'S most popular early songs is called "4th of July, Asbury Park (Sandy)." That he is spending this Independence Day on the shores of the wrong ocean is an irony that escapes no one, including himself. Los Angeles is not terra incognita, but Springsteen does not yet reign here as he does back east, and perhaps the time is auspicious to change that. Although he has been up all night mixing tapes recorded at his last concert (Saturday night, in Berkeley), he is at the pool soaking up the sun by 11:00 A.M.

If God had invented a hotel for rock bands, it probably would look like the Sunset Marquis, where Springsteen and the E Street Band are staying. Nestled on a steep side street just below Sunset Strip, the Marquis is a combination summer camp and commune. Its rooms are laid out around the swimming pool and guests on the first floor use the pool terrace as a sort of patio. In the daytime, the poolside is jammed, and at night, it's easy to tell who's home by the lights inside, behind curtained glass doors. Springsteen, the band, their crew and entourage occupy thirty rooms, including all those around the pool.

At noon, producer/manager Jon Landau, Bruce and I disappear into Springsteen's room to play the Berkeley concert mixes. There are two mixes of an eight-minute rendition of "Prove It All Night" that shatters the LP version, and one mix of an unnamed, shorter instrumental, often called "Paradise by the 'C,' " which opens the second half of his concerts. Even on a small cassette player, it's clear that something considerable is going on.

For years people have been begging Springsteen to make a live album, and "Prove It All Night" shows why. The song is considered the lightest item on *Darkness on the Edge of Town,* his new album, but onstage it becomes what pianist Roy Bittan, for one, thinks is the most exciting song of the show, featuring a lengthy guitar and keyboard improvisation that sounds like an unholy alliance between the Yardbirds and Bob Dylan. When the introduction gives way to the melody of the song, "Prove It" is transformed from something potentially light and dismissible into an emotional crucible. Hearing it, you may wonder if "Prove It All Night" is a hit single, but you *know* it's a great song.

"Paradise by the 'C' " is its alter ego. Only Springsteen, touring behind a new album, would have come up with this to open the second half of the show: a five-minute instrumental featuring Clarence Clemons' sax and Danny Federici's organ, which simultaneously evokes Duane Eddy and Booker T. and the MGs.

Clemons walks into the room with an unbelievably joyous look on his face, and when the tape ends, he takes Bruce by the arm and shouts, "Everybody into the pool!" The next sound is a series of splashes, and in a few moments they reappear, bathing suits dripping, and listen again, then repeat the performance. Soon, the tiny hotel bedroom is crowded with half a dozen people dripping wet and exuberant.

At 6:30 P.M., Bruce is at KMET-FM to do an on-the-air interview with disc jockey Mary Turner. There are a couple of bottles of champagne, which may be a mistake; Bruce gets loose pretty easily. And in fact, he is a little sloshed as the interview begins, but Turner plays it perfectly, fishing for stories. She gets at least one winner.

"When my folks moved out to California," Bruce begins in response to a question about whether he really knows "a pretty little place in Southern California / Down San Diego way" as he claims in "Rosalita," "my mom decided—see my father and I would fight all the time—and she decided that we should take a trip together. She decided that we should go to *Tijuana* [he laughs his hoarse laugh, reserved for the truly absurd]. So we got in the car and drove down there, arguing all the way. First I drove and he yelled at me, and then he drove and I yelled at him.

"Anyway, we finally got there, and of course, my old man is the softest-hearted guy in the world. Within fifteen minutes, some guy has sold him some watch that must've run for all of an hour and a half before it stopped. And then some guy comes up and says, 'Hey, would you guys like to have your picture taken on a zebra?'

"Well, we looked at each other—who could believe this, right? Zebras are in Africa. And so we said, 'Well if you've got a zebra, we definitely want to have our picture taken.' So we give him ten bucks and he takes us around this corner, and he's got . . . he's got a damn donkey with stripes painted on its side. And he pulls out these two hats—one says Pancho, one says

Cisco—I swear—and he sits us on the donkey and takes our picture. My mother's still got that picture. But that is all I knew about Southern California at the time I wrote 'Rosalita.' "

This is the easiest I have ever heard Bruce speak of his father. "Adam Raised a Cain," from the new album, may have exorcised a lot of ghosts. In some of the stories Bruce has told onstage about their relationship, however, his father seems like a demon, which of course, he is not.

In fact, Douglas Springsteen has lived a very rough working-class life. For a great deal of Bruce's childhood, his family (he has two sisters, both younger) shared a house with his grandparents while his father worked at an assortment of jobs—in a factory, as a gardener, as a prison guard—never making as much as $10,000 a year. Later he moved the family from New Jersey to northern California, where he is now a bus driver. Bruce says that the tales of their conflicts are true ("I don't make 'em up"), but that they're meant to be "universal." He is not exactly enthusiastic about discussing the relationship, although in a couple of the songs that did not make it onto *Darkness,* particularly "The Promise" and "Independence Day," he has chronicled his preoccupation with fathers as thoroughly as did John Steinbeck in *East of Eden,* the film that inspired "Adam."

Bruce is so loose by now that when an ad for Magic Mountain's roller coaster—the largest in the world—comes on, he discusses great roller coasters he has known, and his desire to see this one. "Ya wanna date?" he asks Turner, in front of who knows how many listeners. She makes the perfect reply: "Only if we sit in the front seat."

After the interview, we head to the car and a beach house in Santa Monica, where there's a promise of food and fireworks. We race straight out Santa Monica Boulevard to the freeway. It's like something out of a Steve McQueen movie [*Bullitt*]. I haven't spent as reckless a moment as this one in years. But Bruce, who isn't driving, is determined to see those fireworks. "C'mon," he says, over and over again. "I don't wanna miss 'em." He's like a little boy, and the car whips along, straight into a traffic jam at the end of the Santa Monica Freeway, where we can see hints of the fireworks—blue, red, gold, green—cascading out over the ocean.

It's a chill night and the party is outside. Band and crew members shiver on the patio, chewing on cold sandwiches (Swiss cheese, ham, turkey, roast beef) and sucking down beer and soda. Bruce quickly decides this won't do. He heads for the gate leading to the beach. "C'mon," he says to one and all. "Let's walk up to the pier. I want a hot dog."

And so we strike out down the beach. The pier is a mile south, far enough so that its lights are only a glow on the horizon. And covering the beach the entire distance are people shooting off their own fireworks, Roman candles and skyrockets. We haven't gone a hundred yards before the scene has become a combat zone. I suggest a strategic retreat to the highway. Bruce gives me a look. "C'mon, what's the worst that can happen? A rocket upside the head?" He giggles with joy and keeps trudging on through the sand.

The rockets are exploding directly over our heads now, and once in a while, closer than that. A rocket upside the head is not unimaginable. Bruce strikes out closer to the water, where the sand is more firmly packed and the walking is easier. Down here there are other sorts of activity: lovers in sleeping bags and drinkers sitting in sand pits, nursing themselves against the chill with liquor. The rockets, fewer now, drift out into the water to die with a hiss or a fizzle, and Bruce Springsteen moves through it all, just another cloud in a hurricane, a natural force or maybe just another kid.

Two hot dogs with relish and an hour of pinball later, we walk back along the highway to the car and zip back to the hotel. Tour manager Jim McHale, David Landau (Warren Zevon's lead guitarist and Jon's brother) and booking agent Barry Bell are talking in Jon's room when Bruce bursts through the poolside curtains. His face is glowing. "We're goin' to make the hit," he shouts, and ducks back out. McHale's jaw drops and he races from the room. "I think they're going to paint the billboard," says David.

The raid isn't completely a surprise. Sunday night, driving up the Strip on the way to see *The Buddy Holly Story,* Bruce had first noticed the billboard looming above a seven-story building just west of the Continental Hyatt House. Billboards are a Hollywood institution—they're put up for every significant album and concert appearance—and this one uses the *Darkness* cover photo, poorly cropped, to promote both the new record and the group's Forum appearance tomorrow night. As we passed this enormous monument, which rears up forty feet above the building, Bruce had groaned and slumped in his seat. "That is the *ugliest* thing I've ever seen in my *life,*" he said.

The billboard is only a few blocks up the street. According to all accounts, Springsteen, Clemons, bass guitarist Garry Tallent and several crew members approached with some stealth the office building on which the billboard is perched. Much to their surprise, the building was wide open, and the elevator quickly took them to the roof. There, McHale, perhaps figuring that cleverness is better than a bust, quickly organized them. There were twenty cans of black spray paint, quickly distributed, and Bruce, Garry and Clarence quickly took positions on the paperhangers' ledge. Bell was positioned across the street to watch for cops. At a signal from McHale, the painting began: PROVE IT ALL NIGHT spread across the billboard from edge to edge, the middle words nearly lost in the dark photo of Bruce. Then Bruce stood on Clemons' shoulders and painted another legend above NIGHT: E STREET, it said. As they were clambering down, a signal came—the cops. Some headed back for the elevator, but Bruce, Clarence and McHale left Cagney-style, down the outside fire escape. It was a false alarm anyway.

In the hotel lobby at a quarter to three, Bruce is exhilarated. "You shoulda been there," he says, running over the event like a successful general fresh from battle. Was he worried about getting caught? "Naw," he says. "I figured if they caught us, that was great, and if we got away with it, that was even better." He looks down at himself, hands black with paint, boots ruinously dusty from the beach, and laughs. "There it is," he says. "Physical evidence. . . . The only thing is, I wanted to get to my face, and paint on a mustache. But it was just too damn high." He terms the paint job "an artistic improvement."

WEDNESDAY, July 5th: Last night, as we were getting into the car after the KMET interview, Bruce began to talk about the reviews *Darkness on the Edge of Town* has been getting. It is a subject on which he qualifies as something of an expert: more has been written about him—and about what has been written on him—than any other rock performer of recent years, with the possible exception of Mick Jagger. The miracle is, I guess, that the scars barely show—instead, Springsteen looks at the press with avid interest.

"It's a weird thing about those reviews," Bruce says. "You can find any conceivable opinion in them: one guy says the record's exactly like *Born to Run* and it's great, the next one says it's not like *Born to Run* and it's great, the next one says it's not like *Born to Run* and it's awful." This amuses him. The nearly unanimous opinion that the album is grim and depressing doesn't.

It's the title, I suggest. "I know, I know," he says impatiently. "But I put in the first few seconds of 'Badlands,' the first song on the album, those lines about 'I believe in the love and the hope and the faith.' It's there on all four corners of the album." By which he means the first and last songs on each side: "Badlands" and "Racing in the Street," "The Promised Land" and the title song. He is clearly distressed: he meant *Darkness* to be "relentless," not grim.

Later, I ask him why the album lacks the humor that buoys his shows. "In the show, it's a compilation of all the recorded stuff," he says in the halting way he uses when he's taking something seriously. "If you go back to

The Wild and Innocent, 'Rosalita' is there, and all that stuff. But when I was making this particular album, I just had a specific thing in mind. And one of the important things was that it had to be just a relentless . . . just a barrage of the particular thing.

"I got an album's worth of pop songs, like 'Rendezvous' and early English-style stuff. I got an album's worth right now, and I'm gonna get it out somehow. I wanna do an album that's got ten or eleven things like that on it. But I just didn't feel it was the right time to do that, and I didn't want to sacrifice any of the intensity of the album by throwing in 'Rendezvous,' even though I knew it was popular from the show."

The other criticism that is easily made of *Darkness* concerns the repetition of certain images: cars, street life, abandonment by or of women, family and friends. Those who like this call it style; those who don't say Springsteen is drilling a dry hole. But perhaps Springsteen's greatest and most repeated image is the lie.

"It's hard to explain without getting too heavy. What it is, it's the characters' commitment. In the face of all the betrayals, in the face of all the imperfections that surround you in whatever kind of life you lead, it's the characters' refusal to let go of their own humanity, to let go of their own belief in the other side. It's a certain loss of innocence—more so than in the other albums."

I drove out to the Forum this afternoon with Obie. Obie is twenty-five, and she has been Bruce Springsteen's biggest fan for more than a decade. When he was still just a local star, she waited overnight for tickets to his shows to make certain she'd have perfect seats. She is now secretary to Miami Steve Van Zandt, Springsteen's guitarist and manager/producer of Southside Johnny and the Asbury Jukes. This means that while Springsteen is on tour, Obie is the de facto manager of the Asbury Jukes. But she's also something more. She makes some of the jackets and suits Bruce wears onstage. She is also a historian; there are a thousand Asbury Park legends behind her twinkling eyes. More than anything, she is a fan who counts the days between Springsteen shows. Her loyalty is rewarded. Whenever she comes to a show, in any town, the front-row center is reserved for her.

It is partly this that makes Bruce Springsteen so attractive: he is surrounded by real-life characters that form the kind of utopian community most of us lost when we graduated high school; one of the reasons Springsteen is such a singular performer is that he has never lost touch with this decidedly noncosmopolitan gang.

Part of the legend is the E Street Band. "Ya know, you can tell by looking at 'em," Bruce explains to me, "that this isn't a bunch of guys with a whole lot in common. But somehow the music cuts right through all that."

There's a lot to cut. Bassist Garry Tallent is a consummate rockabilly addict who looks the part. He's been known to use Brylcreem. Organist Danny Federici has an angel face that could pass for the kind of tough guy Harvey Keitel plays in *Fingers*. Pianist Roy Bittan and drummer Max Weinberg are seasoned pros, veterans of recording studios and Broadway pit bands. Miami Steve Van Zandt is a perpetual motion machine, a comic version of Keith Richards' Barbary pirate act, with a slice of small-town-boy-made-good on the side. And Clarence Clemons, last of all, dwells in a land all his own, not quite like the universe the rest of us inhabit, though it is seemingly available to all comers. Clemons transforms any room he enters, as a six-foot-plus black man with the bulk of a former football player often can do, but even in his own digs at the Marquis, there's something special happening—his hospitality is perfect, and it is in Clarence's room that the all-night party is most likely to run.

Bruce stands distinctly outside this group. "It's weird," he says, " 'cause it's not really a touring band or just a recording band. And it's definitely me, I'm a solo act, y'know." But there is also a sense in which Bruce Springsteen does not mesh in any society, and it has a great deal to do with what makes him so obsessive about his music.

Before he landed a record contract, all of the Asbury Park musicians held day jobs—Garry Tallent worked in a music store, Clemons was a social worker, Van Zandt was in the construction union. The exception, always, was Bruce, who never held any other job, apparently because he could not conceive of doing anything else. At age eight, when he first heard Presley, lightning struck, and when he picked up the guitar at thirteen, another bolt hit him. "When I got the guitar," he told me Wednesday night, "I wasn't getting out of myself. I was already out of myself. I knew myself, and I did not dig me. I was getting into myself."

By fourteen, he was in his first band; by sixteen, he was so good that when he practiced in his manager's garage, neighborhood kids would stand on milk crates at the windows with their noses pressed to the glass, just to hear. The only other things besides music that ever meant much to him, Springsteen says, were surfing and cars. But nothing—even girls—ever got in the way of his obsession with his music; there is a certain awe in the way that people who have known him for many years speak of his single-minded devotion to playing. It's as if he always knew his destiny, and while this hasn't made him cold—he is one of the friendliest people I know—it has given him considerable distance from everyday relationships. One does not ever think of Bruce Springsteen married and settled down, raising a family, having kids; that would be too much monkey business.

WHAT KEEPS the band so tight is the two-to-three-hour sound check before each gig. Today's began at 3:30 P.M.—it's a 7:30 show on the ticket—and didn't end until nearly seven. In part, these are informal band rehearsals, with Bruce working up new material: as we enter the hall at five, he is singing Buddy Holly's "Rave On," a number he has never done live. But there's more to it than that.

On this tour, Springsteen's sound mixer is Bruce Jackson, a tall blond Australian who worked for Elvis Presley for several years. He is amazed at Springsteen's perfectionism. "At every date," he says, "he goes out and sits in every section of the hall to listen to the sound. And if it isn't right, even in the last row, I hear about it, and we make changes, I mean every date, too—he doesn't let it slip in Davenport, Iowa, or something." Presley, on the other hand, was concerned only with the sound he would hear in the onstage monitors.

("Anybody who works for me," Springsteen says, without a trace of a joke, "the first thing you better know is I'm gonna drive you crazy. Because I don't compromise in certain areas. So if you're gonna be in, you better be ready for that.")

Which perhaps explains the consistently high quality of Springsteen's live performances. I must have seen forty over the years, and no two are alike. Even if the songs are the same, which they hardly ever are, Bruce brings something different to every one. Tonight's is conversational—the loosest I've ever seen, and at the same time, frighteningly intense. He begins immediately after "Badlands," the opening number, by talking about the walk on the beach last night ("It's like a combat zone out there") and makes some self-deprecating remarks about his press attention, which has mushroomed this week; Robert Hilburn had given him a rave advance notice in the Sunday *Los Angeles Times,* and Ed Kociela had more than matched it with a pair of pieces—interview and Berkeley concert review—in Monday's *Herald-Examiner.* In a way, Springsteen was taking Los Angeles by storm, as he had taken New York in August 1975 with the release of *Born to Run* and ten shows at the Bottom Line. There are some who must find such excessive praise threatening or suspicious—though only a fool would think that such enthusiasm could be manufactured—but Bruce defuses it easily: "See all that fancy stuff in the papers about me? Big deal, huh? I gotta tell you, I only levitate to the upper deck on Wednesdays and Fridays. . . . Wednesdays and Fridays, and I don't do no windows."

Perhaps the most nervy and nerve-racking antic Springsteen has retained in making the transition to hockey arenas is his trademark leap into the audience during the third song, "Spirit in the Night." He looks frail—at an extremely wiry and agile five-foot-nine, he is not—and one is always worried that his consummate trust in his fans is going to let him down. But night after night he gets away with it. Somehow. Tonight, the security doesn't get the picture and tries to drag the fans off Bruce as he ascends an aisle deep in the loges. "You guys work here or something?" Springsteen demands. "Get outta here. These guys are my friends." The crowd roars.

His parents have come down from their home near San Francisco for the show, and the evening is sprinkled with allusions to them and his sixteen-year-old sister, Pam. The stories he tells are always among his best moments, but what gets me tonight are the asides and dedications: he tells about the billboard ("We made a few improvements"), about asking Mary Turner for a date, and when he does "For You," he dedicates the song to Greg Kihn, who recorded the song for Berserkley Records a year ago. And because Gary Busey is here, he tells about seeing *The Buddy Holly Story*. It's the perfect review.

"It's funny because I could never really picture Buddy Holly moving. To me, he was always just that guy with the bow tie on the album cover. I liked the picture because it made him a lot more real for me."

But the encores are the evening's highlights. First, "The Promise," a quiet ballad that was one of the first things Springsteen wrote for the new album, and which was finally dropped from it. In an earlier version, "The Promise" was taken by many listeners to be a metaphor for the lawsuit with former manager Mike Appel that delayed production of the new LP for more than a year. But tonight, with a new verse added in the studio, it's obviously about something more universal: "Now my daddy taught me how to walk quiet / And how to make my peace with the past / And I learned real good to tighten up inside / And I don't say nothin' unless I'm asked."

And then, to top it all, he does his two most famous songs, back to back: "Born to Run" and "Because the Night," the latter in a version that shrivels the Patti Smith hit. When the night finally ends, it is with "Quarter to Three," houselights up full and the crowd singing along as spontaneously as I've ever heard 14,500 people do anything.

Backstage I run into Jackson Browne. "Good show, huh?" I say. He looks at me querulously, like I was just released from the nut house. "Uh unh," Jackson says. "Great show."

At midnight, local FM stations broadcast an announcement that Springsteen will play the Roxy, the 500-seat club and record-company hangout on Sunset Strip, on Friday night, one show only. Lines begin forming almost immediately.

THURSDAY, July 6th: Walking through the lobby of the Marquis last night, just after 2:00 A.M., I ran into Bruce, who asked if I wanted to walk over to Ben Frank's for something to eat. On the way I mentioned that there must be a lot of people in line at the Roxy just up the street. Bruce gave me a look. "I don't like people waiting up all night for me," he said.

Bruce ate another prodigious meal: four eggs, toast, a grilled-cheese sandwich, large glasses of orange juice and milk. And the talk ranged widely: surfing (Bruce had lived with some of the Jersey breed for a while in the late Sixties, and he's a little frustrated with trying to give a glimmer of its complexity to a landlocked ho-dad like me), the new album and its live recording ("I don't think I'll ever go back to the overdub method," he said, mentioning that almost all of the LP was done completely live in the studio, and that "Streets of Fire" and "Something in the Night" were first takes). But mostly we talked or rather, Bruce talked and I listened.

Springsteen can be spellbinding, partly because he is so completely ingenuous, partly because of the intensity and sincerity with which he has thought out his role as a rock star. He delivers these ideas with an air of conviction, but not a proselytizing one; some of his ideas are radical enough for Patti Smith or the punks, yet lack their sanctimonious rhetoric.

I asked him why the band plays so long—their shows are rarely less than three hours—and he said: "It's hard to explain. 'Cause every time I read stuff that I say, like in the papers, I always think I come off sounding like some kind of crazed fanatic. When I read it, it sounds like that, but it's the way I am about it. It's like you have to go the whole way because . . . that's what keeps everything *real*. It all ties in with the records and the values, the morality of the records. There's a certain morality of the show and it's very strict." Such comments can seem not only fanatical, but also self-serving. The great advantage of the sanctimony and rhetoric that infests the punks is that such flaws humanize them. Lacking such egregious characteristics, Bruce Springsteen seems too good to be true when reduced to cold type. Nice guys finish last, we are told, and here's one at the top. So what's the catch? I just don't know.

At the end of every show, before the first encore, Bruce stands tall at the microphone and makes a little speech. "I want to thank all of you for supporting the band for the past three years," he concludes and then plays "Born to Run." I wondered why.

"That's what it's about," he said. "Everything counts. Every person, every individual in the crowd counts—to me. I see it both ways. There is a crowd reaction. But then I also think very, very personally, one to one with the kids. 'Cause you put out the effort and then if it doesn't come through it's a . . . it's a breakdown. What I always feel is that I don't like to let people that have supported me down. I don't like to let myself down. Whatever the situation, as impossible as it is, I like to try to . . . I don't wanna try to get by."

And so it was no surprise that, waking up this morning, I found that all hell had broken loose. Only 250 seats for the Roxy show were available for public sale, which meant that a great many of those who had waited up weren't going to get in. And Bruce was not just upset about this; he was angry. It was a betrayal, however well intentioned, and the fact that another 120 tickets would go to fans through radio-station giveaways did not mollify him. People had been fruitlessly inconvenienced by him. It did not matter that at most similar small-club gigs, the proportion of public to industry is reversed. This was *his* show, and it should have been done properly.

F RIDAY, July 7th: Whatever bad blood had erupted from the overnight Roxy fiasco is gone. In its place, one begins to get a sense of Springsteen's impact on L.A. Polaroids snap at the billboard modifications up the Strip, and the band seems prepared for a big night. At 6:00 P.M. there's a media first: Springsteen is interviewed on KABC, the first time he has ever been on TV in any way, shape or form. It's a good interview—"It's probably the only thing that I live for. When I was a kid, I didn't know nothin' about nothin' until rock & roll got into my house. To me, it was the only thing that was ever true, it was the only thing that never let me down. And no matter who was out there, ten people or 10,000 people, there's a lot to live up to. . . . What happens is, there's a lotta trappings, there's a lotta things that are there to tempt you, sort of. It's just meaningless. And I just try to . . . I play Buddy Holly every night before I go on, that keeps me honest."

But even more striking are the filmed performances of "Prove It All Night" and "Rosalita" that accompany the interview. Even on this small screen, Springsteen is a visual natural, mugging like a seven-year-old and leaping like the rocker of someone's dreams; I know why so many film directors, seeing him for the first time, have virtually drooled in anticipation.

After the Forum the Roxy seems cramped. The broadcast is set for nine, but it's quarter past by the time the band takes the stage. The place is packed—even the balcony box above Roy Bittan's piano looks like it is holding twice the customers it was intended for. And while there are celebrities here—Cher and Kiss' Gene Simmons, Jackson Browne, Irving Azoff and

Glenn Frey, Karla Bonoff, Gary Busey, Tom Waits—it is mostly a crowd of kids and young adults.

The crowd rustles as Bruce steps to the mike, but he holds up his hand. "I want to apologize to everybody," he says, "for what happened with the tickets to this show. It was my fault, and I'm really sorry. I wasn't tryin' to make this no private party—I don't play no parties anymore. Except my own." I think that Mrs. Springsteen, sitting in the back, must be very proud to have such a son. And he steps to the mike and sings: "Well-a-well-a little things you say and do . . . " It's "Rave On" and the joint explodes. Garry Tallent, who loves this music as much as anyone I have ever met, is singing the choruses, his face shining. "I've always wanted to sing Buddy Holly on-stage," he tells me later in his quiet way.

But "Rave On" is only the ignition. Having decided to play a special show, Springsteen goes out of his way. He dances on the tabletops, and the crowd leaps to grab him. He adds "Candy's Room," one of the *Darkness* songs he *never* performs, and halfway through the first set, he introduces a "new song that I wrote right after I finished *Darkness*. It's called 'Point Blank,' and it's about being trapped." And he tells a story of a friend of his who has to work two jobs, as does her husband, to make ends meet, and "they're" still trying to take the couple's house away. And when he sings, it's very real, living up to that title: "Point blank, right between the eyes / They got you, point blank / Right between them pretty lies that they tell. . . . No one survives untouched / No one survives untouched / No one survives."

Near the end of the first set, he tells this story: "Last summer, I went driving out in the desert near Reno—we just flew to Phoenix and rented a car and drove around. And in the desert we came upon a house that this old Indian had built of stuff scavenged from the desert. And on his house there was a sign: THIS IS THE LAND OF PEACE, LOVE, JUSTICE AND NO MERCY. And at the bottom of the sign there was an arrow pointing down this old dirt road. And it said: THUNDER ROAD." This gets the biggest hand of the evening.

The second half is, if anything, harder to believe. It begins, after the usual twenty-minute intermission, with Bruce stepping to the mike and saying: "All right all of you bootleggers out there in radioland. Roll them tapes!" And he comes on with a performance that deserves to be preserved: when a guitar has to be sent backstage for repairs, he calls a brief conference, and the band suddenly steps forward and sings, of all things, "Heartbreak Hotel," with Bruce as the very incarnation of his hero. There's an encore performance of "Independence Day," another of those songs that didn't make

Darkness, this one the most moving ballad version of the "Adam Raised a Cain" story I have ever heard. During "Quarter to Three," three hours into the set, Bruce climbs to the balcony and sings a chorus there before he leaps ten feet down to the piano, by some miracle uninjured. The houselights go up, and the kids are on their feet, chanting—no one is going home. And even when the announcement comes that the band has left the building, no one moves. *"Br-u-ce, Bru-ce"* the chant goes on and on, and suddenly the curtain is raised, and there they are (Max Weinberg fresh from the shower). They roll into "Twist and Shout" and finally, nearly four hours after it all began, the show is over.

Los Angeles Times rock critic Robert Hilburn is at a loss for words. "How do I come back and review this show," he says despairingly, "after I just said that the Forum was one of the best events ever in Los Angeles? Who's gonna believe me?" Maybe, I can only suggest, that is everybody else's problem.

PHOENIX, SATURDAY, July 8th: My favorite comment on last night's show came from Max Weinberg on this morning's flight. "You know, I was thinking in the middle of the show that when I was twelve years old, this is *exactly* what I wanted to be doing."

Later, I ask Springsteen why he had apologized. "It just seemed like the only thing to do," he says. "I couldn't imagine not. There was a little naiveté in thinking that the kids are gonna come and when somebody tells them that there's no more tickets, they're gonna go home. They're not. All I know is, it should've been done better."

Still, I suggest, he could have gotten away without an apology. "*I* couldn't have gotten away with it," he says, throwing me a look. "That's all I try to do—live so I can sleep at night. That's my main concern."

It's going to be a task tonight. It was 109 degrees when we got off the plane and into this oven, and a film crew has shown up to shoot tonight's performance for a TV commercial. They'll be at the sound check, and they'll also have cameras—and additional lights—at the show.

Springsteen seems more open and eager to promote *Darkness* than any of his other albums. Despite the massive amounts of ink he has attracted, he has never been a particularly accessible interview, and he has never, ever appeared on TV. I wonder why the change.

"I always had a certain kinda thing about all those things—like the TV ad or this ad or that ad. But I realized shortly after this album came out that things had changed a lot since *Born to Run.* I just stopped taking it as seriously, and I realized that I worked a year—a year of my life—on somethin' and I wasn't aggressively tryin' to get it out there to people. I was super ag-

gressive in my approach toward the record and toward makin' it happen—
you know, nonrelenting. And then when it came out, I went, 'Oh, I don't
wanna *push* it.'

"It's just facing up to certain realities. It was ridiculous to cut off your
nose to spite your face. What it was, was I was so blown away by what happened last time, I initially thought of doing *no* ads. Just put it out, literally
just put it out."

It is the first time I have ever heard Springsteen refer to a negative effect of the past three years of litigation and layoff. It's strange he's not more
bitter, I suggest. "At the time that that went down," he explains, "I wasn't
mentally prepared. I knew nothin' about it. It was all distressing to me. There
were some good times, but what it was, was . . . the loss of control. See, all
the characters [on the LPs] and everything is about the attempt to gain control of your life. And here, all this stuff, whether it had a good effect or a
bad effect, I realized the one thing it did have was it had a bad effect on my
control of myself. Which is why I initially started playing, and why I play.
That's what upset me most about it. It was like somebody bein' in a car with
the gas pedal to the floor."

(I have only heard him explain his relationship with former manager
Mike Appel better on one occasion: "In a way, Mike was as naive as me,"
he said then. " 'You be the Colonel, and I'll be Elvis.' Except he wasn't the
Colonel, and I wasn't Elvis.")

There are of course other reasons for the TV commercial: while Springsteen is enormously popular in certain areas, in others he is all but unknown.
This is particularly true of the South. And it is especially difficult for people who live in the Northeast and Southwest, where Springsteen already is
a star, to grasp his commercial difficulties elsewhere. Anyone who sells out
both the Los Angeles Forum and Madison Square Garden (three nights at
the latter) ought to be a national star, but for a variety of reasons, Springsteen is still not there yet. Most of this has to do with his lack of acceptance
on AM radio—on that side of the dial, he is a virtually invisible quantity:
"Born to Run" made it to Number 17, and "Prove It All Night" will be
fortunate to go that high, principally because both emphasize electric guitars, which makes them hard rock, not exactly what AM program directors
are currently looking for.

In Phoenix, however, all of this can be forgotten. Phoenix was the first
town outside of the New York–New Jersey–Philadelphia–Boston region
where Springsteen became popular. In the words of Danny Federici, "This
is the first place I ever felt like a star." It's hard to believe, driving past these
deserted desert streets at 7:30 on a Saturday evening, that the 10,000-seat

Veterans Memorial Coliseum is sold out. But when the show is over, I know what Robert Hilburn felt.

It's not just that it's another fantastic show. This is another goddamn event, and it goes farther than the Roxy, with all of that show's intimacy, innocence and vulnerability, but with an added factor of pandemonium. It's the sweetest-tempered crowd I've ever seen, and at the same time, the most maniacal. Bruce dedicates the show to the town in memory of the time "when this was about the only place I could get a job," and the crowd gives it back. During "Prove It All Night," three extremely young girls in the front row hold up a hand-lettered sign written on a bedsheet. Quoting the song, it says, JUST ONE KISS WILL GET THESE THINGS FOR YOU. And he gets them, during "Rosalita," one after another, as they race up to kiss him, lightly, on the cheek. A fourth darts up, and just . . . reaches out and touches his hand. And finally, three more race up and bowl him over. ("This *little* girl, couldn't have been more than fifteen, and she had braces on her teeth," Springsteen exclaims later. "And she had her tongue so far down my throat I nearly choked.")

I've never seen anything like this in such a big hall. Before the encores— which include "Raise Your Hand" and the inevitable "Quarter to Three"— are over, not seven, but seventeen girls have climbed up to kiss him, and there are couples dancing, actually jitterbugging, on the front of the stage. The cameramen are torn between filming Bruce, who is pouring it all out, and simply shooting the crowd, which is pushing him farther and farther.

It is a perfect climax to a week of rock & roll unparalleled in my experience. All I know is, it lives up to the grand story Bruce told in the midst of "Growin' Up." The story has become a virtual set-piece by now, but that night he added a special twist. You should get to hear it too. Maybe it fills in some of the cracks, maybe it explains just why Bruce Springsteen pushes people to the edge of frenzy.

It began with a description of his family, house and home, and his perennial battles with his father. "Finally," he says, "my father said to me, 'Bruce, it's time to get serious with your life. This guitar thing is okay as a hobby, but you need something to fall back on. You should be a lawyer'—which I coulda used later on in my career. He says, 'Lawyers, they run the world.' But I didn't think they did—and I still don't.

"My mother, she's more sensitive. She thinks I should be an author and write books. But I wanted to play guitar. So my mother, she's very Italian, she says, 'This is a big thing, you should go see the priest.' So I went to the rectory and knocked on the door. 'Hi, Father Ray, I'm Mr. Springsteen's son. I got this problem. My father thinks I should be a lawyer, and my mother, she wants me to be an author. But I got this guitar.'

"Father Ray says, 'This is too big a deal for me. You gotta talk to God,' who I didn't know too well at the time. 'Tell him about the lawyer and the author,' he says, 'but don't say *nothin'* about that guitar.'

"Well, I didn't know how to find God, so I went to Clarence's house. He says, 'No sweat. He's just outside of town.' So we drive outside of town, way out on this little dark road.

"I said, 'Clarence, are you sure you know where we're goin'?' He said, 'Sure, I just took a guy out there the other day.' So we come to this little house out in the woods. There's music blasting out and a little hole in the door. I say, 'Clarence sent me,' and they let me in. And there's God behind the drums. On the bass drum, it says: G-O-D. So I said, 'God, I got this problem. My father wants me to be a lawyer and my mother wants me to be an author. But they just don't understand—I got this guitar.'

"God says, 'What they don't understand is that there was supposed to be an Eleventh Commandment. Actually, it's Moses' fault. He was so scared after ten, he said this is enough, and went back down the mountain. You shoulda seen it—great show, the burning bush, thunder, lightning. You see, what those guys didn't understand was that there *was* an Eleventh Commandment. And all it said was: LET IT ROCK!' "

■ **RANDOM NOTES** (May 3, 1979)
Bruce Springsteen, rehearsing at his New Jersey home for his next LP with the E Street Band, came onstage at the Fast Lane in Asbury Park to do "Fire" and "Heartbreak Hotel" with Robert Gordon.

■ **RANDOM NOTES** (June 14, 1979)
Bruce Springsteen injured a leg in a recent accident on a three-wheeled, off-the-road machine but was back on his feet shortly thereafter.

■ **RANDOM NOTES** (July 26, 1979)
Bruce Springsteen and the E Streeters were joined by Boz Scaggs and Rickie Lee Jones during during a three-hour jam at the Whisky in L.A. June 3rd to celebrate the wedding of Mark Brickman, Springsteen's lighting director, and June Rudley, the Boss' travel agent. Highlights of the evening were party-out renditions of "Thunder Road" and "Fire," plus lots of Chuck Berry and Little Richard standards.

1978 MUSIC AWARDS

DECEMBER 28, 1978–JANUARY 11, 1979

CRITICS PICKS

BAND OF THE YEAR

Bruce Springsteen and the E Street Band—Possibly rock's most dramatic performer. Bruce's die-cut dialogue with his excellent band turned their live performances into a tour de force.

ALBUM OF THE YEAR

Some Girls (The Rolling Stones)

Runners Up:

Darkness on the Edge of Town—Springsteen came back from the nether world with a dark, self-probing record that detailed the flip side of rock & roll exhilaration with unflinching honesty.

Running on Empty (Jackson Browne)

This Year's Model (Elvis Costello)

Road to Ruin (The Ramones)

Misfits (The Kinks)

1978 MUSIC AWARDS

JANUARY 25, 1979

READERS PICKS

ARTIST OF THE YEAR
Bruce Springsteen
The Rolling Stones
Jackson Browne
The Who
Billy Joel

BAND OF THE YEAR
The Rolling Stones
The E Street Band
The Who
Steely Dan
Little Feat

BEST ALBUM
Some Girls (The Rolling Stones)
Darkness on the Edge of Town
   (Bruce Springsteen)
Running on Empty (Jackson
   Browne)
Who Are You (The Who)
The Stranger (Billy Joel)

MALE VOCALIST
Bruce Springsteen
Jackson Browne
Billy Joel
Mick Jagger
Bob Seger

SONGWRITER
Bruce Springsteen
Jackson Browne
Warren Zevon
Mick Jagger/Keith Richards
Billy Joel

PRODUCER
Peter Asher (for Linda
   Ronstadt)
**Jon Landau (for Bruce
   Springsteen)**
Todd Rundgren (for Meatloaf)
Glimmer Twins (for the Rolling
   Stones)
Alan Parsons (for the Alan
   Parsons Project)

INSTRUMENTALIST
Chuck Mangione (fluegelhorn)
**Clarence Clemons
   (saxophone)**
David Lindley (violin)
Keith Moon (drums)
Jean-Luc Ponty (violin)

SPRINGSTEEN, CBS SUE OVER BOOTLEG ALBUMS

BRUCE SPRINGSTEEN and his record company, CBS Incorporated, are seeking approximately $2 million in damages from an alleged California record bootlegger and four other defendants.

In a civil suit filed in the Federal District Court in Los Angeles, Springsteen and CBS accused Andrea Waters (a.k.a. Andrea Brown and Vicki Vinyl) and the other defendants—Beggar's Banquet, a California retail record outlet; Jim Washburn, manager of Beggar's Banquet's Anaheim store; Fidelatone Manufacturing, a pressing plant in Hawthorne; and Lewis Record Manufacturing in Inglewood—of infringement of copyright, unfair competition, unjust enrichment and unauthorized use of name and likeness, among other things.

The lawsuit was initiated at the request of Springsteen and his manager-producer, Jon Landau. "Bruce spends a year of his life conceiving and executing an album so that it will perfectly reflect the musical statement he wants to make," Landau said. "Then these people come along and confiscate material that was never intended for release on an album, sell it and make a profit on it without paying anyone that's involved. It's just out-and-out theft; somebody has stolen something and we want it back."

According to the complaint filed in court, CBS is seeking $500,000 in damages resulting from the alleged manufacture and sale of four Springsteen bootleg albums—*Fire, Pièce de Résistance, "E" Ticket* and *Live in the Promised Land*—as well as a Cheap Trick bootleg LP, *California Man 1978*. All five albums were said to be manufactured or sold by Waters.

Springsteen is also seeking statutory damages of $50,000 for each of his twenty-five compositions that appear on the albums. Additional damages are being sought for unauthorized use of his name and likeness.

Waters and Beggar's Banquet are both subjects of ongoing FBI investigations into copyright infringement. On June 8th and 9th, the FBI seized twelve tons of bootleg records and manufacturing equipment from their Costa Mesa warehouse in the largest such raid in history.

■ RANDOM NOTES (November 1, 1979)

"It was just between her and me, just boyfriend and girlfriend," claimed Bruce Springsteen after he and his former lady, rock photographer Lynn Goldsmith, got into a very public tussle in front of 20,000 people during the fourth of five MUSE concerts at New York's Madison Square Garden.

Bruce spotted Lynn sitting out in the twelfth row. As a friend explained Springsteen's onstage instincts: "He's superfocused on those front rows, and she was distracting him incredibly." Springsteen said he had personally asked his ex not to photograph him at the Garden. Goldsmith, however—who was in charge of the still photos for the MUSE concerts—says she only agreed not to shoot from the photographers' pit right in front of the stage. Whatever their private deal, Springsteen stormed out into the audience, grabbed her by the arms, wrenched her to her feet, dragged her up onstage and shouted, "This is my ex-girlfriend!" Then he flung her toward the wings, where she was brusquely hustled away. After the show, a clutch of roadies, toadies and subalterns could be heard shouting "macho Boss!" Several women standing backstage with their musician boyfriends were shocked.

Goldsmith was intensely humiliated by the experience, but declined further comment. For Springsteen, though, it was just one of those things. "It was my birthday," he said, "and we were havin' a great time. She was doin' something she said she wouldn't do. I tried to handle it in other ways, but she avoided them. So I had to do it myself."

■ RANDOM NOTES (May 15, 1980)

"The most important thing we have in this state is young people, and we should really do something for them," says New Jersey State Assemblyman Richard Visotcky, who introduced a resolution on April 14th in the state legislature to make Bruce Springsteen's "Born to Run" the official New Jersey theme song. "Why should New Jersey be the casino capital?" he asks. "Why can't we be the rock capital?"

New Jersey currently has no state song. "Born to Run" was suggested to Visotcky by his son, Robert, who works at New York radio station WPLJ-FM. The idea originally came from Carol Miller, a WPLJ DJ. "A few years ago," she says, "I used to joke around on the air, 'All rise for the New Jersey state anthem,' and then I'd play 'Born to Run.' "

Visotcky, 51, says a public hearing on his proposal has yet to be scheduled, but petitions in support of it are already circulating in high schools throughout the state. "I'm getting blasted by all these conservative newspapers. So they don't like the words to the song, so what? If this will get young people more involved, I say let's do it. Everybody wants a better life for themselves, and so 'Born to Run' . . . that says it for all of us."

Bruce Springsteen's long-awaited 1980 tour got off to a stumbling start in Ann Arbor, Michigan, on October 3rd. Until some fans in the front row started singing along, Bruce couldn't remember the words to his opening anthem, "Born to Run." That minor annoyance out of the way, Springsteen and his E Street Band ripped through a three-hour-plus show that leaned heavily on material from his new double album, *The River*, and even included a cameo appearance by local deity Bob Seger.

"The fans wanna hear everything," Springsteen said later. "I know when I get to a concert, I wanna hear the hits—that's why I bought the record. But you can't be afraid to play the new stuff, too. What's to fear—that they're not gonna clap as much?"

True to his words, Springsteen did more than a dozen songs from the new album—six in a row in the second set—and has dropped such old concert favorites as "Spirit in the Night" and "She's the One." In fact, the closing number, "Rosalita," was the only survivor from his first two albums. He did, however, include "Because the Night" and "Fire"—the hits he originally wrote for Patti Smith and Robert Gordon—among the show's more than twenty-five tunes.

Seger arrived at the concert with his long hair shoved up inside a hat and wearing a low-key sports jacket so as not to be recognized. When Springsteen came out for his first encore, he announced, "Although we already played 'Thunder Road,' I met a good friend backstage during intermission, and he's going to come out and sing it with me"—at which point Seger appeared, prompting an outbreak of something like hysteria.

There are no sales figures yet on *The River*, which lists for $15.98, but Springsteen concert tickets are selling phenomenally. New York's Madison Square Garden (where Bruce will play two nights in November and two in December) has received twice as many mail-order requests for his shows as for any other event in the arena's history. And in Los Angeles, where he couldn't sell out a single Forum date two years ago, he's sold out a four-night stand.

FRED SCHRUERS

THE BOSS IS BACK

Bruce Springsteen Hits the Road for His First Tour in Two Years, and Along the Way Gives Ample Life to His Performing Legend

THERE ARE ONLY a couple of small-hall dates on Bruce Springsteen and the E Street Band's 1980 tour. In most cities, the only way to meet ticket demand is for Springsteen and the gang to play the kinds of huge arenas usually reserved for supergroups and pro sports teams. Tonight, backstage after an epic four-hour show in the Milwaukee Arena, it smells like the latter group has just been through.

"That's me," says Springsteen of the liniment smell. "I've got that stuff all over me. To provide some heat on my back. 'Cause otherwise, in three or four hours, I become very similar to this table." His back seems pretty tight right now as he leans forward to knock on the wood table. He says the stiffness is not from his trademark flying leaps onto the speakers. "I think it's just all that breathin'. The whole top of your body goes like *that*," says Bruce, flexing like an already-taut bowstring. "It's mental," an admiring insider says later. "It's intensity."

For the past three shows—in Chicago, St. Paul and Milwaukee—the intensity has been apparent. (Springsteen, in fact, was having so much trouble getting to sleep after the Midwest gigs that he proposed an all-night drive to Milwaukee from St. Paul—"The only car for that would be a Corvette *station wagon*," said road manager Bob Chirmside—but ended up making the one-hour trip by air on a 4:20 A.M. commercial flight.) Springsteen has lent ample life to his performing legend—and with thirty-five or so dates to go, is doing a good job of laying to rest the stigma of being "an East Coast phenomenon"—playing sold-out shows that last a minimum of three and a half hours and are divided into two sets by a break that lets both performer and audience rest. The group does thirty songs in all, and tonight exactly half of them were from Springsteen's new double album, *The River*.

During its two years off the road, the band's only public exposure has been a segment in the *No Nukes* concert movie and a couple of songs on the album. The absence seems only to have built Springsteen's following, for in every "market" in the country, the figures for ticket sales and the album—which shipped gold—are flickering faster than the digit counters on one of the Boss' beloved pinball machines.

Cal Levy, from Electric Factory Productions, brought Bruce to Cincinnati's Riverfront Coliseum in October; he's been promoting concerts in that city since 1975. "In September 1977, Bruce sold 4,000 seats here," he recalls. "In September 1978, he sold 6,630. This past October 4th, he sold 16,300 seats in two hours and forty minutes. We absolutely could have sold out two more shows. I was as surprised as anybody. I told [Springsteen's manager] Jon Landau he should treat this building like the Roxy [a 500-seat club in L.A. where Bruce did a four-night show in 1975] and come in for a week." Similarly, the office of Madison Square Garden promoter Ron Delsener was deluged with enough ticket requests to fill the 18,000-seat arena for sixteen nights. But for Levy, promoter of the December 3rd, 1979, Who concert at which eleven kids were trampled to death in a rush for the door, the Springsteen show was more than Riverfront Coliseum's first sell-out show since that date. "As one local paper put it," Levy explains, "for the first time since December 3rd, people didn't have to look over their shoulders to enjoy themselves. It was so happy yet so controlled. Bruce had those people standing on their seats for the entire show—unless he asked them to sit down. It was almost a feeling of being in a 3,000-seat hall." And as Cincinnati Mayor Jerry Springer said in a radio broadcast, "Rock & roll should never be a defendant in the Who case. Bruce Springsteen showed us that, and we should be grateful to him."

Milwaukee had its own concert problems. The bad memory of a riot last April, when such "special guests" as Bob Dylan and Mick Jagger failed to show up for a New Barbarians concert, had been freshened by a concertgoers' rampage on Thursday, October 9th, six days before Springsteen's date. It seems Black Sabbath bassist Geezer Butler was clocked on the head with a flung beer bottle, and when the rest of the band retreated from the stage after him, the crowd trashed the arena. Just about every cop in the city was called to what local officials called a "miniriot," and some politicians were spoiling to ban rock from the 12,000-seat arena.

Springsteen's representatives thus made a deal to get the band offstage no later than 11:15 P.M. (the concert started a half-hour earlier than usual), but when the time came, Bruce was cranking out an impromptu, rollicking version of "Midnight Hour," and arena president Robert O. Ertl was screaming at tour manager George Travis. "Do you want me to wave him off now?" Travis asked tranquilly, as one wide swath of kids in seats behind the stage swayed back and forth, flinging their hands up in unison on every beat. "He'll come off."

"Oh no," Ertl remembers saying. "He's got the audience up high, he'll have to bring 'em back down." That, admits Ertl, is just what Springsteen did—"beautifully." In fact, some Milwaukee officials felt that Springsteen's concert took the ammunition away from the city's antirock factions.

Dawn Colla, 27, is a mayoral assistant in Milwaukee who came to the arena that night, but she wanted to talk as a fan. She seems to represent the large chunk of Springsteen's growing constituency, which is described by Cal Levy as "salesmen, lawyers—a very *clean* crowd." Said Colla: "I didn't especially like having this guy at the door say, 'Sorry, babe, gotta look in your purse,' but they were frisking everybody. I don't think there's anybody else who could get me and twelve of my friends out. We're all in our late twenties. I'm past going to rock & roll concerts—the last show we all went to was his 1978 show. But you know the guy's trying to knock himself out in every city. He comes out with a double album that costs ten bucks [in fact, Springsteen's $15.98-list, twenty-song LP was selling for less than ten dollars in many stores] after Fleetwood Mac came out with one for fifteen dollars. He doesn't have that phoniness so many acts have. There's a lot of good rock & roll, but the guy's also a poet.

"A lot of the people here are real fans. They're tuned into when the sax is gonna come in, they know all the words—it's like a reunion. There were two kids behind me, eighteen, nineteen, yelling for 'Thunder Road,' and they just went crazy when 'Rosalita' began. But I guess I just look for the poetry. He's saying to people, 'Open your eyes, you have some choices, don't get caught in that group that's gonna be street people all their lives.'"

Springsteen may indeed be one of the few authentic rockers still celebrated by the aging gentry who fueled the Sixties rock & roll explosion. But neither has he lost touch with the kinds of fans who were more than a little put out by the Milwaukee Arena's brand-new ban on beer sales. He seemed to please everybody. He opened his show with "Prove It All Night," did a ferocious rendition of "Badlands"—clutching his guitar across his chest like a priceless talisman as he sang the hushed line, "It ain't no sin to be glad you're alive"—and ended up in the middle of a happy mob in the arena's fifth row of seats to holler "I'm all alone" during "Tenth Avenue Freeze-Out."

"Are ya loose?" Springsteen demanded before going into more somber territory with "Darkness on the Edge of Town" and "Factory." "When I grew up, I used to watch my father go to work every day to a job he hated," he said before "Independence Day." "You're lucky if you got some choices." He played the new "Jackson Cage" to the "excitable bunch" in the cheaper seats just behind the stage, then moved rapidly through "Promised Land" and "Out in the Street" (he had introduced the former song to Chicago by asking, "How many of you guys are living away from home right now?") and played another new song, "Two Hearts." "Racing in the Street" was linked to "The River" by an invocatory few notes from Roy [Bruce calls him "Mr. E=MC Squared"] Bittan's piano. Springsteen then closed the first half of the show with a flurry of leaps, scurryings and knee drops as he and saxman Clarence Clemons played off each other on "Thunder Road" and "Jungleland." During the latter song, the crowd spilled over far enough to block the view of a kid in a wheelchair in the aisle at stage left. Grinning and flinging his hands in the air, he didn't seem to mind.

After the break in Chicago, Bruce had started a dancing frenzy with Elvis Presley's "Good Rockin' Tonight," but in Milwaukee, he chose the new "Cadillac Ranch." Cupping his hands suggestively to sing "Hey little girlie with the blue jeans so tight," he made sure his diction was perfect on the next line: "Drivin' alone through the . . . *Wisconsin* night. . . . " Milwaukee roared. When Clarence Clemons interrupted "Fire" to finish "But your heart stays cool" in a mellifluous bass voice, Springsteen staggered away from the mike, and the crowd screamed with abandon during the long, silent tease before both men made it back to the mike to sing the song's "Romeo and Juliet" verse.

The moment ushered in six songs from the new LP: "Sherry Darling," "I Wanna Marry You" (with a funny spoken intro turning into a beautiful vocal round by Springsteen, Clemons and "Miami" Steve Van Zandt), "The Ties That Bind," "Wreck on the Highway," "Point Blank" and "Crush on You." Springsteen flung his guitar to Clemons early in the latter song, the better to launch into some sidestepping so rapid it was more an athletic feat than a dance. His tight black shirt was soaking wet as he called for "Midnight Hour," then stormed through "Ramrod" and "You Can Look (but You Better Not Touch)." "All those songs—with the exception of 'Midnight Hour'—are new songs," he announced proudly. The lights lowered for a brooding version of "Stolen Car," Garry Tallent's bass rumbling like distant, ominous thunder, and then came the spate of crowd pleasers: "Backstreets," "Rosalita," "Born to Run" and the Mitch Ryder medley. The crowd, seated and attentive for much of the show, then pressed against the stage. "I knew you were out there," said Springsteen. "You're great. Thanks a lot!"

"It was a real warm crowd," Springsteen said backstage as the medicinal rub heated up under a thermal-underwear shirt. "A lot of them have seen us before. I don't think they come to the show at this point with an attitude of 'You have to win me over.' Course, a lot of people bring friends who have never seen us. They must, 'cause a lot of these places we didn't sell out before. So they must be bringing *some*body from *some*place."

His album had been in the stores for only a day, but "Hungry Heart" had already declared itself a single because of radio airplay, and ticket sales were still going through the roof. Where were all those new faces coming from?

"The last tour," he explained, "we played 122 shows, and the band played real hard every single night, you know. Every single night in every town, the band played very hard. And people, I think they just remembered. They remembered, and this time everybody told their friends, 'You just gotta come down to the show.' "

"Where do you reach for the energy to do it?" I asked him. "You're playing nearly four hours, sometimes three nights in a row. Occasionally, you have to be tired."

"The audience brings a lot, even when you think you have nothing left within you. You know, tonight is *tonight,* and what you do tonight, you don't make up for tomorrow, and you don't ride on what you did last night. I always keep in my mind that you only have one chance. Some guy bought his ticket, and there's a promise made between the musician and the audience. When they support each other, that's a special thing. It goes real deep, and most people take it too lightly. If you break the pact or take it too lightly, nothing else makes sense. It's at the heart of everything; I'm not sure how.

"I've got a lot of energy just naturally. But when I get onstage and I'm running on empty, I just think of the promise to the guy or girl who's down there, a promise that's made from hundreds or thousands of miles away. It's no different than if you stood with this person and shook his hand."

PAUL NELSON

THE RIVER ALBUM REVIEW

Let Us Now Praise Famous Men

RUCE SPRINGSTEEN'S *The River* is a contemporary, New Jersey version of *The Grapes of Wrath,* with the Tom Joad/Henry Fonda figure—nowadays no longer able to draw upon the solidarity of family—driving a stolen car through a neon Dust Bowl "in fear / That in this darkness I will disappear." Quite often, he does.

Since *The River* is the culmination of a trilogy that began in high gear with *Born to Run* (1975) before shifting down for *Darkness on the Edge of Town* (1978), you might expect it to stand and deliver weighty conclusions, words to live by. Well, they're there, if you want or need them, and they're filled with an uncommon common sense and intelligence that could only have come from an exceptionally warmhearted but wary graduate of the street of hard knocks. Here's one example: "Now you can't break the ties that bind / You can't forsake the ties that bind." Or: "Two hearts are better than one / Two hearts girl get the job done." Or: "Everybody needs a place to rest / Everybody wants to have a home . . . / Ain't nobody like to be alone." Quoted out of context, without the evocative musical accompaniment of the E Street Band and Springsteen's unsparingly emotional singing, these lines seem incredibly simple yet sturdy. Not very cosmic but they'll do, I suppose, if you feel the necessity to nail some sort of slogan to the wall. Then you can sit back and stare at it and miss the whole point—not to mention the scope—of the album.

Scope, context, sequencing and mood are everything here. Bruce Springsteen didn't title his summational record *The River* for nothing, so getting hit with a quick sprinkle of lyrics is no solution when complete immersion is called for. Each song is just a drop in the bucket, and the water in the bucket is drawn from a river that can take you on a fast but invigorating ride ("Sherry Darling," "Out in the Street," "Crush on You," "I'm a Rocker"), smash you in the rapids ("Hungry Heart"), let you float dreamily downstream ("I Wanna Marry You") or carry you relentlessly across some unknown county line ("Jackson Cage," "Point Blank," "Fade Away," "Stolen Car," "Ramrod," "The River," "Independence Day"). When the surface looks smooth, watch out for dangerous undercurrents. You may believe you're splashing about in a shallow stream and suddenly find yourself in over your head.

Keeping the trilogy in mind, if Springsteen's archetypal journey from innocence (*Born to Run*) to experience (*Darkness on the Edge of Town*) taught him anything, it was that he wasn't even halfway home—that, contrary to what F. Scott Fitzgerald wrote, most American lives *do* have second acts. And that these postexperiential acts are usually the ones in which we either crack up or learn to live with our limitations and betrayals. In a way, Bruce Springsteen's journey started in 1973 with *Greetings From Asbury Park, N.J.*'s "Growin' Up" (in which the singer "found the key to the universe in the engine of an old parked car") and gathered momentum that same year with his "for me, this boardwalk life's through" declaration in *The Wild, the Innocent & the E Street Shuffle*'s "4th of July, Asbury Park (Sandy)" before he saw himself finally "pulling out of here to win" in *Born to Run*'s "Thunder Road." Throughout much of *Darkness on the Edge of Town*, Springsteen discovered the meaning of despair.

What makes *The River* really special is Bruce Springsteen's epic exploration of the second acts of American lives. Because he realizes that most of our todays are the tragicomic sum of a scattered series of yesterdays that had once hoped to become better tomorrows, he can fuse past and present, desire and destiny, laughter and longing, and have death or glory emerge as more than just another story. By utilizing the vast cast of characters he's already established on the earlier LPs—and by putting a spin on the time span—Springsteen forces his heroes and heroines into seeing themselves at different and crucial periods in their lives. The connections are infinite (and, some would say, repetitious).

When an artist ties these kinds of knots around several compositions, it's impressive. But when he also uses jump-cut juxtapositions of mood (the one between "I Wanna Marry You" and "The River" is particularly stunning) and more than a few characters in completely contrasting situations, it's downright brilliant. One labyrinthine example: the randy rocker of "Ramrod," who sings: "Hey, little dolly won't you say that you will / Meet me tonight up on top of the hill / Well just a few miles cross the county line / There's a cute little chapel nestled down in the pines" like he no longer believes a word of it but has to keep pushing anyway or he'll die, is probably the same guy who went racing in the street with his buddy, Sonny, and later sang, in "Darkness on the Edge of Town": "I lost my money and I lost my wife / Them things don't seem to matter much to me now / Tonight I'll be on that hill 'cause I can't stop. . . . " He could easily be the reformed husband in "Drive All Night," too (there's an "on the edge of town" reference).

Though they're separated by eight songs, "Drive All Night" is linked with "I Wanna Marry You" by a set of "my girl" refrains that don't appear on the lyric sheet. Yet the shy, naive narrator of "I Wanna Marry You" (who sweetly and secretly yearns for someone's estranged wife, whom he watches on the street every day) clearly isn't the fortunate protagonist of "Drive All Night." That man wins his wife back. As the reunited couple get ready for bed, they hear a crowd of kids partying in the street. "Fallen angels" and "calling strangers," the husband says. "Let them go . . . do their dances of the dead / . . . There's machines and there's fire waiting on the edge of town / They're out there for hire but baby they can't hurt us now." What he's saying, I'm sure, is that those kids are who we *were,* but we've survived and this is who we *are.* (Check *Darkness on the Edge of Town*'s "Racing in the Street" and "Streets of Fire" for the "angels"-"strangers"-"fire" imagery, and *Born to Run*'s title track for "suicide machines.")

Immediately following the fantasy of "I Wanna Marry You" (whose main character gently debunks the "fairytale" of "true love" while, in fact, daydreaming about achieving it with a total stranger) is the grim reality of "The River," one of the record's two Dreiserian American tragedies and the second chapter of "Racing in the Street." In "The River," there are no idle thoughts about how nice true love might be. Instead, fate and the new Depression shoot the working-class hero and his high-school sweetheart (Mary from "Thunder Road"?) straight between the eyes: "Then I got Mary pregnant / And, man, that was all she wrote / And for my 19th birthday I got a union card and a wedding coat . . . / I got a job working construction for the Johnstown Company / But lately there ain't been much work on account of the economy / Now all them things that seemed so important / Well, mister they vanished right into the air / Now I just act like I don't remember / Mary acts like she don't care."

But, of course, he does remember the good times, and it's killing him: "Now those memories come back to haunt me / They haunt me like a curse / Is a dream a lie if it don't come true / Or is it something worse. . . . "

After "Drive All Night," the singer witnesses—or imagines he witnesses ("there was nobody there but me")—the results of a bloody car crash in which a young man has been either badly hurt or killed. Since he feels personally involved, it frightens him. "Wreck on the Highway" is *The River*'s last song, and this is the album's hard-won, semi-happy ending: "Sometimes I sit up in the darkness / And I watch my baby as she sleeps / Then I climb in bed and I hold her tight / I just lay there awake in the middle of the night / Thinking 'bout the wreck on the highway."

Obviously, there are other ways to ford *The River* and its twenty tunes (e.g., picking out the imagery picked up in John Ford movies would help), but any approach you take is liable to lead in circles. Cars, work and love need the gasoline of the heart to avoid smashing. "Independence Day"— more Dreiser—is both a beginning and an end: one of the greatest ever. As is a scary little *noir* named "Stolen Car" that's wound so tight it practically twitches ("I'm driving a stolen car / Down on Eldridge Avenue / Each night I wait to get caught / But I never do").

Musically, *The River* floats more influences than I'd have thought possible: folk balladry, soul singing and R&B, rockabilly, country music, goofy—or not-so-goofy—teen anthems about cars and death (the terrific "Cadillac Ranch"), Gary "U.S." Bonds, Byrds-like folk rock with ringing twelve-string guitars, party numbers, lots of rock & roll, David Johansen and the New York Dolls ("Crush on You"), Jackson Browne (lyrically, the first half of "The Price You Pay" sounds like a downbeat rewrite of "Before the Deluge"), Elvis Costello (the vocal in "Fade Away")—the list could go on and on.

Throughout much of the LP, producers Bruce Springsteen, Jon Landau and Steve Van Zandt lean toward a live sound, meeting the songs head-on, like the aural equivalent of, say, action-movie director Howard Hawks' camera placement. As a result, though it can't be compared with a Springsteen concert, *The River* seems livelier and more loose than *Darkness on the Edge of Town*. Of the trilogy, I still prefer the innocent zest and relative openness of *Born to Run,* however.

While most of *The River* runs wide and deep, there are a few problems. Ever since he started conceptualizing and thinking in terms of trilogies, Springsteen has lost some of his naturalness and seemed more than a bit self-conscious about being an artist. At times, you think he's closed off his casualness altogether, that he can't bear the idea of playing around with a phrase when he could be underlining it instead. Will we never hear the spring and summer of "Wild Billy's Circus Story," "4th of July, Asbury Park (Sandy)," "Thunder Road" and "Born to Run" again? Must even the brightest days now be touched by autumnal tones and winter light? Bruce Springsteen isn't an old man yet. Isn't it odd that he's trying so hard to adopt the visions of one?

FROM THE STARK, homemade look of their predominantly black-and-white packaging to their gritty, straightforward, to-hell-with-the-state-of-the-art sound, the Clash's *London Calling* and Bruce Springsteen's *The River* are passionately political: i.e., deeply, often desperately concerned with how working-class men and women are getting along in times as troubled as ours. Both Springsteen and the Clash are morally and historically committed to the directness and honesty of rock & roll—and to what this music can mean to those whose hearts are smoldering with anger or shame. In their *Apocalypse Now* manner, the Clash come right out with it, though they're not incapable of dreaming about "Spanish songs in Andalucia / The shooting sites in the days of '39" or recording a tune called "Brand New Cadillac." Next to Bruce Springsteen, however, they sometimes seem very innocent: they still believe in total victory.

Springsteen doesn't. His protagonists—all veterans of their own foreign wars—may hope for the big win, but they've been through the mill (or factory) enough times to realize that even the smallest success can be tremendously shaky. While lines like "Once I spent my time playing tough guy scenes / But I was living in a world of childish dreams / Someday these childish dreams must end / To become a man and grow up to dream again / Now I believe in the end" ring true, such sentiments are usually surrounded by an aura of omnipotent dread that makes them sound more like reveries from the past or wishful thinking than statements about the future. There's nothing apocalyptic or innocent about *The River*. Try listening to it right after *Born to Run* and you'll understand what I mean.

Though I consider *The River* a rock & roll milestone, in a way I hope it's also Independence Day.

FRED SCHRUERS

BRUCE SPRINGSTEEN AND THE SECRET OF THE WORLD

BRUCE SPRINGSTEEN, in the abstract, is just the kind of guy my little New Jersey hometown schooled me to despise. Born seventy-seven days apart, raised maybe fifty miles apart, this beatified greaser and I grew up sharing little more than what came over AM radio. In Mountain Lakes, a community of 4,000, we had a word for people like Bruce: Newarkylanders. The urban canker of Newark-Elizabeth was their state capital, but they lived and played along the boardwalk Jersey shore. They wore those shoulder-strap undershirts some people called "guinea-T's"; we called them "Newarkys." They drove muscle cars and worked in garages and metal shops. They ate meatball subs made of cat parts for lunch, and after work they shouted at their moms, cruised the drive-ins, punched each other out and balled their girlfriends in backseats.

Our contempt for Newarkylanders cut almost as deep as our fear of them. We looked on them as prisoners, a subclass that would not get the college degrees and Country Squires we were marked for. But we realized that prisoners sometimes bust out of their cages with a special vengefulness. The fear was as real as a black Chevy rumbling down your tree-lined block, and inside are six guys with baseball bats and tire irons.

Bruce Springsteen has seen all this from the inside, he's seen the gates swing shut, he's watched people turning the locks on their own cages. You can hear it in his music, a music with shack-town roots; paradoxically, it saved him from that life. I could not have heard his songs, especially the early, wordier ones, and expect our meeting to boil down to the wracking Jersey nightmare of Joe College vs. Joe Greaser.

While even among his ardent fans there are people who say Springsteen has gone to the well too many times for his favorite themes of cars, girls and the night, watching him perform the new songs, I came to believe he really was battering at new riddles: marriage, work and how people in America turn themselves into ghosts.

I would come to understand that this jubilant rock & roll cock of the walk never had cut it as Joe Greaser, that what had fathered his obsessiveness was doing time as a runty, bad-complected kid whom the nuns, girls and greasers had taken turns having no use for. There is finally something irrevocably lonely and restless about him. He's never claimed any different. Springsteen wants to inspire by example—the example of a trashed and resurrected American spirit. "You ask me if there's any one thing in particular," said E Street Band pianist Roy Bittan when we talked about Springsteen's commitment. "There's too many things in particular. He's older and wiser, but he never strays from his basic values. He cares as much, *more,* about the losers than the winners. He's so unlike everything you think a real successful rock star would be."

Springsteen comes down the ramp at the Minneapolis–St. Paul airport and looks down the empty corridor: "No autographs," he says in his characteristic parched cackle. "No autographs, *please.*"

This is exactly what he never says, of course, and when the tour party breaches the corridor's double doors, he greets a pack of young, denim-jacketed guys familiarly. Some are holding copies of *The River,* released just this day and headed very quickly for Number One. As the entourage loads itself into a string of station wagons, a kid who has been hanging at the edge of the pack tells Bruce about a friend who's critically ill in a local hospital. Bruce tells the kid to get his friend's name to him through the record company. Doors are slamming and engines gunning. It's bitter cold. Just another stranger, I think.

Thirty-eight hours later, after performing "Out in the Street" onstage at the St. Paul Civic Center, Springsteen halts the show. "I met a bunch of guys at the airport yesterday coming in. One told me he had a friend who was sick. If that fella who told me his friend was sick will come to the side of the stage during the break, I got something for your friend backstage."

After the kid appeared, and was duly loaded up with autographed mementos, I pondered the gesture. Springsteen could have scribbled his good wishes on an album at the airport and been done with it. But he had left the benediction to be arranged in public. There's a lot of showman in Springsteen, and not a little preacher. Why had he let the anonymous kid slip so close to being forgotten, then given him his last rock & roll rites before the crowd?

"There's not much people can count on today," says Springsteen.

"Everything has been so faithless, and people have been shown such disrespect. You want to show people that somehow, that somewhere, somebody can . . . I guess you just don't want to let them down. That's probably why we come out and play every night, there's that fear, 'cause then nothin' works, nothin' makes sense. As long as one thing does, if there can be just one thing that goes against what you see all around you, then you know that things can be different. Mainly, it's important to have that passion for living, to somehow get it from someplace."

The inescapable cliché about faith is that it can always be doubted. That's the thing about Springsteen—if you pay any attention at all, his lyrics and his every stance will force you into a corner where you must decide whether you believe him or not. I had to believe he wasn't staging the benediction to pump up his image—in the tradition of Babe Ruth socking a homer for a dying child—but for the kid himself. Not to say "rise and walk," but to offer something tangible—the momentary, empathetic suffering of this captive crowd of 15,000. And although most are in their wild age, perhaps some of them might even learn a little charity themselves.

ACCUSE SPRINGSTEEN of being a "star" and he'll flick his hand like he's just been splashed with pigeon shit. He is eager to point out that he has the better deal in the meeting place between fan and star.

"I think the one feeling that's most unique to this job, the best part of the whole thing, is meeting someone like this guy I met the other night who had been on a bus ten hours. He's twenty-one years old, and he just grabs hold of me. We're in a room crowded with people. He's cryin', and he doesn't care. He says, 'It's my birthday,' and I ask, 'How old are you?' He says, 'I'm twenty-one, and this is the most important thing in my life.' And you know they're not kidding when they say it, because you look in their faces and they're so full of emotion.

"You meet somebody, and it's like an open well. In ten minutes I'll know more about him than his mother and father do, and maybe his best friend. All the things it usually takes for people to know each other just go away, because there's this feeling that it's so fleeting. They tell you the thing that's most important to them right away. It's a sobering thing, because you know that somewhere you did *something* that meant something to them. It's just a real raw, emotional thing; it's like the cleanest thing you ever felt. You have a communication, a feeling, and I don't know, you just gotta love the guy. If you don't, there's something the matter with you.

"And it ain't some starry-eyed thing, and it ain't some Hollywood thing, and it ain't some celebrity thing. This guy, he loves you, and what's more, he knows you in a certain way. That's the thing that makes me strong. I get strong when I meet somebody like that."

THERE IS AN OBSESSIVENESS to Springsteen—the underside of his manic onstage energy—that can be a little scary. It seems to spring from flash fires that ignite in his very detailed memory. "There ain't a note I play onstage," he says late one night, "that can't be traced directly back to my mother and father."

We're riding in a rented Winnebago, rocking back and forth in icy crosswinds on a six-hour drive from Pittsburgh to Rochester, New York. We had started the drive at three in the morning, an hour Springsteen takes to like a pup going for a walk. Still buzzed from a show that closed with Elvis Presley's "Mystery Train," he merrily salts some fried chicken and picks up a remembrance. "It was a real classic little town I grew up in, very intent on maintaining the status quo. Everything was looked at as a threat, kids were looked at as a nuisance and a threat. And when you're a kid, your parents become fixtures, like a sofa in the living room, and you take for granted what they do." He lets out one of his oddly mournful laughs. "My father used to drive around in his car, and it would not go in reverse. Heh. I remember pushing it backward; that was just something you did, you didn't even think it was strange."

One of the things that makes Springsteen a whole different species of rock performer is his candor about the numbed, paralytic rage his father, Douglas Springsteen, a bus driver and sometime prison guard, converted to bitterness at a very early age. Bruce will stand on a darkened stage and remember out loud about coming into his house late at night, almost always seeing the kitchen light on, to face his father. One day his aunt showed him a picture of his father, back from World War II, about to marry and start a family that would include Bruce and two sisters. "He looked just like John Garfield, in this great suit, he looked like he was gonna eat the photographer's head off. And I couldn't ever remember him looking that proud, or that defiant, when I was growing up. I used to wonder what happened to all that pride, how it turned into so much bitterness. He'd been so disappointed, had so much stuff beaten out of him by then. . . . "

Sitting in various arenas, ten years gone from my own home, I envy the teenage audience that is hearing Springsteen talk to them about that troublesome blood tie. For many, it is the first time anybody has nosed around in their feelings about their parents; paradoxically, Springsteen's anger seems to set beating, at least for a few moments, a kind of heartsickness that might turn out to be love for those parents. But it's not a Sunday school rap: ". . . so much beaten out of him that he couldn't accept the idea that I had a dream and I had possibilities. The things I wanted, he thought were just foolish. People get so much shit shoveled on 'em every day. But it's just important to hold on to those things. Don't let anybody call you foolish."

He takes the Esquire he has absently, slowly been stroking, shrieks once and slams into "Badlands" and the cathartic, energized slide licks that sound like the hand of God reaching down to rip the tops off fleeing cars: "Poor man wanna be rich / Rich man wanna be king / And a king ain't satisfied / Till he rules everything. . . . "

When he rocks back to goose out the taut guitar break in "Candy's Room," or jumps downstage with harmonica to race Clarence Clemons' sax to the end of "Promised Land," it's invigorating to notice that the guy can *play,* that despite all his steeplechasing and singing, he doesn't come off as a slacker on harp and guitar. Maybe that's because there's nothing ever casual about his attack.

At age nine, Springsteen saw Elvis on *The Ed Sullivan Show.* But in 1959, Bruce found guitar lessons to be "oppressive," his hands were too small, and aspirations toward big-league baseball took over. "I wanted it pretty bad at the time. Every day from when I was eight till thirteen I'd be outside pitching that ball." But the guitar fantasy wouldn't quit. "The best thing that ever happened to me was when I got thrown out of the first band I was in, and I went home and put on 'It's All Over Now' by the Rolling Stones and learned that guitar solo.

"I think when I first started, I wouldn't allow myself to think that someday . . . I just wanted to get in a halfway band, be able to play weekends somewhere and make a little extra dough, working at some job during the week or something. Which is what my parents used to say that I could do. That was allowed. I could do it on weekends, but it was impossible to see or think at the time."

Then it was bars and CYOs and clubs, in and out of various bands, playing, copping licks, going to the Village on Saturdays to catch matinee sets at the Cafe Wha.

"I don't ever remember being introduced to Bruce," says Miami Steve Van Zandt, who lived nearby and shared local guitar hero honors. "I just remember I would go to New York, to the Village, and one day seeing him come walking down MacDougal. We looked at each other like, ah, 'You look familiar' and 'What are you doin' here?' It took a long time to become really close." Stints in bands called the Castiles, Steel Mill, Dr. Zoom and the Sonic Boom followed. And then there was Bruce Springsteen, leader of a band bearing his name.

He signed a management deal with a feisty entrepreneur named Mike Appel on the hood of a car in a dark parking lot. It was a signature that meant Springsteen and band would not make any serious money until the 1978 tour for *Darkness on the Edge of Town,* his fourth album. "People always say, 'Gee, it must have been tough for you.' But I always remember bein' in a good mood, bein' happy even through the bad stuff and the disappointments, because I knew I was ahead of nine out of ten other people that I've seen around me. 'Cause I was doing something that I liked." Appel did get Springsteen face to face with Columbia Records A&R head John Hammond. Springsteen signed on with Columbia Records. After Jon Landau saw him perform at Harvard Square Theatre in 1974, Landau declared, in a review that was a landmark in both men's lives, that Springsteen represented "rock & roll future." They became friends, and Springsteen asked Landau to come into the studio to help him and Appel produce *Born to Run.* Released in late 1975, it quickly went gold.

SPRINGSTEEN IS HAPPY in the front seat of *anything,* and he spends the ride from Rochester to Buffalo, New York, gazing at the sunny, snow-covered fields on either side of the highway. Arriving at the hotel, he tucks his cap under his sweatshirt's hood and invites me for a walk downtown in the "fresh [twenty-two degrees] air." In high boots and a well-broken-in black cloth coat, he looks like a gravedigger off for the winter. He has pored over the local record store's entire cassette case (choosing collections by the Drifters and Gene Pitney) before the guys who work there recognize him. (The cassette I'd found in Springsteen's portable player was Toots and the Maytals' *Funky Kingston.* Springsteen confesses a love for reggae, a music he calls "too complex and too pure" for him to interpret.)

The guys behind the counter put on "Hungry Heart," which has plowed through the charts to Number One. It was a song Springsteen originally didn't even want to have on the album until Jon Landau (now his manager) insisted. Springsteen describes the song as an evocation of what the Beach Boys and Frankie Lymon used to do for him.

Still gimpy from a stumble he'd taken during a show in Washington, he walks on incognito until some jewelry-stand salesgirls corner him for autographs in a bookstore.

We cross the street to McDonald's. "Paradise," he calls it. "I never did get comfortable with places that got the menu in the window," he explains, making two Quarter-Pounders disappear. He looks contentedly around as the munching Buffalonians make no sign of recognizing him. "I love coming to these places where it's nothing but real."

Springsteen works hard at keeping his own life real. His mother is still doing the kind of secretarial work she began at age eighteen, and he predicted that his new money would not make any difference. "What's she gonna do—quit and run around the world and buy things? In a certain way, the money aspect of it is not very useful to them. I gave 'em some money one day and found out later on they didn't spend it. They thought that was gonna be the payoff, you know, there wasn't gonna be anymore. They live around people like them [in San Diego]. The whole thing of driving your folks up to some big house and saying, 'This is yours,' they don't want that. Then it's not them anymore."

Springsteen himself still lives in a rented house near his hometown, with enough acreage to lure him into tearing about on his three-wheel, off-the-road scooter (though he gave his right leg a severe muscle tear by driving it into a tree last spring). Yet, his life at home tends toward more quiet activity, like staying up all night watching late movies, often with his California-based actress girlfriend, Joyce Heiser.

Heiser, to whom Springsteen frequently dedicates "Drive All Night," has been subjected to backstage scrutiny this time around because one theme that takes up a lot of room on *The River* is marriage and relationships—the ties that bind. "That's the hardest thing for me to talk about. I don't know, I'm in the dark as far as all that stuff goes. It took me five albums to even write about it. People want to get involved, not because of the social pressure, not because of the romantic movies that they grew up on. It's something more basic than that, it's very physical and it presents itself. It's just the way men and women are.

"My mother and father, they've got a very deep love because they know and understand each other in a very realistic way. Whatever form relationships take is up to the people involved, I guess. But on the album the characters are wrestling with those questions—the guy in 'Stolen Car,' the guy in 'Wreck on the Highway,' 'Drive All Night,' the guy in 'Sherry Darling,' even. It is a puzzle and a question, it's hard to separate it from the tradition, very hard to separate it from all the impressions that are created in you as you grow older. That's why I wanted 'I Wanna Marry You' and 'The River' together, 'cause they're similar songs, similar feelings.

"Everybody seems to hunger for that relationship, and you never seem

happy without it. I guess that's good enough reason right there. It just got
to a point where all of a sudden these songs about things of that nature started
coming out. I think you do tend to think about that particular thing around
thirty. But even up till then, when I was writing all the earlier songs, 'Born
to Run' and stuff, they never seemed right without the girl. It was just part
of wherever that person was going, that guy was going. It wasn't gonna be
any good without her."

THE NIGHT AFTER John Lennon's murder, Springsteen was scheduled
to play Philadelphia's Spectrum Arena. The band had been onstage
at the Spectrum the previous night when the news came, but, as organist
Danny Federici put it, "They saved it from us till after the show." The next
day, Miami Steve called the tour manager to see if the second night was going
to be postponed. The answer was no. Steve was so upset he went to Springsteen shortly before the show, "saying that I felt really weird about going
onstage, that I couldn't put it together. And he really just reminded me of
why we do what we do, and how it was important to go out that night in
particular. I wish I could remember exactly what he said, like, 'This is what
John Lennon inspired us to do and now it's our job to do the same thing
for these other people, that today it was Lennon and tomorrow it might be
me, and if it is . . .' That's how he does every show, like it was his last. He
lives every minute like it was his last. That's the way to live. It's really lucky
to be close to him at moments like that."

The band took the stage, most of them wearing black. Springsteen went
to the mike. "If it wasn't for John Lennon," he said, "a lot of us would be
in some place much different tonight. It's a hard world that makes you live
with a lot of things that are unlivable. And it's hard to come out here and
play tonight, but there's nothing else to do."

I've seen people digging firebreaks to save their homes, and I've seen
some desperate fist fights, and, God knows, I've seen hundreds of rock &
roll shows, but I have never seen a human being exert himself the way
Springsteen did that night in Philly. His delivery of the last verse of "Darkness on the Edge of Town" was raw with a mixture of anger, grief and determination. I'll remember "Promised Land" for the way the silhouettes in
the top tier of the 18,500-seat arena were standing, striking the air with their
fists. The crowd sang the refrain of "Thunder Road" so hard you could feel
your sternum hum. "I've heard these songs a million fucking times," Miami
would say the next day, "and it was like I never heard 'em before. I've
watched him write, months and months of digging, but last night was a weird

feeling—like you were in exactly the same place he was when he wrote them."

SPRINGSTEEN WORKS from the gut. There seem to be no planks of his ideology that are not nailed down by some hard-core, practical fact of life. There have long been hints that this lover of automobiles doesn't like the big oil companies; for the B side of "Hungry Heart" he chose "Held up Without a Gun," which is partly about gas prices.

Yet many people were surprised when he made his passionate but furtive ideology explicit by joining the lineup for the "No Nukes" concerts at Madison Square Garden. While in Los Angeles in mid–1979, Bruce went to a Jackson Browne concert. Afterward, the MUSE people had a question for him. "They said they needed some help in New York City," he recalls, "and they asked, did we want to help out?"

His manner, as he considers the politics of helping out, is not easy. There seems to be a heavy, slow beat somewhere in his innards before every word he speaks. "There's too much greed, too much carelessness. I don't believe that was ever the idea of capitalism. It's just gotta be voices heard from all places, that's my main concern, and when you're up against big business and politics, you gotta have some muscle.

"People every day in different ways try to talk to people out there. Especially during the elections, they try to appeal to people's secret hearts, you know, with the American dream—really it's the human dream, and everybody knows by now that it ain't about two cars in the garage. It's about people living and working together without steppin' on each other.

"There's a cruel and cynical game that goes on," he continues, letting his hands fall open, as if they could catch hold of whatever is bugging him so deeply. "A game that people with responsibility play with these immense hopes and desires. It's disgusting the disrespect those people with responsibility can have. Like TV. You wonder what's going on in this [NBC-TV chief] Freddy Silverman's head sometimes, like how can he do that? There's some good things on TV, but way too much of it is used to zonk people out.

"So that cynical game goes on; it's like the carrot-in-front-of-the-donkey game. The cynicism of the last ten years is what people adopted as a necessary defense against having tire tracks up and down their front and back everyday."

Springsteen pauses and looks across a table littered with chicken bones and empty soda bottles. Outside the hotel room, Lake Erie's gray expanse is whitening with the dawn.

"That was the spirit of rock & roll when it came in," he goes on, "talking to kids in their secret heart. To promise to somebody that things are gonna be all right, you don't ever have the room to do that. Then you're a politician. All you can do is say there's possibilities, some are gonna stand, some are gonna fall, and then try to say that the search and the struggle is a life-affirming action. Illusions make you weak, dreams and possibilities make you strong. That's what I hope people get from our music. That's what I got from the Drifters, say, 'Under the Boardwalk.' As full as the singer sounds, it always had that little sadness that made you love it, made you recognize it as being true.

"There's this movie, *Wise Blood* [from Flannery O'Connor's story in which a young religious zealot from the deep South blinds himself]. One of my favorite parts was the end, where he's doin' all these terrible things to himself, and the woman comes in and says, 'There's no reason for it. People have quit doing it.' And he says, 'They ain't quit doing it as long as I'm doing it.'

"There's this thing that gets conjured up at night. In fact, to me it's different every night. I was always close to work. I found out very young what makes me happy. I stay very close to that. It just seemed like the secret of the world."

STEVE POND

BRUCE SPRINGSTEEN TAKES ON SCALPERS, WINS BOOTLEG SUIT

TICKET SCALPERS and record bootleggers are the twin parasites of the music business, but no one knew quite what to do about them until Bruce Springsteen came along. Springsteen, whose current tour has become the major concert event of the year, grossing nearly $7 million so far, is fighting back—and winning.

The thirty-one-year-old performer lashed out at scalpers each night of his four-show stand at the Los Angeles Sports Arena last fall, declaring from the stage, "If you've gotta pay $200 to buy a ticket that's marked $12.50, it's not right, and you shouldn't stand for it. Tickets should go to the fans, not the scalpers."

Ticket-scalping is legal in California, so long as it's not done at the site of the event. But Los Angeles was only the most flagrant example of this organized rip-off, which also plagued Springsteen's SRO tour in New York, Chicago, Philadelphia and even Largo, Maryland. Incensed by the situation, Springsteen's promoter, Ron Delsener, hired private investigators to probe the ticket-distribution system in New York and L.A., and contracted an independent accounting firm to disburse the tickets for Springsteen's late-December Nassau Coliseum dates on Long Island.

"If they had gotten the tickets legally, all we could do is argue with the law," says Barry Bell, Springsteen's booking agent. "But the scalpers ended up with blocks of eight to ten tickets in a row for every show, and you can't do that by mailing in requests."

In Los Angeles, Springsteen recorded a radio spot urging fans to support an antiscalping bill that has been introduced in the California State Assembly, and he lent his name to a similar newspaper ad taken out by his local promoter, Wolf and Rissmiller Concerts. Jim Rissmiller says that the ad drew more than 20,000 responses, and State Assemblyman Meldon Levine—the antiscalping bill's author—says he's received more letters of support for the measure than for any similar legislation he's worked on. But, Levine adds, "The scalpers' lobby is one of the strongest in the state. When I introduced my first antiscalping bill in 1977, colleagues came up to me saying, 'That bill of yours hurts my friends.' Unless we get support from the entertainment industry, we'll never overcome that."

In New York, markups of more than two dollars above a ticket's face value are illegal. Still, there were widespread reports of New Jersey scalpers holding large quantities of tickets for the New York shows; scalping is not prohibited in New Jersey. The New York state attorney general is investigating "several hundred complaints" that thousands of seats for Springsteen's four Madison Square Garden shows went to scalpers. One local postal employee was fired when he was found placing his own address labels over all outgoing Springsteen ticket orders. "But mostly," says a Springsteen spokesperson, "we found that Madison Square Garden was incredibly disorganized at filling ticket orders." As for the Long Island shows, "We haven't heard any scalping charges yet. Of course, if we receive enough requests to sell out twenty shows and Bruce only does three, you're still going to get some complaints."

On the bootlegging front, Springsteen and his record company, CBS, won a major victory shortly before Christmas when a federal district court in Los Angeles awarded them $2.15 million in damages from Andrea Waters, former owner of a local record store. Jim Washburn, the store's manager, was ordered to pay $10,750. The two also received $15,750 in additional fines, and they must split the cost of the $105,573 court case.

Waters, sometimes known as "Vicky Vinyl," was charged with producing four Springsteen bootlegs—*Pièce de Résistance; Winterland, 1978; E Ticket;* and *Fire*—and one live Cheap Trick bootleg. Although Washburn and other bootleggers claim that Waters wasn't responsible for the last three records, she was unable to dispute some of the charges after CBS won a summary judgment in the case. She was fined $50,000—the legal maximum—for each of forty-three copyright violations after FBI and other investigators detailed her extensive mail-order operation and a system of storage areas that held up to twelve tons of bootlegs. Washburn says an appeal is likely: "Our options are to appeal or go bankrupt."

Bootleggers claim that their impact on the record business is exaggerated. "It's not a $200-million-a-year rip-off," says one former bootlegger. "But you've gotta be retarded not to make money with boots."

1980 MUSIC AWARDS

MARCH 5, 1981

READERS PICKS

ARTIST OF THE YEAR
Bruce Springsteen
Pink Floyd
The Clash
The Rolling Stones
Queen

BAND OF THE YEAR
The E Street Band
The Rolling Stones
The Clash
Pink Floyd
The Who

BEST ALBUM
Bruce Springsteen: *The River*
Pink Floyd: *The Wall*
The Clash: *London Calling*
Pete Townshend: *Empty Glass*
AC/DC: *Back in Black*
The Rolling Stones: *Emotional Rescue*

BEST SINGLE
Bruce Springsteen: "Hungry Heart"
Queen: "Another One Bites the Dust"
Blondie: "Call Me"
Doobie Brothers: "Real Love"
The Vapors: "Turning Japanese"

MALE VOCALIST
Bruce Springsteen
Jackson Browne
Billy Joel
Bob Seger
Mick Jagger

SONGWRITER
Bruce Springsteen
Pete Townshend
Jackson Browne
Elvis Costello
Billy Joel

PRODUCER
Jon Landau
Nick Lowe
Brian Eno
Phil Ramone
Ted Templeman

CRITICS PICKS

ARTIST OF THE YEAR
Bruce Springsteen
Pink Floyd

BEST ALBUM
The Clash: *London Calling*
Bruce Springsteen: *The River*
Talking Heads: *Remain in Light*
Captain Beefheart and the Magic Band: *Doc at the Radar Station*
Mink DeVille: *Le Chat Bleu*

■ RANDOM NOTES (March 5, 1981)

Bruce Springsteen is producing and contributing songs and backup vocals to an album by Gary "U.S." Bonds, who last hit big in the early Sixties with "New Orleans" and "Quarter to Three." Look for the LP in April.

■ RANDOM NOTES (May 28, 1981)

Ich bin ein Hamburger: Bruce Springsteen kicked off his European tour (postponed for nearly a month due to exhaustion) with a blistering performance in Hamburg, Germany. Der Boss began the three-hour, four-encore show with "Factory" and finished with "Rocking All Over the World," a Creedence Clearwater Revival raveup. Locals gave Springsteen kudos for his soothing way with frenzied Hamburg audiences, which have been getting out of hand ever since the days of Bill Haley.

■ RANDOM NOTES (June 25, 1981)

There's no stopping the Bruce Springsteen European juggernaut. Hottest spot of Bossmania thus far has been Sweden, where one Stockholm daily went so far as to print a full-page canine photo under Bruce's name, much to the initial befuddlement of tour officials. The story? THE DOG WHO ATE THE TICKETS. In concert, Springsteen has been performing two Elvis Presley standards, "I'm Gonna Follow That Dream" and the weepy "I Can't Help Falling in Love With You"—as well as a song he's just written entitled "Bye-Bye, Johnny," said to be about his remembrances of the King (and John Lennon, perhaps?). There's no truth, though, to published reports that had Springsteen starring in a remake of *The Wild One*.

■ RANDOM NOTES (July 23, 1981)

America's greatest source of nonpolluting energy, Bruce Springsteen, left audiences gasping for breath and critics grasping for adjectives after scintillating performances on both sides of the Atlantic last month. The man from Asbury Park, New Jersey, brought his European tour to a spirited climax with four sold-out shows at London's cavernous Wembley Arena, at last purging the memory of his ill-fated, over-hyped dates there in 1975. Among those who ventured backstage after the fourth Wembley gig to wolf down hot dogs and hamburgers were Joe Jackson, Kim Carnes, a pudgy Elvis Costello, former Sex Pistols drummer Paul Cook (sporting a nouveau rockabilly haircut), the Ants sans Adam (the confessed Springsteen buff was sidelined by conjunctivitis and therefore compelled, for *medical* reasons, to don a pirate-style eyepatch), the Pretenders minus Chrissie Hynde, and sizable contingents from the Psychedelic Furs, U2, the Members and the Fabulous Thunderbirds. Most surprised well-wisher of the tour was probably Dave Edmunds, who greeted Springsteen backstage and was given a song written for him by the Boss; most enthusiastic might have been multishow attendee Pete Townshend, who helped close out the tour with a bang by joining Springsteen onstage in Birmingham for a Mitch Ryder medley.

Less than a week later, Springsteen turned up unexpectedly in L.A. for Survival Sunday, a rally sponsored by the Alliance for Survival opposing nuclear power and weapons. Introduced by paraplegic Vietnam vet Ron Kovic, an E-Street Band-less Springsteen stepped out with only a solid-body guitar. "This song's been sung a lot, and it's been misinterpreted a lot," he offered before launching into "This Land Is Your Land." He proceeded to duet on a "real slow" rendition of "Promised Land" with Jackson Browne and teamed up with buddy Gary "U.S." Bonds for a rollicking "Jolé Blon." The show concluded with twenty-seven people—including such *No Nukes* nabobs as Graham Nash, Bonnie Raitt and Stephen Stills—crooning "Brother John Is Gone," a New Orleans funeral standard.

CHRISTOPHER CONNELLY

SPRINGSTEEN RETURNS TO THE ROAD

"I NEVER SEEN *nothing* like this," an ecstatic Bruce Springsteen confided to 20,000 of his closest friends early last month as he kicked off his summer U.S. tour with six sold-out dates at East Rutherford, New Jersey's Brendan Byrne Arena. Springsteen's open-mouthed enthusiasm was clearly directed less at the fine new concert-sports facility than at the overjoyed reaction of his Jersey brethren. "That was the best show ever," he said in his dressing room after the first night's performance. "We couldn't hear each other onstage. I felt like the Beatles."

Even so, the opening set of his three-hour-plus show seemed curiously lackluster. Concentrating on the more pensive, brooding songs in his repertoire ("Darkness on the Edge of Town" and his new Elvis tribute, "Bye-Bye Johnny"), Springsteen remained relatively inert onstage. The most surprising point came before "Independence Day" and its concomitant rap, when he muttered quickly to the crowd, "I'm gonna need a little quiet on this song, thank you." Not a graceless moment, surely, but an off-key one, as if Bruce had lost sight of his fans' savvy. He repeated the line before a solo version of "This Land Is Your Land," replete with characteristic minor chords and overly mournful vocals. Somewhat uninspired renditions of "Badlands" and "Thunder Road" closed out the set, leaving a few Springsteen aficionados knitting their brows worriedly.

But Springsteen and the E Street Band erased all doubts in Act Two. Taking the stage with fire in their eyes, they launched into a whammo streak of ass-shaking rockers: "You Can Look (but You Better Not Touch)," "Cadillac Ranch" (sung by Springsteen while wearing a humongous foam-rubber cowboy hat) and "Sherry Darling." The good-natured Springsteen swagger was back, and when saxman Clarence Clemons, resplendent in a powder-blue polyester suit, swung into "Hungry Heart," the euphoric house screamed out the first verse and chorus to the visible delight of the band.

Much of the rest of the show passed in a blizzard of dancey delight, and for the encore, Springsteen came up with a masterstroke cover: Tom Waits' "Jersey Girl," a bittersweet ballad on the vicissitudes of love in what used to be called the armpit of the nation. Miami Steve Van Zandt then got into the act, crooning his own "I Don't Wanna Go Home," and an extended Mitch Ryder medley brought an end to the proceedings—that is, until a hopped-up Springsteen stopped his bowing and lurched the band into their European tour curtain-closer, a John Fogerty foot-stomper entitled "Rockin' All Over the World."

Later shows had Springsteen juggling the first night's lineup and adding a scintillating new song, "Trapped," reportedly a Jimmy Cliff number re-worked in the searing mode of *Darkness on the Edge of Town*. But not every-thing went his way: During the third show, a firecracker exploded smack in the middle of the emotional "Racing in the Streets," angering Spring-steen and perceivably altering his relationship with the audience for the du-ration of the set.

After inaugurating the Brendan Byrne Arena, Springsteen and the band made an unannounced appearance at the opening of Clarence Clemons' restaurant-club, Big Man's West, in Red Bank. Declaring to the 400 fans who'd braved temperatures in excess of 100 degrees that "this is a night for bar music," Springsteen led the group through Chuck Berry's "Around and Around," Eddie Cochran's "Summertime Blues" and a handful of others before declaring, "Game called on account of heat!" and splitting.

Once done in New Jersey, it was on to Philadelphia for another series of shows, to be followed by similar engagements in Cleveland, Cincinnati, Chicago and a host of cities to be named later. Also on the boards is a ben-efit for Vietnam veterans, the details of which have yet to be announced.

STEVE POND

SPRINGSTEEN, OTHER ROCK STARS RALLY TO HELP VETS

"**B**IG BUSINESSMEN** and political leaders failed to rally behind us," said Vietnam veteran Bobby Muller, speaking to about 15,000 remarkably attentive rock fans on August 20th at the Los Angeles Sports Arena. "And now it ultimately turns out to be the symbol of our generation—rock & roll—that brings us together. . . . This is the first step in ending the silence that has surrounded Vietnam."

To deafening applause, Muller, sitting center stage in a wheelchair, turned over the spotlight to Bruce Springsteen, the first of several rockers to play benefits for the veterans. Minutes earlier, Springsteen had introduced Muller with his own terse, eloquent speech; now, he led the E Street Band into a dark, swelling melody and stepped to the mike to sing, "Long as I remember, the rain's been falling down. . . . " Creedence Clearwater Revival's eleven-year-old "Who'll Stop the Rain" was transformed into a majestic call to arms, and the next two songs deepened the mood: "Prove It All Night" was stripped of its usual joy, and Springsteen came down hard on the lines "If dreams came true, oh wouldn't it be nice / But this ain't no dream we're living through tonight." Then, without pause, he turned toward the two stage-side platforms full of veterans in wheelchairs and on crutches and ripped into "The Ties That Bind": "You been hurt and you're all cried out you say / You walk down the street pushing people out of your way."

All proceeds from the show—the first in a six-night stand for Springsteen at the Sports Arena—will be split between the Vietnam Veterans of America (VVA)—the organization Muller heads—and the Los Angeles Mental Health Clinic (the VVA will receive seventy-five percent of the estimated $100,000 take). Shortly after Springsteen announced his benefit, other musicians came to the aid of the veterans: Pat Benatar's September 20th Detroit performance will benefit the VVA, and Charlie Daniels will give the organization proceeds from a Warner Amex cable TV concert filmed in Saratoga Springs, New York, on September 4th. "I feel that the Vietnam veterans have been the most mistreated and most ignored people I can remember in my lifetime," said Daniels, "and this is the third war I've been through. It's time they were looked after and respected in the way they deserve."

Springsteen became interested in the veterans' plight through his friendship with disabled vet Ron Kovic; he asked his manager, Jon Landau, to research the various veterans organizations to determine which is the most effective, and he decided to do the show after meeting with Muller and VVA vice-president Michael Harbert earlier this summer.

"These are people of our generation—Bruce's, mine," said Landau. "I think Bruce saw a lot of his high-school friends go to Vietnam. It sounds corny, but these people we're trying to help could have been us if the circumstances had been a little different." Landau said he expects Springsteen to continue working for the veterans in different ways; an official Springsteen poster is already for sale, with all proceeds going to the VVA.

Backstage after the Springsteen show, Muller was ecstatic about the support his group is suddenly getting. "We tried everything," said Muller of his three-year-old organization. "Corporations, foundations, direct mail. We got thirty-five editorials in the *Washington Post* in 1978, but we didn't realize a *single* legislative objective. You can't push costly benefit programs through Congress with good arguments. You need political strength, and that means numbers."

With only 8,000 members, the VVA does not have that strength. But after years of maneuvering, the group finally obtained a list of 1 million Vietnam veterans, and money from the concerts will go toward a direct-mailing operation aimed at those vets. Muller said that a goal of 50,000 members by spring and another 100,000 by the end of 1982 is realistic.

"People don't like to think about the Vietnam vets, because everything about the war was negative," he said. "We shouldn't have been fighting, we lost. . . . But Bruce has publicly aligned himself with the lepers of our society and taken us out of the shadows."

Springsteen made his commitment clear in his speech introducing Muller in Los Angeles. "It's like when you're walking down a dark street at night, and out of the corner of your eye you see somebody getting hurt in a dark alley," he said slowly. "But you keep walking on because you think it don't have nothing to do with you and you just want to get home. Vietnam turned this whole country into that dark street, and unless we can walk down those dark alleys and look into the eyes of those men and women, we're never gonna get home."

CHRISTOPHER CONNELLY

SPRINGSTEEN WRAPS UP TOUR

AFTER 139 SHOWS, eleven and a half months on the road and enough fried chicken to feed Latvia for a week, Bruce Springsteen finally wrapped up his 1980–1981 tour with the second of two shows at Cincinnati's Riverfront Coliseum on September 14th. "This has been the best year of my life," said Springsteen, who played to more than a million people during his American and European excursions, at an average venue capacity exceeding ninety-nine percent.

High spirits and high jinks keynoted the final gig. Springsteen seasoned his typical three-hour set with Tommy James and the Shondells' "Mony Mony," which he dropped into his Mitch Ryder medley. (It seems Springsteen first performed the song at a Chicago gig, after band members and associates frantically called coast-to-coast during intermission to find the lyrics.) During one of the encores, two E Street Band crew members disguised as cops began hanging out at both ends of the stage, threatening to terminate the show, which was running overtime. Eventually, the two impostors sprang forward and carried Springsteen to the back of the stage, where he broke away and continued to sing without missing a beat.

After the show, the band repaired to its hotel suite for an intimate but rowdy end-of-the-tour celebration, highlighted by saxophonist Clarence Clemons' lethal Kahuna punch and Springsteen's own party tapes ("heavy on the Dave Clark Five and Jr. Walker," said one attendee). The bash, dubbed "The Concluding Rites of Bossmania 1981," roared on until sunrise, when Springsteen dashed to the windows to shut out the dawn's early light.

Further plans for the band remain sketchy. Springsteen may contribute a cut to Lucy Simon's *In Harmony 2,* a benefit LP for the Children's Television Workshop. His own recording plans are indefinite.

■ RANDOM NOTES (January 21, 1982)

The New York chapter of the National Organization for Women has instigated a letter and phone-call appeal directed at Bruce Springsteen, demanding that he stop referring to women as "little girls" in his songs. "He is writing and singing sexist music," said NOW's New York executive director, Virginia Cornue. The protest is the brainchild of Kathy Tepes, a national NOW consciousness-raising task-force member. "When you call us 'little girls,' " reads one of the three letters Tepes has sent to Springsteen, "you perpetuate the myth that we women do things in a 'small' way." In a postscript, Tepes does some name-changing herself. "To counterbalance your rough and tough image with your nickname, 'the Boss,' I for one call you a Twinkie and Brucie."

A spokeswoman at Springsteen's office defended his use of "little girls," calling it "a rock & roll term." The spokeswoman noted that no calls or letters had yet been received in connection with the appeal, except from a few NOW members wishing to dissociate themselves from the project.

■ RANDOM NOTES (September 16, 1982)

Bruce Springsteen figures to surprise both the public and the recording industry with his new album: it's a solo LP entitled *Nebraska,* recorded at his New Jersey home without the assistance of the E Street Band. Those who've heard it say its mood is personal and darkly ruminative about America as a whole. Many of the songs feature only guitar, harmonica and a vocal, though Springsteen does play some synthesizer on a cut or two. The LP's ten songs were written and recorded earlier this year and were originally intended for use on a rock & roll album with Miami Steve and the boys. Titles of the tracks are "Mansion on the Hill," "Highway Patrolman," "Used Cars," "Open All Night," "My Father's House," "Atlantic City," "State Trooper," about two brothers with different ideas about law and order; "Johnny 99," about an unemployed man who goes on a killing rampage; and "Nebraska," said to be about mass murderer Charlie Starkweather, whose deeds were depicted in the film *Badlands.* The album's final track, "Reason to Believe," offers a ray of hope amid all this sadness: "At the end of every hard-earned day / People find some reason to believe." Though the disc was recorded on a four-track cassette machine, it's said to have studio-quality sound, with Springsteen's vocals out front.

Sure, it's a solo LP—but Bruce Springsteen still needed a little assistance with the title track of his new album, *Nebraska*. Just ask Ninette Beaver, the fifty-five-year-old assignment editor for KMTV news in Omaha, who was the surprised recipient of a call from the Boss last winter. "His name sort of rang a bell," recalls Beaver. Springsteen wanted to talk to Beaver about *Caril,* the book she wrote about the Charlie Starkweather killings (which were also chronicled in the film *Badlands*). Beaver, though, still wasn't sure whom she was talking to. "First I asked him what he did. And he said, 'I'm a musician.' Finally, I just said, 'Honest to God, I know I should know who you are, but I'm just drawing a blank.' And he was just a *doll* about it—really cute." They wound up talking for about half an hour, primarily about Starkweather's companion, Caril Fugate. And the result was "Nebraska."

STEVE POND

NEBRASKA ALBUM REVIEW
Springsteen Delivers His Bravest
Record Yet
★ ★ ★ ★ 1/2*

AFTER TEN YEARS of forging his own brand of fiery, expansive rock & roll, Bruce Springsteen has decided that some stories are best told by one man, one guitar. Flying in the face of a sagging record industry with an intensely personal project that could easily alienate radio, rock's gutsiest mainstream performer has dramatically reclaimed his right to make the records *he* wants to make, and damn the consequences. This is the bravest of Springsteen's six records; it's also his most startling, direct and chilling. And if it's a risky move commercially, *Nebraska* is also a tactical masterstroke, an inspired way out of the high-stakes rock & roll game that requires each new record to be bigger and grander than the last.

Until now, it looked as if 1973's dizzying *The Wild, the Innocent & the E Street Shuffle* would be the last Springsteen album to surprise people. Ensuing records simply refined, expanded and deepened his artistry. But *Nebraska* comes as a shock, a violent, acid-etched portrait of a wounded America that fuels its machinery by consuming its people's dreams. It is a portrait painted with old tools: a few acoustic guitars, a four-track cassette deck, a vocabulary derived from the plain-spoken folk music of Woody Guthrie and the dark hillbilly laments of Hank Williams. The style is steadfastly, defiantly out-of-date, the singing flat and honest, the music stark, deliberate and unadorned.

Nebraska is an acoustic triumph, a basic folk album on which Springsteen has stripped his art down to the core. It's as harrowing as *Darkness on the Edge of Town,* but more measured. Every small touch speaks volumes: the delicacy of the acoustic guitars, the blurred sting of the electric guitars, the spare, grim images. He's now telling simple stories in the language of a

---

*Note: In 1981, ROLLING STONE began using the star rating system; it was discontinued in 1985 and brought back in 1988.

deferential common man, peppering his sentences with "sir's." "My name is Joe Roberts," he sings. "I work for the state."

As *The River* closed, Springsteen found himself haunted by a highway death. On *Nebraska,* violent death is his starting point. The title track is an audacious, scary beginning. Singing in a voice borrowed from Guthrie and early Bob Dylan, he takes the part of mass murderer Charlie Starkweather to quietly sing, "I can't say that I'm sorry for the things that we done / At least for a little while, sir, me and her we had us some fun." The music is gentle and soothing, but this is no romanticized outlaw tale à la Guthrie's "Pretty Boy Floyd." The casual coldbloodedness, the singer's willingness to undertake the role and the music's pastoral calm make Starkweather all the more horrific.

Springsteen follows with another tale of real-life murder, this one involving mob wars in Atlantic City. With "Nebraska" and "Atlantic City," his landscape has taken on new, broader boundaries, and when he begins "Mansion on the Hill" with a reference to "the edge of town," it's clear that his usual New Jersey turf has opened its borders to include Nebraska and Wyoming and forty-seven other states. Crowds on the final leg of his last tour saw hints that Springsteen was heading toward this territory when he talked of Allan Nevins and Henry Steele Commager's history of the United States and Joe Klein's *Woody Guthrie: A Life,* and when he sang the songs of Guthrie, John Fogerty and Elvis Presley, all uniquely American stories.

The keynote lines on *Nebraska*—"Deliver me from nowhere" and "I got debts that no honest man can pay"—each surface in two songs. The former ends both "State Trooper" and "Open All Night," while the latter turns up in "Atlantic City" and "Johnny 99." The album's honest men—and they outnumber its criminals, though side one's string of bloodletters suggests otherwise—are all paying debts and looking for deliverance that never comes. The compassion with which Springsteen sings every line can't hide the fact that there's no peace to be found in the darkness, no cleansing river running through town.

As on *The River,* the most outwardly optimistic songs on the new album are sung by a man who knows full well that his dreams of easy deliverance are empty. In "Used Cars," the singer watches his father buy another clunker and makes a vow as heartfelt as it is heartbreakingly hollow: "Mister, the day the lottery I win / I ain't ever gonna ride in no used car again." And the LP's one seeming refuge turns out to be illusion: in "My Father's House," a devastating capper to Springsteen's cycle of "father" songs, the house is a sanctuary only in the singer's dreams. When he awakens, he finds that his father is gone, that the house sits at the end of a highway "where our sins lie unatoned." By this point, the convicted murderer of "Johnny 99" is one of the few characters who's seemingly figured out how to retain his dignity. He asks to be executed.

If this record is as deep and unsettling as anything Springsteen has recorded, it is also his narrowest and most single-minded work. He is not extending or advancing his own style so much as he is temporarily adopting a style codified by others. But in that decision are multiple strengths: Springsteen's clear, sharp focus, his insistence on painting small details so clearly and his determination to make a folk album firmly in the tradition. "My Father's House" may be the only cut on side two that can stand up to the string of songs that open the record, but inconsistency is perhaps inevitable after that astonishing initial stretch: the title track; "Atlantic City"; and "Highway Patrolman," an indelible tale of the ties that bind and the toll familial love exacts, with one of Springsteen's most delicious, delirious reveries—"Me and Frankie laughin' and drinkin' / Nothing feels better than blood on blood / Takin' turns dancin' with Maria / As the band played 'Night of the Johnstown Flood.'"

By the end of the record, paradoxically, the choking dust that hangs over Springsteen's landscape makes its occasional rays of sunlight shine brighter. In "Atlantic City," for example, a rueful chorus makes the song sound nearly as triumphant as "Promised Land": "Everything dies, baby that's a fact / But maybe everything that dies some day comes back / Put your makeup on, fix your hair up pretty / And meet me tonight in Atlantic City."

Finally, it comes down to that: An old dress and a meeting across from the casino is sometimes all it takes. "Reason to Believe" adds the final brush strokes, by turns blackly humorous and haunting. One man stands alongside a highway, poking a dead dog as if to revive it; another heads down to the river to wed. The bride never shows, the groom stands waiting, the river flows on, and people, Springsteen sings with faintly befuddled respect, still find their reasons to believe. Naive, simple and telling, it is the caption beneath Bruce Springsteen's abrasive, clouded and ultimately glorious portrait of America.

Bruce Springsteen has headed out to Los Angeles to complete his next album with the E Street Band. Before leaving the East, though, the Boss stopped by the Stone Pony in Asbury Park, New Jersey, and played an impromptu fourteen-song set for a stunned crowd of 200 people—who had paid all of two dollars to see local favorites Cats on a Smooth Surface. Backed by the band, Springsteen scored with a raveup version of "Open All Night" from *Nebraska,* another tune entitled "On the Prowl" and a solid selection of oldies, including "Twist and Shout," "Wooly Bully" and "Do You Wanna Dance."

NEBRASKA YEAR-END ALBUM REVIEW

A N ABRASIVE, clouded and ultimately glorious portrait of America, *Nebraska* is a basic folk album on which Bruce Springsteen has stripped his art down to its core. He has used some old tools—a few acoustic guitars, a four-track cassette deck, a plain-spoken folk-music vocabulary—to paint a harrowing, violent picture of a wounded country, albeit a country in which the choking dust makes the occasional rays of sunlight and hope shine brighter. A risky commercial move that worked—it got airplay and sold—*Nebraska* is the bravest of Springsteen's six records. It's also the most startling, direct and chilling.

■ **RANDOM NOTES** (May 12, 1983)

Bruce Springsteen is still in Los Angeles, slaving away on his forthcoming album with the E Street Band, which may make it into the stores before summer's end. Springsteen has played some tracks off the still-untitled LP to such pals as Bob Seger, but apparently isn't satisfied just yet—and any tour, he says, will come afterward. "We'd like to tour," says the Boss, "but it depends on the record. I don't have much control over that myself. I just gotta wait till the record feels right."

Springsteen made those comments at a party following Prince's recent show in Los Angeles, which he attended with his close buddies Mr. and Mrs. Steven Van Zandt. Springsteen's muscles have swelled to Popeye size since he embarked on a weight-training program last year, and one source says he's even passing up junk food, which was his standard cuisine.

1982 MUSIC AWARDS

MARCH 4, 1983

READERS PICKS

ARTIST OF THE YEAR
Bruce Springsteen
The Who
John Cougar
Pete Townshend
Paul McCartney

MALE VOCALIST
Bruce Springsteen
John Cougar
Robert Plant
Roger Daltrey
Paul McCartney

ALBUM OF THE YEAR
Nebraska, **Bruce Springsteen**
It's Hard, The Who
Asia, Asia
Mirage, Fleetwood Mac
Tug of War, Paul McCartney
Combat Rock, The Clash

SONGWRITER OF THE YEAR
Bruce Springsteen

CRITICS PICKS

ALBUM OF THE YEAR
Nebraska, **Bruce Springsteen**
Shoot Out the Lights, Richard and Linda Thompson (tie)
Runners Up:
Imperial Bedroom, Elvis Costello
1999, Prince
The Blue Mask, Lou Reed
Marshall Crenshaw, Marshall Crenshaw

■ RANDOM NOTES (July 7, 1983)

The good news is that Bruce Springsteen has finished his new album, according to one reliable report. The bad news is that he doesn't like it and has decided to write more songs for the record. Springsteen and the band are currently holed up in an East Coast studio, hammering out arrangements of the tunes for the much-delayed LP, which at one point was to have been called *Born in the U.S.A.*

Springsteen has found time to contribute two songs to saxman Clarence Clemons' solo LP, produced by Ralph Schuckett. One of the songs is an instrumental, the other a raveup titled "Save It Up." Springsteen also managed to check out U2, who've been putting on some of the best rock shows in recent memory during their U.S. tour. The Boss was in the audience for their Philadelphia gig, at which the Irish band puckishly dedicated their encore to Steel Mill, one of Springsteen's first Jersey bar bands.

■ RANDOM NOTES (September 1, 1983)

Don't bet the rent on it, but Bruce Springsteen may have turned the corner on his next LP. For the past three weeks, Springsteen, producers Jon Landau and Chuck Plotkin and engineer Toby Scott have been holed up in a New York City studio, mixing some of the tracks that Bruce selected out of the more than thirty he recorded with the E Street Band over the past eighteen months. It could mean that the long-awaited album will be finished by late fall and that Springsteen will hit the road before the year's end—but a spokesperson cautions that the Jerseyite could decide to do even more recording, and that would push the LP and the tour still further back.

On a less surreptitious note, Springsteen joined a bar band, Diamonds, at the Stone Pony in Asbury Park earlier this summer for an impromptu set of rock & roll standards. And one Californian claims to have seen Bruce and Michael Jackson browsing at a newsstand together last month. Bruce accepted kudos from a fan and had only one request: "Please don't ask me about the record."

■ RANDOM NOTES (February 2, 1984)

Not even Bruce Springsteen's own E Street Band knows for sure what's up with his long-delayed new LP. "They talk about it all the time," says one musician who works frequently with the band members, "but they don't even know what's going on. I say, 'What's happening with Bruce's album?' and they say, 'We're cutting more tracks.'" When the album does finally get released, don't expect to hear guitarist Miami Steve Van Zandt on too many cuts, as he hasn't been in the studio with the band for more than a year and a half. Between sessions, Springsteen has found the time to appear in saxman Clarence Clemons' video as a carwash attendant.

■ RANDOM NOTES (March 17, 1984)

Steven Van Zandt (Little Steven or Miami Steve, depending on what part of New Jersey you're in) declares that, contrary to a report in these pages, he has indeed played on a good number of the tracks on Bruce Springsteen's forthcoming album. The LP, says Van Zandt, should be out "sometime this decade. I would not ever bet on Bruce's release date. With forty-two wars going on in the world, I don't worry about it." The official, but cautious, line holds to a June release. Van Zandt will again share production credit on the LP.

Meanwhile, Van Zandt's been shuttling from studio to studio, finishing up his second Little Steven and the Disciples of Soul album. He admits that a Disciples tour is a possibility if Springsteen hits a major block. Either way, says Van Zandt, "I know 1984's gonna be a good year for us. I know this is the best work I've ever done; I'm more focused now, and I know what I'm doing."

■ RANDOM NOTES (May 24, 1984)

Bruce Springsteen's next album, *Born in the U.S.A.,* is finally finished and set for a June release. The single, due out in May, will be "Dancing in the Dark." Other tracks include a raveup titled "I'm on Fire." An East Coast tour is likely to begin in July.

Perhaps in preparation, Springsteen recently took to the stage of his favorite Jersey club, the Stone Pony, where he reeled off an unusual assortment of cover tunes—from the Standells' "Dirty Water" ("New Jersey, that's my home," he sang with a grin) to the ZZ Top steamer "I'm Bad, I'm Nationwide." In other Springsteen news, Springsteen decided not to release the rights to "Streets of Fire" for the soundtrack album of Walter Hill's forthcoming film of the same name.

CHRISTOPHER CONNELLY

"FUN" SPRINGSTEEN ALBUM, TOUR DUE

AFTER WRITING at least sixty songs and spending the better part of two years in the studio, Bruce Springsteen has finally completed his seventh album, *Born in the U.S.A.* The LP will be released early in June; a single, "Dancing in the Dark," which is backed with a nonalbum track called "Pink Cadillac," came out May 10th. A tour is expected to start in July, somewhere in the Midwest, though exact dates and venues are still being considered.

Other than releasing the twelve song titles—"Born in the U.S.A.," "Cover Me," "Darlington County," "Working on the Highway," "Downbound Train," "I'm On Fire," "No Surrender," "Bobby Jean," "I'm Goin' Down," "Glory Days," "Dancing in the Dark" and "My Hometown"— Springsteen's representatives have been tight-lipped about the album.

According to other sources, however, the record marks a significant change in direction from Springsteen's previous albums: *Born in the U.S.A.,* they say, is not a heavy, message-oriented LP. It is simply a lot of fun.

One indication of this is that Springsteen joined mixmaster Arthur Baker one night to prepare a twelve-inch (but nondisco) version of "Dancing in the Dark." "He sort of came up with a password for the evening: 'Later for the subtlety,' " recalled Baker, who added at least fourteen new tracks—from glockenspiels to backup vocals—to the song.

Though many of the album's songs were written in the last few months, some of the material from *Born in the U.S.A.* dates as far back as late 1981, when Springsteen and the E Street Band first assembled at the Power Station in New York to begin recording what was to be a rock & roll album. At the time, Springsteen's songwriting was strongly influenced by his reading of the Southern short-story writer Flannery O'Connor and a book about the Charlie Starkweather killings. The full-band performances of these dark, brooding songs didn't satisfy Springsteen, however, and his solution, of course, was to release his home demos—bare-bones instrumentals and vocals—as the album titled *Nebraska,* in 1982.

Springsteen continued working, and by the end of 1982, he and his band completed a rock & roll album, which was played for musician pals like Bob Seger. But, as is his wont, Springsteen decided not to release the project; instead, he wrote more songs and did more recording. Songs from this aborted 1982 collection also turn up on *Born in the U.S.A.*

Since starting recording in 1981, Springsteen has written between sixty and a hundred songs. In addition, he has spent a considerable amount of time selecting the songs for the album, and even after the record was first turned in to Columbia in late March, an additional song, "No Surrender," was added.

Neither side of the album cover depicts Springsteen's face. The front is a shot of his torso with an American flag in the background; the rear is a picture of Springsteen's rear, jean-clad, with a baseball cap sticking out of one of the pockets. Since completing the record, Springsteen has been relaxing in his New Jersey home; rehearsals for the forthcoming tour will begin as soon as E Street Band sax player Clarence Clemons' tour is finished. In addition, Springsteen is planning to make a video for "Dancing in the Dark." At press time, no director had been selected, though the British team of Kevin Godley and Lol Creme, formerly members of 10cc and directors of Duran Duran's "Girls on Film" video, were considered the front-runners. Feature-film director John Sayles was also a possibility.

Those who've heard the unreleased tracks assert that there is an album's worth of material left over. Springsteen has reportedly discussed releasing some of those songs as early as the end of the year. Sources, however, scotched the persistent rumor that a more dour assortment of songs, purportedly titled *Murder, Inc.,* will be released at tour's end.

■ RANDOM NOTES (June 21, 1984)

When Bruce Springsteen hits the road in July for his 1984 world tour, he won't be accompanied by his longtime guitarist, Steve Van Zandt. Neither side would discuss the split, but both did confirm that Van Zandt, also known as Little Steven, has already scheduled his own U.S. tour, which is also slated to start in July. Right now, it looks as if Springsteen's tour will center on the East Coast during most of the summer and will last at least through late October, when Bruce and his E Street Band will probably play a series of indoor shows in Los Angeles. After the U.S. dates are completed, the tour will move overseas, probably to Australia and Japan.

■ RANDOM NOTES (July 5, 1984)

Time was, the sight of Nils Lofgren sharing a microphone with Bruce Springsteen was a rare occurrence, but last month, the Maryland native was hired to replace guitarist Miami Steve Van Zandt in the Boss' E Street Band. Van Zandt is touring with his Disciples of Soul.

DEBBY BULL

BORN IN THE U.S.A. ALBUM REVIEW
Bruce Springsteen Gives the Little Guy
Something to Cheer About

★ ★ ★ ★ ★

THOUGH IT LOOKS at hard times, at little people in little towns choosing between going away and getting left behind, *Born in the U.S.A.,* Bruce Springsteen's seventh album, has a rowdy, indomitable spirit. Two guys pull into a hick town begging for work in "Darlington County," but Springsteen is whooping with sha-la-las in the chorus. He may shove his broody characters out the door and send them cruising down the turnpike, but he gives them music they can pound on the dashboard to.

He's set songs as well drawn as those on his bleak acoustic album, *Nebraska,* to music that incorporates new electronic textures while keeping as its heart all of the American rock & roll from the early Sixties. Like the guys in the songs, the music was born in the U.S.A.: Springsteen ignored the British Invasion and embraced instead the legacy of Phil Spector's releases, the sort of soul that was coming from Atlantic Records and especially the garage bands that had anomalous radio hits. He's always chased the utopian feeling of that music, and here he catches it with a sophisticated production and a subtle change in surroundings—the E Street Band cools it with the saxophone solos and piano arpeggios—from song to song.

The people who hang out in the new songs dread getting stuck in the small towns they grew up in almost as much as they worry that the big world outside holds no possibilities—a familiar theme in Springsteen's work. But they wind up back at home, where you can practically see the roaches scurrying around the empty Twinkie packages in the linoleum kitchen. In the first line of the first song, Springsteen croaks, "Born down in a dead man's town, the first kick I took was when I hit the ground." His characters are born with their broken hearts, and the only thing that keeps them going is imagining that, as another line in another song goes, "There's something happening somewhere."

Though the characters are dying of longing for some sort of payoff from the American dream, Springsteen's exuberant voice and the swell of the music clues you that they haven't given up. In "No Surrender," a song that has the uplifting sweep of his early anthem "Thunder Road," he sings, "We made a promise we swore we'd always remember: no retreat, no surrender." His music usually carries a motto like that. He writes a heartbreaking message called "Bobby Jean," apparently to his longtime guitarist Miami Steve Van Zandt, who's just left his band—"Maybe you'll be out there on that road somewhere . . . in some motel room there'll be a radio playing and you'll hear me sing this song / Well, if you do, you'll know I'm thinking of you and all the miles in between"—but he gives the song a wall of sound with a soaring saxophone solo. That's classic Springsteen: The lyrics may put a lump in your throat, but the music says, Walk tall or don't walk at all.

A great dancer himself, Springsteen puts an infectious beat under his songs. In the wonderfully exuberant "I'm Goin' Down," a hilarious song that gets its revenge, he makes a giddy run of nonsense syllables out of the chorus while drummer Max Weinberg whams out a huge backbeat. And "Working on the Highway" whips into an ecstatic rocker that tells a funny story, handclaps keeping the time, about crime and punishment. Shifting the sound slightly, the band finds the right feeling of paranoia for "Cover Me," the lone song to resurrect that shrieking, "Badlands"-style guitar, and the right ironic fervor for the Vietnam vet's yelping about the dead ends of being "Born in the U.S.A." Though there's no big difference between these and some of the songs on Springsteen's last rock LP, *The River,* these feel more delightfully offhanded.

The album finds its center in those cheering rock songs, but four tracks—the last two on either side—give the album an extraordinary depth. Springsteen has always been able to tell a story better than he can write a hook, and these lyrics are way beyond anything anybody else is writing. They're sung in such an unaffected way that the starkness stabs you. In "My Hometown," the singer remembers sitting on his father's lap and steering the family Buick as they drove proudly through town; but the boy grows up, and the final scene has him putting his own son on his lap for a last drive down a street that's become a row of vacant buildings. "Take a good look around," he tells his boy, repeating what his father told him, "this is your hometown."

The tight-lipped character who sings "I'm On Fire" practically whispers about the desire that's eating him up. "Sometimes it's like someone took a knife, baby, edgy and dull, and cut a six-inch valley through the middle of my skull," he rasps. The way the band's turned down to just a light rattle of drums, faint organ and quiet, staccato guitar notes makes his lust seem ominous: You picture some pockmarked Harry Dean Stanton type, lying, too wired to sleep, in a motel room.

That you get such a vivid sense of these characters is because Springsteen gives them voices a playwright would be proud of. In "Working on the Highway," all he says is "One day I looked straight at her and she looked straight back" to let us know the guy's in love. And in the saddest song he's ever written, "Downbound Train," a man who's lost everything pours out his story, while, behind him, long, sorry notes on a synthesizer sound just like heartache. "I had a job, I had a girl," he begins, then explains how everything's changed: "Now I work down at the carwash, where all it ever does is rain." It's a line Sam Shepard could've written: so pathetic and so funny, you don't know how to react.

The biggest departure from any familiar Springsteen sound is the breathtaking first single, "Dancing in the Dark," with its modern synths, played by E Street keyboardist Roy Bittan, and thundering bass and drums. The kid who dances in the darkness here is practically choking on the self-consciousness of being sixteen. "I check my look in the mirror / I wanna change my clothes, my hair, my face," he sings. "Man, I ain't getting nowhere just living in a dump like this." He turns out the lights not to set some drippy romantic mood but to escape in the fantasy of the music on the radio. In the dark, he finds a release from all the limitations he was born into. In the dark, like all of the guys trapped in Springsteen's songs, he's just a spirit in the night.

DEBBY BULL

THE SUMMER'S BIGGEST TOURS GET UNDER WAY

Bruce in the Heartland

HIS NEW ALBUM, *Born in the U.S.A.,* is perched at the top of the charts, but it's the songs from *Nebraska,* the album Bruce Springsteen made by just singing along with his acoustic guitar into a little tape deck at home, that are the soul of the shows on his new tour.

With a terrifying dark sound, huge drumbeat and chiming guitar duet by Springsteen and his new sideman, Nils Lofgren, "Atlantic City" is one of the show's most powerful numbers. So is "Mansion on the Hill," performed like a slowly rocked country duet with new backup singer Patti Scialfa. Springsteen introduces it with a story: "My father used to drive me out of town to a big white house. It became very mystical, like a touchstone. And now when I dream, I'm sometimes outside the gate looking in . . . and some times I'm the man inside." That's the compelling paradox of this new roadshow: He sings about the despair that fills you when your dreams let you down, yet he himself has hit the jackpot.

Stinking of Ben-Gay and swaddled in a black leather jacket, Springsteen stretched his legs onto a coffee table in his dressing room after the last of three St. Paul shows. "It's the emotional reality that makes anything real, it's not the details," he said, his voice faint, about why his songs of loneliness and lowly beginnings touch a chord in just about everybody. "Maybe it's your imagination or maybe it's something out of real life, it doesn't matter. It's the inner thing that makes a song real to you. Whether it's 'My Hometown' or something like 'Nebraska' or 'Johnny 99,' you kinda just gotta know what that feels like, somewhere." He let out a gruff laugh. "And everybody does. It's a funny thing. I think if it's real, people will respond."

The *Nebraska* pieces—"I framed them a little bit with the band" is how he described the way they're done—give the show an emotionally darker side that only makes his soaring, uplifting early masterworks like "Badlands" and "Thunder Road" more effective and his new high-spirited rockers like "Working on the Highway" and "Glory Days" more hilarious. Of the thirty

or so songs in the three-and-a-half-hour show, Springsteen and his band perform as many as seven songs from *Nebraska,* about eight from *Born in the
U.S.A.* (which he calls a collection of "survival music"), a handful from *The
River* and a couple from *Born to Run* and *Darkness on the Edge of Town.* He
no longer performs anything off his debut LP, *Greetings From Asbury Park,
N.J.,* and only does "Rosalita" off his second album. For the encores, he's
added a rousing cover of the Stones' "Street Fighting Man," which he says
he performs "because of that one great line—'What can a poor boy do but
sing in a rock & roll band.' " And at the end of every show, he makes a
point of saying, "Let freedom ring."

He hasn't dropped his medley of Mitch Ryder songs, a longtime en-
core piece for him, and it's become kind of a warhorse, as has the overblown
"Jungleland." Far stronger is the new stuff, including a steamy version of
"Pink Cadillac." Springsteen led into it by saying, "I was brought up
Catholic. It seems, according to the Bible, way back when, Eve showed
Adam the apple and Adam took a bite. There's gotta be more to it than that.
Fruit?"

The myth-making tales that he used to introduce the songs with are
gone, but he still takes time between numbers to talk a little about growing
up, his hometown and his relationship with his father. Only "This is about
being so lonesome you could cry" introduces "Nebraska," and "If you've
ever pushed a car down the street and felt like the biggest jerk in the world,
this one's for you" brings on "Used Cars."

The show swings from the gut-wrenching truth of those songs to the
roller-rink organ and garage-band fervor of the *Born in the U.S.A.* rockers.
When he's not out front without his guitar, bending into a ballad, he's in a
frenzied dance around the stage. The best rock dancer around, Springsteen
is showing more confidence than ever before ("I ain't shy *no* more!" he
hollered at one point). It makes for a passionate crowd reaction, but when
a girl climbed onstage to lay a kiss on his lips during the first notes of "Jungleland," he sounded exasperated: "Not while I'm *singin',* baby."

"Jump up and down and scream at the top of your lungs for twenty minutes and see how you feel," Bruce said hoarsely, backstage around two A.M.
one night. Prince was in a nearby room with saxophone player Clarence
Clemons, and off in a hospitality room, Nils Lofgren was talking to the
Celtics' Kevin McHale, a Minnesota boy. Springsteen was drained, but not
as badly as back when he lived on fried chicken and Pepsi. He's a changed
man: he eats vegetables, runs six miles a day, lifts weights. But, he said, "I'm
no fanatic. I still like to eat in diners."

He's been away from the stage since he toured behind *The River* in 1981.

He spent some of that time driving around the States with a friend. "I've always enjoyed traveling like that. It was always kinda liberating for me," he said. "I was only recognized twice. You get out there, and people don't really care that much about two guys just driving."

The appetite he's always had for the road probably comes partly from his ambivalent feelings about his Jersey roots, captured in his new song "My Hometown." "Your home is your home. That's all there is to it," he said. "It's something you carry with you forever, no matter where you go or what you become. There's a lot of conflicting feeling you have about the place. That's just part of it."

Home for him now is affluent Rumson, New Jersey, where he has a house with a pool, and in the driveway, a blue Camaro, a pickup truck and a '64 Chevy convertible, a gift from Gary Bonds. A year or so ago, he realized that his life centered too much on his music and set out to create more of a personal life. Now he invites his friends over for barbecues in the backyard and plays a lot of softball. Lately, he's been reading Flannery O'Connor stories and a book called *Dixiana Moon,* by William Price Fox.

Though Springsteen says rock & roll can express whatever he has to say, other people have approached him about making movies of certain songs. "Part of the thing is that when I write the song, I write it to be the movie— not to *make* a movie, to *be* a movie, like 'Highway Patrolman' or 'Racing in the Street.' It's only six minutes." He laughed. "You could really screw it up in an hour and a half."

He laughs a lot, and the guys in the band say they've never seen him so loose. The changes, even the departure of his guitarist and close friend, Steve Van Zandt (who's touring with his own band, the Disciples of Soul), seem to have presented a heartening challenge. To learn all the songs in a short time, Nils Lofgren moved into Springsteen's house about a month before the tour started. Working Lofgren into the group has been "real natural and easy," Springsteen said. The two have known each other since the late Sixties, "when we auditioned the same night at the Fillmore. I'd always bump into him. It was just somebody that, when I met Nils, we kinda already knew each other. We looked at music in the same way and cared about the same things."

At the last minute, Springsteen also asked singer Patti Scialfa, whom he had heard singing in a bar, to join the tour. "Having a woman up there with us gives it more of a feeling of community," he said.

The rest of the E Street lineup—keyboardists Roy Bittan and Danny Federici, bassist Garry Tallent, drummer Max Weinberg and saxophone player Clarence Clemons—remains the same, and the band has been with

Springsteen for so long that, Bittan said, "It's evolved to the point where it's pretty easy to second-guess him, in some respects. He lets us be creative but gives us signposts along the way. He generally tries to communicate the feeling he's trying to get across. So he'll say, 'We have to play this sparse and simple—we want a lot of space.' "

Born in the U.S.A. is all very early takes of the songs, said Bittan. In fact, the title cut is a first take. "It just never changed," he said. "He showed us the song on the guitar, I played that riff on the synthesizer, we rolled the tape, and that was it."

Springsteen seems to take his new album's reception for granted, and is more pleased that the riskier material from *Nebraska* is a hit. Still, both are about the same kind of people, he believes. He told the *Minneapolis Star and Tribune:* "The last two records felt very real to me in an everyday kind of sense. The type of things that make people's lives heroic are a lot of times very small things. Little things that happen in the kitchen or things between a husband and a wife or between them and their kids. It's a grand experience, but it's not always grandiose. That's what interests me now. There's plenty of room for those types of victories."

After the first show, Springsteen seemed to be feeling that he'd scored a small victory of his own. He'd changed into a threadbare flannel shirt, black jeans and tan boots smushed down around his ankles and uncapped a Heineken. I'd been fiddling with one of his guitar picks and asked if I could keep it to replace one I'd accidentally thrown into the basket at a tollbooth on the New Jersey Turnpike. Bruce looked pleased. "And then the light went green, right?" he said, laughing. "You gotta tell me that's the end of the story."

■ RANDOM NOTES (September 27, 1984)

Backstage after one of his ten record-breaking sold-out shows at Brendan Byrne Arena in New Jersey, Bruce Springsteen said that the rigors of his three-and-a-half-hour performances—an utter joy to watch, as always—have forced him to cut back on his six-miles-a-day running regimen. He also admitted that he'd had some problems doing his new single "Cover Me" live, until he decided to take a cue from mixmaster Arthur Baker's wacky twelve-inch disco version.

■ RANDOM NOTES (October 11, 1984)

Miami Steve Van Zandt was just one of the guests that Bruce Springsteen brought onstage during his ten-date stint in New Jersey; others included Southside Johnny and Springsteen's mother, Adele. Then in early September, Springsteen met Michael Jackson after one of the Jacksons' shows in Philadelphia. Reportedly, the only Springsteen songs Michael said he knew were those recorded by the Pointer Sisters ("Fire") and Donna Summer ("Protection"), but the pair hit it off nevertheless. Said Springsteen later, "He was really gentleman-like."

■ RANDOM NOTES (October 25, 1984)

Who's the right wing's latest darling? Bruce Springsteen, to judge from the recent comments of President Reagan and conservative columnist George F. Will. "If all Americans . . . made their products with as much energy and confidence as Springsteen and his merry band," wrote Will in his September 13th column after attending a Springsteen show, "there would be no need for Congress to be thinking about protectionism." Will admitted he didn't have "a clue about Springsteen's politics."

Six days later, at a New Jersey rally, Reagan did Will one better. America's future, he said, "rests in the message of hope, in the songs of a man that so many young Americans admire, New Jersey's own Bruce Springsteen. Helping you make these dreams come true is what this job of mine is all about."

At press time, there was no comment from the Springsteen camp. And it remained unclear exactly which Springsteen songs Reagan's speech writers had been listening to. When one Reagan-campaign spokesman was informed that the president had referred to Springsteen, he replied: "Omigod. He didn't say 'this gun's for hire,' did he?"

"I'm just a rock & roll singer; I don't get involved in that stuff," said Bruce Springsteen last summer when asked about his political affiliation. So he chose a setting in which he's comfortable—a concert—to comment on Ronald Reagan's citing of him during a recent campaign swing through New Jersey. "The president was mentioning my name the other day, and I kinda got to wondering what his favorite album musta been," said Bruce to a Pittsburgh audience on September 21st. "I don't think it was the *Nebraska* album."

One night later, Springsteen made a subtle but more pointed swipe at Reagan's policies by dedicating "The River" to the United Steelworkers of America's Local 1397, the most activist steel-union local in the country. "Before the show, George Travis [Springsteen's road manager] asked me who I wanted the song dedicated to," said Local 1397's president, Ron Weisen, who declared that, in the Steel City at least, the prez is unpopular: "If Reagan bought a cemetery in Pittsburgh, people would stop dying." After the show, Springsteen posed for pictures with Weisen and the latter's twenty-two-year-old son, Bobby, who was paralyzed a year ago in an accident. ("He was great," said Bobby.)

But despite Springsteen's leftist leanings, he was quick to deny that he had endorsed Walter Mondale. The former vice-president told a cheering crowd in New Jersey on October 1st, "Bruce may have been born to run, but he wasn't born yesterday." A statement from Springsteen's management followed the next day: "Bruce has not, and has no intention of endorsing any political candidate."

KURT LODER

THE ROLLING STONE INTERVIEW: BRUCE SPRINGSTEEN

SEATTLE WAS THE MARKET, but Tacoma was Bruce Springsteen's kind of town. He and the E Street Band had flown in from Vancouver on the second leg of their *Born in the U.S.A.* tour, and immediately everybody got sick. Something in the air. "The Tacoma aroma," locals call it, a lung-raking stench of noxious lumber-milling fumes and other foul industrial emissions that imparted a green-gilled tinge to most members of the Springsteen tour party and made Springsteen himself sick to his stomach. Nevertheless, his first, sold-out show at the 25,000-seat Tacoma Dome went on as scheduled. Springsteen is nothing if not a trouper.

He could have played the Kingdome in Seattle, thirty miles away, where the air is clear and the ambiance more upscale. But the smaller Tacoma Dome has better acoustics, and anyway, Springsteen—although he's something of an upscale guy himself these days—maintains a well-known interest in the embattled world of the working class. Tacoma, in its bilious way, was perfect.

He really was sick, though—white as a sheet when he took the stage and wiped out for sure when he left it four hours later. But he never let it show. He kicked off with a booming, boot-stomping "Born in the U.S.A." and then descended into several songs from his starkly brilliant *Nebraska* album, keeping the audience with him all the way. He's got his raps down on this tour, talking about "powerlessness" at one point and, at another, "blind faith—whether it's in your girlfriend or the government." "This is 1984," he tells the howling crowds, "and people seem to be searchin' for something." In Tacoma, before counting off the haunting "My Hometown," he delivered an extended plug for a community-action group called Washington Fair Share, which recently helped force the clean-up of an illegal landfill and is working to overturn Governor John Spellman's veto of a "right to know" law that would require local industries to inform employees of all toxic chemicals they're being exposed to on the job. "They think that people should come before profit, and the community before the corporation," Springsteen announced. And then added, pointedly, "This is *your* hometown."

This is world-class rock & roll, all right, but something more besides. And in 1984, Bruce Springsteen has become something decidedly more than just another rock star with an album to flog. He is a national presence, his charisma co-opted by as unlikely an adherent as Ronald Reagan—even as Springsteen himself pokes relentlessly through the withered and waterless cultural underbrush of the president's new American Eden. In pursuit of what can only be called his dream, Springsteen has been tenacious: dropping out of Ocean County College in his native New Jersey in 1968 to take his unlikely chances as a songwriting rock & roller and stubbornly waiting out a devastating, yearlong legal dispute with his then manager, Mike Appel, that prevented him from recording for nearly a year in the mid-Seventies. After selling two million copies of his 1980 double album, *The River,* he followed it up with *Nebraska,* a striking, guitar-and-voice meditation on various kinds of pain and craziness in the American hinterlands, and then followed *that* up with *Born in the U.S.A.,* which treats some of the same themes within a full-bore band context and has suddenly become his biggest album to date.

As the tour progressed, Springsteen sat down for interviews in Oakland, California—where he plugged the Berkeley Emergency Food Project—and in Los Angeles, where he maintains a house in the Hollywood Hills. Asked how he keeps his tightly structured stage show fresh down to the last mock-rambling anecdote, he said, "It's a matter of: Are you *there* at the moment? Are you *living* it?" It's a test he appears to pass both on and off the stage.

"BORN IN THE U.S.A.," the title track of your current album, is one of those rare records: a rousing rock & roll song that also gives voice to the pain of forgotten people—in this case, America's Vietnam veterans. How long have you been aware of the Vietnam vets' experience?

I don't know if anybody could imagine what their particular experience is like. I don't think *I* could, you know? I think you had to live through it. But when you think about all the young men and women that died in Vietnam, and how many died since they've been back—surviving the war and coming *back* and not surviving—you have to think that, at the time, the country took advantage of their selflessness. There was a moment when they were just really generous with their lives.

What was your own experience of Vietnam?

I didn't really have one. There wasn't any kind of political conscious-ness down in Freehold in the late Sixties. It was a small town, and the war just seemed very distant. I mean, I was aware of it through some friends that went. The drummer in my first band was killed in Vietnam. He kind of signed up and joined the marines. Bart Hanes was his name. He was one of those guys that was jokin' all the time, always playin' the clown. He came over one day and said, "Well, I enlisted. I'm goin' to Vietnam." I remem-ber he said he didn't know where it *was*. And that was it. He left and he didn't come back. And the guys that did come back were not the same.

How did you manage to escape the draft?

I got a 4-F. I had a brain concussion from a motorcycle accident when I was seventeen. Plus, I did the basic Sixties rag, you know: fillin' out the forms all crazy, not takin' the tests. When I was nineteen, I wasn't ready to be that generous with my life. I was called for induction, and when I got on the bus to go take my physical, I thought one thing: *I ain't goin'*. I had tried to go to college, and I didn't really fit in. I went to a real narrow-minded school where people gave me a lot of trouble and I was hounded off the campus—I just looked different and acted different, so I left school. And I remember bein' on that bus, me and a couple of guys in my band, and the rest of the bus was probably sixty, seventy percent black guys from Asbury Park. And I remember thinkin', like, what makes my life, or my friends' lives, more expendable than that of somebody who's goin' to school? It didn't seem right. And it was funny, because my father, he was in World War II, and he was the type that was always sayin', "Wait till the army gets you. Man, they're gonna get that hair off of you. I can't wait. They gonna make a *man* outta you." We were really goin' at each other in those days. And I remember I was gone for three days, and when I came back, I went in the kitchen, and my folks were there, and they said, "Where you been?" And I said, "Well, I had to go take my physical." And they said, "What hap-pened?" And I said, "Well, they didn't take me." And my father sat there, and he didn't look at me, he just looked straight ahead. And he said, "That's good." It was, uh . . . I'll never forget that. I'll *never* forget that.

Ironic, then, that today you're the toast of the political right, with conservative columnist George Will lauding your recent Washington, D.C., concert and Presi-dent Reagan invoking your name while campaigning in your home state, New Jer-sey.

I think what's happening now is people want to forget. There was Viet-nam, there was Watergate, there was Iran—we were beaten, we were hus-tled, and then we were humiliated. And I think people got a need to feel good about the country they live in. But what's happening, I think, is that

that need—which is a good thing—is gettin' manipulated and exploited. And you see the Reagan reelection ads on TV—you know: "It's morning in America." And you say, well, it's not morning in Pittsburgh. It's not morning above 125th Street in New York. It's midnight, and, like, there's a bad moon risin'. And that's why when Reagan mentioned my name in New Jersey, I felt it was another manipulation, and I had to disassociate myself from the president's kind words.

But didn't you play into the hands of professional patriots by releasing an election-year album called "Born in the U.S.A.," with the American flag bannered across the front?

Well, we had the flag on the cover because the first song was called "Born in the U.S.A.," and the theme of the record kind of follows from the themes I've been writing about for at least the last six or seven years. But the flag is a powerful image, and when you set that stuff loose, you don't know what's gonna be done with it.

Actually, I know one fan who infers from the rump shot on the album cover that you're actually pissing on the flag. Is there a message there?

No, no. That was unintentional. We took a lot of different types of pictures, and in the end, the picture of my *ass* looked better than the picture of my *face,* so that's what went on the cover. I didn't have any secret message. I don't do that very much.

Well, what is your political stance? Election Day is two weeks away: Are you registered to vote?

I'm registered, yeah. I'm not registered as one party or another. I don't generally think along those lines. I find it very difficult to relate to the whole electoral system as it stands. I don't really . . . I suppose if there was somebody who I felt strong enough about at some point, some day, you know . . .

You don't think Mondale would be any better than Reagan?

I don't know. I think there are significant differences, but I don't know *how* significant. And it's very difficult to tell by preelection rhetoric. It seems to always change when they all of a sudden get in. That's why I don't feel a real connection to electoral politics right now—it can't be the best way to find the best man to do the hardest job. I want to try and just work more directly with people; try to find some way that my band can tie into the communities that we come into. I guess that's a political action, a way to just bypass that whole electoral thing. Human politics. I think that people on their own can do a lot. I guess that's what I'm tryin' to figure out now: Where do the aesthetic issues that you write about intersect with some sort of concrete action, some direct involvement, in the communities that your audience comes from? It seems to be an inevitable progression of what our band has been doin', of the idea that we got into this for. We wanted to play because we wanted to meet girls, we wanted to make a ton of dough, and we wanted to change the world a little bit, you know?

Have you ever voted?

I think I voted for McGovern in 1972.

What do you really think of Ronald Reagan?

Well, I don't *know* him. But I think he presents a very mythic, very seductive image, and it's an image that people want to believe in. I think there's always been a nostalgia for a mythical America, for some period in the past when everything was just right. And I think the president is the embodiment of that for a lot of people. He has a very mythical presidency. I don't know if he's a bad man. But I think there's a large group of people in this country whose dreams don't mean that much to him, that just get indiscriminately swept aside. I guess my view of America is of a real bighearted country, real compassionate. But the difficult thing out there right now is that the social consciousness that was a part of the Sixties has become, like, old-fashioned or something. You go out, you get your job, and you try to make as much money as you can and have a good time on the weekend. And that's considered okay.

The state of the nation has weighed heavily, if sometimes subtly, on the characters depicted in your songs over the years. Do you see your albums as being connected by an evolving sociopolitical point of view?

I guess what I was always interested in was doing a *body* of work—albums that would relate to and play off of each other. And I was always concerned with doin' *albums,* instead of, like, collections of songs. I guess I started with *The Wild, the Innocent & the E Street Shuffle,* in a funny way—particularly the second side, which kind of syncs together. I was very concerned about gettin' a group of characters and followin' them through their lives a little bit. And so, on *Born to Run, Darkness on the Edge of Town* and *The River,* I tried to hook things up. I guess in *Born to Run,* there's that searchin' thing; that record to me is like religiously based, in a funny kind of way. Not like orthodox religion, but it's about basic things, you know? That searchin', and faith, and the idea of hope. And then on *Darkness,* it was kind of like a collision that happens between this guy and the real world. He ends up very alone and real stripped down. Then, on *The River,* there was always that thing of the guy attemptin' to come back, to find some sort of community. It had more songs about relationships—"Stolen Car," "The River," "I Wanna Marry You," "Drive All Night," even "Wreck on the Highway"—people tryin' to find some sort of consolation, some sort of comfort in each other. Before *The River,* there's almost no songs *about* relationships. Very few. Then, on *Nebraska* . . . I don't know *what* happened on that one. That kinda came out of the blue.

Wasn't the central inspiration Terrence Malick's "Badlands," the film about mass murderer Charles Starkweather and his girlfriend, Caril Fugate?

Well, I had already written "Mansion on the Hill" during the last tour. Then I went home—I was living in a place called Colts Neck, New Jersey—and I remember I saw *Badlands,* and I read this book about them, *Caril,* and it just seemed to be a mood that I was in at the time. I was renting a house on this reservoir, and I didn't go out much, and for some reason I just started to write. I wrote *Nebraska,* all those songs, in a couple of months. I was interested in writing kind of *smaller* than I had been, writing with just detail—which I kind of began to do on *The River.* I guess my influences at the time were the movie and these stories I was reading by Flannery O'Connor—she's just incredible.

Was there something about Starkweather that struck you as emblematic of the American condition?

I think you can get to a point where nihilism, if that's the right word, is overwhelming, and the basic laws that society has set up—either religious or social laws—become meaningless. Things just get really dark. You lose those constraints, and then anything goes. The forces that set that in motion, I don't know exactly what they'd be. I think just a lot of frustration, lack of findin' somethin' that you can hold on to, lack of contact with *people,* you know? That's one of the most dangerous things, I think—isolation. *Nebraska* was about that American isolation: What happens to people when they're alienated from their friends and their community and their government and their job. Because those are the things that keep you sane, that give meaning to life in some fashion. And if they slip away, and you start to exist in some void where the basic constraints of society are a joke, then life becomes kind of a joke. And anything can happen.

Did the stark acoustic format you eventually chose for "Nebraska" just seem the most appropriate setting for such dark material?

Well, initially, I was just doing songs for the next rock album, and I decided that what always took me so long in the studio was the writing. I would get in there, and I just wouldn't have the material *written,* or it wasn't written well enough, and so I'd record for a month, get a couple of things, go home, write some more, record for another month—it wasn't very efficient. So this time, I got a little Teac four-track cassette machine, and I said, I'm gonna record these songs, and if they sound good with just me doin' 'em, then I'll teach 'em to the band. I could sing and play the guitar, and then I had two tracks to do somethin' else, like overdub a guitar or add a harmony. It was just gonna be a demo. Then I had a little Echoplex that I mixed through, and that was it. And that was the tape that became the record. It's amazing that it *got* there, 'cause I was carryin' that cassette around with me in my pocket without a case for a couple of weeks, just draggin' it around. Finally, we realized, "Uh-oh, that's the album." Technically, it was difficult to get it on a disc. The stuff was recorded so strangely, the needle would read a lot of distortion and wouldn't track in the wax. We almost had to release it as a cassette.

I understand "Born in the U.S.A." was actually written around the time of "Nebraska"; do any other songs on the new album date from that period?

Actually, half of the *Born in the U.S.A.* album was recorded at the time of *Nebraska*. When we initially went in the studio to try to record *Nebraska* with the band, we recorded the first side of *Born in the U.S.A.*, and the rest of the time I spent tryin' to come up with the second side—"Bobby Jean," "My Hometown," almost all those songs. So if you look at the material, particularly on the first side, it's actually written very much like *Nebraska*—the characters and the stories, the style of writing—except it's just in the rockband setting.

You seem to have taken a more spontaneous, less labored approach to recording this album. Max Weinberg says that the title track of "Born in the U.S.A." is a second take—and that he didn't even know the band was going to kick back in at the end until you signaled him in the studio.

Oh, yeah. That entire track is live. Most of the songs on *Born in the U.S.A.* are under five takes, and "Darlington County" is live, "Working on the Highway" is live, "Downbound Train," "I'm on Fire," "Bobby Jean," "My Hometown," "Glory Days"—almost the whole album is done live. Our basic style of recording now is not real tedious. The band is playing really well together, and in five or six takes of a song, they're gonna get it. *Born to Run* was the only album I really did extensive overdubbing on; it's also the only album where I wrote only one more song than we recorded. For *Born in the U.S.A.*, we recorded maybe fifty songs. The recording is not what took the time; it was the writing—and waiting till I felt, "Well, there's an album here; there's some story being told." We record a lot of material, but we just don't release it all.

Bootleg buyers contend that some of your unreleased material is among your best. Does the brisk bootleg trade in your unreleased material annoy you?

I guess nobody likes the feeling that they wrote a song and in some way the song is bein' stolen from them, or presented in a fashion they don't feel they'd want to present it in—the quality isn't good, and they're so expensive. I don't have any bootlegs myself. I always tell myself that some day I'm gonna put an album out with all this stuff on it that didn't fit in. I think there's good material there that should come out. Maybe at some point, I'll do that.

You've turned two of your current hits, "Dancing in the Dark" and "Cover Me," over to producer Arthur Baker to convert into dance-mix singles—with what some of your fans see as bizarre results. What made you want to do that?

I heard this dance mix of Cyndi Lauper's "Girls Just Want to Have Fun" on the radio, and it was incredible. It sounded like fun, so I hooked up with Arthur. He's a character, a great guy. He had another fellow with him, and they were really pretty wild. They'd get on that mixing board and just crank them knobs, you know? The meters were goin' wild.

Did you have input into this?

Not much. The entire thing is Arthur Baker. He's really an artist. It was fun to just give him a song and see what his interpretation of it would be. I was always so protective of my music that I was hesitant to do much with it at all. Now I feel my stuff isn't as fragile as I thought.

You've also started doing videos recently. What do you make of the medium?

Video is a powerful thing, and I wanted to be involved in it in some fashion. But it presents a variety of problems. I didn't want to infringe on my audience's imagination by presenting some concrete image that was a replica of an image in the song, and I didn't want to create *another* story, because I was already tellin' the story I wanted to tell.

For "Dancing in the Dark," you brought in film director Brian De Palma and made a lip-synced concert video. Why?

Brian was great, because I had no time—we were getting ready for our first show—and he came in on real short notice and really took the burden off my shoulders. We did that video in about three or four hours. Lipsyncing is one of those things—it's easy to do, but you wonder about the *worth* of doing it. That video was great, though, because I noticed that most of the people that would come up and mention it to me were people who hadn't heard my other stuff. Very often, they were real little kids. I was on the beach and this kid came up to me—I think his name was Mike, he was like seven or eight—and he says, "I saw you on MTV." And then he says, "I got your moves down." So I say, "Well, let me check 'em out." And he starts doin', like, "Dancing in the Dark." And he was *pretty good,* you know?

You've certainly achieved mass-market success this year. The Born in the U.S.A. Tour is selling out arenas across the country, and the album has sold over five million copies worldwide. Has becoming a rich man changed you at all?

Yeah, there's a change. It doesn't make living easier, but it does make certain aspects of your life easier. You don't have to worry about rent, you can buy things for your folks and help out your friends, and you can have a *good time,* you know? There were moments where it was very confusing, because I realized that I was a rich man, but I felt like a poor man inside.

In what way?

Just my outlook on things in general, because I guess it was formed when I was young. I mean, basically, you know, because of the lawsuit and a bunch of other things—and because of how long it would take me to make records—I didn't get to a situation where I had any dough in the bank till around the *River* tour. And this tour, we've been doin' great so far. But I don't know if money changes you. I guess I don't really think it *does* change you. It's an inanimate thing, a tool, a convenience. If you've got to have a problem, it's a good problem to have.

Obviously you don't spend your money on clothes. What do you do with it?

I'm just figuring that out right now. One of the things I can do is play benefits and help people out that need help, people that are strugglin', you know, tryin' to get somethin' goin' on their own. Money was kind of part of the dream when I started. I don't think . . . I never felt like I ever played a note for the money. I think if I did, people would know, and they'd throw you out of the joint. And you'd deserve to go. But at the same time, it was a part of the dream. Part of like . . .

The pink Cadillac?

Yeah, the pink Cadillac. Me and Steve [Van Zandt, his former guitarist] used to sit around and say, "Yeah, when we make it, we're gonna do this and that. . . ."

What did you plan to do?

Mainly, we planned to be just like the Rolling Stones. They were the band we liked the best at the time. But you grow up, and when you finally put that suit of clothes on, sometimes they don't fit, or they fit differently, and you're a different person, and what you're gonna do is different, I guess. But in general, I do enjoy the success we've had, and the fact that we have an audience, and I've enjoyed the financial success that I've had. It's helped me do some things that I've wanted to do.

Would it be an exaggeration to say that you're a millionaire?

No, no. I definitely got that much.

What's your house in Rumson, New Jersey, like?

It's the mansion on the hill! [*Laughing*] It's the kind of place I told my-self I'd never live in. But before this tour I was lookin' for a big house, 'cause

I was living in a real small house that I rented. I'd always rented, ever since I was a kid, and I realized I'd been playin' for twelve years, and I didn't have any sort of . . . nothin' that was like any kind of *home*. I had a bunch of old cars that I'd collected over the years, old bombs: pickup trucks that I picked up for like $500, a '69 Chevy, an Impala that Gary Bonds gave me and a 1960 Corvette that was one of the few things I got out of *Born to Run*. And all these old cars were stashed away in different people's garages all across New Jersey. So I said, wow, I think I'm gonna get a big house. But what I really wanted to get was a farm with a big barn, where I can build a studio so I don't have to travel to New York to record all the time. Which is what I'm gonna get when I go back after this tour.

So the Rumson house is just a sort of way station?

All my houses seem to have been way stations. That's the kind of person I have been, you know? I don't like feelin' too rooted for some reason. Which is funny, because the things that I admire and the things that mean a lot to me all have to do with roots and home, and myself, personally, I'm the opposite. I'm very rootless in that sense. I never attach myself to any place that I am. I always felt most at home when I was like in the car or on the road, which is, I guess, why I always wrote about it. I was very distant from my family for quite a while in my early twenties. Not with any animosity; I just had to feel loose. Independence always meant a lot to me. I had to feel I could go anywhere, anytime, in order to get my particular job done. And that's basically the way I've always lived. Lately, I've . . . I'm still not . . . I don't know if I'm a big family man. My family's been my band. I've always been that way. I think when I was young, I did it intentionally, because I knew I only had sixty dollars that month, and I had to live on that sixty dollars, and I couldn't get married or I couldn't get involved at the time. And then it just became my way of life, you know? It really became my way of life.

You were never on the verge of getting married?

No. I lived with a girl once. I'd never lived with a girl before. I was in my early twenties, and I'd never even lived with anybody.

How come?

I don't know. I'm not exactly sure. I guess I just wanted to be free to move, a road runner. It's silly, I guess. It sounds silly to me now when I say it. Particularly because I don't really value those ideals. I guess I see fulfillment, ultimately, in family life. That just hasn't been *my* life, you know?

But you're writing all these songs about relationships. What does your mother think about this situation?

I got an Italian *grand*mother, and that's all she asks me. She speaks half Italian and half English, and every time I go over it's "Where's you girlfriend? When are you gonna get married?"

Is it possible for you to have normal romantic attachments?

I guess so. I've had steady girlfriends in the past. I went out with a girl I met at Clarence's club. I'm just not really lookin' to get married at this point. I've made a commitment to doin' my job right now, and that's basically what I do. *Someday,* I'd like to have the whole nine yards—the wife, the kids.

And until then? I'm trying to picture Bruce Springsteen just asking a normal girl for a casual date.

You just do it. You're out in a bar or somethin', and you meet somebody, you can't worry. You gotta go ahead and live your life in as normal a fashion as possible. When I'm out, I don't really think that much about the other part of my life, about how people are looking at me. It's not *relevant,* almost. Somebody may go out with you once or twice because of who you are, but if you're a jerk, they're not gonna want to, because it's not gonna be any fun, you know? That kind of thing wears off pretty quick.

So you're never allowed yourself to become isolated, to slip into the Elvis Presley syndrome?

One of the things that was always on my mind to do was to maintain connections with the people I'd grown up with, and the sense of the community where I came from. That's why I stayed in New Jersey. The danger of fame is in *forgetting,* or being distracted. You see it happen to so many people. Elvis' case must have been tremendously difficult. Because, I mean, I feel the difference between selling a million records and selling 3 million records—I can feel a difference out on the street. The type of fame that Elvis had, and that I think Michael Jackson has, the pressure of it, and the isolation that it seems to require, has gotta be really painful. I wasn't gonna let that happen to me. I wasn't gonna get to a place where I said, "I can't go in here. I can't go to this bar. I can't go outside." For the most part, I do basically what I've always done. I'll walk into a club, and people will just say hi, and that's it. And I'll get up and play.

I believe that the life of a rock & roll band will last as long as you look down into the audience and can see yourself, and your audience looks up at you and can see themselves—and as long as those reflections are human, realistic ones. The biggest gift that your fans can give you is just treatin' you like a human being, because anything else dehumanizes you. And that's one of the things that has shortened the life spans, both physically and creatively, of some of the best rock & roll musicians—that cruel isolation. If the price of fame is that you have to be isolated from the people you write for, then that's too fuckin' high a price to pay.

You must have had a chance to observe Michael Jackson's situation firsthand. Didn't you meet him after a recent Jacksons concert?

I saw them in Philadelphia. I thought it was really a great show. Real different from what I do, but the night I saw 'em, I thought they were really, really good. Michael was unbelievable—I mean *unbelievable*. He's a real gentleman, and he's real communicative . . . and he's *tall,* which I don't know if most people realize.

What bands have you been listening to lately?

I listen to a lot of different types of things. I like U2, Divinyls, Van Morrison. I like the band Suicide.

That makes sense: "State Trooper," one of the songs on "Nebraska," sounds very much like Suicide.

Yeah. They had that two-piece synthesizer-voice thing. They had one of the most amazing songs I ever heard. It was about a guy that murders . . .

"Frankie Teardrop"?

Yeah! Oh, my God! That's one of the most amazing records I think I ever heard. I really love that record.

What about Prince? Have you ever seen him live?

Yeah. He is *incredible* live. He is one of the best live performers I've ever seen in my whole life. His show was funny; it had a lot of humor in it. He had the bed that came up out of the stage—it was great, you know? I think him and Steve, right now, are my favorite performers.

Have you seen "Purple Rain"?

Yeah, it was great. It was like an Elvis movie—a real good early Elvis movie.

You once tried to meet Elvis Presley by jumping over the wall at his Graceland mansion. The attempt failed, but have you met most of your other idols in the music business?

Well, I'm real ambivalent about meetin' people I admire. You know the old saying: Trust the art, not the artist. I think that's true. I think somebody can do real good work and be a fool in a variety of ways. I think my music is probably better than I am. I mean, like, your music is your ideals a lot of times, and you don't live up to those ideals all the time. You try, but you fall short and you disappoint yourself. With my idols, I just like their music. If the occasion comes up, I like to meet them, but I never really seek it out very much, because it's their music that I like in general. People always say they were disappointed by Elvis, they were let down. I'm not sure that's the right way to look at it. I don't think anybody was disappointed by his great records, you know? I think personally it's a hard way to go for everybody out there, and that he gave the best that he had, the best that he could get ahold of.

You, at least, seem unlikely ever to emulate Elvis' drug problems. Is it true that after nearly twenty years in the rock & roll world, you've truly never so much as smoked a joint?

I never did any drugs. When I was at that age when it was popular, I wasn't really in a social scene a whole lot. I was practicing in my room with my guitar. So I didn't have the type of pressure that kids might have today. Plus, I was very concerned with being in control at the time. I drink a little bit now. There's nights when I'll go out and do it up. But not too much when we're touring, because the show is so physically demanding, and you gotta be so prepared.

There's also a notable lack—in your songs, your stage show, your videos—of any sort of exploitative sexual imagery of the kind that routinely spices, say, MTV. Nor do you appear to encourage a groupie scene backstage at your shows. This is unusual for rock, and I wonder if it has anything to do with your growing up with a strong, working mother and two sisters.

I don't know. I think if you just try to have a basic respect for people's humanness, you just generally don't want to do those things. I think it's *difficult,* because we were all brought up with sexist attitudes and racist attitudes. But hopefully, as you grow older, you get some sort of insight into that and—I know it's corny—try to treat other people the way you would want them to treat you.

It's like my younger sister. When I was thirteen, my mother got pregnant again and she really took me through the whole thing. We used to sit on the couch and watch TV, and she'd say "Feel this," and I'd put my hand on her stomach and I'd feel my little sister in there. And from the very beginning, I had a deep connection with her.

One of the best times I can ever remember was when she was born, because it changed the atmosphere of the whole house for quite a while—the old "*Shh,* there's a baby in the house." And I'd watch her all the time, and if she started cryin', I'd run down to see what was the matter. I remember one day I was watchin' her, and she was on the couch and she rolled off and fell on her head—she was about one, still a little baby—and I felt like, "Oh, that's it. Brain damage! My life is over, I've had it!" [*Laughing*] My family moved to California when she was like five or six, and we didn't see each other for quite a while. But every time we did, it was like automatic—like we'd never been apart.

I think that what happens is, when you're young, you feel powerless. If you're a child and you're lookin' up at the world, the world is frightening. Your house, no matter how small it is, it seems so big. Your parents seem huge. I don't believe this feeling ever quite leaves you. And I think what happens is, when you get around fifteen or sixteen, a lot of your fantasies are power fantasies. And I think that's one of the things that gets exploited by some of the more demeaning types of music. If you're a kid, you feel powerless, but you don't know how to channel that powerlessness—how to channel it into either a social concern or creating something for yourself. I was lucky; I was able to deal with it with the guitar. I said, well, I feel weak, but when I do this, when I feel this, when I hold it, I feel a little stronger. I feel like I've got some line on my life. I feel I have some control. That feelin' of weakness, of powerlessness, is there. And I think it gets exploited and misdirected.

One of the problems in the United States is that "united in our prejudices we stand," you know? What unites people, very often, is their fear. What unites white people in some places is their fear of black people. What unites guys is maybe a denigrating attitude toward women—or sometimes maybe women have an attitude toward men. And these things are then in turn exploited by politicians, which turns into fear—knee-jerk fear of the Russians or of whatever *ism* is out there. Or in a very subtle kind of indirect way—like some of our economic policies are a real indirect kind of racism, in which the people that get affected most are black people who are at the lower end of the economic spectrum. And I think somewhere inside, people *know* this—I *really* do. They don't fess up to it, but somewhere inside there's a real meanness in using things this way.

I think it's changing *some*what, but how many times in this election campaign did you hear that the major complaint against Mondale was that he was "wimpish"? It's still a very, very big part of the whole American culture. It's all wrapped up in a variety of different ways in my own music—dealin' with it, fakin' it, tryin' to get *over* fakin' it, tryin' to break *through* it. It's just . . . there's just so much . . . it seems to be . . .

Overwhelming?

Yeah.

What keeps you going at age thirty-five?

I was lucky. During the lawsuit, I understood that it's the music that keeps me alive, and my relationships with my friends, and my attachment to the people and the places I've known. That's my lifeblood. And to give that up for, like, the TV, the cars, the houses—that's not the American dream. That's the booby prize, in the end. Those are the booby prizes. And if you fall for them—if, when you achieve them, you believe that this is the end in and of itself—then you've been suckered in. Because those are the consolation prizes, if you're not careful, for selling yourself out, or lettin' the best of yourself slip away. So you gotta be vigilant. You gotta carry the idea you began with further. And you gotta hope that you're headed for higher ground.

BORN IN THE U.S.A.
YEAR-END ALBUM REVIEW

BRUCE SPRINGSTEEN'S SEVENTH ALBUM made him the mass-appeal, mainstream star his critical claque has always claimed he could be. There are precious few nits to pick here: *Born in the U.S.A.* is simply the most stirring and stylistically cohesive rock record the man has made. The blue-collar themes are familiar, but Springsteen's writing—honed to a fine, harrowing edge on his extraordinary 1982 acoustic album, *Nebraska*—is here boiled down to only the most telling details. Throughout the album, his band—newly streamlined and rich with synthesizers—plays at peak power, with drummer Max Weinberg establishing himself conclusively as the American heir to Charlie Watts. And Springsteen himself sings with a force-of-nature power that's both raw and subtly, intuitively nuanced. Springsteen has always *seemed* to be the embodiment of all that's great about classic rock & roll, but for his detractors that was never enough. In the past he's come off as prolix, pretentiously unpretentious and generally retrogressive. *Born in the U.S.A.,* however, confirms the legitimacy of his vision beyond reasonable argument. Even an Englishman could get into this one.

KURT LODER

BRUCE!

O NE AFTERNOON LAST FALL, Bruce Springsteen sat sipping a beer in a room at the Sunset Marquis hotel in Los Angeles. He wore blue jeans, cowboy boots, a black leather jacket and a newsboy's cap slouched down backward over the bandanna tied around his head. Not one of the great glamour-pusses, you could say. At the peak of his twelve-year recording career, and midway through his most clamorously acclaimed tour with the precision-tooled E Street Band, Springsteen remained as wary as ever of massive success and its attendant seductions. "I never felt I was like an Elvis or a Dylan, or the Rolling Stones," he said. "I don't see myself in that way. I see myself more like a real good journeyman. And that's fine: You do your job real good, you pass on some part of the flame . . . and you stir things up a little bit if you can."

Springsteen's diffidence is a well-known component of what may now be called, with some justification, his legend: the unassuming musical laureate of the working classes. Nevertheless, in 1984, as he began touring in support of *Born in the U.S.A.,* his seventh and biggest-selling album (five million copies so far), the thirty-five-year-old Jersey flash found he had grown from being the country's biggest cult artist—lionized on the East Coast, more patchily appreciated elsewhere—into something very like a national hero. There appeared to be several reasons for this change. On a purely show-biz level, he is one of the most uproariously exciting performers in rock history, and while an ever-shrinking number of skeptics have sometimes found his four-hour shows to be overblown endurance tests, there has never been any doubt about the deep emotional connection he makes with his audiences night after night. More than most major rock stars—Prince and Michael Jackson, the year's two other musical phenoms, come most quickly to mind—Springsteen is publicly perceived as a real and complete person. There is none of Jackson's ethereal remoteness or Prince's sexual threat about him; he still lives in untrendy New Jersey, where he was born and raised, still goes out unguarded to local bars and clubs and still answers what fan mail he can with personal responses. He seems a regular guy. And yet the resonant social vision set out in the best of his new songs—the working-class despair of "Downbound Train"; the painful, betrayed patriotism of his Vietnam-vets anthem, "Born in the U.S.A."; the sense of small-town anomie so piercingly evoked in "My Hometown"—marks Springsteen as a lyrical artist with a unique gift for popular expression. His concern for his characters, and by extension their millions of counterparts in his audience, seems genuine—seems, in fact, the wellspring of his art. As he toured the country, soliciting the realities of unemployment from local union leaders, constantly promoting food banks and other community groups from the stage (and often putting significant amounts of money where his mouth was), he appeared to be striving for a practical realization of the communitarian ideals of the Sixties in the more harshly pragmatic Eighties. Here was art once again stirring up social action, and in a year when the Jacksons were charging thirty dollars to witness their seventy-five-minute show (while Springsteen kept a sixteen-dollar lid on his four-hour spectacles), it proved anew that music can have meaning beyond mere entertainment.

"I want to find out what you can do with a rock & roll band," Springsteen said that afternoon in Los Angeles. "I'm trying to apply the original idea of our band, which was that the possibilities are vast. I first started to play because I wanted to do something good—I wanted to be proud of myself, to feel good about myself. And I found the guitar, and that gave it to me; it gave me my sense of purpose and a sense of pride in myself. And that is the gift of life. It was my lifeboat, my lifeline—my line back into people. It was my connection to the rest of the human race, you know?

"Before that, it was a strange existence. I was a big daydreamer when I was in grammar school. Kids used to tease me, call me 'dreamer.' It's something that got worse as I got older, I think. Until I realized that I felt like I was dying, for some reason, and I really didn't know why. I think that's a feeling that a lot of people have. And so now I go out onstage and I feel like there's people dying out there, there's people really hurt—you know because you feel the same thing. And this is your chance to do something about it. So when I go out onstage at night, I feel like there's really something at stake, that it has some meaning. It's not just another night.

"When I sit down to write, I try to write something that feels real to me. Like, what does it feel like to be thirty-five or something right now, at this point in time, living in America? It's not much more conscious than that. I generally try to write songs that are about real life, not fantasy material. I try to reflect people's lives back to them in some fashion. And if the show is really good, your life should flash before your eyes in some way—

the show's long enough, that's for sure! I think on a night when we're really good, you can come and hopefully you can see your relationships with your parents, brothers, sisters, your town, your country, your friends, everything—sexual, political, the whole social thing. It should be a combination of a circus, a political thing and a spiritual event. And hopefully you'll come and your life will flash before your eyes. That's kind of what I'm out there trying to do, you know?"

That he succeeds, and often brilliantly, is due in large part to his unusual empathy with his audience, his devotion to the otherwise unsung realities of their lives. "I never look out at my crowd and see a bunch of faces," he said. "It's never happened. Any night I've ever been onstage, I see people—individual people in individual seats out there. That's why, before the show, we go out and we check the sound in every section of the room. Because there's some guy sittin' back here, and he's got a girl with him, and, you know, it's like, this is their seat. And what you hope for is that the same thing goes the other way—that when they look up at you, they don't just see some person with a guitar."

That Springsteen is popularly perceived as much more than that is evidenced by his standing in ROLLING STONE's 1984 Readers Poll, which he effectively swept. But along with his burgeoning success has come what would appear to be a personal paradox. With the money rolling in, this determinedly unpretentious chronicler of the working class has become a millionaire. Can he hold on to his soul, to his street-bred ideals, even as he moves into that mansion on the hill he once only dreamed about?

"I know this is idealistic," he said, taking a slug of beer, "but part of the idea our band had from the beginning was that you did not have to lose your connection to the people you write for. I don't believe that fame or success means that you lose that connection, and I don't believe that makin' more money means you lose it. Because that's not where the essence of what you are lies. That's not what separates people. What separates people are things that are in their heart. So I just can never surrender to that idea. Because I know that before I started playing, I was alone. And one of the reasons I picked up the guitar was that I wanted to be part of something. And I practiced and I studied and I worked real hard to do that, and I ain't about to give it up now."

1984 MUSIC AWARDS

FEBRUARY 28, 1985

READERS PICKS

ARTIST OF THE YEAR
Bruce Springsteen
Prince
Cyndi Lauper
Michael Jackson
Huey Lewis

BAND OF THE YEAR
Bruce Springsteen and the E Street Band
Van Halen
ZZ Top
The Cars
U2

MALE VOCALIST
Bruce Springsteen
Prince
David Bowie
Lionel Richie
Billy Idol

PRODUCER
Jon Landau
Trevor Horn
Prince
Quincy Jones
Ted Templeman

ALBUM OF THE YEAR
***Born in the U.S.A.*—Bruce Springsteen**
Purple Rain—Prince
1984—Van Halen
Sports—Huey Lewis and the News
Eliminator—ZZ Top

SINGLE OF THE YEAR
"Dancing in the Dark"—Bruce Springsteen
"When Doves Cry"—Prince
"Jump"—Van Halen
"Let's Go Crazy"—Prince
"Born in the U.S.A."—Bruce Springsteen

CRITICS PICKS

ARTIST OF THE YEAR
Prince
Bruce Springsteen
Tina Turner

BAND OF THE YEAR
Bruce Springsteen and the E Street Band
Los Lobos (tie)
Van Halen
R.E.M.

SONGWRITER
Bruce Springsteen
Prince
Christine Kerr (a.k.a. Chrissie Hynde)
Lou Reed
Laurie Anderson

ALBUM OF THE YEAR
***Born in the U.S.A.*—Bruce Springsteen**
Purple Rain—Prince
Private Dancer—Tina Turner
How Will the Wolf Survive?—Los Lobos
Learning to Crawl—The Pretenders

SINGLE OF THE YEAR
"What's Love Got to Do With It"—Tina Turner
"Jump"—Van Halen
"When Doves Cry"—Prince
"Dancing in the Dark"—Bruce Springsteen
"Pride (In the Name of Love)"—U2

CHRISTOPHER CONNELLY

BRUCE ENDS U.S. TOUR
Springsteen Will Head to Australia
and Japan Next

IT SEEMED A LITTLE ODD that Bruce Springsteen was playing "Santa Claus Is Coming to Town" in late January. But, of course, every day is Christmas for Springsteen: He and the E Street Band grossed approximately $26 million on their forty-five-city, ninety-four-date North American tour. Springsteen finished things up by playing two nights— January 26th and 27th—at the Carrier Dome in Syracuse, New York. Each show drew 39,000 people: the largest audiences of his career. To play the cavernous dome, Springsteen brought in the same sound equipment that had powered the Us Festival—a system twice as big as his usual PA hookup.

Springsteen filled the huge space superbly. Few seemed to object when he bypassed such concert warhorses as "Rosalita (Come Out Tonight)" and "Jungleland." New highlights of the three-and-a-half-hour shows were reworked, twangy versions of "Reason to Believe" and "Working on the Highway," a chilling rendition of Jimmy Cliff's "Trapped" and a sensual delivery of *Born in the U.S.A.*'s fourth single, "I'm on Fire." His comic raps remained pungent and funny; he plugged the local food bank each night; and "Promised Land" was dedicated to his manager-producer Jon Landau's newborn daughter, Kate.

Despite their grueling schedule, the band was in high spirits, and Springsteen appeared rugged and fit. Adding to Springsteen's happy mood may have been the presence of his new girlfriend, actress and model Julianne Phillips. Or was it just coincidence that the first encore both nights was a tender rendition of the Elvis Presley torcher "Can't Help Falling in Love"? At show's end, the mood switched from amorous to clamorous, as Springsteen wrapped things up with John Fogerty's "Rocking All Over the World." And, after a brief respite, the band will be playing shows in Australia and Japan, followed by a European swing slated to end in mid-July. Further American shows were being planned for late summer.

■ **RANDOM NOTES** (March 28, 1985)

Mick and Jerry. Keith and Patti. Billy and Christie. There have been tons of rock star–model trysts—still, who'd expect Bruce Springsteen to jump on the bandwagon? Well, last month, *Good Housekeeping* did name him one of the fifty most eligible bachelors. Gorgeous Julianne Phillips obviously thinks likewise. The Elite model, who starred in .38 Special's video for "If I'd Been the One" and a couple of TV movies, has accompanied him on and off the road since they met in Los Angeles. She could make a model wife.

JOE BREEN

70,000 SEE SPRINGSTEEN OPEN TOUR IN IRELAND

PLAYING BEFORE HIS LARGEST AUDIENCE EVER, Bruce Springsteen opened his European tour on Saturday, June 1st, with a forceful performance on the grounds of an Irish castle. Springsteen, who reportedly was paid some $600,000 for the show, told the ecstatic audience of about 70,000 that it was great to play in the country many of his ancestors came from.

The Boss' first Irish concert took place at Slane Castle, thirty miles northwest of Dublin. It marked the start of an eighteen-date tour that will include three sold-out appearances at London's 70,000-capacity Wembley Stadium in early July, as well as shows in Paris, Munich and Milan.

Looking fit and healthy, Springsteen—accompanied by Julianne Phillips, his wife of a few weeks—arrived in Dublin the day before the concert. That night, after an extensive sound check with the E Street Band, Springsteen reportedly took part in an impromptu jam session at the castle with Eric Clapton and Pete Townshend. The huge international press corps that had descended on the nearby village of Slane was kept well away from the castle, but both Irish morning newspapers featured front-page pictures of Springsteen's arrival in Dublin.

Although 65,000 tickets costing fifteen Irish pounds each (approximately fifteen dollars) had been sold out weeks in advance, local residents had threatened court action to stop the concert, because they feared violence similar to the riots before Bob Dylan's show at the same venue last year. However, they withdrew their objections after promoter Jim Aiken and the castle's owner, Lord Henry Mountcharles, gave assurances of security.

The residents needn't have worried. With a stage that backed onto the river Boyne, the picturesque natural amphitheater was bathed in sunshine as the peaceful crowd thronged the small country roads leading to the site. In an attempt to curb scalping, an additional 5,000 tickets were made available at the gate. Security in and around the castle was tight but not oppressive, and there were no incidents.

Four years ago, during The River Tour, Springsteen would have had trouble attracting half as many people to a show in Ireland. But now, after the success of "Dancing in the Dark" and *Born in the U.S.A.,* he is a major star—a fact that was made evident by the amount of media attention his visit attracted. Newspapers and TV and radio stations from all over Europe had been pumping out Springsteen bios all week, while their reporters scurried about to find some fresh angles on New Jersey's most famous son.

Shortly before the show's 5:00 starting time, members of the media crammed a special VIP area, where they vied with local politicians and businessmen for a prime view of the stage. In addition to an inconspicuous Clapton and a talkative Townshend, the guests included Elvis Costello (disguised as an Orthodox rabbi) and various members of Spandau Ballet, whose singer, Tony Hadley, was later quoted as saying that Queen was still the best live act he had ever seen.

He must have witnessed a different concert, because Springsteen, after a cautious start, put on a show that gradually built toward a thrilling climax. In an attempt to accommodate the enormous crowd, giant Diamond Vision video screens were erected, enabling those at the back to see what the small figures onstage looked like. Up front, it was a tight squeeze, and fans suffering from the intense heat were carried away in a steady stream.

Musically, the show was a triumph—though Springsteen did have to make a few compromises. Playing before 70,000 people in the open air and in broad daylight, he was unable to create his usual feeling of intimacy and community. And although "The River" was especially well received, the crowd responded more readily to the pop appeal of "Dancing in the Dark" and "Hungry Heart" than to his slower, more difficult or emotionally demanding songs. By playing such huge venues, it seems Springsteen has had to sacrifice two of the most important elements of his live shows—total contact with and control of his audience.

He compensated for that by delivering a high-energy, hard-rocking performance. Ably assisted by the E Street Band, Springsteen steamrollered the audience into submission, tearing through memorable versions of "Bobby Jean," "Pink Cadillac," "Cadillac Ranch," "Badlands," "Thunder Road" and many more, before closing the set with a typically robust "Rosalita."

As the crowd screamed for more, Springsteen and company returned for an encore, ending the three-and-a-half-hour performance with their "Twist and Shout"/"Do You Love Me" medley.

The Boss and his band were back in Europe and back in big business.

CHRISTOPHER CONNELLY

STILL THE BOSS
Move into Stadiums Hasn't Blunted Springsteen's Impact

WATCHING BRUCE SPRINGSTEEN from the mezzanine of Philadelphia's Veterans Stadium on August 14th was like watching a bicyclist from an airplane: You could tell what he was wearing, where he was going—and that was about it. Distance was also an issue down front, where blockades had been erected to keep fans a good twenty feet away from the lip of the stage. That separation—unavoidable in a stadium—was troubling, and it recalled the questions that many of Springsteen's fans asked when these stadium shows were first announced: Could he possibly maintain the intimacy that had marked his arena shows? Would the subtlety of his message get lost in such a cavernous expanse? The answer to both questions turned out to be a qualified yes. What the more than 55,000 saw and heard was a slightly diluted show that unquestionably is still rock & roll's best.

In moving to these larger venues, Springsteen opted not to fill the additional space with the sort of stadium-size bombast—flash pots, movable stages—that bands like the Rolling Stones rely on. He did add a long, lower ramp across the front of the stage, with banks of bright footlights illuminating each end. Two large video screens had also been installed on either side of the stage, enabling much of the intraband byplay to be seen in back.

After opening with an initial blast of anthemic rock & roll—"Born in the U.S.A.," "Badlands" and "Out in the Street"—Springsteen switched into his moodier music. In this setting, though, such songs from *Nebraska* as "Atlantic City" and "Johnny 99" seemed distended, blown up too big for their ruminative quality to survive. More effective were "The River," in which Springsteen's opening harmonica wail sounded even more plaintive bouncing off the stadium seats, and "Trapped," a longtime concert favorite that's turned into the show's most harrowing anthem.

While Springsteen's humor flowed freely throughout—"Glory Days" featured a cameo appearance by Father Time, as Springsteen and Clarence Clemons used canes to hobble their "aging" bodies across the stage—he maintained his ability to switch into a darker key at a moment's notice. Before "My Hometown," for example, he carefully cited the names of local food banks and shelters for the homeless and asked for volunteers and donations (without mentioning his five-figure contribution to each organization). Throughout the show, raps like this one were more politically explicit than they've been in the past—and were not as attentively listened to as they once were.

Whatever this audience's fealty to Springsteen's ideals and his perceptions about America's failures, they had come to party. After a forty-five-minute intermission, Springsteen gave them all they could handle. The second set was a junk-rock pig-out, jammed with the loose-limbed, "U.S." Bonds-style songs that dominated *The River*—which proved perfectly suited for a crowd this size. But it wasn't mindless mania, either: Springsteen-inspired singalongs on "Hungry Heart" and "Cadillac Ranch" subverted the stadium's impersonality and created the sort of communal good-time feeling that makes his concerts special.

With the crowd nearly out of breath, Springsteen launched into a rap of uncommon intensity. Eyes cast downward, he told of his mother's trips to the finance company and let the rage at his mother's humiliation build to a higher and higher pitch. This was no idle yarn-spinning. Springsteen seemed almost to be talking to himself, reliving rather than recalling his anger, until he snapped it off with the strains of "I'm on Fire"—building a thoughtful connection between a child's rage and an adult's passion.

From there, it was party time once more. Except for an acoustic "This Land Is Your Land" on the first encore—greeted with more than a few jingoistic yelps—it was straight whoopee to the end: "Born to Run," an earth-shaking "Ramrod" and the "Twist and Shout" medley.

He ended with a cry of "I'm just a prisoner of rock & roll!" But as we know by now, Springsteen is a prisoner of plenty more than that; he's also a prisoner of his phenomenally huge popularity. The show is different now, and so is his life. Can he continue to trust an audience that booed his only reference to his wife? Will he be willing to share his personal life in his newer material, or will his songs tend to fall into mutually exclusive categories of present-day social consciousness and nostalgic reverie?

Based on this show—and a brilliant New Jersey concert a few nights later—the outlook seems very good indeed. He may not be able to toss himself into the crowd like he used to, and he may not play his more lengthy thematic material much anymore. But while Springsteen has remained loyal to his older fans, he hasn't let that loyalty constrain the development of his art or his audience. And while his fans have grown in number, their essential character hasn't changed dramatically, the way Prince's or the Jacksons' fans did during their respective commercial breakthroughs. Because Bruce Springsteen genuinely cares about his audience—and because his audience loves him so fervently—they still seem close to each other. Even from the mezzanine.

JOSEPH DALTON

BRUCE SPRINGSTEEN
MADE IN THE U.S.A.
My Hometown

THE SPIRITUAL CENTER of Freehold, New Jersey, might be the rug factory, on the edge of town. The rug company is long gone, but the factory is still there, a brick reminder, partly filled with small businesses. Freehold is really too small to have neighborhoods, but this part of town is called Texas, perhaps because, to Jersey ears, everyone who moved out of Appalachia to work in the rug factory sounded like John Wayne. There are two Freeholds, actually; out in Freehold township, where the nice suburban homes of commuters into New York butt up against manicured horse farms, they call Freehold borough the hole in the doughnut. That's not really fair; this isn't the Bronx, or East St. Louis. The streets around the rug factory are lined with two-family houses, with neat yards kept by working people who worry that their blue-collar jobs will head south, like the rug company, or to South Korea, or just evaporate. Bruce Springsteen grew up here, in a gray two-family house next door to a Sinclair gas station; this is his hometown.

Not a bad place to grow up, now or twenty years ago, but not a breeding ground for great expectations either. In Freehold, you're expected to go to work instead of college, to make Scotch tape for 3M or instant coffee for Nescafé, and you weren't expected to make a lot of noise about it. Which is what Douglas Springsteen did, coming home from jobs as a factory worker or prison guard or bus driver to sit in his kitchen and think about the world. There was a living room back beyond, but it was for special occasions, and for company; the kitchen, the biggest room in the house and stolen from the set of *The Honeymooners,* was where it all happened. So you walked in, and your dad was sitting there at the kitchen table, reading the newspaper, growing old in a job designed for it. Maybe he said something, like, get a job—or at least a haircut. And you thought, uh-huh: the rug factory. No thanks.

Suddenly it was 1964, and the Beatles hit, and everybody had a guitar.

"Suddenly, there was a band on every street corner," says Vinnie Roslin, who played bass with the first hot local band, the Motifs, and later with Springsteen in a band called Steel Mill.

"I remember the first time I saw the Beatles, on *The Ed Sullivan Show*," says George Theiss. "I got this feeling in my chest, this tightness, almost like I was crying." There was nothing left to do but get a guitar and form a band, play out your gunfighter fantasies, wear Long Rider coats and meet girls. So Theiss did, and that band became the Castiles, after the shampoo he was using. They practiced over on Center Street in Texas, in the half of a two-family house that their drummer, Bart Haynes, lived in.

The Appalachian families had moved on, replaced by Italians, who were being replaced by blacks. It was the era of the transistor radio: Outside of town, country & western reigned, but on the streets of Texas you got Top Forty from the New York stations and, increasingly, soul—Temps, Tops, Otis and Aretha. Jangle it all together, and you've got rock & roll, and on Center Street, the longest street in America because it ran from Texas to Main, it jangled. The Castiles tried to jangle, but, "We were awful," says George Theiss, laughing. The other half of the two-family house was occupied by Gordon "Tex" Vinyard, and he finally came over one night and asked them to knock it off. Theiss came by Vinyard's a couple days later to apologize; they hit it off, and in the end, Vinyard said, hey, if you're going to do this, let's do it right. And they did.

Tex was in his late thirties then, a factory worker who loved kids and had none of his own. He became a legend to Jersey bands; eventually, he would manage more than twenty of them. But the first and possibly the best was the Castiles, and in no time he had cleared out his living room and turned it into a practice hall. The Castiles were going through personnel, and looking for a guitar player. George Theiss was going out with Ginny Springsteen, and somebody else mentioned that her brother, Bruce, played the guitar, so Theiss took him over to meet Tex. Springsteen came in with a borrowed guitar, played a few snatches of songs and wondered if he was in the band. Tex suggested he come back when he'd learned a few songs. Springsteen showed up the next night, played five songs he'd learned off the radio and asked again. An astounded Tex said yeah. Sure.

Vinyard didn't know anything about music, but he knew what he liked, and he liked his opinions. "Tex liked country & western," says George Theiss, laughing. "He couldn't tell you how you were playing the guitar part wrong, but he made us do it again and again until it was right." He sobers up and nods. "An authority figure," he says respectfully.

Tex was a large man, and sometimes he would become impatient and start yelling, say they were acting like kids. His wife, Marion, would come in then, with sodas from Foodtown—they went through cases and cases of Foodtown soda—and say, "Tex, they *are* kids." The Castiles would tease him when he was in a good mood, and call him Flash. The black kids on the block were a little more raffish. They called him Bwana.

There were two sides to him, and on the one side he leaned a little toward George Theiss—a charmer, a lady's man having a time. Theiss would show up ten minutes late for practice, and Tex would yell, "Theiss, that girl better walk herself home tomorrow." But on the other, he leaned toward Bruce Springsteen—shy but very, very serious, a believer in the power of rock & roll, at least in its power to get you out of a two-family house in Freehold. Tex maybe didn't understand rock & roll, but he believed in it too, and that's why he was replacing the shock absorbers on his old Mercury every couple of months after hauling a load of kids and equipment to gigs all over Jersey, or going into debt on a factory worker's salary to buy equipment across the street at Caiazzo's Music Store, getting old man Caiazzo to write out the music to the original songs the band wrote so they could be copyrighted, even paying Ray Cichone, the Motifs' guitar player, to teach Springsteen how to play leads. One observer's estimate is that Tex eventually put $10,000 into the band, in 1965 dollars, for kids who could never have put it together themselves, and he found somebody whose obsession matched his own. When you think of Springsteen as the Boss, remember those black kids on Center Street who called Tex Vinyard Bwana.

Outside the band, at Freehold Regional High School, Bruce didn't make much of an impression. "No, he made no impression at all," says one high school classmate. "He was very shy—no activities, no sports, nothing like that. If he hadn't turned out to be Bruce Springsteen, would I remember him? I can't think why I would." He stops, then says, "You have to remember, without a guitar in his hands, he had absolutely nothing to say." George Theiss went out with Ginny Springsteen for a year and didn't even know Bruce played guitar until someone else told him. "We were trying to be cool," Theiss says, "trying to get by without carrying any books at all, or carrying one, almost like a prop. You would see Bruce, coming down the hall with an armful of books, carrying them up around his chest, like a girl. I thought he was real studious."

He wasn't, but he was an outsider. Freehold High divided into Greasers and Rah-rahs. Rah-rahs wore madras shirts and white pants, were going out with cheerleaders and on to college. Liked the Beatles, the Beach Boys, Jan and Dean. Greasers wore black jeans and white T-shirts, black leather jackets. They were going to work, or to Vietnam; liked the Stones, Motown, the Who. It was a compliment to say of a fellow greaser, "He wears black socks, even in gym class."

The Castiles rode it down the middle, some band members leaning one way, some the other. Bart Haynes, the drummer, Vince Manniello, who replaced him, Bob Alfano, the organist, and Springsteen were the Greasers. George Theiss, who had moved over to rhythm guitar and handled vocals; Curt Fluhr, the bassist; and Paul Popkin, who played tambourines and did some vocals, were the Rah-rahs. But these are arbitrary groupings; the lines shifted all the time, and the band could shift too, depending on where they were playing. Still, there was a time at one Rah-rah stronghold in Sea Bright when the band had to go out the back door and toss the equipment over a barbed-wire fence, with Ray Cichone and Tex standing guard—too much "My Generation."

But there were places to play all over, school dances and CYO dances and YMCA dances. "I saw that 'Dancing in the Dark' video, and I started laughing," says Curt Fluhr. "When he did that dance in high school, he used to call it the boogaloo." There were clubs up and down the Jersey coast, in Red Bank and Long Branch and Asbury Park. There were battles of the bands at the Keyport-Matawan Rollerdrome—the kind of contest where you could hear two bands play "Satisfaction" four times each.

They could play now, although nobody played his own instrument. Curt Fluhr was playing a Silvertone bass Tex owned. Popkin's Stratocaster was played by George Theiss. Springsteen played Theiss' blue solid-body Epiphone. They were in Tex' house five nights a week until eleven or so, joined by as many as twenty other kids, and out a couple times a week at a gig somewhere, then back to Tex' for Foodtown sodas and some of Marion's tunafish sandwiches. There was a teen club in Freehold called the Left Foot, started by a Catholic priest named Father Coleman, with help from Tex— a juice bar, a place for kids to hang out—and the Castiles ruled it. Occasionally, the band went up to New York to play Cafe Wha? in the Village for ten dollars a man. Fluhr laughs, thinking about it. He remembers the night his Hofner bass was stolen offstage, mainly because a waitress took pity on him, gave him his first joint and took him upstairs to meet the Fugs. Glory days.

On the haul up to the city, they would take back roads to avoid the tolls, Springsteen sitting quietly, thinking out songs, and then, in the Village, standing around with his mouth open like the rest of them. There was a gay man named Josie, a West Village legend, who took a liking to Springsteen and would sneak up on him to kiss him. The band would be standing around with slices of pizza in some joint on Bleecker Street, and they'd see Josie coming, and nobody would say a word until Josie had done his work and had run away, giggling. "Even then, I'd have to say Bruce is the most heterosexual person I ever met," says Fluhr, "and he'd get this look on his face that was just . . . incredible." Despite the loner mystique, there was always a girl, lots of them, but Springsteen didn't talk about that either. Back in Freehold for soda and tuna fish, he just quietly slipped away.

Glory days. They were famous. Their hair was down in their eyes, which irritated the Rah-rahs, and everybody else, too. "We were the only five freaks in Monmouth County," says George Theiss, laughing. "And at that time, you had short hair, and were an American, or you didn't, and weren't." It made ordering a cup of coffee interesting, but when the principal of Freehold High called the band in and told them to get haircuts, a petition sprang up—you can't do this, these guys are the *Castiles*—and the order was rescinded. Glory days.

They hung out in Federici's Pizza (no relation to E Street Band keyboardist Danny Federici), acclaimed by Freehold residents as the best pizza anywhere—very thin-crusted pizza, very greasy, the only pizza anywhere that came in a paper bag instead of a box. In the backseat of everyone's car was a circular slick that told you just how highly Federici's pizza was esteemed.

The big acquisition in Freehold was a driver's license, but long after everybody in the band had his, Springsteen was still hitchhiking, incapable of learning to drive. Tex once spent an afternoon with him in the six-acre parking lot at Freehold Raceway, trying to teach him, and came back shaking his head. Every day between May and September, Bruce would take his guitar and hitchhike to the beach. He would get picked up three or four times a year by the cops for hitchhiking, but who cares when you're hearing songs? In September, he always had the best tan.

"You could tell there was something special about him," says Curt Fluhr, a bit abashed. "You had this kid, terribly shy, not terribly attractive, but put a guitar in his hands . . . " And what? "You ever see Bill Bixby turn into the Incredible Hulk?" Fluhr asks. "Put him onstage with a guitar and he lit it up. It was like somebody had plugged him in."

The Castiles made a demo record, paid for by Tex, in a cheap recording studio, but you can hear the power—the slashing leads of a hot seventeen-year-old guitar player and his gritty, high-in-the-throat voice. There was some tension in the band, and that shows up, too. "We weren't the Everly Brothers," says George Theiss, only a bit ruefully. Springsteen wanted to do fewer covers and more of his own songs, and when he did covers, he wanted to do harder music—the Stones and the Who—and he wanted to sing, too. The Castiles' vocalist was Theiss, who has a great voice—a Mrs. Butterworth rock & roll voice, thick and rich—and Tex wanted George to sing.

The end was coming. They had all graduated from high school, except Fluhr, and Springsteen's parents had moved to California. He had stayed behind to attend Ocean County Community College in Toms River (known as Hooper High because it's on Hooper Avenue) and was worried, as they all were, about the draft. Somewhere from those last shows, Theiss says, is a picture of Springsteen giving him the finger onstage. The Castiles played their last gig in August 1968 at the Off Broad Street Coffeehouse in Red Bank.

They went off to do other things. Springsteen became Bruce. The Castiles' first drummer, Bart Haynes, joined the Marine Corps, and was killed in action in Vietnam. Vince Manniello knocked around for a while and now lives at home with his parents in Freehold, helping them run their antique store. Bob Alfano played in local bands, including one with Springsteen called Earth, and is now a milkman living in Asbury Park. Curt Fluhr went up to Boston University, then came back to help his father run the family's fuel-oil business, continuing to play. The fuel-oil business was sold, and Fluhr made a little money and married a former Miss Nashville who is also a former first soprano with the Atlanta Symphony. They're running a country band and thinking about moving south. Paul Popkin and George Theiss enrolled in RCA's electronics school to get deferments, and a year later Popkin was dead, mysteriously, from hepatitis. Theiss got married at nineteen and has stayed married; they have two kids and a nice house in Freehold township with a pool in the back yard. He works as a carpenter, but he keeps on playing rock & roll, and this month he went into the studio to make his first album, with the guys who put Bonnie Tyler on track. He's still a believer in the power of rock & roll. "You can't talk about things," Theiss says. "You have to do them. I just want to do the music."

THE FRIDAY BEFORE THE BORN IN THE U.S.A. TOUR started last summer, Springsteen wanted to rehearse before a live audience, and so the E Street Band went on at the Stone Pony in Asbury Park sometime just after midnight on a hot night. This is Bruce country, a fading shore town where they know their rock & roll, and four hours later, they knew it better. The band was sweating, exhausted, and dragging out the door when Springsteen began yelling at them to come back. They did, and he launched into "Born to Run," and when it was over, they had to carry him outside and drape him over the hood of a car so they could throw buckets of ice water over him.

The Stone Pony is just about the last vestige of the once exploding Asbury Park music scene. The Pandemonium, the Student Prince, the Sunshine Inn—clubs where you heard Top Forty cover bands all summer long, and whatever was happening all winter—they're all gone, victims of Asbury Park's downslide after the riots in 1971. It was always a town for music—Lester Lanin's big band in the Forties, jazz and rhythm & blues clubs on the edge of Asbury's black sections through the middle Sixties, rock & roll after that. The list of people who played standing gigs in Asbury Park includes names as diverse as James Brown, George Benson and Eddie Arnold.

But they're cleaning up the boardwalk now; at one end, the once elegant Berkeley Carteret hotel is being made that way again by a consortium of partners that includes Johnny Cash. Coming down the boardwalk, past Madame Marie's (palms read, fortunes told, see "Sandy," on *The Wild, the Innocent*), you wonder how long the arcades and miniature-golf courses can hold up in the face of gentrification. There may no longer be any room on Ocean Avenue for a mere rock & roll club like the Stone Pony, and although it can resettle inland, it just wouldn't be the same.

But who knows? They probably said the same thing when the Upstage closed. The Upstage was another teen club, a juice bar without a liquor license, open till five on the weekends, started by Margaret Potter and her then-husband, Tom, in 1968. Before that, the Potters ran a hairdressing salon on Cookman Avenue, Studio Six, and spent weekends in clubs, and when the clubs closed, musicians came back to the Potters' apartment for breakfast and to teach Margaret how to play guitar. It evolved into a hangout for musicians and might have gone on like that indefinitely, except that Tom Potter became allergic to hair dye. Two doors down on Cookman Avenue, the Potters found a lease, the second floor over a Thom McAn shoe store, and opened the Upstage. It turned into a folkie coffeehouse, and when the third floor came open, they took that, too. On the third floor, the back wall was covered with tiny speakers—the largest was fifteen inches—and it was there the prototypical Asbury band was born, blaring out of the wall—a big, flathead rhythm section, drums and bass. A saxophone, to blow response to the singer. Keyboards, or an electric piano, or better yet, an organ player on a big B-3, like Booker T. And finally, a funky chunky guitar player for Steve Cropper leads on Strat. After that it was what you could carry—harmonica, another guitar, a horn section. The Upstage became a drop-in, hang-out club for musicians up and down the shore. You paid twenty-five dollars for the year in order to duck the two-dollar cover, and because there was a wall full of speakers, all you had to bring was your guitar.

Margaret Potter remembers the first night Springsteen walked in: "He came up very politely and said, 'Excuse me, but would you mind very much if I borrowed your guitar? The gentleman downstairs said it would probably be okay.' I said sure and stuck around awhile while he plugged in, to make sure he understood the system. He played some blues thing, and I said, 'Oh, Lord,' and went back down to the second floor. Vini Lopez, the first drummer in the E Street Band, was sitting down there, and Miami Steve, and Southside Johnny, all playing Monopoly, which is what you did while you waited to get up, and I told them they had better get upstairs. They were involved in the game, and asked why. I said, 'Hey guys, there's some kid up there who can really play.'" Then, as she turned to leave: "They said, 'Where are you going?' I said, 'Where do you think? Upstairs.'"

At the time, Springsteen was doing his power-trio thing in a band called Earth to get the hard edges out of his system. But that was over soon enough, and his first real band in Asbury Park was something called Child, a band that grew out of the Upstage and the hot players there. Soon enough, they found out there was another band called Child, and they were sitting around the Ink Well coffeehouse in Long Branch, depressed, trying to come up with another name, when an acquaintance came in and asked who died. They stole our name, and we're trying to come up with another one, was the reply. What's the band like? he asked. It's sort of hard, and fast, and . . . heavy. Call it Steel Mill, the friend said. Why? they asked. Well, they're sort of heavy, aren't they? So Steel Mill got a winter rental in Bradley Beach for $125 a month, including a snooker table, which they wore out, since nobody had any money to do anything else, and when they weren't playing snooker, they practiced.

These were serious working musicians, not high-school kids, and Springsteen exhausted them practicing. "He just had this enormous appetite to play," says Vinnie Roslin, the bass player and former member of the Motifs. "He'd play anytime, anywhere, for anybody. He was like a television set with one channel, and on the set was 'practice music.'"

Their manager was a man named Carl West, who ran Challenger Eastern Surfboards. They would surf all summer and then play all winter in the office of West's deserted surfboard factory. But nothing really came of Steel Mill either. West took the band to California to see his old haunts and get rich, but it didn't happen. They got incredible reviews, including a gig at the Fillmore West that caused a *San Francisco Examiner* writer to gush, "I have never been so overwhelmed by totally unknown talent." They tried to get something going with Bill Graham's Fillmore Records, but couldn't, and came home in March, wondering. There were other missteps along the way—they had a chance to play Woodstock, but West blew it off, believing too many people would show up and their equipment would be stolen or damaged. Instead, they played to a handful of people in the Student Prince in Asbury Park. Soon enough, they split up. Some of Steel Mill ended up in the E Street Band—Vini Lopez, the first drummer, and keyboardist Danny Federici. "I've never played in a band so tight," says Roslin. "You could tell when the next guy was going to breathe." Springsteen, he remembers, was completely calm, through all the money troubles and missed opportunities, and one night Roslin asked why. "He just turned to me and said, 'Well. It's like looking up at a light at the end of the tunnel, and what can you do? You just keep walking. And you get there.' " Roslin shakes his head. He's playing bass, here and there, working a day job to keep together and play music at night.

"You just keep walking, and that's what he did," Roslin says. "Remember, one channel."

MERLE GINSBERG

BRUCE SPRINGSTEEN
MADE IN THE U.S.A.

The Fans: Springsteen's Followers
Are Convinced He's Just Like Them

THERE'S NOTHING GENERIC about Bruce Springsteen fans. Unlike Boy George clones, Durannies or Madonna Wanna-Be's, Bruce's legions don't try to dress like him; in fact, they believe he tries to dress like them. They're drawn to Springsteen for precisely the opposite reason that most fans are drawn to a rock star: Instead of offering an escape from the mundane by creating a fantasy world of flash and glitz, Bruce glorifies the ordinariness of life. His fans—like these eleven who were waiting in the parking lot at Giants Stadium, at the Meadowlands, in New Jersey, for Springsteen's August 21st show—come in all ages, from teenyboppers to parents, and from various social and economic backgrounds. What they all have in common is, quite simply, a love for Springsteen's ideals, and his music.

DREW MURRAY, *22, is a mate on a boat out of Atlantic Highlands, New Jersey. He's from the Flatbush section of Brooklyn and just moved to Jersey with his parents and his five sisters. His father is a retired sanitation worker, and his mother is a housewife.*

" 'Born in the U.S.A.' is my favorite Springsteen song. There is no other song, really. Bruce Springsteen is dedicated to his country, and I like that. That's how I feel. He seems very excited when he sings that song, 'cause that's *him,* and he's there for his country. He's just like everybody else—he ain't walkin' around thinkin' he's something special."

JILL ZEITVOGEL, *15, is a junior at Bergenfield High School, in New Jersey. Her father's an air-conditioning salesman, and her mother's a housewife.*

"I got into Bruce through my sister, I guess. And through bein' a Jersey girl, definitely. That's my favorite Bruce song—'Jersey Girl.' I like both the old and the new Springsteen songs—I don't ever get sick of them.

"What do I like about him? He's a fox! He's down-to-earth. He's so cool, he's not like any other rock star. He acts normal. Prince overdresses; he don't dress like a normal person. Bruce'll wear jeans; he don't care. I'm jealous of Julianne Phillips. I'd marry him—he's a fox. He's gorgeous. I seen pictures of him when he wasn't that cute. I guess singing helped him."

LISA BISCARDI, *15, is a junior at Bergenfield High School. Her father's a manager at a computer company, and her mother baby-sits.*
"I've been into Bruce since the *Born to Run* album. I like him 'cause he's gorgeous, and he could sing good—he's my favorite. He's normal. He ain't stuck up like most rock stars. If I met him somewhere, I bet he'd be really cool. I'd love to hang out with him.

"I guess I identify with his patriotic thing, but I don't think about it much—I just like his songs."

LISA REZZONICO, *16, is a junior at Bergenfield High School. Her father owns a butcher store, and her mother's a secretary.*
"Bruce rules! He's been there for so long. He might be twice my age, but it doesn't bother me in the least bit. I like older men."

VICTOR PAPPERT JR., *36, is a disabled vet from Maspeth, Queens. He spent six and a half months in Vietnam, then was classified as disabled. He became an ironworker but, after seven years, quit due to stress and was declared 100 percent disabled. He has a wife and three kids.*
" 'Born to Run' and a couple other of Bruce's songs took my fancy, but 'Born in the U.S.A.,' that really hit home. I admire the man—he's a humanitarian. He focuses on vets 'cause he's an American—he cares what we've done. He doesn't shun us. He's got spirit; he motivates us. I hear he's been givin' to charities; he doesn't have to do that.

"About politics, to tell you the truth, I think he's right and wrong. But he does show a lot of emotion. I used to enjoy Simon and Garfunkel, but Bruce—he gives you the spirit of living. You want to take on the world and challenge it. A lot of disco and punk rock is boring; you don't understand what they say. Bruce has an original outlook on things."

BRENDAN DAVEY, *18, from Yonkers, New York, is attending Fordham University as a freshman, studying liberal arts. His father's a plumber; his mother used to run a deli. Brendan and Paddi Shea have been going out for two years.*
"My sister Mary was into Bruce a long time ago. We had all the albums in our house. 'Rosalita' is my favorite song. I like the way he attracts a lot of energy, and the way he screams into the mike. He brings a lot of people

together, but not like a rough crowd or anything. You don't get a lot of weirdos comin' around, bashing heads, like at some other concerts I been to."

PADDI SHEA, *18, is from Woodlawn, in the Bronx. She is a freshman at Grinell College, in Iowa. Her father, like Bruce's, is a retired bus driver; her mother is a housewife.*

"I've liked Bruce since eighth grade. *The River* is my favorite Bruce record—I love it. It's really nice; it has nice meaning. I like mellow songs.

"He's just a regular person; he doesn't come out with earrings and makeup. He sings about things teenagers like to hear; he seems younger than his age. About his marrying Julianne Phillips, I guess everyone makes mistakes! No, she seems nice. I also love U2, Jackson Browne and even a little Led Zeppelin."

BILL CHAFFEE, *20, hails from Trumbull, Connecticut. He goes to Bryant College, in Rhode Island. His father works for the Connecticut Department of Transportation; his mother's a dental hygienist.*

"I been into Bruce for a couple of years. He's real. 'Rosalita' is my favorite song. I also like Eddie Money, Rush, the Doors, stuff like that."

KEITH DUDZINSKI, *18, is a senior at St. Joseph High School in Trumbull, Connecticut. His father works in the old Bullard's machine-tool works in Fairfield; his mother is a housewife.*

"I've been into Bruce since freshman year. *Greetings From Asbury Park* is my favorite album. I like the older stuff best. I like the way he sings and what he sings about—pure American stuff. He tells a story in every song.

"Bruce's videos are straight out—I like that. He's more mellow, not rock or heavy metal. A lot of my friends are into heavy metal, but I'm not. Hopefully, after high school, I'm thinkin' about playing football. Y'know, glory days."

DAVE OSBORNE, *19, is from Pearl River, in Rockland County, New York. He lives at home and commutes to school at the New York Institute of Technology, where he's studying architecture.*

"I'm a major Bruce fan, a big, big fan. I get duded up for all the shows. I wear the flag to every show, and people come up and pat me on the back and say I look great. Bruce fans are one big family. Everybody's got barbecues in the parking lot before the show; everybody'll give ya a burger or a dog. I've seen him *nine* times, and I saw him front row in Los Angeles. My sister won first prize in the MTV contest, the Bruce Springsteen Roadie Contest, which was to see him anywhere in the country, so we went to L.A.

"I got into Bruce with *Born to Run*—my brother got the album. I love *Darkness on the Edge of Town* and *The River. Greetings From Asbury Park* and *The Wild, the Innocent* are the most incredible albums. It's too bad he never plays any of that stuff; it's so intense.

"I could see him every night. We were on the phone to get tickets about nine or ten hours. Bruce is—he's America. He is exactly what America's all about. He becomes a rock star and writes his dreams. It's like he's your best friend, and you could sit down and talk to him and know everything he's talkin' about. I listen to the Stones, Tom Petty, Jethro Tull, the Who. I like the Heads, Prince, Billy Joel; U2 is really hot, Dire Straits, the Police. But Bruce is the Man, he's *it*. My mother loves Bruce, and she's fifty-two and a librarian. She was really mad I didn't get her a ticket."

A MY HUMAN, *20, lives in New City, New York. She's studying acting and dance at the State University of New York at New Paltz.*

"Dave [Osborne] got me into Bruce. I'm a virgin when it comes to Bruce concerts. I'm really psyched. I've heard about this raw energy and realness—that's what I'm here to see. He's playing for the working man.

"I've heard Springsteen shows compared to Grateful Dead ones, in the sense that it's no frills, and it's the music that is the whole thing. There's a connection between Bruce and the Dead. I guess my favorite Bruce song is 'Spirit in the Night.' I think he's good-looking—and he's got a cute ass, and everyone knows it. He's the most patriotic guy around. I feel patriotic—it's a real turnaround from the hippie days. It's, like, pro being together in a harmonious way. I feel that."

JEFFERSON MORLEY

BRUCE SPRINGSTEEN MADE IN THE U.S.A.

The Phenomenon:
In Their Attempt to Turn Him Into an American Hero, the Media, Politicians and Others Have Missed Springsteen's Real Message

A COUPLE OF ENTREPRENEURS recently had a bright idea sure to appeal to a newly patriotic America. They would produce T-shirts invoking the two heroes of the summer of 1985, two muscular, working-class white guys with bandannas and lingering memories of Vietnam. SPRINGSTEEN: THE RAMBO OF ROCK, the T-shirts proclaimed. In a way, you had to sympathize with the T-shirt hawkers, forced and false as their message might be. Plenty of other clever people, including Lee Iacocca, George Will and Walter Mondale, have tried to grab the Springsteen Phenomenon, and almost all of them have come away with less than they'd hoped. That's because the Springsteen Phenomenon and what Springsteen and his music are all about are two very different things.

The Phenomenon is the media's explanation of Springsteen's new status as "something more than a rock icon, something more than an entertainer" (the *New York Times*). It's also the adulation that kind of coverage encourages. In many respects, this Phenomenon is not unlike the Rambo Phenomenon or the Yuppie Phenomenon or the 1984 Olympics/New Patriotism Phenomenon. Springsteen's working-class origins, his sympathy for Vietnam vets and his desire to feel good about America have made media approval tempting, if facile.

But what is *really* going on "out there" is something very humble, no capital letters, nothing phenomenal and maybe even nothing surprising. Springsteen's music is being shared by a large number of people, and it is making a difference in their lives. We love the bittersweet anthem "Born in the U.S.A.," the reminiscing of "No Surrender," the sheer pride of rocking, the high jinks, the highway, the sorrow. The music is something more than a received pleasure. It touches something you didn't know—or forgot—you had in you.

The media and the businessmen and the politicians cannot fathom all this. The Rambo Phenomenon was easy to handle because fantasies of bitterness and revenge, of exclusion and domination, have shaped public life for the last five years. Springsteen's music and his audience are more elusive because they do not fantasize about revenge or money or social position or glamour or mindless escape or patriotism or any of those things that supposedly everyone wants in 1985.

Baffled by the discrepancy between the familiar explanation and what is really going on, the Phenomenologists take refuge in adulation. *Newsweek* said Springsteen is "a kind of American archetype. He is rock & roll's Gary Cooper." The supermarket tabloid *Star* announced: "He has achieved the stratospheric status we reserve for only our mightiest pop heroes—he no longer needs to use a last name. Madonna, Mick, Tina, Sting . . . Bruce."

What makes the drum roll of that ellipsis, and the RAMBO OF ROCK T-shirt, so poignantly laughable is *not* the glib reverse snobbery which holds that Rambo, Madonna and company are tinsel and Springsteen authentic. Nor is it the meaningless boast that Springsteen "puts on a better show." Springsteen would probably be the first to deny both suggestions.

What is silly is the way these pronouncements earnestly urge Springsteen fans to practice the most cynical self-deception. Springsteen couldn't possibly be what he says he is—"a real good journeyman." He must be something else, a megasuperstar or, bigger yet, an archetype.

The simple truth is, he and his band started out in the bars of the Jersey shore back in the late 1960s and have gotten more popular since. They play rock & roll, not really complicated, in a kind of Sixties style, but they throw in other things, too: Some of Springsteen's songs sound alike, but overall they're pretty great. He recently married a pretty girl from the suburbs. And that's it, nothing more. Why does the Springsteen Phenomenon insist we not take Springsteen at his word?

Perhaps out of habit—a lot of Phenomenons turn out to be fake. Perhaps out of fatalism. You can't help thinking this is why the *Star* article seemed sadly eager to wheel the Boss into Madame Tussaud's: "Brucemania, like Michaelmania of last year, will no doubt subside and the fanfare will fade, but true fans will always cherish. . . . " Springsteen may sing, "I don't want to fade away," but he's sure to fail.

Also, just maybe, the Phenomenon is subconsciously hostile to its subject. To make Springsteen something he's not, to make him a liar, is to get rid of him. Springsteen confronted the built-in obsolescence offered by the Phenomenon when Lee Iacocca reportedly offered him $12 million for the right to use "Born in the U.S.A." in a Chrysler commercial. One imagines the offer was appallingly sincere. Iacocca might have really thought that he was just doing his part (he himself a much-admired Phenomenon) for the country and for Springsteen. He might have truly believed that those few seconds would help people keep feeling good ("Chrysler's back" and "America's back") and at the same time Do Good by reducing the trade deficit caused by the yellow man.

Of course, if you're a twisted and bitter individual, you might think that Iacocca wanted nothing more than to prove who's really the Boss, that he wanted the power to discard Springsteen into the oblivion of old ad slogans. And if you're not that cynical, you might wonder if it makes any difference. In any case, Springsteen answered Iacocca with three words, rock lyrics from before there was rock music: *No thanks, mister.*

If some have missed Springsteen's truth by elevating him, others have missed it by trivializing him. Reporter Sara Rimer closed her August 16th article in the *New York Times* by quoting a fan: "It's rock & roll. It's just rock & roll." This is closer to the truth in that Rimer understands Springsteen's uniqueness begins in his music. But her insinuation is as false as the Rambo T-shirt.

We can be fairly sure that the fan Rimer was quoting meant something like, "Don't deny Springsteen's truth by making him something he isn't." In other words, if you're not going to shut up, Walter and Ronald, don't bother coming to the party. As for you, Rambo, please check your grenade launcher at the door. But we can be fairly sure that our unthinkingly dutiful *New York Times* reporter was quoting the fan for the purpose of saying, "Everybody knows rock is basically trivial but, hey, that doesn't mean it can't be fun for a night." Rimer's implication here is utterly wrong. And if she doesn't know it, she should just ask Bruce Springsteen.

"Until I realized that [rock music was my connection to the rest of the human race], I felt like I was dying, for some reason, and I didn't really know why," Springsteen told ROLLING STONE's Kurt Loder last fall. Some of Springsteen's most touching and thrilling songs are about wryly ("Glory Days") or chillingly ("State Trooper") recognizing that you are dying. Sure, some of Springsteen's other songs are "just" rock & roll: fast cars ("Cadillac Ranch") and girls ("Rosalita"). All of them helped save Bruce's life and change ours.

What unites these songs is not the genius of some godlike superstar nor some progressive political sensibility, but a very out-of-fashion, much-derided article of faith from the Sixties: the promise and power of rock music. Rock & roll is fun, but it is also something more: a means of holding on to life, of blasting away self-deception, joining with others and discovering why one should keep on living. Its spirit is democratic, its pain redeemable, its joys communal. If it were "merely" rock & roll, then Springsteen's talk of dying would be phony or foolish. It's a special pleasure to note that George Will and President Reagan have corroborated for us that Springsteen's music is neither pretentious nor phony.

Plenty of Springsteen's more politically inclined fans (myself included) pouted when Will claimed Springsteen on behalf of Reaganism last fall. In retrospect, though, I think we should thank Will. Of course, Americans were "gettin' manipulated and exploited" (Bruce's words) by the Reaganites' sudden attention. And Will and the fashionable conservatives did not dare resurrect their 1984 hucksterism in the summer of 1985. But their attempted co-optation and its failure provided inadvertent acknowledgment from an unlikely source of what is "political"—and powerful—about Springsteen's music.

Imagine, for a moment, that it is 1965 and you pull aside former actor Ronald Reagan after he has just denounced Martin Luther King. "I have bad news, sir," you tell him. "Twenty years from now there will be a guy who is very popular with people of all ages and who plays one of those electric guitars at deafeningly loud levels. He'll give piles of money to union bosses. He'll have a colored guy in his band. He'll tell everybody in sight that this three-chord racket saved his life. And people will take him seriously!"

Reagan asks if the guy will sing any better than that awful guy on the radio, Bob Dillon (sic). "Well, a little. But there's more. This guy, call him Bruce—no, he's not a queer, thank God, sir—will be a national hero. He'll be on the cover of magazines, the toast of political columnists. Conservatives will be scared to attack him. Democratic, even Republican presidential candidates, will try to associate themselves with him."

"This is exactly what I've said all along," Reagan says with a grim laugh. "America's on a perilous path, and if we are to rescue our country from such a liberal, decadent future, well, like I say: There *are* simple answers. There just aren't easy answers."

The conservatives' testimonials to Springsteen are a useful reminder that even the most powerful and fashionable people have to admit that what is absurd, scorned, silly, impractical, can come smashingly true. Even they have to recognize that the outsiders, the people who are scorned by conventional wisdom—losers, sad highway patrolmen, former high-school baseball players, even humiliated criminals—are worthy and can command the attention of people who run the country. It's no accident that the Reaganites tried to snatch Springsteen and haul him into the country club. They may have been ever so slightly worried.

That Springsteen's music is a triumph of the spirit of the Sixties is the one thing that the Springsteen Phenomenon could not bear to admit. Not the Sixties spirit as it exists behind glass in the museum—peace, drugs, liberation, love beads, long hair. That's all part of the Sixties Phenomenon and doesn't mean much to those of us who were in second grade in 1965. Not the Sixties spirit as renovated in the Yuppie Phenomenon. But the Sixties spirit as it arrived belatedly in a small, unpolitical New Jersey town, the same way it arrived belatedly in countless other places. It has something to do with liberation and something to do with self-respect. It is the spirit that says you can't start a fire sitting around crying of a broken heart.

■ RANDOM NOTES (November 21, 1985)

When Bruce Springsteen asked Patti Scialfa to sing on the E Street Band's world tour, she lost it completely—her voice, that is. "I had nodes. I went to specialists in New York who told me I could only handle folk music! It was a literal 'You'll never sing again.' But I found a special voice teacher and learned his method. I had to stop talking on the telephone; forget drinking or smoking. When Bruce hired me, I was still in a very bad state and getting hoarse. He didn't know it—when he heard me, my voice was fine. I didn't talk at the beginning of the tour; I'd go home after shows; I'd sleep all day. And it worked. I got it back, *better*."

Patti started singing with her brother's band when she was fifteen, in Oakhurst, New Jersey. Later she sang on the streets of New York with two girlfriends. "On a good night we made a hundred apiece." Then Patti sang lead vocals for David Sancious, and in 1980 the three girls toured with the Asbury Jukes. She also sang on David Johansen albums. One night, Bruce heard her sing at the Stone Pony. "He came up to me afterward and told me he thought I sang nicely. It was a great moment for me, because I'd had so many disappointments. About a year later he called up and said, 'C'mon over.' I just sat around with Bruce and Roy Bittan and Nils Lofgren and sang casually. He asked me back a few days later and just said, 'Wanna come out?' The great thing about working with Bruce is, he gives you such acceptance. Inside that, you can regain all your faith." Now that the tour is over, Patti has sung backup on the new Rolling Stones record, and she is about to record her first solo album. "I was eighteen, taking demos around. I wasn't ready—*then*."

■ YEAR-END RANDOM NOTES (December 19, 1985)

Somewhere along the endless highway of *Born in the U.S.A.*, Bruce Springsteen crossed that magic white line between the rock & roll future and the eternal present. With album sales certified at ten million and a fifteen-month megatour rewiring the planet's concert circuitry, Bruce ceased to be a mere rock & roll phenomenon and became, quite simply, a fact of life. As the songs from *Born in the U.S.A.* poured out of every speaker cone in America, the Boss became a beneficent big brother, as essential—and unavoidable—as the air we breathe.

Rock vids by big-name directors—especially John Sayles' "Glory Days," wherein a radiant Boss flashes like a neon ad for America itself—completed Springsteen's transformation from a scrounging Seventies cult hero into a full-blown Eighties working-class matinee idol.

As he refused political and commercial co-optation (spurning Lee Iacocca's bid to license the rights to "Born in the U.S.A." for Chrysler), Bruce continued to exemplify the best qualities of the American spirit. He looms large as the most reliable champion We the People have in the Eighties. This boss works for us.

■ RANDOM NOTES (December 19, 1985–January 2, 1986) ALTARED STATES

We got our first look at her when Bruce Springsteen took model and actress Julianne Phillips to the Grammy awards in February. There had been other girls in Bruce's life—actress Joyce Hyser, photographer Lynn Goldsmith—but this just smelled *serious*. *Paparazzi* shots of Bruce traveling with Julianne began to appear. In early May, rumor crept out that Julianne, twenty-five, just might make a model wife. Jersey girls all over the world were distraught.

The press prepared a major onslaught on Lake Oswego, Oregon, Julianne's hometown, on May 15th, the date the ceremony was expected to occur. The couple, however, beat them to the punch and tied the knot just after midnight on Monday, May 13th, at Our Lady of the Lake Church. After the wedding, Julianne's face graced more magazine covers than when she was an Elite model. "It's real important, but I don't want *that* to be why people are interested in me," she says of her new role of Boss woman. "I want to be thought of as an actor." She has a part in the upcoming Blake Edwards film *A Fine Mess* and has done a couple of television movies. Of course, her most famous role was her cameo as Bruce's wife in his "Glory Days" video.

■ **RANDOM NOTES** (January 16, 1986)

Bruce Springsteen and Willie Nelson placed ads in *Variety*, the *New York Times*, the *St. Paul Dispatch* and the *Asbury Park Press* asking the 3M Company not to shut down a plant in Springsteen's hometown of Freehold, New Jersey. The plant, which manufactures audio and video recording tape, is set to start laying off people on March 1st, and as many as 330 employees will lose their jobs. . . . "My Hometown," the Springsteen song about the closing of a Freehold textile mill in 1964, has become the seventh single off *Born in the U.S.A.* The LP has now sold more than ten million copies in the States, making it the fourth best-selling album of the past decade. Only Michael Jackson's *Thriller*, Fleetwood Mac's *Rumours* and the *Saturday Night Fever* soundtrack have outsold it.

■ **RANDOM NOTES** (February 27, 1986)

Rhino Records is releasing *Cover Me*, an LP of Bruce Springsteen songs done by other performers. Among the cuts are "Because the Night" by Patti Smith, "Fire" by Robert Gordon, "Johnny 99" by Johnny Cash, "Atlantic City" by Zeitgeist, "From Small Things (Big Things One Day Come)" by Dave Edmunds, "This Little Girl" by Gary "U.S." Bonds and "Hearts of Stone" by Southside Johnny and the Asbury Jukes.

DAVID FRICKE

THE LONG AND WINDING ROAD

The Members of the E Street Band Look Back at the Fifteen-Month Tour that Made Bruce Springsteen a National Hero

T HE SHOW WOULD BE well into its fourth hour, the musicians visibly wilting under the hot lights and the damp weight of their own sweat as they summoned up the energy for that last blast of "Born to Run." But Bruce Springsteen would never say, "Enough," until the last member of the audience keeled over in joyous exhaustion. After each encore, every night for nearly a year and a half during his 1984–85 world tour, Springsteen called his E Street Band into a brief huddle backstage.

"We had a saying," explains saxman Clarence Clemons. " 'Are they still on their feet? Yeah, let's go back and get 'em. Can they still raise their hands? If they can, we haven't done our job.' When we finally saw the guys in the front row falling down, lying over each other, then we said, 'Okay, they've had enough. Let's go home.' "

Having started the Born in the U.S.A. Tour in St. Paul, Minnesota, on June 29th, 1984, Springsteen and the E Street Band didn't go home until October 2nd, 1985—after their last four shows drew more than 330,000 people to the Los Angeles Memorial Coliseum. Their labors, of course, did not go unrewarded. *Born in the U.S.A.* sold more than ten million copies in the United States alone, becoming the biggest-selling album in the history of Columbia Records. The tour grossed $80 to $90 million from ticket sales ($34 million of that came from Springsteen's stadium shows in only four-teen cities). Bruce was the people's choice in ROLLING STONE's 1985 Read-ers Poll, sweeping the Artist, Male Vocalist, Songwriter and Best Live Performance of the Year categories. And in the Critics Poll, he shared Artist of the Year honors with miracle worker Bob Geldof, while the E Street Band—Clemons, drummer Max Weinberg, keyboardists Roy Bittan and Danny Federici, bassist Garry Tallent, guitarist Nils Lofgren and vocalist Patti Scialfa—tied for Band of the Year with Irish pals U2. In short, Bruce Spring-steen was indisputably the Boss in 1985.

The sales figures and tour grosses tell, however, only the accountants' side of the story. Whether it was the June '84 warm-up date at the Stone Pony in Asbury Park, New Jersey, or the outdoor concert in Göteborg, Sweden, where Springsteen performed under the burnt-orange rays of the midnight sun, his shows were do-it-till-you-drop spectaculars, parties already way out of bounds by the time he trotted out the old bar-band standbys ("Twist and Shout," "Devil With a Blue Dress On"). One night in Japan, Springsteen brought a young girl up onstage, as he did everywhere, to do the twist with him on "Dancing in the Dark." "She was good, too," Clemons recalls, "but as soon as she got offstage, she collapsed. She fell right over."

The fun of falling over never obscured Springsteen's unmistakable message—you've got to stand tall in spite of it all—in songs like "Born in the U.S.A.," the bouncy "Working on the Highway" and his electrified *Nebraska* meditation "Mansion on the Hill." Springsteen took it upon himself to set the example, giving his usual 110 percent during an '84 show in Tacoma, Washington, even though he was suffering from a debilitating virus. In the face of *Rambo*-mania and the misrepresentation of his *Born in the U.S.A.* message by nearsighted conservatives, he plugged Vietnam-veterans organizations, local food banks and community-action groups while quietly pledging his own money to many of these causes. And in a year when Live Aid proved what a world community of rock fans could accomplish, Springsteen demonstrated night after night what just one die-hard rock fan could do.

"I don't really think I could live with myself if I did it any other way," Springsteen told ROLLING STONE early in the tour, describing his faith in the power of music and how that faith manifests itself in his performances. "A lot of what I do up there I do for myself, because you go out there and your pride is on the line, your sense of self-respect, and you feel like 'Hey, there's something important happening here.' You have a chance to do something. And you wanna make the best of it."

"It takes a lot of courage to believe as strongly as he does," remarks Patti Scialfa, whom Springsteen hired after hearing her sing at a Stone Pony jam session one Sunday night in 1983. "It made every show special to me because you carried that belief with you. It was great to be going around making music that had such a strong center of faith. It made every show seem to have so much more depth. It wasn't just a musical expression; you were working your heart muscles, too."

SPRINGSTEEN DIDN'T WASTE too much energy on rehearsals for his massive tour. In May of '84, he convened the E Street Band at Big Man's West, Clarence Clemons' club in Red Bank, New Jersey. The purpose was a combination jam session and audition for Nils Lofgren. It was the first time

Springsteen and the band had played together in a live setting since The River Tour in 1981. Yet as soon as Springsteen counted off "Prove It All Night," "It was like we'd never stopped," says Max Weinberg. "We looked around at each other like 'Wow, that's what we've been missing.' "

Weinberg had undergone five hand operations for tendinitis prior to the Born in the U.S.A. Tour, but he was ready to play. (During the last nine months of the tour, however, he had to tape the ring finger of his left hand around the drumstick because he couldn't bend the finger at all.) After that Red Bank jam session, he says, the band rehearsed for four or five days in New Jersey before heading to central Pennsylvania for three days of dress rehearsals with full sound and lights.

"It was maybe eight or nine rehearsals altogether," Weinberg recalls. "And that's a lot. On the River tour, we rehearsed four days. On the Born to Run Tour, we didn't rehearse at all. We went right from the last record-ing session to a rehearsal room at eight in the morning. We ran through the set and played that night."

"We know each other so well," says organist Danny Federici, who has played with Springsteen for eighteen years, "that we can tell what song we're going to play just by the way Bruce counts it off or the way he wants it by the intensity with which he counts it off. Bruce would go, 'One, two, three, four,' and we'd all play the same song. We didn't discuss what it would be."

The secret, according to Clarence Clemons, a member of Springsteen's band for fourteen years, is simple: "When you learn a Bruce Springsteen song, it's like learning to ride a bike. You don't forget it."

But newcomers Scialfa and Nils Lofgren—the first new E Street mem-bers in ten years—didn't have a lot of time to learn. Lofgren had met Spring-steen in 1969 at the Fillmore West in San Francisco, where Bruce's band Steel Mill was playing an audition. They kept bumping into each other on the Northeast college circuit in the early Seventies, so when Lofgren got a call from Springsteen, right before the rehearsals, asking him to replace the departing Miami Steve Van Zandt, "I was familiar with a lot of the famous songs. But I wasn't exactly ready to step into the guitar parts." Lofgren paid a visit to a Springsteen tape collector he knew in Washington, D.C., and borrowed bootleg recordings of a 1981 *River* show and *Born in the U.S.A.,* which hadn't even been released yet. He worked up chord charts for about fifteen songs, then went to New Jersey the next day.

"People ask me to compare playing with Neil Young and Bruce," notes Lofgren, who has recorded and toured extensively with Young. "To me, if you gotta label it, Bruce plays melodic rock & roll—melodies with tough rhythms. His songs are more structured. So it was easy for me to know when to step in and step out. Originally, all I did was cop some of the important guitar parts that Bruce and Steve had done on the records. At least it was something they wrote, and it wouldn't throw anybody. It seemed to be a safe place to start."

Scialfa, a graduate of Asbury Park High School, had in fact auditioned for Springsteen twice previously—before *Born to Run* was released and earlier, when he was leading a big band called Dr. Zoom and the Sonic Boom. But she was thrown straight into the deep end when she joined the tour on five days' notice. She spent the first three weeks singing from "cheat sheets," with the lyrics printed in bold letters and specific cues written in the margins. Her biggest problem onstage, though, was concentrating on her parts with all of that E Street energy whipping around her.

"There was one time where I forgot to sing because I was so absorbed in watching and listening," Scialfa remembers. "But I felt confident inside because Bruce was so confident. I'd try to lock in with him. I'd watch his back, watch him breathe."

The first American leg of the tour totaled ninety-four shows in forty-five cities. It climaxed on January 26th and 27th, 1985, with two concerts at the cavernous Carrier Dome in Syracuse, New York. The crowds there—39,000 people each night—were the largest of Springsteen's career up to that time. They were also a sign of things to come.

For Federici, the first leg was the hardest part of the tour, "because we were doing a lot more one-night stands in real close cities, flying out and playing the next day." But there was little rock & roll backstage monkey business; the entire organization, from Springsteen on down, was a model of efficiency.

"When you go backstage at a Bruce Springsteen show, you don't see a circus," declares Clarence Clemons. "Everybody has a job to do, and everybody goes about it seriously. Bruce instills the moral fiber that runs through the whole organization."

Each of the members of the E Street Band prepared for the evening's work in his or her own quiet way. Clemons, a recent convert to the Indian guru Sri Chinmoy, meditated for about a half hour and received a massage before every show. A few band members warmed up with a game of ping-pong. Backstage guests were usually escorted to a hospitality suite, well stocked with food and drink, where they awaited visits from Springsteen and the band.

It was often an all-star crunch. Elizabeth Taylor, Don Rickles, John McEnroe and Jack Nicholson, with Meryl Streep on his arm, were among the nonrock stars who attended. Royalty included Princess Stephanie and Prince Albert of Monaco, who attended the Paris show, and purple potentate Prince of Minneapolis, who showed up in Clarence Clemons' dressing room there and complimented Clemons' Swedish wife, Christina, on her dress.

Clemons says one of the high points of the tour for him was when Sean Connery, "*the* James Bond, came back and said he really admired me." But did it ever get crazy backstage with all those luminaries jockeying for position? "No," he says serenely, "*we* were the luminaries. They came to our gig."

No one enjoyed those gigs more than the musicians themselves. "Nils said it in a fantastic quote," notes Weinberg. "He said it's like you get up there with Bruce and they've given you four hours to live. And this is your four hours. Now what are you going to do with your time?"

To a man—and woman—the E Streeters agree that out of the approximately 150 shows they performed in 1984 and 1985, they didn't have a single bum night. Led by Springsteen, with a calm assurance born of nearly twenty years at center stage, they displayed a consistency each night that was equal parts technique and telepathy. The "stump the band" aspect of the group's mid-Seventies concerts—when Springsteen would suddenly alter the set in midshow, calling out an old cover or a forgotten LP track—tapered off as the band went into stadiums. "For the sake of projecting to 50,000 people, you needed more structure," claims Weinberg. Yet, while ninety percent of every show ran like clockwork, Springsteen always left an extra ten percent, Lofgren says, "to goof with."

For example, there was the night at Giants Stadium in New Jersey when the band was set to play "I'm on Fire," from *Born in the U.S.A.,* and Springsteen abruptly called out "Fire" instead. At one of the last shows on the tour, Springsteen had finished the last encore when someone in the crowd threw an artificial leg onstage. "A whole leg," recalls Weinberg, marveling. "Bruce picks it up and says, 'We've got to play one more for this guy.' So we all run back to our instruments, but what the hell are we gonna play? Bruce looks at the leg and says, 'Fellas, "Stand on It." ' "

AFTER COMPLETING the U.S. arena tour in Syracuse, the band took a six-week breather during February and March before taking on the rest of the world. Springsteen's international itinerary included spring and summer swings through Britain, Europe and countries like Australia and Japan where the group had never performed before.

But Springsteen's rock & roll gospel of self-respect and emotional lib-eration needed no translation. Japanese, Australian and European audiences easily grasped the universality of his frank, lyric portrayal of the tarnished American dream—the dashed hopes and defiant aspirations. Clarence Clemons was astonished to see young Japanese fans waving American and Japanese flags sewn together during shows there. In Milan, Italy, 60,000 peo-ple sang "My Hometown" with Springsteen while, ironically, an American serviceman near the foot of the stage stood at attention, holding the Stars and Stripes for the entire show.

"You could hear the whole audience singing," Max Weinberg re-members. "The idea of community in rock & roll is never more apparent than when something like that happens. The things we've seen from our vantage point onstage are irreplaceable memories."

"I wish some of the politicians had seen these things," declares Clemons. "Those kids didn't understand the words to 'Born in the U.S.A.,' but they understood what we were singing about. Those things Bruce sings about, attention to self and country, pertain not only to America. They pertain to everybody."

Clemons remembers swooping down in a helicopter over Slane Castle, near Dublin, Ireland, awed by the sight of over 70,000 people gathered there for the band's show. "It wasn't only the sheer volume of numbers, but the sheer volume of harmony and peace. The next day I was in a cab going to the airport, and the driver turned to me and said: 'You were better than the pope. You brought the North and the South together, and there were no fights.' And that's what it's all about. That's why we knock ourselves out."

Audiences responded everywhere. At a race track in Brisbane, Australia, Springsteen asked the crowd to raise their hands in the air during "Twist and Shout." "They were so tightly packed together," says Weinberg, "they couldn't get their hands down. They were standing there in front of us, wav-ing their hands. I felt, 'Wow, this must have been what Beatlemania was like.' They were completely freaking out." The normally reserved Japanese, he adds, "were the best dancers I've ever seen. And they knew all the words."

The decision by Springsteen and his manager, Jon Landau, to play large, outdoor venues, first in Europe and then in the States, was not made lightly. Springsteen worried about the loss of intimacy and the often inferior sound quality at stadium rock shows. "But there was a time when Bruce didn't want to go into arenas because of the same argument," Garry Tallent points out. "We had to take the shot. Some intimacy was lost," he admits, "but something was there to replace it—the event itself. We pulled it off."

To compensate for the increased distance between band and audience, Springsteen doubled the size of his sound system and added giant video screens to broadcast the action onstage to the back rows. Danny Federici says some of the band members also made slight adjustments in their stage wear. "We'd wear more vivid colors so we could be seen. I remember telling Garry, 'That shirt's a little too busy; they won't see you in the back.' We tried to get our clothing together a little bit better, wear more outrageous shirts."

"When you play big places like that, there's a tendency to think that if you jump around a lot, people are going to notice you more," explains Nils Lofgren, a veteran of stadium shows with Neil Young. "But in those places, it doesn't matter, because twenty or thirty rows out you still look like a dot. The best thing for us to do, with the video cameras there, was to do exactly what we normally did—be ourselves and let the cameras pick it up."

Max Weinberg dubbed the U.S. outdoor stadium shows that wound up the tour in September and October the Pestilence Tour. At the Cotton Bowl in Dallas, the band was attacked by a horde of crickets that got in the musicians' hair, on Weinberg's drum kit and even down the back of Springsteen's shirt while he was getting sentimental in "My Hometown." In Philadelphia, the temperature onstage registered 106 degrees. In Denver, the mercury plummeted to 35 degrees, with snow to boot. The weather was fine in Miami; unfortunately, the Orange Bowl there did not have an electrical system adequate for high-volume rock & roll. Diesel generators were brought in to take up the slack and set up behind the stage. Says Weinberg, groaning, "Those fumes were killing us."

Throughout the tour, the Springsteen road crew numbered between thirty and forty members. (By comparison, the Who traveled with a crew of ninety on their 1982 farewell U.S. tour.) The sound, lights and band gear filled nine tractor-trailers; the three separate outdoor stages used for the stadium shows took up another fifteen trucks. Often, while a crew was dismantling a stage in one stadium, Springsteen was performing on a second one in another city and a crew member was overseeing construction of a third stage in the next scheduled venue. Although the crew usually had two days to set up the entire production, they set a record at Giants Stadium when, because of a conflict with a football game there, they put up the stage, sound, lights and instruments in only seventeen hours.

Springsteen probably set a record, quite unintentionally, for breaking female hearts when he married actress and model Julianne Phillips last spring. But the betrothal didn't come as a real surprise to the E Street Band. "Seeing the look in their eyes before they were married reminded me very much of me and my wife, Becky," says Max Weinberg. Clarence Clemons knew it was coming after Springsteen played godfather at the christening of Clemons' third son, Christopher, in Hawaii early last year.

"When he was holding the kid," Clemons recalls, smiling, "I looked into his eyes and thought, 'Well, he's gone.' Two weeks later he called me up and said, 'Big Man, I'm gettin' married.' I said, 'I know.' "

W HEN THE TOUR FINALLY ENDED in Los Angeles last October, Springsteen and the E Street Band felt, in Max Weinberg's words, "incredibly drained but incredibly buzzed." The length of the tour and of the shows themselves had a kind of reverse effect on the band. Charged by the unflagging energy of their leader and their audiences, they actually thrived on the physical and psychological demands made on them.

"Of course, you get exhausted," admits Clemons. "You want to pass out. I came close a couple of times. But you're filled with something, that feedback that comes from the audience. You feel so strong that if somebody shot you with a gun you could keep going."

Everybody has settled down in recent months, at least for the time being. While Springsteen enjoys married life at his home in Rumson, New Jersey, the members of the E Street Band are using their extended vacation to indulge their own interests. Both Clemons and Nils Lofgren managed to squeeze recording sessions into tour breaks last year that resulted in solo albums—Lofgren's lively rock-out *Flip* and Clemons' ebullient pop outing *Hero*. Spurred by the Top Twenty success of his duet with Jackson Browne, "You're a Friend of Mine," Clemons will be taking most of his *Hero* studio band on the road for a summer tour. The Big Man may also take up a large chunk of your television screen; he's in the running for future guest-star roles in *Hill Street Blues* and *Miami Vice*. But in keeping with his spiritual rebirth, he insists, "I'll never do a role I wouldn't want my guru to see. I won't be a coke dealer, I won't be a pimp."

Lofgren recently spent a working holiday at Neil Young's ranch in northern California, writing material for a solo album to be recorded by spring. He is a permanent member of the E Street Band, though. "I didn't want to be a gun for hire for eighteen months. I'll be there whenever they play."

Patti Scialfa is shopping a demo tape of original material. She wants to release an album this summer. Danny Federici bought a house in his old home town of Flemington, New Jersey; an electronics enthusiast, he installed a recording studio where he composes instrumental music—for television soundtracks, he hopes. Garry Tallent has ambitions in record producing. He just finished production on a charity-rock single by Jersey Artists for Mankind (JAM), featuring Southside Johnny, assorted Jukes, jazz guitarist Tal Farlow and Nils Lofgren.

Roy Bittan continues to do sessions, and Max Weinberg worked as both drummer and mixing assistant of the debut album of highly touted Philly rocker John Eddie. Weinberg, who published a book called *The Big Beat,* a collection of interviews he conducted with great rock drummers, is also touring as a solo act—on the college lecture circuit, talking about both his drumming and life with you-know-who.

But Springsteen only has to nod his head and everyone will jump back to E Street again. At a New Year's Eve party for the band at his home, Springsteen suggested getting together periodically for jam sessions, hinting that he already had some new material ready. "There isn't anybody in the E Street Band who wouldn't immediately drop what they're doing," declares Weinberg. In fact, they were all very sorry to see the tour end.

"On the last night, I cried," Weinberg admits. "There's a video clip that I saw on *Entertainment Tonight.* We were all lined up, and I can see tears in my eyes. I can see tears in everybody's eyes. When Bruce was singing 'Glory Days' and he turned around and said the line, 'Boys, we're going home now,' it really struck home."

1985 MUSIC AWARDS

FEBRUARY 27, 1986

ARTIST OF THE YEAR
Bruce Springsteen
Phil Collins
Sting
Bob Geldof
Madonna

SINGLE OF THE YEAR
"Money for Nothing"—Dire
    Straits
"We Are the World"—USA for
    Africa
**"Glory Days"—Bruce
    Springsteen**
"Shout"—Tears for Fears
"Sun City"—Artists United
    Against Apartheid

BAND OF THE YEAR
U2
Dire Straits
The E Street Band
Tears for Fears
Talking Heads

BEST MALE SINGER
Bruce Springsteen
Sting
Phil Collins
Bono
Paul Young

VIDEO OF THE YEAR
"Take on Me"—A-ha
"Money for Nothing"—Dire
    Straits

**"Glory Days"—Bruce
    Springsteen**
"Don't Come Around Here No
    More"—Tom Petty and the
    Heartbreakers
"Sun City"—Artists United Against
    Apartheid

BEST SONGWRITER
Bruce Springsteen
Sting
Phil Collins
Mark Knopfler
Bono

BEST-DRESSED MALE
David Bowie
Sting
Bruce Springsteen
Prince
Phil Collins

BEST DRUMMER
Phil Collins
Tony Thompson (the Power Station)
**Max Weinberg (the E Street
    Band)**
Larry Mullen Jr. (U2)
Neil Peart (Rush)

BEST BASS PLAYER
John Taylor
Sting
Adam Clayton (U2)
Garry Tallent (the E Street Band)
Geddy Lee (Rush)

BEST LIVE PERFORMANCE
**Bruce Springsteen and the E
    Street Band**
U2
Tina Turner
Prince and the Revolution
Sting

WORST-DRESSED MALE
Prince
David Lee Roth
Dee Snider
Bruce Springsteen
Boy George

SEXIEST MALE ROCK ARTIST
Bruce Springsteen
Sting
George Michael
Paul Young
Prince

**BEST KEYBOARD
    PLAYER**
Howard Jones
Nick Rhodes (Duran Duran)
Stevie Wonder
**Roy Bittan (the E Street
    Band)**
Billy Joel

ARTIST OF THE YEAR
Bruce Springsteen
Bob Geldof (tie)

BAND OF THE YEAR
The E Street Band
U2 (tie)

BEST MALE SINGER
Bruce Springsteen

BEST LIVE PERFORMANCE
**Bruce Springsteen and
    the E Street Band**

KURT LODER

LIVE SPRINGSTEEN!
Five-Record Set Due This Fall

I

T'S OFFICIAL: BRUCE SPRINGSTEEN will be back in the record racks—and back onstage, too—before Thanksgiving. Within the next few weeks, Columbia Records will release *Bruce Springsteen & the E Street Band Live/1975–85,* a collection of in-concert performances—and the long-awaited answer to many a Springsteen fan's dreams—in a boxed set in three formats: five LP discs, three cassettes and three CDs. All will be accompanied by a thirty-six-page booklet.

The material will span Springsteen's recording career and will include, for the first time on a nonbootleg release, his versions of "Fire" and "Because the Night" (originally written for Robert Gordon and Patti Smith) and the powerful concert renditions of "Born to Run," "Hungry Heart" and the memorable show opener "Born in the U.S.A." In all, there will be some forty tracks; the retail price had not been decided at press time.

A live Springsteen album has always seemed a natural ploy for such an acclaimed concert performer, but Springsteen has resisted the notion for thirteen years. He only began considering the possibility at the end of his last tour, in October 1985. What is presumably a vast backlog of concert tapes was subsequently audited, edited and digitally mixed and mastered at studios in Los Angeles and New York. Some of the tracks reportedly date back to Springsteen's club days. No new material will be included, and there will be no accompanying videos, either short or long form.

There will, however, be Springsteen in the flesh. On Monday, October 13th, Bruce will join with Neil Young, Don Henley, Tom Petty, Nils Lofgren and comic Robin Williams for an all-acoustic benefit concert at the Shoreline Amphitheatre, promoter Bill Graham's 15,000-capacity venue in Mountain View, California, forty minutes south of San Francisco. Proceeds from the concert, organized by Young's wife, Pegi, will go to the Bridge School, a Bay Area organization involved in the education of handicapped children. (The Youngs' eight-year-old son suffers from cerebral palsy.) The show, produced by Graham, will consist of brief sets—twenty to twenty-five minutes—by each of the artists. Tickets, at twenty-one dollars each, were briefly available by mail until September 22nd; a Shoreline spokeswoman doubted that any would be left for box-office sale on the day of the event.

MICHAEL GOLDBERG

THE SPRINGSTEEN CHRISTMAS
Initial Orders for Live Five-Record Compilation Top the Million Mark

AT PRESS TIME, record retailers around the country were predicting that *Bruce Springsteen & the E Street Band Live/1975–85* would generate the biggest volume in preorders, in terms of dollars, of any LP in history. Columbia Records, Springsteen's label, was planning to ship more than 1.5 million copies of the five-album boxed set, and the company has reportedly stockpiled an additional 2 million copies so it will be able to quickly fill reorders. At a cost of approximately nineteen dollars per set to retailers, the album has already brought in nearly $30 million in preorders.

From the moment the album's November 10th release was announced, executives at record chains have been raving about its sales potential, proclaiming it the "ultimate Christmas gift." Reminiscing about the days when the Beatles would release a highly anticipated album just before Christmas, Tower Records president Russ Solomon called the Springsteen set "this year's Beatles album."

To sell the record—which is expected to carry a retail price of between twenty-five and thirty-five dollars—Columbia has orchestrated a major advertising and merchandising campaign that ad directors at several major labels estimate could cost the company as much as $2 million or $3 million. During Thanksgiving weekend alone, Columbia hopes to reach "40 to 50 million consumers." Columbia wouldn't comment on what it's spending, but the company did note that TV-ad buys on *Late Night With David Letterman* and the *Today* show mark "the first time CBS has ever used national network TV to advertise a release."

A full-color, four-page "marketing overview" noting various "selling points" was sent to record stores nationwide. "All told, [the album] represents the definitive performance package from the ultimate American rock & roll performer," reads the text. "As a result, you can count on it being *the* biggest holiday gift of 1986, as well as the major release throughout 1987."

The set includes a thirty-six-page booklet of photographs and song lyrics; the forty songs, which run three hours and twenty minutes, cover

Springsteen's entire career. Columbia is also releasing a single from the set—Springsteen's cover of Edwin Starr's 1970 hit "War." (The flip side will be a 1980 live performance of "Merry Christmas Baby," a Charles Brown classic also recorded by Elvis Presley and Otis Redding.) A video of the single, which will include some live footage and may in some way underline the antiwar message of the song, is set to be released before Christmas.

W HEN BRUCE SPRINGSTEEN ended his 1984–85 world tour, he had no intention of releasing a live album. In fact, he had no intention of doing anything other than just unwinding after a triumphant but grueling few years of recording and touring. While relaxing, he began listening to live tapes, rough mixes from the just-completed tour. Soon, a source close to Springsteen indicates, he realized that "an album could be made that, in addition to being a retrospective, would be both something very forward-looking—and a unique and personal statement."

No more than six weeks after the tour ended, Springsteen began to seriously consider releasing a live album. By January of this year, Springsteen and his manager, Jon Landau, got together and acknowledged that they were, in fact, making a record. Along with coproducer Chuck Plotkin, they reviewed and analyzed more than thirty three-and-a-half-hour live shows, dating from 1975 club dates at the Roxy in Los Angeles to the concluding outdoor stadium performance of the 1984–85 tour at the L.A. Coliseum. There were, for example, thirty versions of "Rosalita (Come Out Tonight)" to choose from; they settled on a 1978 version from the Roxy because it sounded the freshest, the most authentic.

By early March, they had the songs and the running order—five and a half records' worth of material. (One song that didn't make the final edit is a ten-minute version of "Incident on 57th Street," which will be released in England as the B side of the "War" twelve-inch.) Springsteen spent April and May in the studio—at both the Record Factory in Los Angeles and the Hit Factory in New York—reviewing master tapes and doing what one source called an "incidental and negligible amount of overdubbing."

Beginning in June, Springsteen, Landau and Plotkin spent ten weeks working with Bob Clearmountain, who mixed the collection at the Right Track studio in New York. They finished in early October, one year after Springsteen first began listening to the live material—and just in time to prepare for the Bridge School benefit concert that he'd agreed to play in California.

The album opens with an acoustic version of "Thunder Road" from 1975 and closes with "Jersey Girl" from the Born in the U.S.A. Tour. Almost all of the songs on the album have already been released in studio versions, the only exceptions being "War," "Fire," "Seeds," "This Land Is Your Land," "Because the Night," "Paradise by the 'C,' " "Raise Your Hand" and "Jersey Girl" (a live version of "Jersey Girl" did appear as the B side of Springsteen's "Cover Me" single). Such unreleased Springsteen originals as "Rendezvous," "The Promise" and "Don't Look Back" aren't on the album, nor are most of the more than 100 cover tunes he's performed over the last decade—like the Beatles' "Twist and Shout," Mitch Ryder's "Devil With a Blue Dress On/Good Golly Miss Molly," Gary "U.S." Bonds's "Quarter to Three" and John Fogerty's "Rockin' All over the World."

Unlike Springsteen's live shows, the album does not conclude with a high-energy rock & roll medley of cover songs. "He wanted to ease out of the record a little more focused on the content and emotion, rather than going for the total excitement thing," said the source. " 'Jersey Girl' felt like a better ending to the record than 'Twist and Shout.' "

For those involved in making the album, it was an intense nine months of work. "One of the things that happens when you work for Bruce, you go down—as if in a submarine—for a period of time, and when you resurface, you realize that you've let the rest of your life go to seed," says Chuck Plotkin. "Whenever I've finished working on a project, it takes six to eight weeks to regain my bearing. My tax returns are always late. I'm scrambling around to pay my bills. I get home from New York, and the phone's been shut off, the gas doesn't work. We worked hard."

But Plotkin felt the effort was worth it. "Someone hears Bruce is doing a live record," he says. "Is there any way for it not to be disappointing, really, given the level of expectation that one has to have? Yet the only thing I can tell you for sure—the damn thing is *not* disappointing!"

DAVID FRICKE

BRUCE SPRINGSTEEN & THE E STREET BAND LIVE/1975—85 ALBUM REVIEW

Bruce Looks Down the Long Road

I**T'S NOT ENOUGH.** By anyone else's standards, of course, *Bruce Spring-steen & the E Street Band Live/1975—85* is an embarrassment of riches—five albums and ten years' worth of barroom, hockey-arena and baseball-stadium dynamite; greatest hits, ace covers, love songs, work songs, out-of-work songs—the ultimate rock-concert experience of the past decade finally packaged for living-room consumption, a special gift of thanks to the fans who shared those 1,001 nights of stomp and sweat and the best possible consolation prize for the poor bastards who could never get tickets.

Still, Bruce Springsteen could have filled another five-record set with what's missing from this one. Particularly conspicuous in their absence are still-unreleased gems like "The Fever" and "Rendezvous," as well as vintage showstoppers like "Jungleland" and "Kitty's Back," a song that used to inspire lengthy E Street flights of hot jazz fancy in its mid-Seventies heyday. It is also a little disappointing that Springsteen has not included any recordings from the blazing five-alarm shows of 1973 and '74 that led the critic Jon Landau, later his manager, to write the infamous, ultimately prophetic line: "I saw rock & roll future and its name is Bruce Springsteen." Instead, this boxed set starts in 1975 with the Born to Run tour, when the "future" had already arrived on wings of rueful media hype.

Regrettably, *Live/1975—85* has been dropped in our laps with the same attendant hysteria. But minor caveats about content aside, it's going to take more than cheap overkill, like all-Bruce radio and *USA Today*'s ludicrous Elvis-versus-Bruce readers poll, to eclipse the sheer physical wallop of *Live/1975—85* and the spectral wonder of its forty songs, not to mention the incomparable charisma of the singer. If nothing else, this set is an extraordinary demonstration of how Springsteen's telepathic command of a concert audience has increased in direct proportion to the size of his stage. In his rousing cover of Eddie Floyd's 1967 Stax hit "Raise Your Hand," an encore recorded at the Roxy, in Los Angeles, in 1978, Springsteen doesn't just ask for a show of hands—he *demands* it. "You think this is a free ride?" he bellows before giving the crowd one last blast. "You want to play, you got to pay!" Six years later, in a big New Jersey arena, he strips "No Surrender" to its naked, valiant core, backed by just guitar, harmonica and the massed hush of 20,000 people holding their breath.

Loosely chronological in structure, this set also charts the evolution of Springsteen's lyric themes from early Great Escape anthems ("Growin' Up," "Thunder Road") to the macrocosmic resonance of *Born in the U.S.A.,* with its gritty telegraphic novellas of average Joes and Josephines up against a wall of irrevocable economic change and eroding social values. At the same time, this *Bruceograph*-style overview plots his corresponding progression from fanciful, often mischievous overarranging—the revved-up boardwalk baroque of "Rosalita (Come Out Tonight)"—to the knuckle-sandwich sound of "Cover Me" and the previously unreleased "Seeds." By the time he took the big leap into outdoor stadiums in 1985, documented with heady 3-D frenzy on sides seven through ten, Springsteen was having no trouble zapping fans half a mile away with his short-story rock & soul.

To be sure, the '78 Roxy version of "Spirit in the Night," the most enduring of Springsteen's florid love-and-wheels narratives, is certainly a cracker, distinguished by Max Weinberg's drop-kick drumming and Clarence Clemons's lusty foghorn sax. Yet "Racing in the Street," Springsteen's grim *Darkness* portrait of a generation racing to a dead end, draws its power from a deeper well, palpably accelerating with pensive desperation as Danny Federici's sorrowful organ clouds over Roy Bittan's ballerina piano figure. And any idiot who still believes "Born in the U.S.A." is all stars and stripes will definitely get baked by the fiery rage and sense of utter betrayal at its core, vividly illustrated by Springsteen's rockets'-red-glare guitar solo and the atomic E Street crescendo that detonates the theme's climactic reprise.

In some instances, it's the little details and subtle flourishes on *Live/1975–85* that bring Springsteen's vision to life. He practically scrapes the pit of his desire with a gravelly, almost laryngitic vocal on the '75 Roxy version of "Thunder Road" ("Roy Orbison singing for the lonely / Hey that's me and I want you only"), accompanied only by piano and the delicate tingle of Federici's glockenspiel. His solo rendition of Woody Guthrie's "This Land Is Your Land," taken at a slower, more thoughtful pace, amplifies not only Guthrie's fierce democratic pride but also the song's unspoken promise of a brighter future ("And a voice was sounding / As the fog was lifting / Saying this land was made for you and me"). And although it doesn't have any words, the quickie instrumental "Paradise by the 'C,' " with its R&B bluster and frat-rock sass, speaks volumes about Springsteen's pre-glory days in North Jersey seaside clubs. It doesn't take much to imagine the crowd at the old Upstage in Asbury Park tanking up to this one.

Two of the album's finest moments aren't even musical. Springsteen's opening rap to "The River," delivered over a twelve-string guitar reverie by Nils Lofgren, is a poignant ramble about his father—the tensions, the petty disagreements and, ultimately, the reconciliation. With "War," however, Springsteen gets right to the point, dedicating it to the post-Vietnam kids in the crowd ("The next time they're gonna be lookin' at you") before leading the E Street Band into an explosive reading of the 1970 Edwin Starr hit with his best tonsil-ripping yell and plenty of spitfire guitar.

All this and—finally!—"Because the Night" and "Fire," too. *Live/1975–85* could have done with a few less *Born in the U.S.A.* numbers— eight of the album's twelve songs are reprised here—and maybe a few more covers, particularly Springsteen's highly personalized renditions of the Animals' "We Gotta Get Out of This Place" and Bob Dylan's "I Want You." But it seems churlish to carp about titles when there is so much raw power, lyric honesty and spiritual determination packed into this box. For best results, just pretend you're at the foot of the stage. Then, as Springsteen instructs in "Spirit in the Night," "stand up and let it shoot right through you."

ANTHONY DeCURTIS

1986 MUSIC AWARDS: ARTIST OF THE YEAR

A Record 19,000 Readers Vote, and Their Choice Is Bruce

FOR THE THIRD CONSECUTIVE YEAR, and for the sixth time in nine years, ROLLING STONE's readers have voted Bruce Springsteen Artist of the Year—an extraordinary index of how deeply Springsteen has penetrated American culture and the souls of his fans. After all, Springsteen was virtually invisible through most of 1986. He made a single live appearance, at a benefit concert in California for handicapped children, and gave no interviews. His last album of new songs, *Born in the U.S.A.*, was released nearly three years ago.

Still, as everyone knows, the *Bruce Springsteen & the E Street Band Live/1975–85* boxed set dominated record sales, radio play and the lives of rock cognoscenti for the last two months of 1986. From any other living artist, such a set would have seemed close to the ultimate cynical gesture: an expensive multialbum collection of greatest hits, recorded live and released around Christmas time for maximum commercial impact; a set that contained only one new song and a smattering of predictable covers (a Motown tune, a Stax/Volt song, a folk chestnut, a feeling singer-songwriter finale); the perfect way to follow up and cash in on the biggest-selling record of his career.

But from Springsteen it was a masterful triumph—not merely the performance album anticipated from the earliest "you gotta see him live" days of his recording career and foreshadowed in hundreds of cherished bootlegs, but the celebration of his attaining the heights his ambition always demanded that he strive for. This Artist of the Year award is his fans' confirmation that Springsteen deserves this stature—it's a lifetime-achievement award, really, a resounding thank-you.

But Springsteen's career, let alone his lifetime, isn't nearly over, and the question that shadows the success of *Live/1975–85* is "Where does he go from here?" With characteristic go-for-broke determination, his unfailing instinct for upping the ante at every crucial turn, Springsteen has brought himself face to face with this question. The scope of *Live/1975–85,* which starts with the national breakout of the *Born to Run* tour and ends with *Born in the U.S.A.*'s national conquest, defines a full ten-year period as the era of Bruce Springsteen—and simultaneously declares an end to that era. The slate swept clean, anything less than a dramatic new beginning would be worse than anticlimactic. It would be a failure to meet his own challenge, the be- trayal of his promise to himself.

Meeting the challenge and delivering on the promise, however, are complicated by the enormous, and enormously divergent, expectations Springsteen's audience has of him. Like every artist who has attained suc- cess on such a massive scale—Elvis Presley and Michael Jackson represent other vivid examples—Springsteen embodies a plethora of contradictions. In the public's eye, he is both easygoing and fiercely aspiring, both an or- dinary working-class guy and a multimillionaire. He inspires millions of fans to feel an intense personal relationship with him, but he is, in fact, insulated and remote. He is rarely seen in public, virtually never speaks to the media and releases albums infrequently. He is both a rebel and a patriot, claimed by the political left and right. He is life-size and larger than life.

Similar contradictions inform the public's perception and understand- ing of Springsteen's music. The basic meanings of Springsteen's songs seem clear, but somehow those meanings double back on themselves in troubling ways. In song after song, Springsteen demands that his characters, and by extension his listeners, "show a little faith," believe in themselves, dare to hope and struggle and win. As a corollary to this, he displays a profound, unpatronizing compassion for people whose circumstances make the achievement of such faith unbearably difficult. According to Springsteen's values, nobody should have to be a hero just to lead a decent life—and lead- ing a decent life is its own kind of heroism.

But in a society that dangles the prospect of upward mobility as one of its more intoxicating opiates, Springsteen's idealistic calls to raise yourself up are easily—perhaps even willfully—misread. For a disturbingly large portion of Springsteen's audience—particularly among the gang that signed on in the wake of *Born in the U.S.A.*—spitting in the face of these badlands means something like "going for it" or "getting yours." Pulling out of here to win means going where the action is hotter in order to score that BMW or close that key real-estate deal. Distortions like these—along with Spring- steen's own miscues, like using the American flag as a stage backdrop— account for the otherwise puzzling attraction Springsteen holds for youth- ful, and not so youthful, conservatives.

After the grand summary statement of *Live/1975–85,* Springsteen is looking squarely down the double barrel of these contradictions, which he has so far been content to hold in tense suspension rather than force to resolution. Unlike such artists as Bob Dylan, Talking Heads and David Bowie, Springsteen has followed the populist path of building his career by steadily expanding his audience—not by shedding some fans and adding new ones with each successive album release. Inclusiveness is at the heart of his vision; breaking with any portion of his audience will not come easily or naturally to him. But the political bite of "Seeds," the only new song on the five-LP set; the pointed stage rap that precedes the "War" single and video; and the very choice of "War" as a single suggest that Springsteen is presenting a sterner challenge to many of his followers.

Springsteen's elaborate, Spectorian sound has become increasingly streamlined; it has been honed to such a fine compactness that it's hard to imagine how it could change in any significant way without seeming forced. But if Springsteen should decide it's time for a change, will he want the E Street Band to accompany him? Will the band members, who have projects of their own under way, want to stick around for the Sturm und Drang of launching the next stage of the Springsteen saga? And if the music should change, will Springsteen's fans, many of whom display an irritating resistance to new sounds and seem insistent on becoming the Deadheads of the Eighties, be receptive to it?

Whenever he's been on the spot in the past, Springsteen has always found a way to rise to the occasion. Questioning has dogged him all down the line, not only from doubters but also from worried, ultimately hopeful supporters. Could he ever be more than a Northeast regional artist? Could he ever make an album to match his live shows? Would he be able to follow up *Born to Run?* Could he come back after being hyped too much too soon, or after his excruciating management and legal problems? Springsteen has ridden roughshod over every one of those questions with brilliant records, committed performances and the sheer force of his personality.

But never before has there been so much belief and so many hungry hearts at stake. It's exhilarating and a little frightening. Given Springsteen's recording history, it is unlikely that he'll release a new album in 1987. What appears more certain is that the next time the 1986 Artist of the Year issues the invitation to "climb in," not everybody will be going along for the ride. And for the career of Springsteen the artist, not the media projection or the fantasy figure, that may be a good thing.

1986 MUSIC AWARDS

FEBRUARY 26, 1987

READERS PICKS

ARTIST OF THE YEAR
Bruce Springsteen
Peter Gabriel
Phil Collins
Madonna
Steve Winwood

ALBUM OF THE YEAR
Bruce Springsteen & the E Street Band Live/1975–1985—Bruce Springsteen
5150—Van Halen
So—Peter Gabriel
Lifes Rich Pageant—R.E.M.
Invisible Touch—Genesis

BEST BAND
Genesis
Van Halen
R.E.M.
The E Street Band
U2

BEST MALE SINGER
Peter Gabriel
Bruce Springsteen
Phil Collins
Steve Winwood
Robert Palmer

BEST SONGWRITER
Phil Collins
Billy Joel
Paul Simon
Bruce Springsteen
Holly Knight

BEST REISSUE ALBUM ARTIST
Then and Now . . . The Best of the Monkees—the Monkees
Every Breath You Take: The Singles—the Police
Bruce Springsteen & the E Street Band Live/1975–85—Bruce Springsteen and the E Street Band

BEST ALBUM COVER
Eat 'Em and Smile—David Lee Roth
Third Stage—Boston
5150—Van Halen
True Blue—Madonna
Bruce Springsteen and the E Street Band Live/1975–85—Bruce Springsteen and the E Street Band

BEST LIVE PERFORMANCE
Bruce Springsteen and the E Street Band
Genesis
Van Halen
U2
R.E.M.

WORST DRESSED MALE ROCK ARTIST
David Lee Roth
Prince
Billy Idol
Elton John
Bruce Springsteen

SEXIEST MALE ROCK ARTIST
Bruce Springsteen
Jon Bon Jovi
David Lee Roth
Sting
Don Johnson

ANTHONY DeCURTIS

NO HOME-VIDEO RELEASE LIKELY FOR SPRINGSTEEN FOOTAGE

THE VIDEO DIRECTOR FOR BRUCE SPRINGSTEEN'S Born in the U.S.A. Tour is currently editing and cataloging material from the tour, including a selection of some forty songs from four shows at Giants Stadium, in New Jersey, and four shows at the Los Angeles Memorial Coliseum. A spokesperson for Springsteen, however, insists that the artist has "absolutely no plans" to release a live-concert home videotape.

Arthur Rosato—who directed the videos for "My Hometown" and "War" and edited the video for "Fire"—taped performances by Springsteen and the E Street Band in Australia, Europe and the U.S. during the Born in the U.S.A. Tour. Since the tour ended in Los Angeles on October 2nd, 1985, he's been working with the footage he gathered, using the New Jersey facilities of NFL Films. "My job, now that the tour's over, is to go through and catalog everything," Rosato says. "I've been editing stuff, just so that it makes sense to them, and I show it to them as we go along. As for the future, they could release something tomorrow if they decided."

Video footage of the sort that Rosato is compiling comes in handy for recording artists, even when no commercial compilation is released. As with "War" and "My Hometown," live material can always be used to promote singles, and news programs, documentaries and other types of programming frequently make use of live tapes provided by artists or their management. Rosato also points out that Springsteen has been taped and filmed on other tours. "It's just that right now it's more noticeable," he says. "People want to know what's going on more."

Rosato, who has filmed artists on tour for about twelve years and has done a great deal of work for Bob Dylan, says that Springsteen's management company, Jon Landau Management, will occasionally contact him and ask to see specific songs and that he sometimes sends Landau a particular performance that he finds interesting.

"It's like home movies. In general, if you know the way Bruce oper-ates—you can see with his five-record set, it took him ten years to come out with some of that stuff," Rosato says. "There's nothing that I know is imminent."

MICHAEL GOLDBERG

BRUCE LIVE SET SLIPS

CBS Creates Program to Deal With
Returns of the Bruce Albums

CLOSE TO THREE-QUARTERS OF A MILLION COPIES of Bruce Springsteen's highly touted five-disc album, *Bruce Springsteen & the E Street Band Live/1975–85,* are beginning to gather dust at record stores around the country. More than 3 million copies of the best-selling boxed set in history have already been purchased in the United States, but recently sales have slumped dramatically. During March and April, the album dropped from Number 43 to Number 104 on *Billboard*'s Top Pop Albums chart. Russ Solomon, the president of the Tower Records chain, says the set "went up like a skyrocket and came down about as fast."

Worried that panicky retailers would try to return massive numbers of the album (the estimated 700,000 unsold Springsteen sets represent a potential loss of about $14 million), CBS Records has placed an indefinite moratorium on returns. But in an attempt to keep retailers happy, CBS has extended credit to the record stores equal to the number of sets on their shelves and will not bill them for those albums until October. CBS is obviously hoping that the sets will sell in the next six months if they remain in the stores.

Some retailers say that in an attempt to revive consumer interest in the set, CBS is planning a new marketing strategy that will capitalize on upcoming Springsteen projects, including a rumored long-form live video, a TV special with interview and live-performance footage and a possible tour. Springsteen's management denies plans for a tour or long-form video but says that a TV special remains a possibility.

"[CBS] is trying to get themselves in a position where they'll be able to come back with it [the album] next [holiday] season and have as successful an item as they did last year," says Mario DeFilippo, the vice-president of purchasing for Handleman Company, the nation's largest record rack jobber.

Despite all of the media hoopla surrounding its release, the set has not sold as well as expected. It apparently appealed to a hard-core Springsteen audience of about 3 million fans. So far, of the two singles released from the set, only "War" was a substantial hit. "Fire" stalled before reaching the Top Forty—the first Springsteen single to miss the Top Forty since "Badlands," in 1978. They seemed to have done little to broaden the appeal of the album. By contrast, *Born in the U.S.A.*, which generated seven hit singles, has sold over 10.5 million copies in the United States.

Still, several major retailers believe that the set can be a big seller for them this Christmas. "A lot of fans will have worn the record out," says Tower executive Stan Goman. "They'll want to get another copy for Christmas."

DAVID FRICKE

THE 20 GREATEST CONCERTS: BRUCE SPRINGSTEEN AND THE E STREET BAND

The Bottom Line, New York City, August 13th–17th, 1975

A S PART OF ITS TWENTIETH-ANNIVERSARY CELEBRATION, ROLLING STONE commemorated the greatest live rock performances of the last two decades. ROLLING STONE editors' criteria: "the most exciting, musically outstanding and historically significant concerts." According to David Fricke, "Our selection highlights the lasting impact and pivotal artistic contributions of the musicians . . . captured in their finest performances."

F OR FIVE NIGHTS DURING THE SUMMER OF 1975, the ultimate rock & roll bar band played in the ultimate bar. More than 5,000 people passed through the doors of New York's Bottom Line to see Bruce Springsteen and the E Street Band over the course of their ten shows there that week. Of those, at least 1000 were record-company executives, radio programmers, retail salesmen and critics waiting to see if this boardwalk bard and his gang of road warriors measured up to the advance hype. Another half a million or so fans in the tri-state area heard the early show on the third night broadcast live on WNEW-FM.

Never had so much expectation been crammed into such a tiny space. And for Springsteen, an East Coast cult hero who had yet to get within shouting distance of the Top Ten, the stakes were never higher. The year before, critic Jon Landau had hailed the New Jersey singer-songwriter as "rock & roll future." (Landau later became Springsteen's manager.) Yet with three years of hard gigging behind him and *Born to Run* about to hit the stores, Springsteen knew the August 13th–17th Bottom Line stand was his big chance to prove to the industry, the pen pushers and the fans that he was primed for conquest here and now. "It was our big chance to crack it," says E Street sax man Clarence Clemons. "We were right on the verge. If we had flopped at the Bottom Line, it would have been very detrimental to us emotionally.

"But we were pretty well locked into what we were doing," he says. "We knew what we wanted, and we knew that we were good. And this was our chance to shine, to show the world we were ready."

THE WORLD, HOWEVER, WAS NOT PREPARED for the jubilant energy, taut drama and emotional resonance of Springsteen's turnpike adventures and tenement operas. WNEW DJ Dave Herman admits going to the band's opening night at the Bottom Line with a real "show me" attitude. All doubt evaporated as soon as Springsteen sat down at the piano and uncorked a stark, poignant solo version of "Thunder Road." "The intensity of this man at the piano was overwhelming," Herman says. "I'd never seen a standing ovation for an opening number before." Then the E Street Band kicked in, and Springsteen started dancing on the tables. "Within fifteen minutes," Herman says, "I realized I'd never seen anything like this before." The next morning, he publicly apologized over the air for ignoring Springsteen's talent for so long.

The way Springsteen worked that tiny room, climbing on top of Roy Bittan's piano and whirling around the two big columns on either side of the stage, was wonder enough. But as Dave Marsh wrote in his original ROLLING STONE review of the shows, Springsteen was "the living culmination of twenty years of rock & roll tradition." From the rousing covers of Jackie DeShannon's "When You Walk in the Room" and Gary "U.S." Bond's "Quarter to Three" to the seashore melancholy of "4th of July, Asbury Park (Sandy)" and the highway roar of "Born to Run," Springsteen and the E Street Band wrapped up the troubles and dreams of every rock & roll generation, and the result was an unforgettable celebration of love and hope.

Considering how much he had riding on the Bottom Line engagement, Springsteen showed no signs of panic going into the shows. "If he did feel some anxiety, he never let it show," Clemons says. "You always saw the strong leader in him, and you knew what you had to do. You knew you had to be sharp just to keep up with him."

"If anything, I think we might have attacked the songs a little too hard to begin with," organist Danny Federici says, "because we were so over-anxious to get out there and do our best."

"When we'd come out and slam into 'Spirit in the Night,' you really had to be dead not to get into it," says drummer Max Weinberg. "It was just overwhelming. My heart would begin to beat so fast. I would get so psyched up, the adrenalin would start to pump in the anticipation of playing. We hit the stage and blew the people back in their chairs. Once we did that, it was our audience."

"The first night was great because of the impact that show had," Clemons says. "But after that, it started to get better, and by the third night it was really starting to show in that confinement. We would have killed them if we'd stayed at the club any longer."

The ten Bottom Line shows, which averaged two hours apiece, took their toll even on the superhuman E Street Band. Weinberg says the whole group was sick the next week in Atlanta. But the reward was not long in coming. *Born to Run* quickly went gold, and *Time* and *Newsweek* ran simultaneous cover stories. Anyone who didn't know Bruce Springsteen's name before he played the Bottom Line couldn't help knowing it soon after.

Indeed, Dave Herman was so excited the night of WNEW's broadcast that he couldn't even say the star performer's name correctly. Herman, who was doing the station's backstage play-by-play, says Springsteen was so wired after the last encore that he "was jumping up and down like a prizefighter after a big win, punching the air with both hands." Then Springsteen went into his dressing room, where there was a radio tuned in to the broadcast.

"In all of my excitement," says Herman, "over the air I said, 'Bruce Spring*street* and the E *Steen* Band.' He opened the door, jumped out and said, laughing, 'Gimme a break! Gimme a break! At least get the name right!' "

■ RANDOM NOTES (June 4, 1987)

What do you do on a Sunday night in Asbury Park, New Jersey? If you head over to the Stone Pony bar, you can catch Cats on a Smooth Surface playing their regular gig. And if you're as lucky as a couple hundred Garden Staters were recently, you may catch a bit of rock & roll history. On April 12th, Bruce Springsteen and most of the E Street Band (except for Clarence Clemons and Nils Lofgren) took the stage just before the midnight hour. They rolled through a sweaty hour-plus set of originals ("Light of Day," "Stand on It," "Darlington County," "My Hometown" and "Glory Days") and golden oldies ("Lucille," "Carol," "Wooly Bully" and "Twist and Shout"). After *that,* the Boss told the crowd, "Don't leave yet." Turns out Jon Bon Jovi was lurking in the wings. He joined Springsteen for a rendition of "Kansas City," then Jon and his guitarist, Richie Sambora, and his drummer, Tico Torres, tackled Tom Petty's "Breakdown." According to Stone Pony regular Kerry Layton, a very good time was had by all—"for the bargain price of four bucks!"

■ RANDOM NOTES (July 16–30, 1987)

Bruce Springsteen has been busily recording in Los Angeles, and among the songs he's been working on are some country-tinged tunes. Springsteen called on steel guitarist Jay Dee Maness, a Nashville studio veteran and a member of Chris Hillman's Desert Rose Band, to help out. Evidently, Springsteen "is recording a lot of different things, some country and some not," according to one source. "He told Jay Dee he was going to record the kind of album he wanted to do and take his time." Harp player Jimmie Wood and violinist Richard Greene have also joined in Springsteen's sessions.

THE TOP 100:
THE BEST ALBUMS OF THE
LAST TWENTY YEARS

IN 1987, ROLLING STONE ASKED seventeen rock writers to submit nominations for the 100 greatest albums of the last twenty years—albums initially released between 1967 and 1987. Five of Bruce Springsteen's LPs made the cut.

#8 Born to Run

Born to Run wasn't the album that proved Bruce Springsteen was a classic rocker; to anybody who was listening, *The Wild, the Innocent & the E Street Shuffle* had already done so two years earlier. But *Born to Run* was the record that demanded that *everybody* who cared about rock & roll come to terms with a scruffy twenty-six-year-old from the Jersey shore. Bold, grandiose, melodramatic and inescapably powerful, it was an oversize record that caused an oversize reaction: rave reviews, sold-out concerts, even Springsteen's simultaneous appearance on the covers of *Time* and *Newsweek*.

Song for song, *Born to Run* may not be Springsteen's best album, but it is a benchmark work in a way that few albums are, a record that can summon up the excitement of a few months in late 1975 as easily as *Sgt. Pepper* can bring back the summer of 1967. The only other Springsteen work that has had similar force as a pop event is *Born in the U.S.A.*, and the similarity of the two titles is no accident. It's also no accident that ten years after *Born to Run,* Springsteen was still closing the first half of his shows with "Thunder Road" and putting his encores in high gear with "Born to Run": More than anything on the first two albums, these songs are the basis for everything that followed in Bruce Springsteen's career.

When he recorded them, though, Springsteen was simply a cult favorite trying to get on with a career. His first two albums had been critical successes but commercial flops; when he and coproducer-manager Mike Appel went into the studio in mid–1974 to record his third album, they quickly recorded the ragged but riveting title track, then stalled. They had the songs: Onstage, Springsteen had already performed early versions of "Thunder Road," "Jungleland" and "She's the One." And Springsteen knew what he was after: "He said he wanted a record where the singing sounded like Roy Orbison and the music sounded like Phil Spector," says E Street Band keyboardist Roy Bittan. They spent months recording take after take, but the songs simply wouldn't come.

By the spring of 1975, Springsteen knew he needed an outside ear, and he turned to writer-producer Jon Landau. "Bruce just seemed to be a little blocked in certain respects," says Bittan, "and Jon coming into the picture helped tear down some walls." With Landau coproducing, they moved from the comparatively low-rent 914 Sound Studios, in the suburbs of New York City, to the more professional Record Plant, in Manhattan, and signed on a twenty-two-year-old engineer named Jimmy Iovine.

"It was really hard," says Iovine, who went on to produce Patti Smith, Tom Petty and many others. "God, it was hard. We worked very slowly, and he had a picture in his head of what he wanted. But all of us were young and inexperienced, so we had to go the long way to do anything."

In constructing the dense, thickly layered sound of *Born to Run,* Springsteen relied far more on overdubs than he ever had or ever would again, recording basic tracks of piano, bass and drums, then layering on guitars, extra keyboards and horns. "Bruce was trying to make the kind of record people hadn't heard on the radio in a long, long time," says Iovine. He was also trying to make a flat-out rock & roll record, to showcase the hard edges that dominated his live shows but hadn't been captured on either of his first two albums.

Bittan says the recording process was difficult. "We were recording epics at the time," he says. "I mean, 'Jungleland' and 'Backstreets' are not easy songs to record. It's like trying to drive a Grand Prix course: Every time you go around one turn, there's another."

Springsteen would recall the sessions as "*the* most intense experience I ever had. . . . Some of the stuff that was in the air in that studio was *deadly*." The LP was finished in a feverish marathon: "At the end," says Iovine, "we mixed the album in nine days straight, maybe leaving the studio for a few hours to go home. We even slept there. We had to get it finished, Bruce had shows booked. But he had a picture in his head, and as tired as he was, he wouldn't let go of that picture."

The album may be Springsteen's most romantic and exultant, but it also has a restless, unsettled air. It's fitting that in the album's very first line (from "Thunder Road"), a woman slams her door and stands outside, mulling over a ride toward an uncertain deliverance. Salvation, refuge and escape are always just around the corner or down the street—and if real satisfaction is nebulous, the album is fueled by the risky exhilaration of the open road.

The lyrics of *Born to Run* energize some classic young-American archetypes, and the album's music does the same with the sounds that nurtured Springsteen—the brazen nerve of Elvis Presley, the monumental heartache of Roy Orbison, the trashy songs of dozens of British Invaders and American one-hit wonders. "Thunder Road" soars with a grace that lends credence to the vow "It's a town full of losers / And I'm pulling out of here to win"; "She's the One" is powered by a truly savage Bo Diddley riff; "Backstreets" uses stately, majestic music to underline a story of a passion that's too desperate to last. In the aftermath of such songs, Bruce Springsteen's cult status couldn't last either.

#28 *Born in the U.S.A.*

It looked as if Bruce Springsteen had boxed himself in after releasing *Nebraska,* a bleak album of demos: He had dug so deep inside himself that a return to arena rock could have been problematic. Yet he re-emerged with a wide-ranging album that combined somber surveys of a troubled America with lighthearted party noise. It dominated the charts for more than a year and instated him as a pop icon without compromising his working-class roots.

During the two years it took to complete the album, Springsteen's longtime friend and band mate, guitarist Steve Van Zandt, departed for a solo career, and the future of the E Street Band seemed in jeopardy. Springsteen's musical direction wavered as he polled numerous people about song selection. Manager Jon Landau, worried that the record was sounding retrogressive, hounded Springsteen into including "Cover Me," a disco-flavored tune he'd originally penned for Donna Summer. Landau also demanded and got a hit single, "Dancing in the Dark," which, for all its synthesized radio catchiness, has tough-minded lyrics ("I ain't nothing but tired / Man, I'm just tired and bored with myself") and bitter vocals to match.

As the album yielded more hits, its soul—that of the Springsteen who had made *Nebraska*—became evident to millions. "Glory Days" admits that "time slips away" and can leave one with only rehashed memories. "My Hometown" has echoes of *The Last Picture Show* in its ode to the past. And the furious title song, misinterpreted by some as a blindly patriotic anthem, is in fact a defiant cry by a Vietnam vet who's endured the world's harshness. The band's performance of the song—actually a leftover from *Nebraska* that hadn't worked acoustically—is probably the closest the band will ever come to replicating its concert sound in a studio setting.

It's a sign of the album's strength that its seven hit singles don't even include some of the best cuts—the melancholy "Downbound Train" and the thinly disguised farewell to Van Zandt, "Bobby Jean." With *Born in the U.S.A.,* Springsteen incorporated the sensibility of his personal, bare-bones folk album into full-blown rock & roll, proving that a musician needn't be plastic to become a superstar.

#40 *Darkness on the Edge of Town*

It didn't have the overall impact of *Born to Run* or *Born in the U.S.A.*; it didn't contain any major hits; and when it was released, it didn't even sell as well as the decidedly uncommercial *Nebraska.* But for Bruce Springsteen, *Darkness on the Edge of Town* was a pivotal album: On it he put aside both the multilayered sound and the mythic cityscapes of its predecessor, *Born to Run,* and shortened his songs and toughened his outlook. *Darkness* was designed, Springsteen has said, to be *relentless,* and that's precisely what it is. Focusing intently on characters who struggle to retain some hope in the midst of situations that offer none, it was the album that pointed the way toward the Springsteen of today.

When he made the record, Springsteen was twenty-eight years old, and he had a lot to prove. Three years earlier he had made the covers of *Time* and *Newsweek,* but the ensuing fuss had led some doubters to charge that CBS Records hype was responsible; then he was prevented from recording a followup album because of a bitter, lengthy lawsuit with his former manager.

When Springsteen finally went into the studio, he was in one of his most prolific periods. In these sessions he cut songs that other people wound up recording, songs that ended up on *The River,* songs that he had been performing live and songs that never surfaced legitimately. Because they didn't tell the story he wanted to tell, Springsteen never seriously considered using sure hits like "Fire" on the album. After months of juggling, he found the combination he was looking for; one of his last moves was to drop "The

Promise" and replace it with the title track. "Darkness," "Badlands" and "The Promised Land" were grimly defiant assertions of faith, while "Racing in the Street" movingly acknowledged that hitting the road—long a favorite Springsteen image—may exact a heavy toll but in the end it's better than sitting at home and slowly dying.

"It's less romantic," Springsteen later told one reporter. "There's less of a sense of a free ride than there is in *Born to Run*. There's more of a sense of 'If you wanna ride, you're gonna pay. And you'd better keep riding.' "

Afterward, Springsteen hit the road for his first full-scale arena tour, and he came back a star. It seems odd now to imagine a time when Bruce Springsteen had to prove he wasn't a hype—but there was such a time, and with *Darkness on the Edge of Town* and its subsequent tour, he proved it. All night, and then some.

#51 *The Wild, the Innocent & the E Street Shuffle*

"Walk tall," murmurs Bruce Springsteen on "New York City Serenade," the closing song on his second album, "or baby, don't walk at all." It might have been a message to himself, as the record had to overcome the new-Dylan hype and commercial failure of his debut, *Greetings From Asbury Park, N.J.* Virtually abandoned by both radio and his record company, the scrawny, bearded street kid rose to the challenge and walked tall. "I started slowly to find out who I am," he has said, "and where I wanted to be. It was like coming out of the shadow of various influences and trying to be yourself." Though still verbose and sometimes murkily recorded, *The Wild, the Innocent & the E Street Shuffle* reveals a soaring, sprawling romanticism, and the E Street Band (albeit an early version) sounds looser and more spontaneous than on *Greetings*.

The song "4th of July, Asbury Park (Sandy)" typifies the complexity of Springsteen's songwriting. His vivid descriptions of the boardwalk's sights and sounds ("our carnival life on the water") serve as background for the impassioned plea "Love me tonight, and I promise I'll love you forever." He's not just another kid with a throbbing libido glorifying youth: The song's protagonist realizes forlornly that he must "quit this scene," and he invites Sandy to share the ride toward adulthood.

The other extended songs—"Kitty's Back" and all of side two—are similarly novellalike in their ability to encompass character, mood and setting. Yet they never fall into pretentiousness and never fail to rock out. The album showcases the versatile band: Clarence Clemons' full-bodied sax, Danny Federici's melancholic accordion, David Sancious' jazzy keyboards. And Springsteen's own distinctively hard-edged guitar sound stands out, especially on "Kitty's Back" and the classic "Rosalita (Come Out Tonight)."

On the brink of failure, Springsteen proved himself a poet with this album and paved the way for his national breakout.

#63 *The River*

On *The River,* his only double album, Bruce Springsteen attempted to stave off the isolating grimness so powerfully rendered on his previous LP, *Darkness on the Edge of Town,* by reasserting the values of committed relationships and rock & roll celebration. That he only half succeeded makes *The River* a compellingly fragmented, nervously unbalanced statement. In the fissures that open between the album's frat-rock raveups, declarations of the ties that bind and restless bolts into lonely freedom, fascinating revelations emerge about Bruce Springsteen's divided soul.

"I did the *Darkness on the Edge of Town* thing, and with *The River* thing I allowed some light to come in, part of the time," Springsteen says in Dave Marsh's book *Glory Days.* "I had to—had to. In a funny way, I felt that I didn't have the center, so what I had to do was I had to get left and right, in hope that it would create some sort of center—or some sense of center." Bruce Springsteen had released only one album since *Born to Run* in 1975. His extensive touring had ended in late 1978. As a result the album had all the earmarks of a major event, and when "Hungry Heart" became a Top Ten single, Springsteen achieved mass success for the first time.

In American culture the river is an image that extends at least back to Mark Twain's mighty Mississippi, and it's one of the world's oldest metaphors for the all-encompassing flow of life itself. Springsteen required a concept of that scale and significance to contain all the contradictory currents of *The River.* While "I Wanna Marry You" is a touchingly modest proposal of marriage as a comforting hedge against the world's uncertainties, "Stolen Car" suggests that "something" in life finally makes connection impossible. Rockers like "Sherry Darling" and "Cadillac Ranch" offer girls, cars, music and fun as a rather manic solace until the larger philosophical issues can be resolved.

"People want to be part of a group yet they also want to disassociate themselves," Springsteen says of *The River* in *Glory Days.* "People go through those conflicts every day in little ways. . . . I wanted to get part of that on the record—the need for community, which is what 'Out in the Street' is about. Songs like 'The Ties That Bind' and 'Two Hearts' deal with that, too. But there's also the other side, the need to be alone."

Springsteen would explore "the need to be alone" to an almost frightening degree on his next album, *Nebraska*. *Born in the U.S.A.* would champion the "need for community." Both records find their sources in the fertile dichotomies of *The River*.

KURT LODER

TUNNEL OF LOVE LP
DUE FROM SPRINGSTEEN

SUDDENLY, A NEW BRUCE SPRINGSTEEN ALBUM is on the way. It's titled *Tunnel of Love,* and it is *not* a collection of songs about American angst and alienation, nor is it a-bristle with arena-rock anthems
of the sort that kept 1984's *Born in the U.S.A.* on the charts for more than
two years. Instead, the new LP—the ninth release of Springsteen's fourteen-
year recording career—is said to be largely about love, a subject in which
he's apparently developed a renewed interest since his marriage to model
Julianne Phillips. It's not a solo Bruce outing, like his 1982 release *Nebraska,*
but neither is it exactly a standard band opus (members of the E Street Band
play on the record, but in shifting configurations). Produced by the usual
studio team of Bruce, the engineer Chuck Plotkin and Springsteen's manager, Jon Landau, *Tunnel of Love* is said by those few people who have heard
it to be Springsteen's most sensually direct work to date. At press time, the
album's cover art was being rushed into production to enable CBS Records
to ship the LP to stores this fall—in plenty of time for the Christmas gift-
giving season. (Last year's Springsteen blockbuster—the five-disc, boxed-
set retrospective *Bruce Springsteen & the E Street Band Live/1975–85*—is still
in oversupply at many shops, and CBS is encouraging retailers to cut the
set's price to around $14.95 for the upcoming holidays.)

In recording the tracks for *Tunnel of Love,* Springsteen drew on the talents of such disparate musicians as the onetime Seatrain violinist Richard
Greene, harmonica player Jimmie Wood and Jay Dee Maness, a Nashville
studio veteran who currently holds down the steel-guitar slot in Chris Hillman's Desert Rose Band. Despite Springsteen's use of such offbeat instru-
mentation, *Tunnel of Love,* by all accounts, is not a "country" album. (In fact,
both Maness—who made the mistake of gabbing to the press about the sessions—and Greene are absent from the record's final mix.)

Whatever lyrical or stylistic surprises the new record may hold in store, it promises to be, at heart, more of the same thing that Springsteen has always delivered: Call it Bruce music. And that, for most folks, will be more important, and certainly more interesting than all the media hoopla that will inevitably erupt around it.

MIKAL GILMORE

TWENTIETH ANNIVERSARY SPECIAL
Bruce Springsteen Q & A

IN ROLLING STONE'S SPECIAL TWENTIETH ANNIVERSARY ISSUE (the last of four), editors chose thirty-three individuals "whose work has stood out and whose voices have often been heard in the pages of ROLLING STONE, to talk about their experiences during the past two decades, their understanding of what has survived and what they see ahead." Bruce Springsteen was selected as one of those "who have helped to shape rock & roll, as well as American culture and politics," a list which also included Bono, Jesse Jackson, Pete Townshend, Tom Wolfe, William Burroughs, Lou Reed, Bob Dylan, Sting, Keith Richards, Mick Jagger, Paul McCartney, and George Harrison, among others.

THE 1960s ARE OFTEN idealized as times of great innocence and wonder. Although your own work has been recorded in the Seventies and Eighties, some of your best songs seem haunted by the strife of that era. Looking back, do you see the Sixties as a period in which a great deal was at stake in American culture?

I think that in the Sixties there was a rebellion against what people felt was the dehumanization of society, where people were counted as less than people, less than human. It was almost as if there were a temper tantrum against that particular threat. In the Sixties moral lines were drawn relatively easily. "Hey, this is wrong, this is right—I'm standing *here*!" That idea busted up nearly every house in the nation. And people expected revolution. I think some people thought it was going to happen in an explosive burst of some sort of radical, joyous energy, and that all the bullshit and all the Nixons were going to be swept away, and, man, we were going to start all over again and do it right this time. Okay, that was a childlike fantasy. But a lot of those ideas were good ideas.

It's funny, but because of the naiveness of the era, it's easily trivialized and laughed at. But underneath it, I think, people were trying in some sense to redefine their own lives and the country that they lived in, in some more open and free and just fashion. And *that* was real—that desire was real. But I think that as people grew older, they found that the process of changing things actually tends to be *un*romantic and not very dramatic. In fact, it's very slow and very small, and if anything, it's done in inches.

The values from that time are things that I still believe in. I think that all my music—certainly the music I've done in the past five or six years—is a result of that time and those values. I don't know, it seems almost like a lost generation. How do the ideals of that time connect in some pragmatic fashion to the real world today? I don't know if anybody's answered that particular question.

One of the central events that inspired the idealism of that era—the war in Vietnam—was also the most horrific thing to happen to this society in the last twenty years. It tore us apart along political and generational lines, but it also drew a hard line across the nation and forced many of us to take a clear stand.

That's true: That *was* the last time things ever felt that morally clear. Since then—from Watergate on down—who or what the enemy is has grown more obfuscated. It's just too confusing. But you can't wait for events like Vietnam, because if you do, then maybe 55,000 men end up dying and the country is left changed forever. I mean, that experience is *still* not over. And without those particular memories, without the people who were there reminding everybody, it would've happened again already, I'm sure. Certainly, it would have happened in the past eight years if they thought they could have gotten away with it.

So what went wrong? Why is it that so few of the brave ideals of those times carried over to the social and political realities of today?

I think the problem is that people yearn for simple answers. The reason the image of the Reagan presidency is so effective is that it appeared to be very simple. I think that's also the whole reason for the canonization of Oliver North: He said all the right words and pushed all the right buttons. And people yearn for those sorts of simple answers. But the world will never ever be simple again, if it ever was. The world is nothing but complex, and if you do not learn to interpret its complexities, you're going to be on the river without a paddle.

The classic thing for me is the misinterpretation of "Born in the U.S.A." I opened the paper one day and saw where they had quizzed kids on what different songs meant, and they asked them what "Born in the U.S.A." meant. "Well, it's about my country," they answered. Well, that *is* what it's about—that's certainly one of the things it's about—but if that's as far in as you go, you're going to miss it, you know? I don't think people are being taught to think hard enough about things in general—whether it's about their own lives, politics, the situation in Nicaragua or whatever. Consequently, if you do not learn to do that—if you do not develop the skills to interpret that information—you're going to be easily manipulated, or you're going to walk around simply confused and ineffectual and powerless.

People are being dumped into this incredibly unintelligible society, and they are swimming, barely staying afloat, and then trying to catch on to whatever is going to give them a little safe ground.

I guess when I started in music I thought, "My job is pretty simple. My job is I search for the human things in myself, and I turn them into notes and words, and then in some fashion, I help people hold on to their own humanity—if I'm doing my job right."

You *can* change things—except maybe you can affect only one person, or maybe only a few people. Certainly nothing as dramatic as we expected in the Sixties. When I go onstage, my approach is "I'm going to reach just one person"—even if there's 80,000 people there. Maybe those odds aren't so great, but if that's what they are, that's okay.

Was that what you had in mind at the end of the last tour, when before performing Edwin Starr's "War," you told your audience to think twice about committing itself to any of America's future military involvements?

With that, I guess we were playing the percentages, you know? [*Laughs.*] I mean, I've met people on the street who I could tell misunderstood my work, and I've also met people who have understood it. It was the same thing when we'd play in a club—it was just fewer numbers. But when we started to do "War," which we only did the last four nights of the whole tour, I was looking for some way to reshape that part of the show to make it as explicit as I could, without sloganeering. But "War" . . . a lot of people heard it, and some people didn't hear it. I'm sure that when we're on tour, I'll be singing that song again. And maybe people that didn't hear it will hear it differently this time. My job is to try to make sure that they do. I never thought, "Well, I'll do this because this feels like the *right* thing to do." I did it because it was the *only* thing that I felt I could do. I think that people get tired and frustrated. I learned that again during the week when Oliver North was testifying. It was a frustrating time. I was walking around arguing with everybody [*laughs*]. It was like "I don't *believe* this is happening." It reminded me that you've got to wake up in the morning and go to work again.

You keep talking about your involvement in rock & roll as a job. That's a far cry from the view that many of us had in the Sixties, when we looked upon artists—such as Bob Dylan—not so much as people performing a job but as cultural revolutionaries.

Dylan was a revolutionary. So was Elvis. I'm not that. I don't see myself as having been that. I felt that what I would be able to do, maybe, was redefine what I did in more human terms than it had been defined before, and in more everyday terms. I always saw myself as a nuts-and-bolts kind of person. I felt what I was going to accomplish I would accomplish over a long period of time, not in an enormous burst of energy or genius. To keep an even perspective on it all, I looked at it *like* a job—something that you do every day and over a long period of time.

To me, Dylan and Elvis—what they did was genius. I never really saw myself in that fashion. I'm sure there was a part of me that was afraid of having that kind of ambition or taking on those kinds of responsibilities.

"Born to Run" was certainly an ambitious record. Maybe it wasn't revolutionary, but it was certainly innovative: It redefined what an album could do in the Seventies.

Well, I was shooting for the moon, you know? I always wanted to do that too, on top of it. When I did *Born to Run,* I thought, "I'm going to make the greatest rock & roll record ever made." I guess what I'm saying is, later on my perspective changed a bit so that I felt like I could maybe redefine what doing the particular job was about. So that it does *not* have to drive you crazy or drive you to drugs or drinking, or you do not have to lose yourself in it and lose perspective of your place in the scheme of things. I guess I wanted to try and put a little more human scale on the thing. I felt that was necessary for my *own* sanity, for one thing.

I was always afraid of those things, of the forces that you set loose in people. In this job, part of what you do is excite people. And you don't know what people are going to do when they get excited. My idea was that when I went on a stage, I wanted to deliver my best to pull out the best in *you,* whatever that may be. But sometimes you don't do that. Sometimes you just pull out someone's insanity—you don't know *what* you're going to pull out or what will come to the surface.

Your next record, "Darkness on the Edge of Town," sounded far less hopeful than "Born to Run." Several critics attributed the sullen mood to the long stall between the records—that ten-month period in which a lawsuit prevented you from recording. What really was happening on "Darkness"?

That was a record where I spent a lot of time focusing. And what I focused on was this one idea: What do you do if your dream comes true? Where does that leave you? What *do* you do if that happens? And I realized part of what you have to face is the problem of isolation. You can get isolated if you've got a lot of dough or if you don't have much dough, whether you're Elvis Presley or whether you're sitting in front of the TV with a six-pack of beer. It's easy to get there. On that record it was like "Well, what I've done, does it have any greater meaning than that I've made a good album and had some luck with it?" I was trying to figure out that question, which is really one I'm still trying to figure out.

James M. Cain once wrote of "the wish that comes true, for some reason a terrifying concept." He said that readers realized that "the characters cannot have this particular wish and survive." Yet you seem to have achieved your wishes without losing your way.

I guess I consider myself one of those people that that happened to. And you have to decide: Does that leave you with a certain responsibility? I know that before *Darkness,* I was writing songs where people were trying to escape all the time and were also searching. But once that happens, once you break those ties to whatever it is—your past—and you get a shot out of that community that you came up in, what are you going to do *then*? There *is* a certain frightening aspect to having things you dreamed were going to happen *happen,* because it's always more—and in some ways always less—than what you expected. I think when people dream of things, they dream of them without the complications. The real dream is not the dream, it's life without complications. And *that* doesn't exist.

For me, the Seventies were a time I spent dealing with what had happened to me and trying to figure out where that fit in with everybody else. Because the irony of the entire situation is that the thing you did in order to be with people, and to be of use to people, is that same thing that—if you do it well enough—ends up making you forever different in some fashion. And it isolates you in that way. That was something that I was fighting against when I was young, and the way I fought against it was with my guitar. I was saying, "Hey, let me in—I got something to say, I wanna say it, I wanna talk to somebody."

I used to think that fame, on its best day, is kind of like a friendly wave from a stranger standing by the side of the road. And when it's not so good, it's like a long walk home all alone, with nobody there when you get there. And I guess what I wanted to figure out is, what happens if you dream that dream? What happens if you dream of having some real effect on people's lives and then you meet people who say that's what you have had?

I remember the night that I got married. I was standing at the altar by myself, and I was waiting for my wife, and I can remember standing there thinking, "Man, I have everything. I got it all." And you have those moments. But you end up with a lot more than you expected. I guess I wouldn't trade it for anything, but it's a strange job, you know?

On each of your records since "Darkness"—"The River," "Nebraska" and "Born in the U.S.A."—you managed to write about hard working-class realities in ways that sounded surprisingly immediate, coming from a rich, well-known pop star.

Was there something about moving into fame and wealth that caused you to identify more closely with the world you were leaving behind?

I think it's probably a normal reaction. I mean, the circumstances of your life are changing, and what they are changing to is unknown to you, and you have never known closely anyone else who has had the same experience. On one hand you cannot hide in the past. You can't say, "Well, I'm the same old guy I used to be." You have to go ahead and meet that person who you're becoming and accept whatever that's about. I always wanted to live solidly in the present, always remember the past and always be planning for the future. So from *Darkness* to *The River,* I was attempting to pull myself into what I felt was going to be the adult world, so that when things became disorienting, I would be strong enough to hold my ground. Those were the records where I was trying to forge that foundation and maintain my connections and try to say, "Well, what is this going to mean? Maybe what this is all going to mean is up to me."

With the later records, that resolve seemed to have more and more political resonance. In 1979 you took part in the No Nukes benefit concert, and in November 1980 you made some scathing remarks onstage in Arizona on the evening following Ronald Reagan's election. How did events of recent years inspire your new-found political concern and awareness?

I think my response was based on an accumulation of things. I never considered myself a particularly political person. I wasn't when I was younger, and I don't think I really am now. But if you live in a situation where you have seen people's lives wasted . . . I think the thing that frightened me most was seeing all that waste. There wasn't any one specific thing that made me go in that particular direction, but it seemed like if you're a citizen, and if you're living here, then it's your turn to take out the garbage. Your tour of duty should come around.

It just seemed that people's lives are being shaped by forces they do not understand, and if you are going to begin to take a stand and fight against those things, you got to *know* the enemy—and that's getting harder to do. People are so easily affected by buzzwords; they're getting their button pushed with *God, mother, country, apple pie*—even in soda commercials. And so it's like "Where is the real thing? Where is the real America?"

What's also disturbing is the casualness with which people are getting used to being lied to. To me, Watergate felt like this big hustle was going down. And in the end it seemed to legitimize the dope dealer down on the street. "Hey, the president's doing it, so why can't I?" I guess we're pretty much left to find our way on our own these days. That sense of community that there was in the Sixties made you feel like there were a lot of people along for the ride with you. It felt like the whole country was trying to find its way. You do not have a sense that the country is trying to find its way today. And that's a shame. As a result, I think you feel more on your own in the world today. Certainly, *I* feel more isolated in it.

Maybe everybody's just got to grab hold of each other. The idea of America as a family is naive, maybe sentimental or simplistic, but it's a good idea. And if people are sick and hurting and lost, I guess that it falls on everybody to address those problems in some fashion. Because injustice, and the price of that injustice, falls on everyone's heads. The economic injustice falls on everybody's head and steals everyone's freedom. Your wife can't walk down the street at night. People keep guns in their homes. They live with a greater sense of apprehension, anxiety and fear than they would in a more just and open society. It's not an accident, and it's not simply that there are "bad" people out there. It's an inbred part of the way that we are all living: It's a product of what we have accepted, what we have acceded to. And whether we mean it or not, our silence has spoken for us in some fashion. But the challenge is still there: Eight years of Reagan is not going to change that.

That seemed part of what "Nebraska" was about: a reaction to the Reagan years. Was that how you intended people to see that record?

In a funny way, I always considered it my most personal record, because it felt to me, in its tone, the most what my childhood felt like. Later on, a bunch of people wrote about it as a response to the Reagan era, and it obviously had that connection.

I think people live from the inside out. Your initial connection is to your friends and your wife and your family. From there your connection may be to your immediate community. And then if you have the energy and the strength, then you say, "Well, how do I connect up to the guy in the next state or, ultimately, to people in the world?" I think that whatever the political implications of my work have been, they've just come out of personal insight. I don't really have a particular political theory or ideology. It came from observations, like, okay, this man is being wasted. *Why* is this man being wasted? This person has lost himself. Why is that? And just trying to take it from there. How does my life interconnect and intertwine with my friends and everybody else? I don't know the answers yet. I'm a guitar player—that's what I do.

But millions of people see you as more than a guitar player. In fact, many see you as nothing less than an inspiring moral leader. But there's a certain irony to being a modern-day hero for the masses. Back in the Sixties nobody ever spoke of the Beatles or the Rolling Stones or Dylan as being overexposed. Yet these days, any pop artist who has a major, sustained impact on a mass audience runs the risk of seeming either overly promoted by the media or too familiar to his audience. In recent years, performers like you, Michael Jackson, Prince and Madonna have all faced this dilemma. Do you ever feel that you're running the danger of overexposure?

Well, what does that mean? What is "overexposed"? It really has no meaning, you know? It's kind of a newspaper thing. I just ignore it, to be honest with you. I make the best records I can make. I try to work on them and put them out when it feels right and they feel like they're ready. That's what it is—not whether I'm overexposed or underexposed or not exposed. It's like "Hey, put the record on. Is it good? Do you like it? Is it rockin' ya? Is it speaking to you? Am I talking to you?" And the rest is what society does to sell newspapers or magazines. You gotta fill 'em up every month. You have an entire counterlife that is attached to your own real life by the slimmest of threads. In the past year, if you believe what was in the newspapers about me, I'd be living in two houses that I've never seen, been riding in cars that I've never had [*laughs*]. This is just what happens. It's, like, uncontrollable: The media monster has to be fed.

So all that sort of stuff, if you believe that it has anything really to do with you, you know, you're gonna go nuts. In the end, people will like my records and feel they were true or feel they weren't. They'll look at the body of work I've done and pull out whatever meaning it has for them. And that's what stands. The rest is transient. It's here today and gone tomorrow. It's meaningless. Whether Michael Jackson is sleeping in a tank or not, what does it mean to you? It's just a laugh for some people; that's all it really is. And I feel like, hey, if it's a laugh for you, then have one on me. Because when you reach for and achieve fame, one of the byproducts of fame is you *will* be trivialized, and you will be embarrassed. You *will* be, I guarantee it. I look at that as a part of my job. And I ain't seen nothing compared to, you know, if you look at Elvis's life or even Michael J.'s. I've had it pretty easy, but I know a little bit of what it's about. These things are gonna happen, and if you don't have a strong enough sense of who you are and what you're doing, they'll kick you in the ass and knock you down and have a good time doing it. That's the nature of our society, and it's one of the roles that people like me play in society. Okay, that's fine, but my feeling is simple: My work is my defense. Simple as that. I've done things I never thought I'd be able to do, I've been places I never thought I'd be. I've written music that is better than I thought I could write. I did stuff that I didn't think I had in me.

You've also come to mean a lot to an awful lot of people.

That's a good thing, but you can take it too far. I do not believe that the essence of the rock & roll idea was to exalt the cult of personality. That is a sidetrack, a dead-end street. That is not the thing to do. And I've been as guilty of it as anybody in my own life. When I jumped over that wall to meet Elvis that night [at Graceland], I didn't know who I was gonna meet. And the guard who stopped me at the door did me the biggest favor of my life. I had misunderstood. It was innocent, and I was having a ball, but it wasn't right. In the end, you cannot live inside that dream. You cannot live within the dream of Elvis Presley or within the dream of the Beatles. It's like John Lennon said: "The dream is over." You can live with that dream in your heart, but you cannot live inside that dream, because it's a perversion, you know? What the best of art says is, it says, "Take this"—this movie or painting or photograph or record—"take what you see in this, and then go find your place in the world. This is a tool: go out and find your place in the world."

I think I made the mistake earlier on of trying to live within that dream, within that rock & roll dream. It's a seductive choice, it's a seductive opportunity. The real world, after all, is frightening. In the end, I realized that rock & roll wasn't just about finding fame and wealth. Instead, for me, it was about finding your place in the world, figuring out where you belong.

It's a tricky balance to do it correctly. You got to be able to hold a lot of contradictory ideas in your mind at one time without letting them drive you nuts. I feel like to do my job right, when I walk out onstage I've got to feel like it's the most important thing in the world. Also I got to feel like, well, it's only rock & roll. Somehow you got to believe both of those things.

FRED GOODMAN

LOW-KEY START FOR *TUNNEL OF LOVE*

BRUCE SPRINGSTEEN'S NEW ALBUM, *Tunnel of Love,* received a warm welcome from record buyers, but retailers say the album's ultimate commercial success hinges on whether radio cuddles up to its next couple of singles.

"It's doing nicely and should definitely be our number-one record out of the box," says Kevin Hawkins, the product manager for the 133-store Record Bar chain, which is based in Durham, North Carolina. "But now that the hard-core fans have it, it's up to the next few singles and videos to determine how it does."

A video for the first single, "Brilliant Disguise," has been completed but is not expected to be ready for release during the song's tenure as a single. "Tunnel of Love" will probably be the next single released from the album.

Jeff Lega, the manager of Jack's Music in Red Bank, New Jersey—the heart of Springsteen country—characterizes the release of *Tunnel of Love* as comparatively low-key. "The excitement and hysteria of the live album just wasn't here," he says. Lega estimates that his store sold approximately 2,000 copies of the five-record set, *Bruce Springsteen & the E Street Band Live/1975–85,* on the first day of its release, compared with 500 copies of *Tunnel of Love.*

At Maryland's thirty-store Kemp Mill Records chain, vice-president Howard Appelbaum says *Tunnel of Love* was the number-one record "by far" in its first week of release. But while Appelbaum believes the record is artistically strong, he's not sure how well it will ultimately sell. "The first week's sales were on Bruce's name rather than the music," he says. "*Tunnel of Love* is an intimate record and will take longer to get into people's heads. We'll have to wait to see what the demand is."

While a source at Columbia Records says that *Tunnel of Love* had an initial shipment of approximately 2 million copies—enough to certify it as double platinum—the label appears more concerned with letting the album find its own level than with hyping it: One retailer says that despite the fact that

Tunnel of Love outsold all other albums at his stores during its first week of release, CBS did not actively solicit the shops to report the album as its number-one seller to the *Billboard* charts. By contrast, he says, CBS did request the retailers' support to ensure Michael Jackson's album *Bad* debuted in the chart's top slot.

■ RANDOM NOTES (November 19, 1987)

The audience included Billy Idol, Sandra Bernhard, Dennis Quaid, Harry Dean Stanton, Leonard Cohen and Richard Thompson, but the real star power was onstage at L.A.'s Coconut Grove when Cinemax taped its tribute to Rock and Roll Hall of Famer Roy Orbison (to air early next year). In addition to Elvis Presley's old band (guitarist James Burton, drummer Ronnie Tutt, bassist Jerry Scheff and pianist Glen Hardin), Orbison was backed by Bruce Springsteen, Elvis Costello and Tom Waits. Supporting vocalists were Jackson Browne, J.D. Souther, Bonnie Raitt, Jennifer Warnes, k.d. lang and Steve Soles, best known for appearing in Bob Dylan's Rolling Thunder Revue. The group ran through almost twenty Orbison classics, including "Only the Lonely," "Running Scared," "Blue Bayou" and "In Dreams," plus a few new songs, including one written by Costello.

The all-stars, though, didn't spend much time in the spotlight: all of the lead vocals were done by the man in the black fringed jacket and shades, sounding almost exactly the way he did thirty years ago. "I said to those guys, 'You wanna go up against Orbison?'" said musical director T Bone Burnett, laughing. "Not only is he just about the only one of the rock & rollers his age who's still alive, but he still sings those songs in the same key as the originals. *Nobody* does that."

Every time Orbison effortlessly hit one of his high notes, he drew a huge grin from Springsteen, who shared a mike with Orbison on "Uptown" and "Dream Baby" and took guitar solos on "Ooby Dooby" and "Oh, Pretty Woman." "It was fun," said Springsteen afterward, his arms draped around Orbison's neck. "Lotta fun, playing guitar with James Burton and just *being* there with this guy." Then the Boss headed out the door, still humming "Dream Baby."

STEVE POND

TUNNEL OF LOVE ALBUM REVIEW
Bruce's Hard Look at Love

S O BRUCE SPRINGSTEEN MET A GIRL, fell in love, got married and made an album of songs about meeting a girl, falling in love and getting married. And if you think it's that cut and dried, you don't know Springsteen. Far from being a series of hymns to cozy domesticity, *Tunnel of Love* is an unsettled and unsettling collection of hard looks at the perils of commitment. A decade or so ago, Springsteen acquired a reputation for romanticizing his subject matter; on this album he doesn't even romanticize romance.

Tunnel of Love is precisely the right move for an artist whose enormous success gloriously affirmed the potential of arena rock & roll but exacted a toll on the singer. *Born in the U.S.A.* sold 12 million copies mostly because it was the best kind of thoughtful, tough, mainstream rock & roll record—but also because it was misinterpreted and oversimplified by listeners looking for slogans rather than ideas. When Springsteen hit the road to support that album, his sound got bigger, his gestures larger, his audience huger. The five-record live set that followed that tour was a suitably oversize way to sum up Bruce Springsteen, the Boss, American Rock Icon.

But where do you go from there? Trying to top *Born in the U.S.A.* with another collection of rock anthems would have been foolhardy artistically; on the other hand, to react the way Springsteen did after the breakthrough 1980 success of *The River*—with a homemade record as stark and forbidding as *Nebraska*—would have turned an inspired gesture into a formula. So *Tunnel of Love* walks a middle ground. The most intelligently arranged album Springsteen has made, it consists mostly of his own tracks, sparingly overdubbed; he uses the members of the E Street Band when they fit. It's not, as was rumored, a country album, though Springsteen sings it in the colloquial, folkish voice he used on *Nebraska,* and it's not a rock & roll album, though "Spare Parts" and "Brilliant Disguise" come close to the full-bodied E Street Band sound.

Instead, this is a varied, modestly scaled, modern-sounding pop album; it is a less ambitious work than *Born in the U.S.A.,* but its simpler sound is perfectly suited to the more intimate stories Springsteen is telling. Although you could often hear the sweat on his previous records, this LP came surprisingly quickly and feels effortless and elegant rather than belabored. Crucially, it demystifies Springsteen's often arduous album-making process.

But energy rather than elegance is what sold *Born in the U.S.A.*; the scaled-down *Tunnel of Love* is thus a chancier commercial proposition. The songs are the kind that many of the fans at the last tour's stadium shows talked through. Listeners who turn to Springsteen for outsize gestures and roaring radio rock may well be confused or even irritated by these more somber miniatures and may insist on reading a first-rate song collection as an aberration.

Initially, in fact, *Tunnel of Love* sounds not only modest but also playful, giddy and lightweight. "Ain't Got You" is a funny, partially a cappella Bo Diddley-style rocker that jokes about Springsteen's wealth ("I got a pound of caviar sitting home on ice / I got a fancy foreign car that rides like paradise") but expresses yearning for the one thing money can't buy (i.e., "you"). In the next two songs, "Tougher Than the Rest" and "All That Heaven Will Allow," Springsteen is head over heels in love, convinced that the sun will shine as long as he's got the right woman by his side. Those three songs are a light, romantic, lovely beginning, and then it all comes crashing down.

Bobby said he'd pull out Bobby stayed in
Janey had a baby it wasn't any sin
They were set to marry on a summer day
Bobby got scared and he ran away.

The song, "Spare Parts," is a roadhouse rocker reminiscent of Dylan's "Highway 61 Revisited"; the sound is abrasive and harsh; the story is bleak; and the moral is hard: "Spare parts / And broken hearts / Keep the world turnin' around."

From that point on, times are tough. In "Cautious Man," the main character has LOVE tattooed on one hand, FEAR on the other (Springsteen's lift from the film *The Night of the Hunter,* in which Robert Mitchum played a preacher with LOVE and HATE tattooed on his knuckles). The relationships in "Two Faces," "Brilliant Disguise" and "One Step Up" ("and two steps back") are crumbling as trust gives way to betrayal and recrimination: "Another fight and I slam the door on / Another battle in our dirty little war." In the title song, Springsteen voices a fear that underlies the entire album: "It's easy for two people to lose each other in / This tunnel of love."

But these are not "Baby, you done me wrong" songs. They're not about the outside forces that threaten relationships but about the internal demons that keep people uncertain of love, skeptical that they can ever truly touch another human being. It is an album about loneliness and solitude in the midst of what promised to be bliss. A pivotal moment comes halfway through "Brilliant Disguise," when the singer stops questioning his lover and turns upon himself: "I wanna know if it's you I don't trust / 'Cause I damn sure don't trust myself." More than any record since his first, it is an album in which you can hear Springsteen's Catholic upbringing: Again and again lovers pray for deliverance, romance is depicted as a manifestation of God's grace, and love brings with it doubt and guilt.

Of course, the religious images and the frequent references to weddings will tempt those who want to think these songs tell us about Springsteen's own recent marriage. But to read *Tunnel of Love* as a report from the marital front is far too facile and ignores the fact that Springsteen was telling similar stories as far back as *Darkness on the Edge of Town,* in 1978. Since then, he has written about the promises our country makes to its people and the way it reneges on those promises, about the dreams our land inspires and the things that stifle those dreams and about the glory in simply persevering. On *Tunnel of Love,* Springsteen is writing about the promises people make to each other and the way they renege on those promises, about the romantic dreams we're brought up with and the internal demons that stifle those dreams. The battleground has moved from the streets to the sheets, but the battle hasn't changed significantly.

And in "Valentine's Day," the last song on the record, Springsteen quietly reaffirms the glory of persevering. In the song, the singer drives a long, lonely highway and thinks about his girl, terrified of losing her and grappling with all the uncertainty that's surfaced throughout the album. Finally, he shrugs aside the doubts and makes a final plea: "So hold me close honey say you're forever mine / And tell me you'll be my lonely valentine." It's a partial return to the touching naiveté of the album's first three songs, but at this point it sounds like deliberate, hard-earned naiveté.

More than any other song, however, it is "Walk Like a Man"—the track that ends side one—that has the feel of outright autobiography. Yet another song about his father—sung from the vantage point of the son's wedding day—it moves to as lovely an arrangement as Springsteen has ever crafted: a steady drumbeat with distant echoes of "Racing in the Street," a gentle wash of synthesizer, a lulling melody. Every incident rings true, and every line seems open, genuine and artless ("So much has happened to me / That I don't understand"). It is perhaps the most compassionate and affecting song

Springsteen has written to his father, but at its center is a devastating question that reverberates through the entire album:

> *I remember ma draggin' me and my sister up the street to the church*
> *Whenever she heard those wedding bells*
> *Well would they ever look so happy again*
> *The handsome groom and his bride*
> *As they stepped into that long black limousine*
> *For their mystery ride?*

There's the heart of the album: an uncertain journey down a dangerous, dark highway. The album doesn't make it sound like an easy trip—but then, it's been a long time since Bruce Springsteen has written about free rides of any sort. One of the wonders of *Tunnel of Love* is that in the end, he convinces us that the mystery ride just might be worth the toll.

DAVID FRICKE

TUNNEL OF LOVE YEAR-END ALBUM REVIEW

O R "THE WILD, THE INNOCENT AND THE HORIZONTAL RUMBA." The crucial studio followup to *Born in the U.S.A.* was very much a political record, only this time Springsteen explored the politics of the mattress and the heart. Although it was essentially divided into can't-live-with-her and can't-live-without-her songs, *Tunnel of Love*—despite its hollowed-out, predominantly acoustic sound—was a lot more complicated than that. As Springsteen sang in the title track, "The house is haunted and the ride gets rough." It certainly didn't get much rougher than the sexual treachery and broken promises in "Spare Parts": "Bobby said he'd pull out Bobby stayed in. . . . They were set to marry on a summer day / Bobby got scared and he ran away."

Yet for every moment of confusion ("Brilliant Disguise"), frustration ("One Step Up") and regret ("Two Faces"), there was one of humor (the bluesy, Diddleyish "Ain't Got You"), invigorating lust ("Tougher Than the Rest") or romantic renewal ("Cautious Man"). The notable lack of a wailing, full-strength E Street Band prompted comparisons to the stark, empty-prairie sound of *Nebraska*. But *Tunnel of Love* was a lot richer than that. There are a million ways to say, "I love you," in rock & roll. Springsteen just concentrated on the simple ones and endowed them with a quiet, formidable power that made *Tunnel* a sometimes rough but wholly unforgettable ride.

■ RANDOM NOTES (January 14, 1988)

Although details were not available at press time, Bruce Springsteen will likely launch a tour of small venues soon. Rumors indicate that he will not be backed by the entire E Street Band but will perform either solo or with a few musicians.

■ RANDOM NOTES (February 11, 1988)

Bruce Springsteen will begin his Tunnel of Love Express Tour in late February. Contrary to prior reports of a solo tour, he'll be playing with the entire E Street Band at arena-size venues in over twenty cities. They plan to play an average of two shows per city. (At press time, no dates were available.)

■ RANDOM NOTES (March 24, 1988)

Bruce Springsteen's Tunnel of Love Express Tour continues to expand and is now expected to run at least through the end of May in the U.S., with a European jaunt likely to follow. In New Jersey, former E Street Band guitarist Steve Van Zandt is directing rehearsals of the band—which will include a five-piece horn section and, possibly, some background singers. Van Zandt may join Springsteen for part of the tour.

Word is that Springsteen will be performing very little solo material and altering his repertoire considerably. Some oft-performed numbers are being dropped, although "Born in the U.S.A." is reportedly among the tunes the expanded band will play.

Tickets for the tour's first three shows, at the Centrum, in Worcester, Massachusetts, sold out in two hours. Additional New York-area dates are anticipated for mid-May. Springsteen is reportedly insisting on a 95 percent split with promoters; the industry norm for artists of his stature is 90 percent.

1987 MUSIC AWARDS

MARCH 10, 1988

READERS PICKS

ARTIST OF THE YEAR
U2
R.E.M.
Madonna
Bruce Springsteen
Bon Jovi

BEST ALBUM
Joshua Tree—U2
Document—R.E.M.
***Tunnel of Love*—Bruce
Springsteen**
*A Momentary Lapse of
Reason*—Pink Floyd
Whitesnake—Whitesnake
Hysteria—Def Leppard
Sign o' the Times—Prince
Tango in the Night—
Fleetwood Mac
. . . Nothing Like the Sun—
Sting
Bad Animals—Heart

BEST SINGLE
"With or Without You," U2
"Where the Streets Have No
Name," U2
"I Still Haven't Found What I'm
Looking For," U2
"The One I Love," R.E.M.

"Here I Go Again," Whitesnake
**"Brilliant Disguise," Bruce
Springsteen**
"Touch of Grey," the Grateful
Dead
"Alone," Heart
"I Want Your Sex," George
Michael
"Learning to Fly," Pink Floyd

BEST MALE SINGER
Bono
Bruce Springsteen
Sting
John Cougar Mellencamp
George Michael

WORST MALE SINGER
Michael Jackson
Bruce Willis
Bruce Springsteen
Bon Jovi
Prince

BEST SONGWRITER
Bono
Bruce Springsteen
Sting
Prince
John Cougar Mellencamp

BEST ROCK COUPLE
David Coverdale and Tawny
Kitaen
Jim Kerr and Chrissie Hynde
Madonna and Sean Penn
**Bruce Springsteen and
Julianne Phillips**
Tommy Lee and Heather
Locklear

**BEST DRESSED MALE ROCK
ARTIST**
David Bowie
Sting
Bruce Springsteen
Bono
Jon Bon Jovi

**WORST DRESSED MALE
ROCK ARTIST**
Michael Jackson
Prince
Bruce Springsteen
Billy Idol
David Lee Roth

SEXIEST MALE ROCK ARTIST
Bono
George Michael
Jon Bon Jovi
Sting
Bruce Springsteen

CRITICS PICKS

BEST ALBUM
***Tunnel of Love*—Bruce
Springsteen**
The Joshua Tree—U2
Sign o' the Times—Prince
Robbie Robertson—Robbie
Robertson
Pleased to Meet Me—the
Replacements

Bring the Family—John Hiatt
By the Light of the Moon—
Los Lobos
Document—R.E.M.
Franks Wild Years—Tom
Waits
Babble—That Petrol Emotion

BEST SINGLE
**"Tunnel of Love," Bruce
Springsteen**
"Luka," Suzanne Vega
"The One I Love," R.E.M.
"Sign o' the Times," Prince
"Faith," George Michael

BEST SONGWRITER
Bruce Springsteen

STEVE POND

BRUCE'S "EXPRESS" HITS THE ROAD IN HIGH GEAR

"**R**EADY FOR A DATE?"

Bruce Springsteen had been out of circulation for some time when he used those words to kick off the first show of the Tunnel of Love Express. Taking the stage of the Centrum, in Worcester, Massachusetts, for his first tour in two and a half years, rock's most acclaimed showman began the four-month series of shows with a warm, generous set marked by some missing Springsteen standards, a handful of new songs and unexpected choices and much of the *Tunnel of Love* album.

The result wasn't as anthemic, oversize or topical as the Born in the U.S.A. Tour; instead, it was a three-hour reflection on love, commitment and family. And at the end of the evening the thirty-eight-year-old rocker dropped to his knees and, rather than shouting out his traditional battle cry ("I'm just a prisoner . . . of *rock & roll!*"), roared his new motto: "I'm just a prisoner . . . of *love!*"

In many ways the Tunnel of Love Express looks to be a calmer tour than the exhausting fifteen-month extravaganza that began early in the summer of 1984. For one thing, it simply won't play to as many people: Where the last leg of the Born in the U.S.A. Tour found Springsteen playing stadiums holding as many as 100,000 people, this time he's sticking to 12,000-to-20,000-seat indoor arenas.

Of course, the tour is still surrounded by a certain amount of frenzy. The 39,000 tickets for the three Worcester shows sold out in less than two hours. Local papers incessantly ran Springsteen stories. And many scalpers were asking upward of $200 per ticket.

This tour showcases *Tunnel of Love*, a subtle, ballad-heavy album less obviously suited to the stage than were the rock anthems of *Born in the U.S.A.* Springsteen made the album's low-key songs the heart of his show and augmented them with some surprising song choices, including a few B sides ("Be True" and "Roulette," the flip sides of "Fade Away" and "One Step Up," respectively), songs he'd given away ("Light of Day," the title track from last year's Michael J. Fox–Joan Jett movie) and brand-new tunes (Springsteen's reworking of "Geno Is a Coward," an obscure soul song by Geno Washington, and "Part Man, Part Monkey," an infectious reggae original).

The show began with Springsteen and his band buying tickets from an onstage carnival barker, and the evening quickly took on a warm, romantic air with tunes like "Be True" and "All That Heaven Will Allow." But then Springsteen shattered the calm with two of his angriest topical songs, "Seeds" and "Roulette," and followed those with "Cover Me."

The crux of the first set—which included "Brilliant Disguise" and ended with "War" and "Born in the U.S.A."—came when Springsteen told a meandering story about a childhood encounter with domestic violence. The story cut to the quick when he described returning to his old neighborhood and finding "the people in those houses were strangers, just like me, doing the best that they could to hold onto the things that they loved." Then he strummed his guitar and sang "Spare parts / And broken hearts / Keep the world turning," providing the theme for a set that dealt with desperately trying to hang onto loved ones in the face of personal and social calamities.

The set didn't make its points as succinctly as it might have, but that will undoubtedly come in time. And in other ways, Springsteen was already in fine shape: The five-man horn section was smoothly integrated into the material, and one-time backup singer Patti Scialfa played rhythm guitar, frequently shared the microphone with Springsteen and took her place as his main foil in a set that was, after all, about relationships between men and women.

The second set, which opened with the gentle strains of "Tougher Than the Rest," was an hour-long look at the various sides of desire, from flirtation (a playful version of "You Can Look [but You Better Not Touch]") to obsession ("I'm on Fire," a rampaging version of "She's the One"). By turns humorous, touching and raucous, it found the E Street Band and the horn section fleshing out the *Tunnel of Love* songs with fuller and more emphatic but still restrained arrangements.

Some fans might have noticed what was missing: "Badlands," "Thunder Road," "The Promised Land" and other standards. But doing those songs might well have trapped Springsteen in a show similar to those of his past tours. And yet at the end of the evening, Springsteen found a way to rework at least one old anthem, and in the process he created a moment as moving as almost anything he's done onstage.

"When I was twenty-four, I wrote this song," he said, strumming his guitar. "It was about a guy and a girl who wanted to run and keep on running. . . . It was my song. And maybe it was your song, too. But as I got older, I realized that I really didn't want it to be."

With that he turned "Born to Run" from a roaring anthem into a bittersweet acoustic ballad. He slowly sang the familiar lines, the crowd joined in on the choruses, and what was once a hymn to the open road became an extraordinary elegy to lost innocence. And when he followed it with joyous versions of "Hungry Heart," "Glory Days" and a full-band arrangement of Elvis Presley's "Can't Help Falling in Love," the show took on a lovely glow.

Naturally, he didn't stop there: In case anybody doubted that the guy could still rock the house down, he tore into "Rosalita (Come Out Tonight)" and his "Devil with a Blue Dress On" medley. The horn section made these warhorses sound fresher than they have for some time. In a way, those songs felt anticlimactic after the earlier, more affecting moments, but at the same time they brought back some of the old-style Springsteen. Opening-night glitches aside, it was a night that suggested the prisoner of love can be just as remarkable as the prisoner of rock & roll ever was.

STEVE POND

BRUCE SPRINGSTEEN'S *TUNNEL* VISION

After the Mammoth Success of *Born in the U.S.A.*, the Rocker Took a Hard Look at His Career and Decided to Bring His Music Back Down to Human Proportions

THE AUDIENCE CONSISTS OF HIS SOUND CREW, his sax player's wife and son and a couple dozen ushers and security guards. But that doesn't stop Bruce Springsteen, who's turning in an extraordinary performance at the Omni, in Atlanta. He's in the middle of a late-afternoon sound check—not one of the marathon sound checks for which Springsteen used to be known but an hour-long chance to refresh his music by playing oldies or current favorites or whatever pops into his head.

Springsteen stands in the middle of the huge white stage in jeans and a long-sleeved white shirt, laughing as he tries to piece together half-remembered lyrics, joking when a band member tosses out the riff from a familiar oldie and muttering, "Okay, what next?" when he finishes a tune. It's a country and folk set: the Everly Brothers, Hank Williams and some lesser-known choices. Some songs fizzle out after a verse or two; every so often, though, Springsteen and the band instinctively craft a full-bodied arrangement, grab a song and claim it as their own.

That happens during "Across the Borderline," a six-year-old song by Ry Cooder, John Hiatt and Jim Dickinson from the movie *The Border*. A plaintive lament about Mexicans in search of an American paradise, the song is one of Bruce's current passions: One person in Springsteen's entourage says he's driven everyone crazy playing it in the van.

So when Springsteen sings its opening lines, the members of the band quickly latch on to the slow groove; they've heard this one before. Guitarist Nils Lofgren picks up a slide and adds an aching counterpoint to Springsteen's vocals. By the first chorus, this has become a performance to break hearts: "When you reach the broken promised land / Every dream slips through your hand / And you'll know that it's too late to change your mind / 'Cause you've paid the price to come so far / Just to wind up where you are / And you're still just across the borderline."

Like the best of Springsteen's own music, this is a song with a deep sense of consequences. Not only do its lines about shattered dreams and broken promises recall his songs, but the song seems to speak directly to the experience of a man who dreamed of becoming a rock star, then became the biggest; who found himself feeling isolated and empty and fought that by reassessing his work, then by turning to his marriage; who at age thirty-eight has set aside his fervent belief that rock & roll can save you in favor of the more sober idea that love *might* save you—if you work at it hard and long enough.

"I guess I used to think that rock could save you," he says later. "I don't believe it can anymore. It can do a *lot*. It's certainly done a lot for me—gave me focus and direction and energy and purpose. I suppose, when I was a kid, it was your best friend: your new 45, man, that was your best buddy.

"But as you get older, you realize that it is not enough. Music alone—you can take some shelter there, and you can find some comfort and happiness, you can dance, you can slow-dance with your girl, but you can't hide in it. And it is *so* seductive that you want to hide in it. And then if you get in the position of somebody like me, where you *can* if you want to, you really can."

He stops himself. "Well, you *think* you can, anyway. In the end you really can't, because no matter who you are, whether it's me or Elvis or Michael Jackson, in the end you really can't. You can use all your powers to isolate yourself, to surround yourself with luxury, to intoxicate yourself in any particular fashion that you so desire. But it just starts eating you away inside, because there is something you get from engagement with people, from a connection with a *person,* that you just cannot get anyplace else. I suppose I had a moment where I kinda crashed into that idea, before I was married. . . .

"It's just confusing. Even the type of connection you can make in your show, which is *enormous,* you can't live there. You have three hours onstage, and then you got the other twenty-one. You may know exactly what you're doing in those three hours, but you better figure out what you're gonna do in them other twenty-one, because you can't book yourself around the clock."

"THE FIRST THING I DID," Springsteen says, "was make everyone stand in a different place." It was the first day of rehearsals for the Tunnel of Love Express, and he knew it was time for a show that would be drastically different from the stadium-rock blowouts that had followed his album

Born in the U.S.A.—especially since those shows had themselves been similar to the acclaimed concerts he'd been doing ever since he started playing
large arenas in 1978.

So he moved the members of the E Street Band out of the places most
of them had occupied onstage for the past thirteen years: drummer Max
Weinberg moved to the side; pianist Roy Bittan and keyboardist Dan Federici traded places; so did guitarist Nils Lofgren and bassist Garry Tallent;
sax man Clarence Clemons shifted from Bruce's right to his left; and singer
Patti Scialfa picked up a guitar, moved into Clarence's old position and became Springsteen's new onstage foil. A horn section recruited from the New
Jersey bar band La Bamba and the Hubcaps took up the rear. Springsteen
had tried this once before—at the beginning of the rehearsals for the Born
in the U.S.A. Tour—but back then, he says, the band "flipped."

This time the musicians, who knew that their boss had considered a solo
acoustic tour, quickly adjusted to the change. Springsteen knew what he
didn't want—"I made a little list of stuff I couldn't imagine playing," he
says—but when manager Jon Landau said it was time to start booking
the tour, he didn't know what he wanted. "I said, 'I don't know if I have
a show, I don't know if I have a *set,*'" says Springsteen with a laugh. "Jon
said, 'Well, you know, that's your job, you've been doing it a long time,
you do it good, so it'll happen.' So I took his word for it."

Two and a half months later, when he takes the stage of the Omni,
Springsteen has a show. It rocks almost as much as his past concerts, but it's
also far more intimate: where his last tour, which played some huge outdoor stadiums, explored the ideas of community and society, this tour,
which is limited to indoor arenas, focuses on desire, commitment and family. The first set is part relationship songs from the *Tunnel of Love* album. It's
part B sides and outtakes: "Be True" and "Roulette" were both recorded
for *The River.* (Springsteen now says, "Both of those songs should have been
on *The River,* and I'm sure they would have been better than a couple other
things that we threw on there.") And at the end of the set are a couple of
barn burners from the Born in the U.S.A. Tour. Songs that have served as
longtime Springsteen staples are missing, for the most part replaced by music
that is hard, dark and almost claustrophobic: Each gentle, nostalgic moment
is shattered by colder, more fearful songs.

Near the end of the set, pianist Roy Bittan plays a pastoral melody, and
Springsteen steps to the mike. The monologue he delivers, ostensibly about
the unmarried mother who's the central character in "Spare Parts," could
just as easily deal with a rock & roll star who's determined to do something
different.

"The past is a funny thing," he says, as the crowd quiets down and Bittan plays softly. "The past is something that seems to bind us all together with memory and experience. And it's also something, I guess, that can drag you down and hold you back as you get stuck in old dreams that just break your heart over and over again when they don't come true."

A brutal version of "Spare Parts" follows, then an angry "War"—no introduction needed, what with Ronald Reagan's troops sitting in Honduras—and finally, just before intermission, "Born in the U.S.A." Three years ago, this song was the hard-fought call to arms that began virtually all of Springsteen's shows; now, coming at the end of a set that dwells on devastating personal and social struggles, it lacks any suggestion of the patriotism that some people insisted on reading into it on the last tour. Musically as exultant as ever, "Born in the U.S.A." suddenly hits home as an agonized, brutal modern-day blues.

"WHEN WE PLAYED THAT FIRST SET IN REHEARSAL," Springsteen says, "I said, 'Yeah, that's good.' " Sitting in the semidarkness of his backstage dressing room in Atlanta, he drops his voice to a gravelly whisper. "It felt real new, real modern to me. I figure some people will wrestle with it a little bit." He breaks the spell with a loud, hoarse laugh. "But that's okay."

It's shortly after one in the morning, and the rest of the E Street Band is gone. There's nobody around in the Omni dressing rooms marked HORNS, PATTI, BAND and MOKSHAGUN (the name given to Clarence Clemons by his guru, Sri Chinmoy, whose framed picture sits next to a lighted candle in Clemons' dressing room). The Springsteen tour is low-key, calm and precisely organized; if there weren't a show tomorrow, they'd already be flying to the next city or flying home to Jersey for a day or two.

Now Springsteen sits back in an overstuffed chair, clad in black slacks, a black dress shirt, a black leather blazer and the silver-tipped black cowboy boots he wears onstage; he has a gold wedding band on his left hand and a single diamond stud in his left ear. He drinks a Heineken very slowly and occasionally takes a pretzel from the small bowl on his coffee table. Behind him, a portable heater glows red. The room is austere: a curtain in front of the door, a folding rubdown table, a buffet table lightly stocked with food and drink.

Though he doesn't look tired, Springsteen speaks slowly, fighting his impulse to ramble. Most of the time he's serious and philosophical, though the nervous, wheezing belly laugh with which he constantly interrupts both his jokes and his most thoughtful and revealing comments suggests he can't take himself too seriously.

"The idea on this tour," he says, "is that you wouldn't know what song was gonna come next. And the way you do that is you just throw out all your cornerstones, the stuff that had not become overly ritualized on the Born in the U.S.A. Tour but would have been if we did it now. It would have been pushin' the buttons a little bit, you know?" Springsteen and the band had more rehearsals for this tour than for all their previous tours combined. In the process, songs were dropped as Springsteen found his themes, and certain tunes "stopped making emotional sense." The last song to go was "Darlington County," which he'd added to lighten a set he finally decided he didn't want to lighten.

"That sense of dread—man, it's everywhere," he says, staring at the wall of his dressing room. "It's outside, it's inside, it's in the bedroom, it's on the street. The main thing was to show people striving for that idea of home: people forced out of their homes, people looking for their homes, people trying to build their homes, people looking for shelter, for comfort, for tenderness, a little bit of kindness somewhere."

Springsteen doesn't vary the show much from night to night, because he feels it is "focused and specific." At its heart are echoes of the struggle that he went through when he began to live out the rock & roll dream that had driven him since he was a high schooler growing up near the Jersey shore. "I guess you get to a place where your old answers and your old dreams don't really work anymore," he says, "so you have to step into something new. For me, there was that particular moment when I had to put my old dreams down, because I had grown beyond them. I suppose I had a particular time when I felt pretty empty."

For Springsteen, that time came after the break-through success of the two-record set *The River,* when he recorded the stark, haunted folk songs that made up his 1982 album *Nebraska.* "I suppose that's where some of that record came from," he says. "I took a little trip across the country, 'cause I felt very isolated." He pauses. "So you start taking those steps outward. That's where you gotta go. And you reach a point where there's a person who says, 'I can show you these other things, but you have to trust me.'"

That person was Julianne Phillips, an actress-model he met in 1984 in Los Angeles and married the following May. The songs that followed, the songs that make up *Tunnel of Love,* focus on the perils of adult romance and commitment. "I wanted to write a different kind of romantic song, one that took in the different types of emotional experiences of any relationship where

you are really engaging with that other person and not involved in a nar-
cissistic romantic fantasy or intoxication or whatever.

"In my life previously, I hadn't allowed myself to get into a situation
where I would even have cause to reflect on these things. When I was in
my twenties, I was specifically *avoiding* it." He laughs. "It was like 'I got
enough on my hands, I ain't ready for that, I don't write no marryin' songs.'
But when this particular record came around, I wanted to make a record
about what I felt, about really letting another person in your life and trying
to be a part of someone else's life. That's a frightening thing, something that's
always filled with shadows and doubts and also wonderful things and beautiful things."

He laughs again. "It's difficult, because there's a part of you that wants
the stability and the home thing, and there's a part of you that isn't so sure.
That was the idea of the record, and I had to change quite a bit to just get
to the point to write about that stuff. I couldn't have written any of those
songs at any other point in my career. I wouldn't have had the knowledge
or the insight or the experience to do it."

And does he think he's found the home he sings about onstage? "Sometimes I really do," he says quietly. "I don't believe that you find something
and there it is and that's the end of the story. You have to find the strength
to sustain it and build on it and work for it and constantly pour energy into
it. I mean, there's days when you're real close and days when you're real far
away. I guess I feel like I know a lot more about it than I ever did, but it's
like anything else: You gotta write that new song every day."

He grins. "I guess, gee, I've been married for three years, just about.
And I feel like we just met."

RIGHT OFF THE BAT, the second set at the Omni violates a given of any
Bruce Springsteen concert: It starts not with a flat-out rocker but with
a measured, emphatic version of the *Tunnel of Love* ballad "Tougher Than
the Rest." It's followed by a thundering rendition of the thirteen-year-old
"She's the One"; the original neo-rockabilly arrangement of "You Can Look
(but You Better Not Touch)"; a rollicking overhaul of "Geno Is a Coward," an old Geno Washington number; a sinuous new reggae original, "Part
Man, Part Monkey"; and the rockers "Dancing in the Dark" and "Light of
Day." But it's "Walk Like a Man," full of telling autobiographical detail and
plaintive yearning—"I pray for the strength to walk like a man," sings
Springsteen, who worried about being too direct and personal when he
wrote the song—that brings the set's tales of desire to a head.

For an encore, Springsteen walks out with an acoustic guitar. "When I was sittin' at home, thinkin' about comin' out on tour and trying to decide what I was gonna do," he says, "I thought, 'Well, I gotta sing a new song.' That's my job. But this is an old song. I wrote this song when I was twenty-four years old, sitting on the end of my bed in Long Branch, New Jersey, and thinking, 'Here I come, world.' " A giggle. "When I wrote it, I guess I figured it was a song about a guy and a girl who wanted to run and keep on running."

A huge cheer; the crowd knows what's coming. "But as I got older, and as I sang it over the years, it sort of opened up, and I guess I realized that it was about two people out searching for something better. Searching for a place they could stand and try and make a life for themselves. And I guess in the end they were searchin' for *home,* something that I guess everybody looks for all their lives. I've spent my life looking for it, I guess. Anyway, this song has kept me good company on my search. I hope it's kept you good company on your search."

The acoustic version of "Born to Run" that follows is elegiac and antiromantic, the kind of haunting moment that wins Springsteen and his audience the right to celebrate. And they do—with "Hungry Heart" and "Glory Days" and finally with "Rosalita (Come Out Tonight)" and the "Detroit medley," Springsteen's customary encore of rock and R&B standards, including "Devil With a Blue Dress."

And as Springsteen gives this determinedly new show a very old ending, in the middle of a rock & roll maelstrom in which he almost seems to turn his back on the hard lessons that preceded the celebration, he shouts out just how this stuff fits in. He introduces "Rosalita" as "the best love song I *ever* wrote!" And before the "Detroit medley," he shouts, "But that's not the end of the story. They got in their car, they drove down the road, they went into a little bar, there was a band there, the band leader shouted, 'One, two, three, four! Devil with a blue dress . . .' " Every love story, it seems, deserves a happy ending—and as a coda to this dark, dark ride, Bruce Springsteen is grinning like a fool and doing the boogaloo and writing *his* happy ending.

THERE'S A STEINWAY BABY GRAND in the living room and a guitar case by the couch, but the music in Bruce Springsteen's posh hotel suite comes from a small boom box blaring out a tape of Chicago blues. It's almost time for another sound check, and the remnants of Springsteen's most recent meal sit on his dining-room table: a box of Shredded Wheat, a cereal bowl in which uneaten strawberries sit in a small pool of milk. Twenty-five floors, one private elevator and a couple of receptionists and security guards away from the fans outside Atlanta's Ritz-Carlton, Springsteen sits in an armchair in blue jeans, a pin-striped white shirt and his silver-tipped cowboy boots, nursing a chocolate milkshake and talking about his career.

To some, *Tunnel of Love* is a foolish move: an album of intimate ballads from a guy who broke things wide open with an album of rockers. The tour isn't the juggernaut its predecessor was, and the album has sold considerably less than *Born in the U.S.A.*—although Springsteen clearly prefers it to the earlier record, which he shrugs off as "a rock record." He says, "I never really felt like I quite got it, though 'Born in the U.S.A.' and 'My Hometown' made it feel more thematic than it probably was." Is the quintessential mainstream American rock hero now just another guy with an album in the Top Twenty and a tour in the local arenas?

"I don't really have a desire to have some super big-selling record," he says. "I mean, I enjoyed *Born in the U.S.A.*, and it did bring a new audience to me, some who will fall away and some who will stick around for the rest of the show. I don't consider *Tunnel of Love* a small record, but I suppose it doesn't reach out and grab you by the throat and thrash you around like *Born in the U.S.A.*

"I wouldn't *mind* having another big record like that. But my main concern is writing that new song that has that new idea, that new perspective. To me, that is the essence of my job." He chuckles. "Also, you want to rock people. That's my job, too. So that makes you want to write a *fast* song."

But for now, the most moving moment of his show may well be the fast song slowed down, the song about running that's become a song about home. "I wanted to separate 'Born to Run' from any way we've ever done the song before," Springsteen says. "I didn't want to crash into it like some old anthem or something, and I wanted to give people a chance to reexperience the song. And myself, too." He grins. "I guess in that song I asked every question I've been trying to answer since I was twenty-four. I was young, and those were the things I wanted to know. And fifteen years down the line, you understand much clearer what those things are, and what they cost, and their importance. And I suppose, when I play the song now, I would imagine that you get some sense of that.

"I asked myself those questions at that age, and I really did faithfully, I feel, do everything I could to find some answers. The way you keep faith with your audience is not by signing autographs; it's by keeping faith with that initial search you set out on. I suppose this show is a—it's not a resolution by any means, but it is what I've learned and what I know."

But can Bruce Springsteen, a multimillionaire rock star in his penthouse suite, remain close to his audience while his images have been appropriated by politicians and television commercials? After all, Springsteen may have added "Backstreets" to his set after a fan sent him a letter explaining how much the song meant to him and his friends—but when he tells that story, even Springsteen is amazed that the fan managed to penetrate security and get the letter to his hotel room.

"In some ways," he stammers, "there's not a lot of difference. I still go out, meet people. With the size of the thing, the way that you counteract that is by becoming more intimate in your work. I suppose that's why after I did *Born in the U.S.A.,* I made this intimate record. I made a record that was really sort of addressed to my core audience, my longtime fans."

He frowns. "The size is tricky, it's dangerous. You can become purely iconic, or you can become just a Rorschach test that people throw up their own impressions upon, which you always are to some degree anyway. With size, and the co-option of your images and attitudes—you know, you wake up and you're a car commercial or whatever. And the way I think the artist deals with that is just reinvention. You've got to constantly reinvent, and it's a long trip, it's a long drive."

If there was ever a point when his relationship with the audience would have changed, he adds, it would have been during the *Born to Run* furor of 1975—the covers of *Time* and *Newsweek,* the move from clubs to theaters, the charges that he was a record-company hype—rather than the *Born in the U.S.A.* explosion of a decade later.

"Obviously, the *Born in the U.S.A.* experience had its frightening moments," he says. "But I had a real solid sense of myself by the time I was thirty-five. When I was twenty-five, I thought that I would slip away. . . . Also, when I was twenty-five, I just worked all the time, because I had nothing else going. I think at this point in my life I've gotten to the place where I want a *real* life, which is something you've got to cut out for yourself. And I've been lucky: Most of my fans, most of the people I meet wish you the best. Then you meet people that—your real life is an intrusion upon their fantasy, and they don't like that."

He laughs uproariously. "But, hey, that's not my problem. So anyway, along the road I probably come in contact with fans a little less than I used to, but outside of the details of the thing, I think my basic feelings and attitudes toward my audience haven't really changed. I guess I still feel like one of them, basically."

And this, it seems, is why the new Bruce Springsteen still pulls out those warhorses at the end of the night, the reason the guy who refuses to do "Badlands" and "Thunder Road" and "Jungleland" winds up every show with "Rosalita" and half an hour of the "Detroit medley."

"That's the trick of the show," he says. "The most important song, re-ally, is 'Devil With a Blue Dress.' " He laughs heartily, savoring the seem-ing silliness of that idea. "Because the show really builds up to the moment when the houselights come up. The lights come up, and the stage slips back into the crowd, and the audience comes forth, and that *is* the event. You would think the end of the show is about excitement, but it's really not. It's about emotion. Because that's when people are the most visible, when they're the most vulnerable, the *freest*.

"That's when things sit in a certain perspective. You can look up, *way* up, and you see some guy, and he waves to you, and you wave back—and in a funny kind of way, you know, that's the idea of the whole night. And the thing that keeps it from being just an aerobic exercise is the rest of the show, which resonates underneath that and gives those songs, which appear to be kind of thrown off, emotional meaning and emotional life.

"And in a funny way, with all the stuff I sing about for the whole rest of the night, I'm not sure I say anything that's more important than that par-ticular moment."

■ RANDOM NOTES (May 19, 1988)

After a recent Bruce Springsteen show in Landover, Maryland, Fawn Hall, former loyal secretary and shredder to Oliver North, wanted to go backstage to meet the singer. According to the *Boston Globe,* an attendant conveyed her wishes to Springsteen and returned with the following message from the man himself: "I don't like Ollie North, and I don't approve of the things you did. I'm a Democrat, and I have nothing to say to you." A few nights earlier, Springsteen told a New Jersey audience, "Don't vote for that fuckin' Bush."

■ RANDOM NOTES (June 16, 1988)

"Everyone's standing in different places," says backup singer and guitarist Patti Scialfa, downplaying her very prominent role in Bruce Springsteen's Tunnel of Love Express Tour. The willowy Scialfa now takes her place right next to Springsteen onstage, and she seems to have replaced Clarence Clemons as Bruce's main sidekick. The thirty-year-old singer recently signed her own record deal with Columbia. "I wanted to make a personal record," she says. She's written all of the material for the album, which she describes as "a romantic record." Scialfa plans to go into the studio before the Tunnel of Love Express heads off to Europe this summer. As for the musicians, she doesn't rule out members of the E Street Band. Springsteen's involvement thus far has been as an adviser. "He gives great advice. He's helped me pick out the material for the record. He goes over it, listens to my material and gives me direction with it." But even if her solo career takes off, Scialfa says that she will always be available to sing with Bruce. "It's satisfying, just to be able to be a part of his music. I feel like it's a gift, you know?"

■ RANDOM NOTES (August 11, 1988)

In the wake of his separation from his wife, Bruce Springsteen, who has long made a point of keeping his personal life private, has suddenly seen it splashed across the pages of almost every tabloid. It began when rumors of his breakup with Julianne Phillips surfaced in May. Those rumors became front-page news when pictures emerged of Springsteen and backup singer Patti Scialfa nuzzling poolside in Rome. According to Phillips's manager, the couple have been separated since April. The tabloids reported that Springsteen had left his wife because she was more interested in a career than in having kids. But Springsteen stated through his record company that the issue of having children had no role in the separation and that he fully supported Julianne's pursuit of her career. "My sense is that he's very upset that a lot of the coverage has been negative toward Julianne," said a Springsteen spokesperson.

FRED GOODMAN

WHERE ARE THEY NOW?
E Street Band Alumni

VINI LOPEZ REMEMBERS PLAYING A GIG with Bruce Springsteen one New Year's Eve at a club called the Student Prince, in Asbury Park, New Jersey. "Nobody came," he says. "We had a good old time, but nobody came."

It's impossible to picture Springsteen playing to an empty house these days. But during the five years that Lopez—nicknamed Mad Dog by Springsteen, who was fond of introducing Vini onstage as a "homicidal, paranoid-schizophrenic Catholic"—drummed for Springsteen, the biggest problem the group had was making enough money to eat.

"When the first album came out, I was making $35 a week playing with Bruce," says Lopez. "Then it went up to $50 when we did *The Wild, the Innocent & the E Street Shuffle*. The most I ever got was $110." Today, Lopez works as a caretaker on an estate in Brewster, New York, but still occasionally gigs around the Jersey Shore.

It was in 1968, at the Upstage, a club located above a Thom McAn shoe store in Asbury Park, that Lopez first hooked up with Springsteen. "Bruce was always real straight," says Lopez. "The guitar and his songs were all he cared about. He wanted it real bad, and I knew he would go far." Lopez went on to back Springsteen in a succession of bands that included Child, Steel Mill, Dr. Zoom and the Sonic Boom, the Bruce Springsteen Band and the original E Street Band.

"On the road, I roomed with Garry Tallent and Clarence Clemons," Lopez says. "But Clarence snored, and I used to wind up sleeping in the truck." Money was still tight even after Bruce signed to Columbia, and Lopez remembers fishing for his dinner. "Clarence could really cut fish," he says. "His dad had a fish market in Norfolk, Virginia."

Although Lopez was replaced as the band's drummer in February of 1974, he remains proud of his E Street days. "I guess I could've been bitter," he says, "but I prefer not to let it affect me that way. I don't remember any bad shows. We always tried our best, even in rehearsals. We wanted to please Bruce."

Several other E Street alumni have carved out their own careers. Miami Steve Van Zandt, of course, metamorphosed into Little Steven. Keyboardist David Sancious—whose mother's house, on E Street, in Belmar, New Jersey, was the group's rehearsal spot and namesake—formed a jazz-fusion group called Tone. Sancious, who has also toured as a member of Peter Gabriel's band, now lives in Kingston, New York.

It was Sancious who brought drummer Ernest "Boom" Carter, an Asbury Park native, into the E Street band as a replacement for Lopez. Although Carter spent less than a year in the band, he recorded the most famous drum part in the Springsteen catalog: the pounding introduction to "Born to Run."

Carter, who left with Sancious to play in Tone, later played with Southside Johnny and the Asbury Jukes and a New Jersey band called the Fairlanes. He recently appeared on Steve Forbert's album *Streets of This Town*. He says his only regret is that he never received a gold record for his work on *Born to Run*. "It would be nice to have a million dollars in the bank," he says, "but if I didn't leave, I wouldn't have the ears I have now and the tools to express myself."

Although vocalist Patti Scialfa is currently in the limelight with the E Street Band, she is not the first female member of the group. That distinction belongs to Suki Lahav, a violinist whose first husband, Louis Lahav, was the engineer on Springsteen's first two albums. An Israeli, Suki now lives in Jerusalem, where she teaches violin and writes lyrics for Israeli pop singers.

A member of the E Street Band for just "four or five months," Suki actually spent a couple of years around the band because of her former husband's involvement. On record, she contributed the violin introduction to "Jungleland."

Suki says Springsteen is quite popular in Israel. "I'm not surprised at all at how big he has become," she says. "I'm just very proud of him. For me, it's kind of like the success of a big brother."

MICHAEL GOLDBERG

SPRINGSTEEN EP DUE

Four-Song Release Keyed to Start of Human Rights Now! Tour

IN ANTICIPATION OF HEADLINING Amnesty International's Human Rights Now! Tour, Bruce Springsteen will release a four-song EP to benefit the organization at the end of August.

The highlight of the record is an anthemic version of Bob Dylan's classic protest song "Chimes of Freedom" that Springsteen performed July 3rd in Stockholm after announcing his participation in the Amnesty International tour. The EP will also include live versions of "Tougher Than the Rest," "Be True" and the acoustic version of "Born to Run" that has been a show stopper during Springsteen's Tunnel of Love Express tour. The three additional songs were recorded in April during Springsteen's L.A. concerts.

" 'Chimes of Freedom' is the song Bruce has adopted as a key song for what he'll be doing for the Amnesty tour," says a source close to Springsteen's management. "It symbolizes his connection to Amnesty." Springsteen has also apparently decided to include the song in his current repertoire: He recently performed it during his concert at East Berlin's Velodrome Stadium, which attracted 160,000 fans.

In Europe, a different version of the twelve-inch EP—tentatively planned to feature live and studio versions of "Spare Parts" and a live version of "Cover Me," in addition to "Chimes of Freedom"—will be released. Both versions of the record will probably be available on CD. Although Springsteen is donating his royalties to Amnesty International, fund raising is not the chief reason for releasing the recordings.

"Bruce thought it would be great to get some new music out," says the management source. "It seemed like a great idea to get some new music out in anticipation of the Amnesty appearances that would draw attention to the tour."

Springsteen is said to be excited about collaborating with some of the other artists. And instead of his usual three-plus hours, Springsteen will be limiting himself to a one-hour set of hits and material suitable to the tour.

TOP 100 SINGLES OF THE LAST TWENTY-FIVE YEARS

FOR A TRIBUTE TO THE ROCK & ROLL 45, ROLLING STONE writers and editors chose the top 100 singles of the twenty-five years spanning 1963 to 1988. Bruce Springsteen scored a song in the top ten.

#9 "Born to Run"

Introducing "Born to Run" on his Tunnel of Love tour, Bruce Springsteen identified the anthem as his favorite among his songs. "I don't know if it's my *best*," he said, "but it surprises me how I knew so much about what my life was about at that time."

The song that would finally free Springsteen from being viewed as just another neo-Dylan was almost never released at all. He worked on recording "Born to Run" for a staggering five months, but it also took sheer chance and a college undergraduate to change the course of his career.

In 1974, Springsteen remained mired in cult-hero status, and relations with his label, Columbia, were strained. When his second album, *The Wild, the Innocent & the E Street Shuffle,* hadn't sold well, his manager, Mike Appel, had sent Columbia executives bags of coal for Christmas; soon the label was suggesting that Springsteen make his next record using session musicians instead of the E Street Band.

That was too drastic, but changes were needed. Praising the second album, the critic Jon Landau wrote that the drummer, Vini Lopez, was "the album's consistent weak spot" and called the recording "a mite thin or trebly-sounding." Springsteen seemed to agree: Before the third album, Lopez was replaced by Ernest "Boom" Carter, and the idea while recording the first track for the album was to make it sound as big as possible. Springsteen has said his goal was to sing like Roy Orbison, with words like

Bob Dylan's and a sound like Phil Spector's early-Sixties productions.

The song that the twenty-four-year-old Springsteen had written fully embodied his vision of the tenuous American dream: It's an emotional, imagistic plea to a girl from "a scared and lonely rider" trying to break out of a "death trap" small town, driving his "suicide machine" on highways "jammed with broken heroes."

Springsteen, the E Street Band—Carter, Garry Tallent, Danny Federici, Clarence Clemons and David Sancious—and coproducer Appel returned to 914, a studio in Blauvelt, New York, where the first two albums had been recorded.

The singer knew, says Appel, that "this song would set the tone for the entire album and for his career from that point forward." This fact weighed heavily on the recording, which took as long as most entire albums do. "It was more than just cutting a song," says Louis Lahav, who engineered the sessions. "It was this *thing* you believed in so much—like a religion."

Appel had recently met Jeff Barry, cowriter of many of Phil Spector's hits, and they had discussed how Spector had achieved his trademark Wall of Sound. Springsteen and Appel strove to re-create these techniques for "Born to Run": keeping the piano pedal down to generate a heavy drone, overdubbing numerous guitars, saxophones and strings and laying on heavy echo and reverb. The song's blaring "Da Doo Ron Ron" inspired opening, for instance, was achieved by enhancing Clemons' multiple baritone sax tracks with Sancious' synthesizer. Also prominent is a Spectorish glockenspiel.

"It was a sixteen-track," says Lahav, "but it was *packed,* like a thirty-two-track today." Adds Appel, "You couldn't relax in the mix for a second."

Columbia thought the result was too long for a single, but the overlaid tracks rendered the song unremixable and uneditable, and the label withheld funds for the rest of the album. So Appel released a cassette of the song to a few dozen radio stations, which gladly played it; this only angered Columbia further.

Springsteen and the E Street Band returned to the college circuit to pay the rent; at Brown University the singer gave an interview to the school paper complaining that the new president of CBS Records, Irwin Segalstein, didn't care about artists and wanted to drop him. Unbeknownst to Springsteen, Segalstein's son—a Springsteen fan—was attending Brown at the time and, appalled to read about his father's actions, called home to complain. Segalstein, in turn, called Appel, who threatened more damning press; ultimately a thawing out was achieved. Columbia loosened the purse strings;

Max Weinberg and Roy Bittan replaced Carter and Sancious. Jon Landau came on as a coproducer (and ultimately became Springsteen's manager), and the sessions moved to New York City. Landau tried to remix "Born to Run," but he realized that, like a Spector recording, it was what it was.

Over the years the song has accrued richer meaning for Springsteen. He says that he chose to play "Born to Run" acoustically on the *Tunnel of Love* tour because "I wanted to give people a chance to reexperience the song. And myself, too. Before, people would experience just the song's visceral power, that thrust toward the sense of individual freedom. . . . The way I'm doing it now, there's a sense of consequences."

"When I wrote it, it was about a guy and a girl that wanted to run and keep on running," Springsteen told one audience this year. "As I got older, I realized how much that was me, and how much I didn't want it to end up *being* me."

As Springsteen says, "If 'Born to Run' said, 'I want this'—whether it was individual freedom, home, friendship, love or the search for something better—fifteen years down the line you understand much clearer what those things are and what they cost. And their importance. And that's growin' up!"

■ RANDOM NOTES (October 6, 1988)

"I'm pretty angry at all of this business about a rivalry between Bruce and myself—maybe this will put an end to it," said Sting prior to his show at New York's Madison Square Garden, where Bruce Springsteen joined him onstage to sing "The River."

Their duet was a gesture to promote Amnesty International's Human Rights Now! Tour, which they're headlining along with Peter Gabriel, Tracy Chapman and Youssou N'Dour. Sting says that he and Bruce may swap songs on the tour, but there's one song from Bruce's repertoire he won't touch. "I don't think I could sing 'Born in the U.S.A.' with any conviction," he says.

After the show, Sting, Bruce and their respective girlfriends, Trudie Styler and Patti Scialfa, were joined by Madonna and Jodie Foster at a dinner party at the Canal Bar. At dinner, Sting said of Bruce's performance, "He sings so loud, I couldn't believe it!"

■ RANDOM NOTES (NOVEMBER 3, 1988)

"The great challenge of adulthood," said Bruce Springsteen during the Philadelphia press conference for Amnesty International's Human Rights Now! Tour, "is holding on to your idealism after you lose your innocence and believing in the power of the human spirit. . . . Amnesty International is an organization that reaffirms that power."

The tour, featuring Springsteen, Peter Gabriel, Sting, Tracy Chapman and Youssou N'Dour, has followed a grueling travel schedule that one day included breakfast in Paris, lunch in Budapest and dinner in Torino, Italy. "The logistics of flying around 170 people with 350 bags is a nightmare," said Sting's saxophonist, Branford Marsalis. To maintain their sanity on the long flights, the bands and crew members sometimes "act like adolescents—having pillow fights and stripping and doing wild shit," he said. "Everybody except the front guys."

Backstage at the Philly show, Sting's *Bride* costar, Jennifer Beals, said she was "too scared" to meet Springsteen. "You know when you're almost on the verge of idolizing someone?" she said. Also roaming the backstage area were members of the Hooters, Eric Stoltz, Mary Stuart Masterson and Elizabeth McGovern. Gabriel gave the night's most moving set, which included a duet of "Don't Give Up" with Chapman. Also notable was Springsteen's rare performance of "Jungleland." "That brought back all the great memories of all the great times we played that song," said saxman Clarence Clemons.

After the show, Springsteen and Patti Scialfa appeared in the lobby bar of their hotel, where they socialized with Amnesty organizers, including U.S. Amnesty head Jack Healey, a driving force behind the tour. A few days later, at the Oakland show, Joan Baez, a special guest of the U.S. tour, and Springsteen performed a duet of "Blowin' in the Wind."

■ RANDOM NOTES (November 17, 1988)

Not so Boss: CBS is taking heat for its recently released CD-3 of Bruce Springsteen's *Chimes of Freedom* EP. Two selections were edited because of the format's twenty-one-minute time limit, and many Springsteen fans are up in arms. Trimmed off were one verse of "Tougher Than the Rest" and Springsteen's poignant spoken introduction to "Chimes of Freedom." The disc also has none of the colorful graphics found on the record and cassette. Springsteen was consulted, however, and the decision was made to edit rather than drop one song altogether (or not issue a CD at all). "Believe me, we went through a lot trying to figure out how to do this," says one CBS executive involved. "It wasn't a lightly made decision." As for the packaging, the label's primary objective is keeping the price down to help the new configuration's chance for survival. "We recognize it's a severe compromise," says Jerry Shulman, vice-president of marketing development for CBS, "but our ultimate objective is to provide incredible sound at incredible prices."

■ RANDOM NOTES (JANUARY 12, 1989)

Bruce Springsteen and Julianne Phillips have reached an out-of-court divorce settlement (though nothing's been signed). The terms are being kept confidential. Other Bruce news: Springsteen joined Southside Johnny onstage at the Stone, in San Francisco.

JIM FARBER

SPRINGSTEEN'S *VIDEO ANTHOLOGY/1978—88* VIDEO REVIEW

IF YOU WANT TO TEST THE LIMITS of Bruce Springsteen's credibility (as so many do these days), watch his videos. In this anthology of eighteen clips, our "down-to-earth everyman" takes on the medium of self-loving calculation—and wins! This triumph is all the more amazing considering that Springsteen has benefited so profoundly from the star-faking machinery of the video years. His ascent to super-duper stardom paralleled the arrival, circa 1984–85, of MTV as a major marketing force in the music industry. Still, watching this collection, one can't help recognizing that Springsteen's honesty overcomes the medium's contrivance.

Springsteen can communicate his message as deeply with his face and body as with his voice. In the clip for "I'm on Fire," Springsteen's eyes relate the inner life of the character he is singing about, mixing equal parts lust and self-doubt. What is most amazing is that Springsteen's charisma, even at its most spectacular, seldom overwhelms the tales of the everyday men and women who people his songs. There are exceptions: In "My Hometown," for example, his sexual allure overpowers the lyrics of the song. Still, when Springsteen indulges his erotic side, as he does in "Fire," he does it with wit.

Like "Fire," the majority of the pieces are live, dating back to a primitive "Rosalita (Come Out Tonight)," from 1978. Also included is Arnold Levine's wonderful short for "Atlantic City," which contrasts the city's forgotten poor with its new citadels of misdirected hope. Springsteen doesn't appear in "Atlantic City"—which says something about his opinion of videos at the time—but by 1984 he was serving up video iconography as self-conscious as "Born in the U.S.A." Such posing could have compromised Springsteen's populism, but clips like "Born to Run," from 1987, show why it didn't. "Born to Run" offers a typically adoring compilation of concert scenes, but the effect is unique for this simple reason: The sense of identification that Springsteen inspires in his audience has blurred the line between performer and viewers so completely that the videos that exalt him do just the same for us.

■ **RANDOM NOTES** (April 20, 1989)

Bruce Springsteen, who's been hanging out in L.A. with Harley rider Mickey Rourke, brought Patti Scialfa to a party for boxer Ray "Boom Boom" Mancini at Rourke's club, Rubber. Springsteen took the stage with the house band to sing "C.C. Rider."

■ **RANDOM NOTES** (May 4, 1989)

Bruce Springsteen, who recently took the stage at the L.A. club Rubber to sing "C.C. Rider" with the house band, the Mighty Hornets, is on the West Coast with Patti Scialfa while she lays down demo tracks for her solo album. There are no details yet on Springsteen's involvement in the project. Springsteen was also among the guests—including Tom Petty and Bob Seger—who gathered at the Reel Inn, in Malibu, for producer Jimmy Iovine's thirty-sixth birthday bash.

■ **RANDOM NOTES** (May 4, 1989)

Two former roadies for Bruce Springsteen—Michael Batlan and Douglas Sutphin—had several charges against their former boss thrown out by a New Jersey judge recently. Included among those charges was one in which the two sought punitive damages of $6 million. Still pending is a charge dealing with a denial of overtime pay. Batlan and Sutphin contend that although Springsteen paid them a total of $250,000 in severance pay when they left his employ in 1985, they were subject to arbitrarily docked paychecks and that a promised raise for Batlan was never delivered. Batlan and Sutphin also claim that their work as roadies was covered by federal hour-and-wage laws and that they are entitled to retroactive overtime pay. Although that is not generally the practice in the tour business, Springsteen's attorneys say that the plaintiffs do have a legal right to overtime, if indeed they can prove they worked overtime. The case, which could go to a jury as early as July, might necessitate an appearance on the witness stand by Springsteen.

■ **RANDOM NOTES** (August 10, 1989)

Bruce Springsteen is back to his old stage-hopping tricks. He dropped in at the Stone Pony, in Asbury Park, three times recently: joining Killer Joe Delia's band, featuring Max Weinberg; playing with Nils Lofgren and his band; and taking the stage with Bobby Bandiera. His next stop was at Neil Young's Jones Beach concert, where the pair did an acoustic version of "Down by the River." Finally he was back in Jersey (Atlantic City this time) to join Jackson Browne for a three-song encore.

■ **RANDOM NOTES** (September 21, 1989)

Bruce Springsteen and his E Street Band donated over $206,000 in royalties from the EP *Chimes of Freedom* to Amnesty International, marking the biggest donation ever made to the organization. Besides the Amnesty gift, Springsteen recently made contributions to a factory workers' resource center in New Jersey, a California hospital where his father underwent surgery and a TV news program about South Africa. Meanwhile, the rocker is still wrangling in court with ex-roadies who claim he owes them back pay; he was recently ordered by the court to turn over some of his tax records.

■ **RANDOM NOTES** (November 16, 1989)

On the eve of his fortieth birthday, Bruce Springsteen made it back to his old stomping grounds, Asbury Park's Stone Pony. There he joined Jimmy Cliff, who is touring in support of his new album, *Images,* onstage to sing Cliff's "Trapped," which Springsteen covered on the album *We Are the World.* Cliff then led the crowd—which included Patti Scialfa, Springsteen's mother and sister—in singing "Happy Birthday" to Bruce.

The next night, Springsteen celebrated at McLoone's Rum Runner, a bar near his Rumson, New Jersey, home. He played for an hour with the help of Roy Bittan, Max Weinberg, Garry Tallent, Steve Van Zandt and Patti Scialfa. Springsteen also called on manager Jon Landau to play guitar and his uncle Warren to sing backup. Halfway through the eight-song set he left the stage to slow-dance with his mother, Adele, as Scialfa and Van Zandt sang "Stand by Me." Springsteen told the crowd, "I'm forty years old, but damn, I'm still handsome!"

TOP 100 ALBUMS OF THE EIGHTIES

A T DECADE'S END, ROLLING STONE editors chose the best albums of the Eighties. Bruce Springsteen showed up four times.

#6 *Born in the U.S.A.*

"I had written a catchy song," Bruce Springsteen recalled in an interview last year with ROLLING STONE, "and I felt it was a really good song, probably one of my best since 'Born to Run.' I knew it was going to catch people—but I didn't know it was going to catch them like *that,* or that it was going to be what it was."

Born in the U.S.A.—the album, the song and the sixteen-month tour—turned out to be the breakthrough that Springsteen fans had been expecting for a decade. The influential Jersey musician became the world's biggest rock star—and a bona fide American icon, to boot.

As a result, Springsteen found himself dominating the album charts in 1984 and 1985. He hit the Top Ten seven times and wound up in heavy rotation in the theretofore unfamiliar terrain of MTV. The album inspired those who knew what his bitter, tough-minded songs were really saying (from numerous songwriters to novelist Bobbie Ann Mason, whose *In Country* owes a debt to the LP), as well as many others who misinterpreted and exploited the cover's American-flag imagery (among them, both 1984 presidential candidates and countless advertising agencies and jingle writers).

For Springsteen, who'd been catapulted into the media spotlight almost ten years earlier, when his album *Born to Run* landed him simultaneously on the covers of *Time* and *Newsweek, Born in the U.S.A.* afforded him an opportunity to do it over again, older and wiser and not so awestruck by the machinery of fame. "The *Born in the U.S.A.* experience obviously had its frightening moments," Springsteen told ROLLING STONE. "But I was thirty-five, and I had a real solid sense of myself by that time. With *Born in the U.S.A.*, I had a chance to relive my 1975 experience when I was calm and completely prepared and went for it. It was like 'Great. We're selling all those records? Dynamite.' "

But it took Bruce Springsteen a long time and a lot of soul-searching to get to the point where he was willing to welcome that kind of stardom. *Born to Run* was followed by two years of legal difficulties and, finally, the grim, relentlessly downbeat *Darkness on the Edge of Town*. The commercial breakthrough of *The River* was answered by the bleak acoustic album *Nebraska*. But when it came time to assemble a new album, Springsteen's choice was clear: If he was ever going to make a blockbuster rock record, this would have to be the one.

Besides, he already had most of the songs. Springsteen and the E Street Band had recorded seven of the songs on *Born in the U.S.A.* prior to the release of *Nebraska* in a three-week blitz in May 1982: "Glory Days," "I'm Goin' Down," "I'm on Fire," "Darlington County," "Working on the Highway," "Downbound Train" and—most crucial of all—"Born in the U.S.A."

Springsteen originally recorded the last of these on the acoustic demo tape that became *Nebraska,* but he quickly abandoned that version, feeling it didn't really work in that format. At the start of the May sessions with the full band, Springsteen revived the song in a new, electric arrangement. "Bruce started playing this droning guitar sound," says drummer Max Weinberg. "He threw that lick out to [keyboardists] Roy [Bittan] and Danny [Federici], and the thing just fell together.

"It absolutely grabbed us. We played it again and got an even better groove on it. At the end, as we were stopping, Bruce gave me the high sign to do all these wild fills, and we went back into the song and jammed for about ten minutes, which was edited out. I remember that night as the greatest single experience I've ever had recording, and it set the tone for the whole record. That track was so special; it was really something to live up to."

For a while, though, Springsteen was ambivalent about following through with the rock record whose tone had been so dramatically set by "Born in the U.S.A." "He spent a good deal of time after the release of *Nebraska* feeling very close to that album," says Springsteen's manager, Jon Landau, who coproduced *Born in the U.S.A.* "I don't think he was ready to suddenly switch back into the 'Born in the U.S.A.' mode."

Springsteen drove to Los Angeles, where he began recording demos on his own, most of them closer in sound and spirit to *Nebraska* than to *Born in the U.S.A.* Some, like "Shut Out the Light," eventually appeared as B sides; others, such as "Sugarland" and his overhaul of Elvis Presley's "Follow That Dream," never appeared.

When he returned to recording with the E Street Band, the sessions were marked by prolific songwriting and a freewheeling approach on the part of Springsteen. "I remember one night when we were completely packed up to go home and Bruce was off in the corner playing his acoustic guitar," says Weinberg. "Suddenly, I guess the bug bit him, and he started writing these rockabilly songs. We'd been recording all night and were dead tired, but they had to open up the cases and set up the equipment so that we could start recording again at five in the morning. That's when we got 'Pink Cadillac,' 'Stand on It' [both used as B sides] and a song called 'TV Movie.' . . . Bruce got on a roll, and when that happens, you just hold on for dear life."

In the end, though, most of the sessions were inconclusive. Of the dozens of songs he recorded from mid-1982 to mid-1983, only "My Hometown" would make *Born in the U.S.A.*'s final cut.

Eventually, Landau and coproducer Chuck Plotkin convinced Springsteen that the best songs were from the May 1982 sessions. Late in the recording process, however, Springsteen wrote a few more standouts, including "Bobby Jean," his benediction to guitarist Steve Van Zandt, who'd left the band to pursue a solo career, and "No Surrender," an optimistic raveup. The album slowly and painstakingly assumed a shape with the help of band members, colleagues and friends who were asked to vote for their favorites from about twenty contenders.

Born in the U.S.A. appeared to be finished, but then Landau, in an exchange that he admits was "testy, by our standards," told Springsteen that the album needed another song. He had a list of requirements: It should unify the record, it should be written in the first person, and it should capture where Bruce was at that point in time. Springsteen objected—"The obvious response is, 'Hey, if that's what you want, then write it yourself,' and I got a little bit of that in this case," says Landau—but three days later Springsteen played Landau a new song born of his frustration and confusion. Its title was "Dancing in the Dark." With that, his blockbuster was finished.

Born in the U.S.A. was Springsteen's triumph, though he doesn't regard it as his best work. "That was a *rock* record," he says from the vantage point of four years later. "When I put it on, that's kind of how it hits me: That's a rock record. And the bookends ["Born in the U.S.A." and "My Hometown"] sort of covered the thing and made it feel more thematic than probably it actually was, you know? But I never really felt like I quite got it."

Still, if Springsteen looks back at *Born in the U.S.A.* as merely "a rock record," it should be pointed out that this was the album that defined how hard a record could rock, how much a rock record could say and what impact a rock record could have.

#25 *Tunnel of Love*

Bruce Springsteen wasn't a romantic young kid anymore. He couldn't write songs about hitting the road with his girl, because as he got into his late thirties, that wasn't the kind of thing that appealed to a married millionaire. So on the heels of his commercial blockbuster *Born in the U.S.A.* and the ensuing live boxed set that summarized and closed the chapter on the past ten years, Bruce Springsteen made a low-key, intimate record about adult relationships. "It's easy for two people to lose each other in this tunnel of love," he sings ominously in the title track.

"When I wrote the record," he told ROLLING STONE after its release, "I wanted to write a different type of romantic song, one that I felt took in the different types of emotional experiences of any real relationship. I guess I wanted to make a record about what I felt. Really letting another person into your life, that's a frightening thing. That's something that's filled with shadows and doubts, and also wonderful things and beautiful things, things you've never experienced before and things you cannot experience alone."

Tunnel of Love deals mostly with shadows and doubts. Ten years after *Darkness on the Edge of Town,* Springsteen was singing in the voice of a man who, in the words of the remarkable "Brilliant Disguise," is "lost in the darkness of our love." At the center of the album is "Walk Like a Man," an open account of his wedding day. Surrounding the hope at the heart of that song are songs whose characters can barely keep their hopes alive: "Tunnel of Love," "One Step Up," the searing, hard-luck rocker "Spare Parts" and the fearful late-night reverie "Valentine's Day."

"I suppose it doesn't have the physical 'reach out and grab you by the throat and thrash you around' of, say, *Born in the U.S.A.,*" said Springsteen. "*Tunnel of Love* is a rock record, but most of the stuff is midtempo, and it's more rhythm oriented, very different. It was more meticulously arranged than anything I've done since *Born to Run.* I was into just getting the grooves."

It also came quickly. Unlike the modus operandi for most of his albums, Springsteen wrote only three or four extra songs, and he recorded the album swiftly, cutting most of the tracks in a small studio at his home in New Jersey. It was a quintessentially low-tech studio: It wasn't air-conditioned; Springsteen's Corvette had to be moved out of the way to do some piano overdubs; and if a car driving by honked its horn, the take would have to be redone.

Springsteen's first series of demos included nine of the album's twelve songs. "Brilliant Disguise" and "One Step Up" came later, and "Tunnel of Love" was written when Springsteen decided that it would make a good album title and set about composing a song with that name.

Most of the tracks were recorded, instrument by instrument, by Springsteen himself; though he later brought in E Street Band members and the odd outsider to add parts or replace drum machines, other musicians were used sparingly, and the entire band never played together. As a result, *Tunnel of Love* has an intimacy perfectly suited to the tales being told by a rock star determined to return to a more human scale in his music.

"The way you counteract the size [of stardom] is by becoming more intimate in your work," he said. "And I suppose that's why after I did *Born in the U.S.A.,* I made an intimate record . . . a record that was really addressed to my core audience, my longtime fans."

#43 Nebraska

First, he sat on a rocking chair in his New Jersey bedroom, strumming an acoustic guitar and singing into a tape recorder. Then he stuck the cassette (sans case) in his back pocket and carried it around for a couple of weeks. Next, he tried to teach the songs to the E Street Band. Finally, several soul-searching months later, Bruce Springsteen decided that his next album was going to be the cassette tape he'd kept in his pocket.

That tape would become *Nebraska,* an album full of dark, desperate tales from a rock & roll star who'd decided that some stories are best told simply, by a man and his guitar. Commercially, it was a daring move. In 1982, Springsteen was at the point where a strong rock album would have cemented the breakthrough he'd made with *The River,* released in 1980, which yielded his first Top Ten hit, "Hungry Heart." But he was growing increasingly disturbed by the currents in Ronald Reagan's America and was unable to retain his youthful belief that rock & roll could make everything right. "There was a particular moment when I said, 'Oh, my ideas that have sustained me have sort of failed,' " he said later. "I had a particular time when I felt pretty empty and very isolated, and I suppose that's where some of that record came from."

He listened to Hank Williams, Johnny Cash and more obscure folk and country singers. He saw movies like John Huston's *Wise Blood* and Terence

Malick's *Badlands,* which sparked his interest in the 1958 murder spree of Charlie Starkweather and Caril Fugate. Back home in New Jersey, he wrote more than a dozen shattering, plain-spoken songs about murder, despair and isolation. On January 3rd, 1982, he sang them, one after another, into a four-track tape recorder.

He planned to teach them to the E Street Band, but somehow the songs that were so haunting in their rough, unaccompanied versions didn't sound right with fuller arrangements. "It became obvious fairly soon that what Bruce wanted on the record was what he already had on the demo," says drummer Max Weinberg. "The band, though we played the hell out of them, tended to obscure the starkness and the vibe he was going for."

Eventually, Springsteen returned to the acoustic demos, deciding to release them as is. *Nebraska* was a grim record for a grim time. It was both a courageous album and an influential one, presaging the frank, narrative songwriting and spare presentation of such late-Eighties folk stylists as Tracy Chapman and Suzanne Vega. Its ghostly aura even pervaded the work of U2 and John Cougar Mellencamp. But it was, above all, a profoundly personal statement from an artist who was unsettled by all he saw around him—and decided he couldn't look away.

#86 *The River*

He was a major rock & roll star. His records were FM-radio staples. He sold out coliseums. His live shows were legendary. But by 1980, Bruce Springsteen had not yet placed a single in the Top Twenty, and he hadn't really made an album that fully captured the bracing live sound of the E Street Band.

The River changed all that. The album is the work of a top-notch rock band playing live in the studio. Over the course of two discs, Springsteen displays a little bit of everything that drew people to him. If songs like "Jackson Cage," "Point Blank" and "Independence Day" recall the grim, relentless *Darkness on the Edge of Town,* tunes like the frat rocker "Sherry Darling" and the Number Five hit "Hungry Heart" are lighter and more buoyant. And if the sheer giddiness of "Crush on You" and "I'm a Rocker" make *The River* sound like Springsteen's party record, sobering character sketches like the title track and "Stolen Car" argue otherwise.

The album didn't come easily to Springsteen. "I search for that internal logic that connects everything," he said later. "And if it comes real naturally, it's great. With *The River,* man, forget it. It took many months. *Years,* you know?"

All in all, the album consumed more than a year in the studio, in excess of $500,000 in recording costs and what Springsteen remembers as "about ninety songs" that were rehearsed and either recorded or rejected. In the spring of 1979, Springsteen and the band began cutting songs like "The Ties That Bind" and "Roulette" (a savage rocker that would remain unreleased for eight years). By that fall, Springsteen and his coproducers, Jon Landau and Steve Van Zandt, had compiled a single-disc album that was to include "Hungry Heart," a rockabilly arrangement of "You Can Look (But You Better Not Touch)" and the still-unreleased gems "Cindy" and "Loose Ends." But when they returned to the studio after playing two No Nukes concerts in New York with other concerned musicians, Springsteen decided he didn't want to put the finishing touches on that record. Instead, he was looking for something richer and more expansive—something that would take close to another year to finish.

"I was trying to answer 'Where are these people going now?' " he said. "I had an idea where they were going, but I wasn't really sure. I guess I didn't know where *I* was going, you know?"

On *The River,* Springsteen accepts the fact that contradictions and paradoxes can be part of his music because they're part of everyday experience, and the decision to make a two-record set gave him the space to let his characters go just about everywhere. The trip encompasses a hard-rocking visit to "Cadillac Ranch" and the disquieting vision at the heart of the stark finale, "Wreck on the Highway."

"Bruce Springsteen didn't title his summational record *The River* for nothing," wrote Paul Nelson in his ROLLING STONE review of the album. "Each song is just a drop in the bucket, and the water in the bucket is drawn from a river that can take you on a fast but invigorating ride, smash you in the rapids, let you float dreamily downstream or carry you relentlessly across some unknown county line."

ROB TANNENBAUM

SPRINGSTEEN GOES IT ALONE

Rocker Will Search for a New Direction
Without the E Street Band

BRUCE SPRINGSTEEN HAS REACHED a musical crossroads. After sixteen years with the E Street Band, he has served notice to the band members that he will not be working with them on his next album, fueling speculation that his next recording may show a substantial change in direction.

Since his involvement in last year's Amnesty International Human Rights Now! Tour, Springsteen has expressed a desire to expand the scope of his music. That, combined with his rapid rise to superstardom and very public divorce from Julianne Phillips, may have caused a kind of midlife career crisis. He has no firm plans to begin recording, and his next album may be a long time coming.

"You always have to grow and go through changes," says Nils Lofgren, guitarist with the E Street Band. Lofgren, like the other members of the band, got a call from Springsteen in October, informing him of Springsteen's recording plans. "Right now he's just a little . . . he's searching. He's allowed to be confused. He specifically said, 'I'm just gonna do some experimenting and try recording some songs with some different players.'" Lofgren adds that Springsteen has written "a couple" of new songs.

Jon Landau, Springsteen's manager, says Springsteen hasn't actually begun to record but has been "giving some thought to what approach he might want to take musically."

Since the Amnesty tour ended in October 1988, Springsteen has been on a sabbatical from touring and recording. He has spent much of that time in Los Angeles, where he is rumored to be producing a solo album for girlfriend Patti Scialfa. Two tracks are known to have been recorded by Scialfa: a version of Nanci Griffith's "Gulf Coast Highway" and the Springsteen song "Burning Love." The latter track has already circulated among Springsteen fanatics.

Springsteen has recorded his own version of Elvis Presley's "Viva Las

Vegas" for an all-Elvis compilation that will be released in England in February to benefit the Nordoff-Robbins Music Therapy Foundation, which
aids autistic and other severely handicapped children. None of the E Street
Band members appear on the recording. Springsteen's backing band—which
was assembled by producer Chuck Plotkin, a longtime associate, and Toby
Scott, his engineer—is made up of a number of West Coast session all stars:
former Toto drummer Jeff Porcaro, bassist Bob Glaub and keyboardist Ian
McLagan. Landau stresses that the "Viva Las Vegas" band is not Springsteen's
"new band."

Springsteen has long encouraged the members of the E Street Band to
pursue individual projects. After the Amnesty tour, bassist Garry Tallent
moved to Nashville, where he is active as a producer; Lofgren and saxophonist Clarence Clemons recently toured with Ringo Starr, with whom
they hope to release an already-recorded live album and then cut a studio
album. The outlook for the E Street Band members' solo recording careers
is a bit cloudier, though: Clemons' *Night With Mr. C,* his third solo album
for Columbia Records, was a flop, failing to even make *Billboard*'s Top 200
album chart, and it appears unlikely that the label will want another album.
Lofgren played several East Coast clubs with his brother Tom's band in December but has been unable to find a label for his next solo album. In addition, he and pianist Roy Bittan are coproducing sessions in Los Angeles
for actress Stepfanie Kramer, the star of the TV show *Hunter.*

Max Weinberg, who reenrolled last year at Seton Hall University, in
Orange, New Jersey, graduated in December with a degree in communi-
cations and plans to go to law school. But he remains hopeful that Springsteen will reenlist him as his drummer.

"You can never be sure what Bruce is gonna do next," says Weinberg,
who joined the band in 1974. Although Weinberg says he's "not waiting
around," he also adds that he's "not packing away my drums."

Springsteen's relationship with the E Street Band has been ambiguous
since 1982, when he decided that the demo tapes he recorded by himself
for *Nebraska* were better than the band versions of the same songs. After that
album was released, according to Dave Marsh's Springsteen biography *Glory
Days,* Springsteen considered making another album without the band.
Tunnel of Love, his most recent record, was made with minimal input from
most of the band members.

But the pivotal factor in Springsteen's reevaluation of the band may have
been the Amnesty International tour, which was the first time he'd toured
with other musicians since 1973. "In rock & roll, you work in a very iso-

lated environment," he said when the Amnesty caravan began. "You move from town to town, but you're basically with the same group of thirty people. I wanted to look outward."

During the tour, Springsteen formed a friendship with Sting, who, he once joked, "tutors me on what's wrong with my music." Subsequently, Springsteen showed signs of broadening his musical horizons. Sting often dueted with him on "The River," a song that also featured Shankar, the Indian-born violinist from Peter Gabriel's band. Branford Marsalis, Sting's saxophonist, joined the E Streeters, along with percussionists from Gabriel's and Youssou N'Dour's bands.

"The end of this tour marks my graduation of sorts," Springsteen said a year ago. "And I hope that I will be able to go back home and in my music write about a different sensibility that I felt on this tour."

■ RANDOM NOTES (February 8, 1990)

Although he'd recently served notice to the members of the E Street Band that he wouldn't be using them on his next album, Bruce Springsteen showed up to jam with his longtime sax man Clarence Clemons during the Big Man's solo show at the Ventura, California, Concert Theater last December. The former Boss played "Glory Days" and "Cadillac Ranch" with Clemons—who was earlier joined onstage by Jackson Browne and Daryl Hannah for "You're a Friend of Mine." All four closed the show with "Sweet Little Sixteen."

Clemons says he was shocked when Springsteen told him of his solo plans. "My emotions ran the gamut from being angry to being hurt to being happy. But now I'm over it. It was like a mother hen kicking the little chicks out of the nest, saying, 'You've grown now. It's time to stand on your own feet.' "

■ RANDOM NOTES (September 6, 1990)

Bruce Springsteen and Patti Scialfa became the parents of a baby boy, Evan James, on July 25th.

■ NOTABLE NEWS (August 9, 1990)

As this issue went to press, the leader of the 2 Live Crew, Luther Campbell, was making plans to release a solo single, "Banned in the U.S.A.," on the Fourth of July. The song—attributed to Luke, Featuring 2 Live Crew—is to be released by Atlantic Records in partnership with Luke Records and borrows heavily from Bruce Springsteen's best-selling "Born in the U.S.A."

Springsteen granted Campbell permission to use the backing track of "Born in the U.S.A." in late June. Almost immediately, Jack Thompson, the Florida lawyer who is spearheading the anti-Crew campaign, said Springsteen was aiding "racist stereotyping of blacks, mental molestation of children and the encouragement of the sexual abuse of women." In an interview with the *Los Angeles Times,* Thompson added, "Bruce and Luther can go to hell together."

Springsteen's management said copyright approval was granted to Campbell because "Banned in the U.S.A." was a "quality" song. There were other considerations as well. "Bruce is not unmindful of the fact that Luke is on the spot," said Springsteen's manager, Jon Landau. "He's happy to lend a hand."

The single focuses on the censorship issue, and an accompanying music video is to feature performance footage, along with news clips of the band's recent arrest in Florida.

MIKAL GILMORE

BRUCE SPRINGSTEEN: WHAT DOES IT MEAN, SPRINGSTEEN ASKED, TO BE AN AMERICAN?

In a special issue that surveyed the music of the Eighties, ROLLING STONE's Mikal Gilmore
looked at Springsteen's very important place—musically and ideologically—
in that decade's sociopolitical climate.

O N THE NIGHT OF NOVEMBER 5TH, 1980, Bruce Springsteen stood onstage in Tempe, Arizona, and began a fierce fight for the meaning
of America. The previous day, the nation had turned a fateful corner: With a stunning majority, Ronald Reagan—who campaigned to end
the progressive dream in America—was elected president of the United
States. It was hardly an unexpected victory. In the aftermath of Vietnam,
Watergate, the hostage crisis in Iran and an economic recession, America
developed serious doubts about its purpose and its future, and to many vot-
ers, Reagan seemed an inspiring solution. But when all was said and done
the election felt stunning and brutal, a harbinger of the years of mean-
spiritedness to come.

The singer was up late the night before, watching the election returns,
and stayed in his hotel room the whole day, brooding over whether he
should make a comment on the turn of events. Finally, onstage that night
at Arizona State University, Springsteen stood silently for a moment, fin-
gering his guitar nervously, and then told his audience: "I don't know what
you guys think about what happened last night, but I think it's pretty frightening." Then he vaulted into an enraged version of his most defiant song,
"Badlands."

On that occasion, "Badlands" stood for everything it had always stood
for—a refusal to accept life's meanest fates or most painful limitations—but
it also became something more: a warning about the spitefulness that was
about to visit our land as the social and political horizon turned dark and

frightening. "I wanna spit in the face of these badlands," Springsteen sang with an unprecedented fury on that night, and it was perhaps in that instant that he reconceived his role in rock & roll.

In a way, his action foreshadowed the political activism that would transform rock & roll during the 1980s. As the decade wore on, Springsteen would become one of the most outspoken figures in pop music, though that future probably wasn't what he had in mind that night. Instead, Springsteen was simply focusing on a question that, in one form or another, his music had been asking all along: What does it mean to be born an American?

WELL, WHAT DOES IT MEAN TO BE BORN IN AMERICA? Does it mean being born to birthrights of freedom, opportunity, equity and bounty? If so, then what does it mean that many of the country's citizens never truly receive those blessings? And what does it mean that in a land of such matchless vision and hope, the acrid realities of fear, repression, hatred, deprivation, racism and sexism also hold sway? Does it mean, indeed, that we *are* living in badlands?

Questions of this sort—about America's nature and purpose, about the distance between its ideals and its truths—are, of course, as old as the nation itself, and finding revealing or liberating answers to those questions is a venture that has obsessed (and eluded) many of the country's worthiest artists, from Nathaniel Hawthorne to Norman Mailer, from John Ford to Francis Coppola. Rock & roll—an art form born of a provocative mix of American myths, impulses and guilts—has also aimed, from time to time, to pursue those questions, to mixed effect. In the 1960s, in a period of intense generational division and political rancor, Bob Dylan and the Band, working separately and together, explored the idea of America as a wounded family in albums like *The Basement Tapes, John Wesley Harding* and *The Band;* in the end, though, artists shied from the subject, as if something about the American family's complex, troubled blood ties proved too formidable. Years later, Neil Young (like the Band's Robbie Robertson, a Canadian obsessed by American myths) confronted the specter of forsworn history in works like *American Stars 'n' Bars, Hawks and Doves* and *Freedom.* Yet, like too many other artists or politicians who have come face to face with how America has recanted its own best promises, Young finally didn't seem to know what to say about such losses. In some ways, Elvis Presley, a seminal figure for Springsteen, came closest to embodying the meaning of America in his music. That's because he tried to seize the nation's dream of fortune and make himself a symbol of it. It's also because once Presley had that dream, the dream found a way of undoing him—leading him to heartbreak, decline, death. American callings, American fates.

Bruce Springsteen followed his own version of the fleeting American dream. He grew up in the suburban town of Freehold, New Jersey, feeling estranged from his family and community, and his refusal to accept the limits of that life fueled the songwriting in his early, largely autobiographical LPs. Indeed, records like *Greetings From Asbury Park, N.J., The Wild, the Innocent & the E Street Shuffle* and *Born to Run* were works about flight from dead-end small-town life and thankless familial obligations, and they accomplished for Springsteen the very dream that he was writing about: That is, those records lifted him from a life of mundane reality and delivered him to a place of bracing purpose. From the outset, Springsteen was heralded by critics as one of the brightest hopes in rock & roll—a songwriter and live performer who was as alluring and provoking as Presley and as imaginative and expressive as Dylan. And Springsteen lived up to the hoopla: With his 1975 album, *Born to Run,* Springsteen fashioned pop's most form-stretching and eventful major work since the Beatles' *Sgt. Pepper's Lonely Hearts Club Band.* But for all the praise and fame the album won him, it couldn't rid Springsteen of his fears of solitude, and it couldn't erase his memory of the lives of his family and friends. Consequently, his next LP, *Darkness on the Edge of Town,* was a stark and often bitter reflection on how a person could win his dreams and yet still find himself dwelling in a dark and lonely place—a story of ambition and loss as ill-starred and deeply American as *Citizen Kane.*

With *The River,* released in 1980, Springsteen was still writing about characters straining against the restrictions of their world, but he was also starting to look at the social conditions that bred lives split between the dilemmas of flight and ruin. In Springsteen's emerging mythos, people still had big hopes, but they often settled for delusional loves and fated family lives. In the album's haunting title song, the youthful narrator gets his girlfriend pregnant and then enters a joyless marriage and a toilsome job in order to meet his obligations. Eventually, all the emotional and economic realities close in, and the singer's marriage turns into a living, grievous metaphor for lost idealism. "Now, all them things that seemed so important," sings Springsteen. "Well, mister, they vanished right into the air / Now I just act like I don't remember / Mary acts like she don't care." In *The River*'s murky and desultory world, people long for fulfillment and connections, but as often as not they end up driving empty mean streets in after-midnight funks, fleeing from a painful nothingness into a more deadening nothingness.

The River was Springsteen's pivotal statement. Up to that point, he had told his tales in florid language, in musical settings that were occasionally operatic and showy. Now he was streamlining both the lyrics and the music into simpler, more colloquial structures, as if the realities he was trying to dissect were too bleak to support his earlier expansiveness. *The River* was also the record with which Springsteen began wielding rock & roll less as a tool of personal mythology than as a means of looking at history, as a way of *understanding* how the lives of the people in his songs were shaped by the conditions surrounding them and by historical forces beyond their control.

This drive to comprehend history came to the fore during the singer's remarkable 1980–1981 tour in support of *The River*. Springsteen had never viewed himself as a political-minded performer, but a series of events and influences—the near-disaster at the Three Mile Island nuclear reactor and his subsequent participation in the No Nukes benefit, at New York City's Madison Square Garden in September 1979—began to alter that perception. Springsteen read Joe Klein's biography of folk singer Woody Guthrie and was impressed with the way popular songs could work as a powerful and binding force for political action. In addition, he read Ron Kovic's harrowing personal account of the Vietnam War, *Born on the Fourth of July*. Inspired by the candor of Kovic's anguish— and by the bravery and dignity of numerous other Vietnam veterans he had met—Springsteen staged a benefit at the L.A. Sports Arena in August 1981 to raise funds and attention for the Vietnam Veterans of America. On one night of the Los Angeles engagement, Springsteen told his audience that he had recently read Henry Steele Commager and Allan Nevins's *Short History of the United States* and that he was profoundly affected by the book. A month earlier, speaking of the same book, he had told a New Jersey audience: "The idea [of America] was that there'd be a place for everybody, no matter where you came from . . . you could help make a life that had some decency and dignity to it. But like all ideals, that idea got real corrupted. . . . I didn't know what the government I lived under was doing. It's important to know . . . about the things around you." Now, onstage in Los Angeles, getting ready to sing Woody Guthrie's "This Land Is Your Land," Springsteen spoke in a soft, almost bashful voice as he told his audience: "There's a lot in [the history of the United States] . . . that you're proud of, and then there's a lot of things in it that you're ashamed of. And that burden, that burden of shame, falls down. Falls down on everybody."

IN 1982, AFTER THE TOUR ENDED, Springsteen was poised for the sort of massive breakthrough that people had been predicting for nearly a decade. *The River* had gone to the top of *Billboard*'s albums chart, and

"Hungry Heart" was a Top Ten single; it seemed that Springsteen was finally overcoming much of the popular backlash that had set in several years earlier, after numerous critics hailed him as rock & roll's imminent crown prince. But after the tour, the singer was unsure about what direction he wanted to take in his songwriting. He spent some time driving around the country, brooding, reading, thinking about the realities of his own emotional life and the social conditions around him, and then he settled down and wrote a body of songs about his ruminations. On January 3rd, 1982, Springsteen sat in his home and recorded a four-track demo cassette of the new songs, accompanied for the most part only by his ghostly sounding acoustic guitar. He later presented the songs to Jon Landau and the E Street Band, but neither Landau nor the musicians could find the right way to flesh out the doleful, spare-sounding new material. Finally, at Landau's behest, Springsteen released the original demo versions of the songs as a solo effort, entitled *Nebraska*. It was unlike any other work in pop-music history: a politically piercing statement that was utterly free of a single instance of didactic sloganeering or ideological proclamation. Rather than preach to or berate his listeners, Springsteen created a vivid cast of characters—people who had been shattered by bad fortune, by limitations, by mounting debts and losses—and then he let those characters tell the stories of how their pain spilled over into despair and, sometimes, violence.

There was a timeless, folkish feel to *Nebraska*'s music, but the themes and events it related were as dangerous and timely as the daily headlines. It was a record about what can occur when normal people are forced to endure what cannot be endured. Springsteen's point was that until we understood how these people arrived at their places of ruin, until we accepted our connection to those who had been hurt or excluded beyond repair, America could not be free of such fates or such crimes. "The idea of America as a family is naive, maybe sentimental or simplistic," he said in a 1987 interview, "but it's a good idea. And if people are sick and hurting and lost, I guess it falls on everybody to address those problems in some fashion. Because injustice, and the price of that injustice, falls on everyone's heads. The economic injustice falls on everybody's head and steals everyone's freedom. Your wife can't walk down the street at night. People keep guns in their homes. They live with a greater sense of apprehension, anxiety and fear than they would in a more just and open society. It's not an accident, and it's not simply that there are 'bad' people out there. It's an inbred part of the way that we are all living: It's a product of what we have accepted, what we have acceded to. And whether we mean it or not, our silence has spoken for us in some fashion."

"NEBRASKA" ATTEMPTED TO MAKE a substantial statement about the modern American sensibility in an austere style that demanded close involvement. That is, the songs required that you settle into their doleful textures and racking tales and then apply the hard facts of their meaning to the social reality around you. In contrast to Springsteen's earlier bravado, there was nothing eager or indomitable about *Nebraska*. Instead, it was a record about people walking the rim of desolation who sometimes transform their despair into the irrevocable action of murder. It was not exulting or uplifting, and for that reason, it was a record that many listeners respected more than they "enjoyed." Certainly, it was not a record by which an artist might expand his audience in the fun-minded world of pop.

But with his next record, *Born in the U.S.A.*, in 1984, Springsteen set out to find what it might mean to bring his message to the largest possible audience. Like *Nebraska, Born in the U.S.A.* was about people who come to realize that life turns out harder, more hurtful, more closefisted than they might have expected. But in contrast to *Nebraska*'s killers and losers, *Born in the U.S.A.*'s characters hold back the night as best they can, whether it's by singing, laughing, dancing, yearning, reminiscing or entering into desperate love affairs. There was something celebratory about how these people face their hardships. It's as if Springsteen were saying that life is made to endure and that we all make peace with private suffering and shared sorrow as best we can.

At the same time, a listener didn't have to dwell on these truths to appreciate the record. Indeed, Springsteen and Landau designed the album with contemporary pop styles in mind—which is to say, it was designed with as much meticulous attention to its captivating and lively surfaces as to its deeper and darker meanings. Consequently, a track like "Dancing in the Dark"— perhaps the most pointed and personal song Springsteen has ever written about isolation—came off as a rousing dance tune that worked against isolation by pulling an audience together in a physical celebration. Similarly, "Cover Me," "Downbound Train" and "I'm on Fire"—songs about erotic fear and paralyzing loneliness—came off as sexy, intimate and irresistible.

But it was the terrifying and commanding title song—about a Vietnam veteran who has lost his brother, his hope and his faith in his country—that did the most to secure Springsteen's new image as pop hero and that also turned his fame into something complex and troubling. Scan the song for its lyrics alone, and you find a tale of outright devastation: a tale of an American whose birthrights have been paid off with indelible memories of violence and ruin. But listen to the song merely for its fusillade of drums and firestorm of guitar, and in a political climate in which simple-minded patriotic fervor had attained a startling credibility, it's possible to hear the singer's roaring proclamation—"I was *born* in the U.S.A."—as a fierce, patriotic assertion. Indeed, watching Springsteen unfurl the song in concert—slamming it across with palpable rage as his audience waved flags of all sizes—it was possible to read the song in both directions. "Clearly the key to the enormous explosion of Bruce's popularity is the misunderstanding [of the song "Born in the U.S.A."]," wrote critic Greil Marcus during the peak of Springsteen's popularity. "He is a tribute to the fact that people hear what they want."

One listener who was quite happy to hear only what he wanted to was the syndicated conservative columnist George Will, who, in the middle of the 1984 campaign that pitted Walter Mondale against Ronald Reagan, attended a Springsteen show and liked what he saw. In a September 14th, 1984, column, Will commended Springsteen for his "elemental American values" and, predictably, heard the cry of "Born in the U.S.A." as an exultation rather than as pained fury. "I have not got a clue about Springsteen's politics, if any," Will wrote, "but flags get waved at his concerts while he sings about hard times. He is no whiner, and the recitation of closed factories and other problems always seem punctuated by a grand, cheerful affirmation: 'Born in the U.S.A.!' "

Apparently, Reagan's advisors gave a cursory listening to Springsteen's music and agreed with Will. A few days later, in a campaign stop in New Jersey, President Ronald Reagan declared: "America's future rests in a thousand dreams inside your hearts. It rests in the message of hope in songs of a man so many young Americans admire: New Jersey's Bruce Springsteen. And helping you make those dreams come true is what this job of mine is all about."

It was an amazing assertion. Clearly, to anybody paying attention, the hard-bitten vision of America that Springsteen sang of in "Born in the U.S.A." was a far cry from the much-touted "new patriotism" of Reagan and many of his fellow conservatives. And yet there was also something damnably brilliant in the way the president sought to attach his purpose to Springsteen's views. It was the art of political syllogism, taken to its most arrogant extreme. Reagan saw himself as a definitional emblem of America; Bruce Springsteen was a singer who, apparently, extolled America in his work; therefore, Springsteen must be exalting Reagan—which would imply that if one valued the music of Springsteen, then one should value (and support) Reagan as well. Reagan was manipulating Springsteen's fame as an affirmation of his own ends.

A few nights later, Springsteen stood before a predominantly blue-collar audience in Pittsburgh and, following a rousing performance of "Atlantic City," decided to respond to the president's statement. "The president was mentioning my name the other day," he said with a bemused laugh, "and I kinda got to wondering what his favorite album might have been. I don't think it was the *Nebraska* album. I don't think it was this one." Springsteen then played a passionate version of "Johnny 99," a song about a man who commits impulsive murder as a way of striking back at the meanness of the society around him—a song he wrote, along with other *Nebraska* tunes, in response to the malignant political atmosphere that had been fostered by Reagan's social policies.

Springsteen's comments were apt: Was *this* the America Ronald Reagan heard clearly when he claimed to listen to Springsteen's music? An America where dreams of well-being had increasingly become the province of the privileged and where jingoistic partisans had determined the nation's health by a standard of self-advantage? When Reagan heard a song like "My Hometown," did he understand his own role in promoting the disenfranchisement the song described?

But Reagan's attempt to co-opt Springsteen's message also had some positive side effects. For one thing, it made plain that Springsteen now commanded a large and vital audience of young Americans who cared deeply about their families, their futures and their country and that Springsteen spoke to—and perhaps *for*—that audience's values in ways that could not be ignored. The imbroglio also forced Springsteen to become more politically explicit and resourceful at his performances. After Pittsburgh, he began meeting with labor and civil-rights activists in most of the cities he played, and he made statements at his shows, asking his audience to lend their support to the work of such activists. He also spoke out more and more plainly about where he saw America headed and how he thought rock & roll could play a part in effecting that destiny. One evening in Oakland, when introducing "This Land Is Your Land," he said: "If you talk to the steelworkers out there who have lost their jobs, I don't know if they'd believe this song is what we're about anymore. And maybe we're not. As we sit here, [this song's promise] is eroding every day. And with countries, as with people, it's easy to let the best of yourself slip away. Too many people today feel as if America has slipped away and left them standing behind." Then he sang the best song written about America, in as passionate a voice as it had ever been sung.

But none of this was enough. In November 1984, Ronald Reagan was reelected president by an even more stunning mandate than the first time. It seemed plausible that many (if not most) of the millions of fans of voting age who made *Born in the U.S.A.* such a huge success cast their votes for the man to whom Springsteen so obviously stood in opposition. Perhaps it nettled him, but Springsteen was finally facing the answer to the question he had been asking during the length of the decade: To be born in America, to be passionate about the nation's best ideals, meant being part of a nation that would only believe about itself what it wanted to believe. It also meant that one still had to find a way to keep faith with the dream of that nation, despite the awful realities that take shape when that dream is denied.

IN 1984, AMERICA HAD NOT HAD ENOUGH of Ronald Reagan, or it would not have reelected him. It had also not had enough of Bruce Springsteen: After an international tour, he returned to the States a bigger, more popular artist than ever. It may seem like a contradiction that a nation can embrace two icons that differed so dramatically, but the truth is, Reagan and Springsteen shared an unusual bond: Each seemed to stand for America, and yet each was largely misunderstood by his constituency. Reagan seemed to stand for the values of family and improved opportunity at the same time that he enacted policies that undermined those values. Springsteen seemed to stand for brazen patriotism when he believed in holding the government responsible for how it had corrupted the nation's best ideals and promises.

To his credit, Springsteen did his best to make his true values known. In the autumn of 1985, he embarked on the final leg of his Born in the U.S.A. Tour, this time playing stadium-size venues that held up to 100,000 spectators. Playing such vast settings was simply a way of keeping faith with the ambition he had settled on a year or two earlier: to see what it could mean to reach the biggest audience he could reach. It was also an attempt to speak seriously to as many of his fans as possible, to see if something like a genuine consensus could be forged from the ideals of a rock & roll community. And of course, the gesture also entailed a certain risk: If Springsteen's audience could not—or would not—accept him for what he truly stood for, then in the end he could be reduced by that audience.

In some surprising respects, Springsteen's ambition succeeded. At the beginning of the stadium swing, many fans and critics worried that he would lose much of his force—and his gifts for intimacy and daring—by moving his music to such large stages. But if anything, Springsteen used the enlarged settings as an opportunity to rethink many of his musical arrangements, transforming the harder songs into something more fervid, more moving, more aggressive than before and yet still putting across the more rueful songs from *The River* and *Nebraska* with an uncompromised sensitivity. If anything, he made the new shows count for more than the election-year shows, if only because he recognized that addressing a larger audience necessarily entailed some greater responsibilities. In Washington, D.C., on the opening night of the stadium shows, Springsteen told a story about a musician friend from his youth who was drafted and who, because he did not enjoy the privilege of a deferment, was sent to Vietnam and wound up missing in action. "If the time comes when there's another war, in some place like Central America," Springsteen told his audience of 56,000, "then you're going to be the ones called on to fight it, and you're going to have to decide for yourselves what that means. . . . But if you want to know where we're headed for [as a country], then someday take that long walk from the Lincoln Memorial to the Vietnam Veterans Memorial, where the names of all those dead men are written on the walls, and you'll see what the stakes are when you're born in the U.S.A. in 1985." For the last dates of the tour, at the Los Angeles Memorial Coliseum, he added Edwin Starr's 1970 hit "War" to the show, coming down hard on the lines "Induction, destruction / Who wants to die."

Later, at the end of the last show in L.A., Springsteen stood before his band, his friends and his audience and said: "This has been the greatest year of my life. I want to thank you for making me feel like the luckiest man in the world." Indeed, Springsteen had begun the tour as a mass-cult figure; he was leaving it as a full-fledged pop hero—a voice of egalitarian conscience unlike any that rock had yielded before, with a remarkable capacity for growth and endurance.

In short, Springsteen seemed to emerge from the tour occupying the center of rock & roll, in the way that Presley or the Beatles had once commanded the center. And yet the truth was, in the pop world of the 1980s, there was no center left to occupy. Rock was a field of mutually exclusive options, divided along racial, stylistic and ideological lines. In fact, by the decade's end, even the American and British fields of rock—which had dominated the pop world thoroughly for a quarter-century—were gradually losing their purism and dominance as more adventurous musicians began bringing African, Jamaican, Brazilian, Asian and other musical forms into interaction with pop's various vernaculars. In modern pop, America no longer overwhelmed the international sensibility.

In any event, Springsteen seemed to step back from rock & roll's center at the same moment that he won it. In 1986, he assembled a multidisc package of some of his best performances from the previous ten years of live shows—a box set intended to be a summation of his artistic growth and his range as a showman. It was the most ambitious effort of his career but also the least consequential. It didn't play with the sort of revelatory effect of his best shows or his earlier albums, and it didn't captivate a mass audience in the same way, either. Then, the following year, Springsteen released the album *Tunnel of Love*. Like *Nebraska, Tunnel of Love* was a more intimate, less epic statement than its predecessor—a heartbreaking but affirming suite of songs about the hard realities of romantic love. Maybe the record was intended to remind both Springsteen and his audience that what ultimately mattered was how one applied one's ideals to one's own world—or maybe the songs were simply about the concerns that obsessed Springsteen most at that time.

At the end of the decade, Springsteen was on tour again. Reluctant to continue playing oversize venues, he returned to the arena halls where he had done some of his most satisfying work in the years before and restored a more human scale to his production. It was another election year, and while he still spoke out about issues from time to time, Springsteen seemed wary of being cast as merely a rock politician or statesman. Perhaps he realized that America's political choices just couldn't be affected very tellingly from a rock & roll stage, or maybe he was simply discouraged by what he saw around him. To be sure, there was plenty to be disheartened about: It was a season when Oliver North enjoyed status as a cultural hero and when George Bush turned patriotism and flag-waving into viciously effective campaign issues.

At the same time, Springsteen remained committed to the idea of turning the rock & roll audience into an enlightened and active community. After the Tunnel of Love Tour, he headlined Amnesty International's Human Rights Now! world tour in the fall of 1988. Along with Live Aid, the Amnesty tour was one of the most ambitious political campaigns in rock's history. And the fact that it could occur at all and could reach an audience that was both massive and ready was in some ways a testament to the sort of idealism that Springsteen had fought for throughout the 1980s.

Which is to say, despite the currents of history, Springsteen kept faith with a difficult quest. In the midst of a confusing and complex decade, he wrote more honestly, more intelligently and more compassionately about America than any other writer of the decade. And after he did so, he set about the business of tending to his own life. An act like that is neither a retreat nor a failure. Instead, it is a way of refusing to be broken by the dissolution of the world around you. It is a way of saying that, sooner or later, you have to bring your dreams of a better world into your own home and your own heart, and you have to see if you can live up to them. All in all, that isn't such a bad way to finish off one decade. Or to begin another.

ANTHONY DeCURTIS

SPRINGSTEEN RETURNS

"WHEN EVERYBODY STARTS BELIEVING those big illusions," said Bruce Springsteen from the stage of the Shrine Auditorium, in Los Angeles, "you end up with a government like the one we've had for the past decade." The occasion was the second of two benefit concerts given by Springsteen, Bonnie Raitt and Jackson Browne on November 16th and 17th for the Christic Institute, an organization that is pursuing a lawsuit against a group of United States–sponsored covert operatives for allegedly bombing a press conference in Nicaragua in 1984. The song Springsteen was introducing was "Reason to Believe," from *Nebraska,* and the specific illusion he referred to was the American government's belief in its inalienable right to police the world and shape the destiny of other sovereign nations.

Springsteen's endorsement of the Christic Institute and its conviction that an ongoing conspiracy of government officials and former military and intelligence officers has played a major role in American foreign policy over the past three decades represents a far more radical stance than he has ever before taken. In his characteristic fashion, however, Springsteen managed to put a human face on the array of complex, far-ranging political issues the Christic Institute lawsuit addresses. His two masterful solo acoustic sets—his first live appearances since the close of the Amnesty International Human Rights Now! world tour in October of 1988—were breathtakingly moving explorations of how self-deceit, romantic illusions and fantasies of control corrupt the bedroom and the boardroom, personal as well as political affairs, and poison human experience. With remarkable emotional sophistication, Springsteen was able to dramatize both the damage such illusions inflict and the difficulty and pain involved in giving them up for a real world that is far from a utopia.

The first evening's show was more taut and gripping, if less relaxed, than the second. Walking out of the wings to center stage without an introduction, his hair grown long and swept back, Springsteen was clearly tense.

Strumming an acoustic guitar, he mentioned not having "done this in a while" and told the audience, "If you're moved to clap along, don't—it'll mess me up." He then set the tone for the night with a stark, intense—and simply spectacular—reading of "Brilliant Disguise," a song about the virtual impossibility of understanding your own emotions, let alone another person's. His singing strong and supple, Springsteen incited howls of excitement with the subtlest gestures, such as sliding his voice into a fragile falsetto on certain line endings. "Is it me, baby, or just a brilliant disguise?" Springsteen nearly whispered to the crowd of 6,200 people witnessing his return to the public eye. The question seemed far from innocent a little later when, after a fan screamed, "We love you, Bruce," Springsteen responded, without a shred of irony, "But you don't really *know* me."

A modified arrangement of "Darkness on the Edge of Town" was somewhat less successful—it would work far more effectively the next night—but a haunted "Mansion on the Hill," with Springsteen providing a plaintive harmonica solo, proved riveting. The singer bemoaned how "over the past decade the country's been sold an illusion of itself" and praised the Christic Institute for "trying to make us grow up" by way of leading into "Reason to Believe," which he souped up with a chilling slide-guitar part.

The set took an amusing turn when Springsteen—obviously in a 2 Live Bruce mood—hauled out a song he'd written the night before called "Redheaded Woman," which he dedicated to "my two favorite redheads:" Bonnie Raitt and, of course, Patti Scialfa. "Well, now, listen up, stud, your life's been wasted," Springsteen wailed over a propulsive rockabilly beat, "till you been down on your knees and tasted a redheaded woman." In "57 Channels," another funny new song with a rockabilly feel, Springsteen described shooting out his television Elvis style because "there's fifty-seven channels, man, and nothing on."

The fun halted with a heart-stopping version of "My Father's House," which Springsteen prefaced with a wrenching description of how, "three or four times a week," late at night, by himself, he used to drive past the houses in which he grew up with his parents. Concerned, he consulted a psychiatrist, who explained that "something went wrong" in those houses, something broke down, and that Springsteen was driven to return to the scene in a desperate, compulsive effort to "make it right." "But," the psychiatrist concluded, "you can't." The song ends: "My father's house shines hard and bright / It stands like a beacon calling me in the night / Calling and calling so cold and alone / Shining across this dark highway where our sins lie unatoned."

The degree to which Springsteen's tangled feelings about his parents

have been reactivated—possibly by his having a child of his own—was evident the following night, when he replaced "My Father's House" with "The
Wish," a poignant song about his mother. "If pa's eyes were windows into
a world so deadly and true," he sang, accompanying himself on guitar.
"You couldn't stop me from looking, but you kept me from crawling
through." While Springsteen's struggle with his tormented feelings about
his father fuels his greatest art—"My Father's House" is, significantly, a far
more compelling song than "The Wish"—his feelings about his mother account for the sweeter, more vulnerable aspects of his personality.

On Friday night, Springsteen moved over to the piano after "My Father's House" for "Tenth Avenue Freeze-Out." Despite the raw energy of
Springsteen's R&B-flavored rendition, that song—along with the spellbinding, introspective version of "Thunder Road" he performed later, also
at the piano—essentially served as an elegy for the E Street Band. Hearing
Springsteen belt out a line like "When the change was made uptown / And
the Big Man joined the band" as he sat alone on the large, dark stage was a
powerful moment. "I'm all alone, I'm on my own," he sang. "And I can't
find my way home."

Brilliant, spare versions of "Atlantic City" and "Nebraska" framed Friday night's biggest surprise: the rarely performed "Wild Billy's Circus Story,"
from *The Wild, the Innocent & the E Street Shuffle*. A new song called "When
the Lights Go Out"—about deception, corruption of spirit and the darker
elements within us—followed "Nebraska." "Thunder Road"—which
Springsteen stopped midsong because he forgot the lyrics, shaking his head
and saying, "I knew this would happen"—came next, and a stunning,
mournful "My Hometown," performed on piano, closed the set proper.

For his encore, Springsteen played a new song at the piano, a stirring
ballad called "Real World," which he cowrote with E Street Band pianist
Roy Bittan and dedicated on Saturday night to Patti Scialfa, who was backstage with their new baby, Evan James. A bracing, hymnlike love song, "Real
World" is about abandoning fairy-tale fantasies and accepting the limits and
delights of the possible. "Ain't no church bells ringing, ain't no flags un-
furled," sang the man whose storybook marriage ended bitterly and whose
most popular tour became an orgy of flag-waving. "Just me, you and the
love we're bringing into the real world."

Jackson Browne and Bonnie Raitt—whose opening sets were strong
but, unfortunately, entirely overwhelmed by Springsteen's performance—
then joined Springsteen for a rousing cover of Bob Dylan's "Highway 61
Revisited." The trio alternated lead vocals and harmonized on the choruses.
Browne's driving acoustic rhythm guitar—Springsteen played harmonica and

Raitt rattled a tambourine—turned Dylan's blackly humorous tale of profit frenzy and war fever into an insinuating boogie workout. With Browne playing piano, Springsteen playing acoustic guitar and Bonnie Raitt playing slide guitar, the night ended with a feeling rendition of Ry Cooder's "Across the Borderline." A song about Central and South American immigrants who come to Texas to find a "broken promised land," it provided a touching multicultural complement to the domestic dislocation of Springsteen's "My Hometown."

On Saturday night, in addition to substituting "The Wish" for "My Father's House," Springsteen deleted "Wild Billy's Circus Story" and "Atlantic City" and added "State Trooper," a stately, dignified reading of "Tougher Than the Rest" and a new song called "Soul Driver." Taken together, the two shows—beginning with a "Brilliant Disguise" and ending in the "Real World"—demonstrated that Springsteen's ability to seize the moment onstage and make palpable the meaning of potent emotional and social issues has not at all diminished. He continues to look deep inside himself and find a world there, a world we can enter to learn a bit about how a life proceeds, to learn a bit about ourselves and our own world.

"I built a shrine in my heart / It wasn't pretty to see / Made out of fool's gold, memory and tears cried," Springsteen sang in "Real World." "Well, now I'm heading over the rise." It's a necessary trip, and with as much conviction as ever, he's taking us along with him.

■ **NOTABLE NEWS** (August 8, 1991)

Greatest Show on Earth? Mike Appel, Bruce Springsteen's former manager, told the fanzine *Backstreets* that if he had continued as manager, Springsteen would have done a "tent tour," complete with a midway, following the release of *Born to Run.* "What could have been more newsworthy than Springsteen in a tent?" Appel thinks Springsteen's current manager nixed it. "The thinking on the other side of the fence might have been that this is one more example of Colonel Tom Parker, Circus Parker, Mike Appel making a circus act out of Bruce Springsteen." Anyone wonder why Springsteen changed managers?

■ RANDOM NOTES (August 8, 1991)

Jersey's blue-collar poet laureate Bruce Springsteen wed Patti Scialfa Saturday, June 8th, in an early evening ceremony, on the grounds of the couple's sprawling Beverly Hills estate. Among the approximately ninety guests were Jackson Browne, Daryl Hannah, John Fogerty, Bonnie Raitt and Michael O'Keefe. News reports state that the couple hired a helicopter to thwart press coverage of the blessed event—at which former E Street Band members Steven Van Zandt, Danny Federici and Roy Bittan performed. The couple has a one-year-old son, Evan James.

■ RANDOM NOTES (October 27, 1991)

The lawsuits between Bruce Springsteen and two of his former roadies were settled out of court six days before the case was to go to trial in early September. Michael Batlan and Doug Sutphin sued Springsteen for, among other things, not paying them overtime during the Born in the U.S.A. Tour (Batlan received $125,000 in severance pay and Sutphin $100,000 when Springsteen let them go) and making them pay for replacing his canoe, which was destroyed because of their neglect. Springsteen filed a countersuit after Batlan admitted in a deposition that he took tapes of an album's worth of unreleased Springsteen songs cut during sessions leading up to the release of Born in the U.S.A. In addition, Batlan took four of Springsteen's notebooks—including lyrics and titles—and sold them for about $28,000. Details of the settlement have not been revealed, but it is believed the former roadies received a relatively small cash payment. A statement issued by Parcher and Hayes, the legal firm representing Springsteen, said that it had recommended settling "as a matter of principle" even though the judge had already dismissed much of the plaintiffs' overtime case and was "inclined to grant most of the remaining dismissal relief requested by Mr. Springsteen."

■ RANDOM NOTES (February 20, 1992)

Rock & reproduction: Bruce Springsteen and Patti Scialfa delivered their second child, a girl, in shorter time than it's taken to give birth to either of their albums.

MICHAEL GOLDBERG

DOUBLE DOSE OF SPRINGSTEEN

FOUR AND A HALF YEARS AFTER RELEASING his last album, 1987's *Tunnel of Love,* Bruce Springsteen is returning to action with not one but two albums of new songs. The albums, *Human Touch* and *Lucky Town,* will be released simultaneously in the early spring. It is expected that a world tour—Springsteen's first since he disbanded the E Street Band—will start in the U.S. by the summer.

Unlike Guns n' Roses' *Use Your Illusion I* and *II,* which were basically two halves of a double album, the Springsteen discs are said to be distinctly separate albums, each with its own character and sound. One source who has heard the LPs described them as "different in sound—but both are rock albums." Thematically, they are said to be related in much the same way that *Born in the U.S.A.* was related to *Nebraska.* "Both have reflective material and potential singles," said another source. "What really differentiates them is the point of view of the writing, the perspective Bruce brings to the material."

Human Touch includes fourteen songs recorded at a number of Los Angeles studios, including A&M Studios, in Hollywood. It was produced by Springsteen, manager Jon Landau, Chuck Plotkin and former E Street Band member Roy Bittan. In addition to "Real World," "Soul Driver" and "57 Channels"—all of which Springsteen performed at two 1990 benefits for the Christic Institute at the Shrine Auditorium, in Los Angeles—the album includes "Cross My Heart," "Gloria's Eyes," "With Every Wish," "Roll of the Dice," "All or Nothin' at All," "Man's Job," "I Wish I Were Blind," "Long Goodbye," "Real Man," "Pony Boy" and the title track.

Lucky Town, produced by Springsteen with additional production assistance by Landau, Plotkin and Bittan, is made up of ten songs: "Better Days," "Local Hero," "If I Should Fall Behind," "Leap of Faith," "Big Muddy," "Living Proof," "Book of Dreams," "Souls of the Departed," "My Beautiful Reward" and the title track.

With the exception of "Roll of the Dice" and "Real World," which

Springsteen wrote with Bittan, all of the songs were written solely by Springsteen.

Springsteen apparently settled on the musicians for his first post-E Street Band efforts quite painlessly. He initially worked with session drummer Jeff Porcaro on a version of "Viva Las Vegas" that appeared on the Elvis Presley tribute album *The Last Temptation of Elvis;* things "clicked," according to a source, and Springsteen brought Porcaro back for the *Human Touch* sessions.

In addition to Porcaro, Springsteen used bassist Randy Jackson and keyboardist Bittan as the core band on *Human Touch.* Another former E Street Band member, David Sancious, plays some keyboards on the album, and Mark Isham plays trumpet. Springsteen's wife, Patti Scialfa, contributes vocals, as do Bobby Hatfield of the Righteous Brothers, Sam Moore of Sam and Dave and Bobby King, who's best known for his work with Ry Cooder.

Springsteen spent more than a year writing and recording *Human Touch.* His approach to making the album was to write and record a batch of songs, then take a break, then head into the studio again to record another batch. The album, which he began in January 1990, was essentially finished by the spring of 1991, but Springsteen wanted one more song to round it out. Instead of a single song, he composed an entire album's worth, and by last summer he had decided to release them both.

Lucky Town was recorded at Springsteen's home studio, in Los Angeles, in about eight weeks. The core musicians and singers who appear on the album are Bittan, Jackson, Scialfa, drummer Gary Mallaber and vocalists Lisa Lowell and Soozie Tyrell.

With one or two exceptions, Springsteen plays all of the rhythm and lead guitar on both albums. "There is a lot of guitar on the albums," said a source. "A lot of lead guitar, a lot of great guitar."

At press time, cover art hadn't been finalized. Springsteen had participated in a number of photo sessions, including one with Annie Leibovitz, who shot the covers of *Born in the U.S.A.* and *Tunnel of Love.* The first single from the albums is expected out by the end of March, and a video was being directed by Meirt Avis, who has worked with U2 and who directed some of the videos from *Tunnel of Love.* Neither Springsteen's management nor his label, Columbia Records, however, would identify which song had been selected as the single. In fact, security around the project is so tight that one source at Sony Music said Columbia Records president Don Ienner has been using code words when referring to the albums and single so as to prevent media leaks.

It is believed that Springsteen will begin a world tour in the U.S. no later than the summer. Promoters expect Springsteen to play multiple dates at arenas. It is thought that at least some of the musicians who played on the albums will join Springsteen on the road, although one source said Porcaro won't be touring.

Springsteen last toured in 1988, when he and the E Street Band headlined Amnesty International's Human Rights Now! world tour. Since then, he has undergone numerous changes in his personal life. Springsteen and actress Julianne Phillips were divorced in March 1989, and he subsequently married Scialfa. They have had two children, Evan James and Jessica Rae.

In a prepared statement, Springsteen said, "I'm excited about being finished and am looking forward to getting out on the road."

■ **RANDOM NOTES** (April 2, 1992)

You know it's almost spring when Bruce Springsteen begins popping his head up above ground. And because he's Bruce Springsteen, he has the ability to take small, uninhabited bars and ruin them forever by producing floods of fans hoping that one day he may return. At the latest formerly out-of-the-way haven—the Maple Leaf, in New Orleans—Springsteen sat in for a pair of songs, including "Save the Last Dance for Me," with the local band the Iguanas.

JAMES HENKE

BRUCE'S LUCKY TOUCH
Two New Albums Put Springsteen Back in the Rock & Roll Spotlight

T HE LONG WAIT IS OVER, Bruce Springsteen is back, and he hasn't forgotten how to rock.

That message came through loud and clear on March 4th, when two new Springsteen songs, "Human Touch" and "Better Days," began dominating radio. By the end of that week, "Human Touch" was the most-added song on Top Forty, album-rock and adult-contemporary stations.

According to *Radio and Records,* 91 percent of all album-rock stations that report to the magazine were programming "Human Touch," making it the Number One song on that format. ("Better Days" entered *R&R*'s album-rock chart at Number Five.) At Top Forty, or CHR, radio, 177 of 230 reporting stations added "Human Touch" its first week out. "It's a hell of an accomplishment," said Joel Denver, *Radio and Records'* CHR editor, "particularly at a time when it's not hip to be rocking out on CHR."

In fact, radio's response to the single seemed to dispel some music-industry doubts about how well Springsteen would fare this time out, given that it's been nearly five years since he released his last studio album, *Tunnel of Love,* and that many of his songs are now tackling more obviously adult themes. The week before the double-A-sided single was released, *Billboard* magazine had reported that pop radio was "concerned about overexposure of past Springsteen hits and his current relevance to its audience." *Billboard* also reported that Sony Music, Springsteen's label, had decided to play it safe, limiting initial shipments of the two albums to 1.5 million each (*Tunnel of Love* sold about 3 million copies).

"They [Sony] don't want too many albums in the field," said Russ Solomon, owner of the Tower Records chain. "With Michael Jackson, they shipped 4 million, and they haven't sold them off yet. If an album is sitting around in large quantities in a record store, it looks stale."

Solomon added that Springsteen's long layoff was cause for some concern: "Whether the fans who are now five years older care that much, I don't know." But Solomon and other retailers were still optimistic that Springsteen's new albums, *Human Touch* and *Lucky Town*, would do very well when they reach the stores on March 31st. "Great artists have tremendous followings," Solomon said, "and Springsteen certainly is a great artist. These records could take off like nobody's business."

"We think they're going to be monstrous," said Lew Garrett, vice-president of purchasing for the Camelot chain. "Springsteen appeals to a demographic that has money in their pockets and isn't afraid to spend it."

Though early reports had indicated that *Human Touch* and *Lucky Town*—Springsteen's tenth and eleventh albums—were vastly different in style, both are essentially straight-ahead, guitar-driven rock LPs, and there are no dramatic departures from his previous work. But the breakup of the E Street Band following the Human Rights Now! Tour in 1988 gave Springsteen the freedom to record with different musicians for virtually the first time in his career, and there are a few songs on the two albums that probably would not have surfaced on an E Street album.

Springsteen, who's now forty-two, began making *Human Touch* in late 1989, using a core group that included former E Street Band member Roy Bittan on keyboards and sessionmen Jeff Porcaro (of Toto fame) on drums and Randy Jackson (who's worked with Journey, among others) on bass. The first song they recorded was "Roll of the Dice," a rousing rocker written by Springsteen and Bittan that would not have sounded out of place on an E Street Band album.

The LP includes several other uptempo tracks: "Soul Driver," which features Sam Moore, formerly of Sam and Dave, on vocals and David Sancious, an early E Street Band member, on Hammond organ; "Gloria's Eyes," one of several tracks on which Springsteen serves up some stinging guitar; "The Long Goodbye," another guitar-heavy rocker; the more soulful "Real World"; and "All or Nothin' at All," a two-chord scorcher.

The album's funniest track is "57 Channels," which opens with Bob Glaub's thumping bass line and tells the story of a man who "bought a bourgeois house in the Hollywood Hills," installed cable TV and then a satellite dish ("home entertainment was my baby's wish"), only to find that "there was 57 channels and nothin' on." He finally buys a .44 Magnum, "and in the blessed name of Elvis, well, I let it blast."

In a more serious vein is "With Every Wish," a spare, haunting ballad that features Springsteen on acoustic guitar, Mark Isham on trumpet, Kurt Wortman on drums and Doug Lunn on bass. Musically, it recalls *Born to Run*'s "Meeting Across the River." The lyrics deal with wishes that come true: "Before you choose your wish, son / You better think first / With every wish there comes a curse."

Springsteen finished *Human Touch*—which includes fourteen songs and contains nearly an hour of music—in early 1991. But almost immediately he had an unexpected burst of creativity and began writing again. One of the first songs he came up with was "Living Proof." For a while, he considered adding it to *Human Touch,* but the song—obviously inspired by his young son, Evan James—didn't seem to fit. "There was a different voice there," said a source familiar with the project. "It became apparent that something had happened, that he was in a different mode."

Springsteen went on to record the ten songs on *Lucky Town,* including "Better Days," in about eight weeks, working at his home in Los Angeles. Bittan and Jackson rejoined him, but Porcaro was unavailable, so drummer Gary Mallaber, whose résumé includes stints with Van Morrison and the Steve Miller Band, was recruited.

The album has a loose, stripped-down sound, especially compared to the more polished *Human Touch.* It includes two beautiful ballads: the love song "If I Should Fall Behind," with Springsteen on bass and acoustic guitar, and "Book of Dreams," a touching wedding-day portrait. There are other overt allusions to Springsteen's family life: In "Souls of the Departed," a rocker, he sings about a seven-year-old boy who was murdered in a Compton, California, schoolyard, then adds: "As I tuck my own son in bed / All I can think is what if it'd been him instead."

One source summed up the difference between the albums by saying that on *Human Touch,* Springsteen is "struggling for the meaning of happiness: What does it mean to be a man?" On the second album, "he's realized he's happy, and he's trying to find out what that means."

Springsteen is expected to be on the road by the summer, but at press time tour plans were still being worked out.

■ RANDOM NOTES (May 28, 1992)

On the road again. For the past couple of months, Bruce Springsteen has been auditioning and rehearsing musicians in Los Angeles for a North American tour that is expected to begin in late summer or early fall. According to one source, former E Street Band keyboardist Roy Bittan is the only musician featured on Springsteen's new albums, *Human Touch* and *Lucky Town,* who will be in the touring band. No other former members of the E Street Band are expected to join Springsteen on the road. Bittan and Springsteen have been assembling a backing band that is expected to consist of a second guitarist, a bassist, a drummer and several background vocalists. A source said that the band members will be relatively unknown but seasoned "road guys." Springsteen is expected to concentrate almost exclusively on material from the new albums, although he will throw in a few old favorites. As for the followup to "Human Touch," at press time a source said that the likely candidate is "57 Channels (and Nothin' On)."

■ RANDOM NOTES (June 25, 1992)

Before his first-ever TV performance on *Saturday Night Live,* Bruce Springsteen got down to the Bottom Line. As a tuneup for the tube, His Bruceness played a surprise show at the downtown-New York club that ran through an hour and a half of his new material (he's got two albums' worth of the damn stuff) and helped set the stage for his first tour in four years.

ANTHONY DeCURTIS

HUMAN TOUCH AND *LUCKY TOWN* ALBUM REVIEWS

New Bruce: Lose Your Illusions

Human Touch

★ ★ ★ ★

Lucky Town

★ ★ ★ ★ 1/2

WITH HIS TWO NEW ALBUMS—his first in nearly five years and first as a declared solo artist—Bruce Springsteen completes an emotional triptych begun in 1987 with *Tunnel of Love*. On that album, "Tougher Than the Rest" articulates the early Springsteen code on love: Commitment is a triumph of the will. You make a vow, you keep it. But at the center of that album stand three songs—"Tunnel of Love," "Two Faces" and "Brilliant Disguise"—that suggest the virtual impossibility of knowing yourself well enough (let alone another person) to make any vow meaningful forever. To enter the tunnel of love is to take a night journey on which the definitions of your identity dissolve and you encounter aspects of yourself that seem profoundly foreign and disturbing. In short, *Tunnel of Love* is a study of deception—and more chillingly, self-deception—in matters of the heart.

Human Touch (begun in 1989, completed in early 1991) and *Lucky Town* (recorded in a two-month burst shortly after *Human Touch*) describe the effort of building a realistic life after the code has been shattered, in Springsteen's case by an affair and a divorce. Intriguing companion pieces, they're *Lose Your Illusion I* and *II*.

Beginning with the pulsing title track, which stands among Springsteen's best work, the fourteen songs on *Human Touch* explore the movement from disenchanted isolation to a willingness to risk love and its attendant traumas again. At first the moves are tentative, motivated more by loneliness—a need for "a little of that human touch"—than by love's golden promise or, even more remote, the prospect of actual lasting happiness with another human being. Also, as the bluesy "Cross My Heart" makes clear, the certainties of the past ("Once you cross your heart / You ain't ever supposed to lie") are starting to be replaced by a more shaded outlook: "Well you may think the world's black and white / And you're dirty or you're clean / You better watch out you don't slip / Through them spaces in between."

Aptly, the introspective, self-questioning mood of *Human Touch* shifts near its midpoint with "Roll of the Dice," the most generic-sounding Springsteen rocker—glockenspiel and all—on either of these albums. With renewed energy, even optimism, the singer accepts the emotional dangers of love and his own failings ("I'm a thief in the house of love / And I can't be trusted"), stops fretting and determines to get on with living. The superb "Real World" then offers an inspiringly lucid vision of a love that can side-step fantasy to take a dignified place in "the real world," and the slamming "All or Nothin' at All," graced by a soaring, catchy chorus, insists on commitment rather than flees it.

After that, however, both "Man's Job" and "Real Man" flirt perilously with soft, contemporary clichés about masculinity ("If I can find the guts to give you all my love / Then I'll be feelin' like a real man"). Fortunately, Springsteen stops short of songs about his inner child or flagging self-esteem. The slick, annoyingly seductive keyboard riff of "Real Man" also ventures closer to Phil Collins territory than anything Springsteen has done before. More positively, "Pony Boy," a traditional tune performed acoustically by Springsteen on guitar and harmonica, with his wife, Patti Scialfa, providing harmony, closes *Human Touch* on a tender, disarming note.

The childlike charm of "Pony Boy" provides an effective, understated transition to *Lucky Town,* on which Springsteen examines his life as a family man, negotiates a truce with his demons and achieves a hard-won sense of fulfillment. Dedicated to Scialfa and the couple's two children, the album's ten songs paint a convincing—and only rarely cloying—portrait of domestic life and its contents. The rousing opener, "Better Days," ably sets the tone; it's a bracing antinostalgia blast that asserts: "These are better days baby / Better days with a girl like you." The song also takes on with impressive candor the Springsteen myth ("It's a sad funny ending to find yourself pretending / A rich man in a poor man's shirt") and the immeasurable degree of his material comfort ("A life of leisure and a pirate's treasure / Don't make much for tragedy").

With characteristic sure-footedness, however, Springsteen does not permit heartfelt satisfaction to slip into self-satisfaction. If "Leap of Faith," "If I Should Fall Behind," "Living Proof" and "Book of Dreams" all convey a nearly swooning appreciation of the pleasures that a settled home life affords,

"The Big Muddy," "Souls of the Departed" and "My Beautiful Reward" intimate that, for Springsteen at least, the attainment of love is inextricable from the fear of its loss. A brooding blues evocatively colored by Springsteen's acoustic slide guitar, "The Big Muddy" takes a knowing look at infidelity, greed and moral compromise, concluding, "There ain't no one leavin' this world buddy / Without their shirttail dirty / Or their hands bloody." The churning, guitar-driven "Souls of the Departed" depicts the singer, one of "the self-made men" in the Hollywood Hills, under siege as violence rages in the Middle East and, closer by, in East Compton. The death of a child in a barrio shooting causes him to wonder, in an aching drawl, "Tonight as I tuck my own son in bed / All I can think of is what if it would've been him instead."

"My Beautiful Reward," an elegant, folkish ballad, ends *Lucky Town* on an almost surreally unsettled note. The calm, gentle music belies dreamlike imagery of falling, wandering and abandonment. The striking verse that closes the song and the album—"Tonight I can feel the cold wind at my back / I'm flyin' high over gray fields my feathers long and black / Down along the river's silent edge I soar / Searching for my beautiful reward"— harks back to the restlessness at the heart of *Human Touch* and hints of a darkness on the edge of *Lucky Town*.

Musically, neither of these two albums represents much of a departure for Springsteen, despite the breakup of the E Street Band. Produced by Springsteen, Jon Landau, Chuck Plotkin and former E Street Band keyboardist Roy Bittan, *Human Touch* is more richly textured than *Lucky Town,* which Springsteen recorded in his home studio and pretty much produced himself, with help from the other three men. Along with the impeccable Bittan on keyboards, the studio pros on hand for *Human Touch*—bassist Randy Jackson and drummer Jeff Porcaro—do fine; Porcaro even manages on occasion to approach the muscle and finesse of the brilliant E Street Band drummer, Max Weinberg. Springsteen handles virtually all instruments except drums (played by Gary Mallaber) on *Lucky Town* with expressiveness and flair; on both albums his guitar playing is plentiful and gripping, a cry from the soul.

Without question, the aesthetic and thematic aims of *Human Touch* and *Lucky Town* would have been better realized by a single, more carefully shaped collection that eliminated their half-dozen or so least essential songs. But taken together, the two albums chart the fascinating progress of one of the most compelling artists of our time, a man who has found what he was looking for and who is searching still.

JAMES HENKE

BRUCE SPRINGSTEEN:
THE ROLLING STONE INTERVIEW

"IN THE CRYSTAL BALL, I SEE ROMANCE, I see adventure, I see financial reward. I see those albums, man, I see them going back up the charts. I see them rising past that old Def Leppard, past that Kriss Kross. I see them all the way up past 'Weird Al' Jankovic, even. . . . Wait a minute. We're slipping. We're slipping down them charts. We're going down, down, out of sight, into the darkness. . . . "

It was June 5th, and as Bruce Springsteen was performing "Glory Days" near the end of a live radio broadcast from a Los Angeles sound stage, he finally offered his commentary on the much-publicized failure of his latest albums—*Human Touch* and *Lucky Town*—to dominate the charts in the same way that some of their predecessors had. Thankfully, Springsteen demonstrated that while he may have lost a little of his commercial clout, he hasn't lost his sense of humor.

The show, in front of about 250 invited guests and radio-contest winners, was a "dress rehearsal" meant to introduce his new band—keyboardist Roy Bittan, guitarist Shane Fontayne, bassist Tommy Sims, drummer Zachary Alford, singer-guitarist Crystal Taliefero and vocalists Bobby King, Gia Ciambotti, Carol Dennis, Cleo Kennedy and Angel Rogers—and to stir up excitement for his summer tour of the States. He succeeded on both counts. The concert proved that even without the E Street Band, Springsteen is still a masterful performer; in fact, his new band rocks harder, and musically it challenges him more than his previous group. And he still has more than a few loyal fans: The day after the radio broadcast, he sold out eleven shows at New Jersey's Brendan Byrne Arena (more than 200,000 tickets) in just two and a half hours.

Even so, it has been an unusually trying season for Springsteen. Though *Human Touch* and *Lucky Town* entered the charts at Numbers Two and Three, respectively, they quickly slipped and eventually dropped out of the

Top Forty. On top of that, some segments of the media seemed to be reaping pleasure from Springsteen's relative lack of success (and indeed, it is relative: Each of the albums has sold more than 1.5 million copies). One magazine, *Entertainment Weekly,* even put Springsteen on its cover with the headline WHAT EVER HAPPENED TO BRUCE?

But things could be worse, as Springsteen well knows. For the past several years, he has been waging a far tougher battle—trying to repair what had become a badly damaged personal life. "I was real *good* at music," he says, "and real *bad* at everything else."

Onstage, of course, Springsteen could do it all; offstage, it was a different story. Something of a loner by nature, he had difficulty maintaining any kind of long-term relationship. Even as he was preaching about "community" during his *Born in the U.S.A.* tour, he himself was keeping his distance from just about everyone. And when he wasn't working, he wasn't happy.

When he hit the road in 1988 to support his *Tunnel of Love* album, the cracks in Springsteen's personal life were beginning to show. His marriage to actress Julianne Phillips had begun to deteriorate, and thanks to the tabloids, it soon became public knowledge that he was seeing E Street Band singer Patti Scialfa. When he got off the road in late 1988 after playing a series of shows for Amnesty International, Springsteen hit rock bottom.

Gradually, he began to regain control of his life. He went into therapy. He got divorced from Phillips and eventually married Scialfa. He parted ways with the E Street Band. He left New Jersey and moved to Los Angeles. And with Scialfa, he fathered two children: Evan James, who's almost two, and Jessica Rae, who was born last New Year's Eve.

Springsteen's personal trials are documented on *Human Touch;* his victory over those trials is the subject of *Lucky Town.* The jury is still out on whether his U.S. tour, which kicks off on July 23rd in New Jersey, will resuscitate those albums. But there's no question that Springsteen himself is the happiest he's been in a long time. Over the course of three lengthy interviews in Los Angeles and New York—the first in-depth interviews he's done since 1986—he outlined in great detail what he calls "the biggest struggle of my life," and he addressed a variety of other subjects, ranging from rap music to the presidential race.

The music scene has changed a lot since you last released an album. Where do you see yourself fitting in these days?

I never kind of fit in, in a funny kind of way. In the Seventies the music I wrote was sort of romantic, and there was lots of innocence in it, and it certainly didn't feel like it was a part of that particular time. And in the Eighties, I was writing and singing about what I felt was happening to the people I was seeing around me or what direction I saw the country going in. And that really wasn't in step with the times, either.

Well, given the response to your music then, I think you fit in pretty well during the Eighties.

Well, we were *popular,* but that's not the same thing. All I try to do is to write music that feels meaningful to me, that has commitment and passion behind it. And I guess I feel that if what I'm writing about is real, and if there's emotion, then hey, there'll be somebody who wants to hear it. I don't know if it's a big audience or a smaller audience than I've had. But that's never been my primary interest. I've had a kind of story I've been telling, and I'm really only in the middle of it.

At the same time, your new albums haven't fared as well on the charts as most people expected, and you've had to endure some sniping from the media. How do you feel about that?

I try not to get involved in it. It does seem to be out there in the air, for everybody and anybody, but I don't take it that personally. I mean, if you spend any time in Los Angeles, you see that a lot: "Great, you're a tremendous success—now *fail!*"

There's a media game that's played out there, and I guess it sells newspapers and magazines. But it's not central to who I am or what I do. You make your music, then you try to find whatever audience is out there for it.

Do you think that a teenager who's into rap or heavy metal would be interested in your new albums?

I don't know. And I don't know if you can generalize like that. I think some yes and some no. All I can do is put my music out there. I can't contrive something that doesn't feel honest. I don't write demographically. I don't write a song to reach these people or those people.

Of course, I'm interested in having a young audience. I'm interested in whoever's interested in what I'm doing. And what I have to say is "This is how I've grown up. Maybe this will have some value. These are the places I've been, and these are the things I've learned."

But I want to sing about who I am now. I want to get up onstage and sing with all of the forty-two years that are in me. When I was young, I always said I didn't want to end up being forty-five or fifty and pretending I was fifteen or sixteen or twenty. That just didn't interest me. I'm a lifetime musician; I'm going to be playing music forever. I don't foresee a time when I would not be onstage somewhere, playing a guitar and playing it loud, with power and passion. I look forward to being sixty or sixty-five and doing that.

For the first time in about twenty years you're embarking on a tour without the E Street Band. What led to your decision to get rid of them?

At the end of the Born in the U.S.A. Tour and after we made the live album, I felt like it was the end of the first part of my journey. And then, for the Tunnel of Love Tour, I switched the band around quite a bit. I switched where people had stood for fifteen years, just trying to give it a different twist.

But you can get to a place where you start to replay the ritual, and nostalgia creeps in. And I decided it was time to mix it up. I just had to cut it loose a little bit so I could have something new to bring to the table. I wanted to get rid of some of the old expectations. People were coming to my shows expecting to hear "Born to Run" or stuff that I wrote fifteen or twenty years ago. And I wanted to get to a spot where if people came to the show, there'd be a feeling of like, well, it's not going to be this, it's going to be something else.

Did you call each of the guys to give them the news?

Oh, sure, yeah. Initially, some people were surprised, some people were not so surprised. I'm sure some people were angry, and other people weren't angry. But as time passed, everything came around to a really nice place. I mean, I wasn't the guy writing the check every month. Suddenly, I was just Bruce, and some of the friendships started coming forward a little bit. And it was interesting, because we hadn't had that kind of relationship. We had all been working together for so long that we didn't really have a relationship outside of the work environment.

You mentioned the Born in the U.S.A. Tour as marking the end of one phase of your career. How did the enormousness of that album and tour affect your life?

I really enjoyed the success of *Born in the U.S.A.*, but by the end of that whole thing, I just kind of felt "Bruced" out. I was like "Whoa, enough of that." You end up creating this sort of icon, and eventually it oppresses you.

What specifically are you referring to?

Well, for example, the whole image that had been created—and that I'm sure I promoted—it really always felt like "Hey, that's not me." I mean, the macho thing, that was just never me. It might be a little more of me than I think, but when I was a kid, I was a real gentle child, and I was more in touch with those sorts of things.

It's funny, you know, what you create, but in the end, I think, the only thing you can do is destroy it. So when I wrote *Tunnel of Love,* I thought I had to reintroduce myself as a songwriter, in a very noniconic role. And it was a relief. And then I got to a place where I had to sit some more of that stuff down, and part of it was coming out here to L.A. and making some music with some different people and seeing what that's about and living in a different place for a while.

How's it been out here, compared with New Jersey?

Los Angeles provides a lot of anonymity. You're not like the big fish in the small pond. People wave to you and say hi, but you're pretty much left to go your own way. Me in New Jersey, on the other hand, was like Santa Claus at the North Pole [*laughs*].

What do you mean?

Hmm, how can I put it? It's like you're a bit of a figment of a lot of other people's imaginations. And that always takes some sorting out. But it's even worse when you see yourself as a figment of your own imagination. And in the last three or four years, that's something I've really freed myself from.

I think what happened was that when I was young, I had this idea of playing out my life like it was some movie, writing the script and making all the pieces fit. And I really did that for a long time. But you can get enslaved by your own myth or your own image, for the lack of a better word. And it's bad enough having other people seeing you that way, but seeing yourself that way is really bad. It's pathetic. And I got to a place, when Patti and I hooked up, where I said I got to stop writing this story. It doesn't work.

And that's when I realized I needed a change, and I like the West. I like the geography. Los Angeles is a funny city. Thirty minutes and you're in the mountains, where for 100 miles there's one store. Or you're in the desert, where for 500 miles there's five towns.

So Patti and I came out here and put the house together and had the babies and . . . the thing is, I'd really missed a big part of my life. The only way I could describe it is that being successful in one area is illusory. People think because you're so good at one particular thing, you're good at many things. And that's almost always not the case. You're good at that particular thing, and the danger is that that particular thing allows you the indulgence to remove yourself from the rest of your life. And as time passed, I realized that I was using my job well in many ways, but there was a fashion in which I was also abusing it. And—this began in my early thirties—I really knew that something was wrong.

That was about ten years ago?

Yeah, it started after I got back from The River Tour. I'd had more success than I'd ever thought I'd have. We'd played around the world. And I thought, like, "Wow, this is it." And I decided, "Okay, I want to have a house." And I started to look for a house.

I looked for two years. Couldn't find one. I've probably been in every house in the state of New Jersey—twice. Never bought a house. Figured I just couldn't find one I liked. And then I realized that it ain't that I can't *find* one, I couldn't *buy* one. I can find one, but I can't buy one. Damn! *Why is that?*

And I started to pursue why that was. Why did I only feel good on the road? Why were all my characters in my songs in cars? I mean, when I was in my early twenties, I was always sort of like "Hey, what I can put in this suitcase, that guitar case, that bus—that's all I need, now and forever." And I really believed it. And really lived it. Lived it for a long time.

In a ROLLING STONE *cover story from 1978, Dave Marsh wrote that you were so devoted to music that it was impossible to imagine you being married or having kids or a house. . . .*

A lot of people have said the same thing. But then something started ticking. It didn't feel right. It was depressing. It was like "This is a joke. I've come a long way, and there's some dark joke here at the end."

I didn't want to be one of those guys who can write music and tell stories and have an effect on people's lives, and maybe on society in some fashion, but not be able to get into his own self. But that was pretty much my story.

I tend to be an isolationist by nature. And it's not about money or where you live or how you live. It's about psychology. My dad was certainly the same way. You don't need a ton of dough and walls around your house to be isolated. I know plenty of people who are isolated with a six-pack of beer and a television set. But that was a big part of my nature.

Then music came along, and I latched onto it as a way to combat that part of myself. It was a way that I could talk to people. It provided me with a means of communication, a means of placing myself in a social context—which I had a tendency not to want to do.

And music did those things but in an abstract fashion, ultimately. It did them for the guy with the guitar, but the guy without the guitar was pretty much the same as he had been.

Now I see that two of the best days of my life were the day I picked up the guitar and the day that I learned how to put it down. Somebody said, "Man, how did you play for so long?" I said: "That's the easy part. It's stopping that's hard."

When did you learn to put the guitar down?

Pretty recently. I had locked into what was pretty much a hectic obsession, which gave me enormous focus and energy and fire to burn, because it was coming out of pure fear and self-loathing and self-hatred. I'd get onstage and it was hard for me to stop. That's why my shows were so long. They weren't long because I had an idea or a plan that they should be that long. I couldn't stop until I felt burnt, period. Thoroughly burnt.

It's funny, because the results of the show or the music might have been positive for other people, but there was an element of it that was abusive for me. Basically, it was my drug. And so I started to follow the thread of weaning myself.

For a long time, I had been able to ignore it. When you're nineteen and you're in a truck and you're crossing the country back and forth, and then you're twenty-five and you're on tour with the band—that just fit my personality completely. That's why I was able to be good at it. But then I reached an age where I began to miss my real life—or to even know that there was another life to be lived. I mean, it was almost a surprise. First you think you are living it. You got a variety of different girlfriends, and then, "Gee, sorry, gotta go now." It was like the Groucho Marx routine—it's funny, 'cause it runs in my family a little bit, and we get into this: "Hello, I came to say I'd like to stay, but I really must be going." And that was me.

What was it that woke you up to the fact that you were missing something or had a problem?

Unhappiness. And other things, like my relationships. They always ended poorly; I didn't really know how to have a relationship with a woman. Also, I wondered how can I have this much money and not spend it? Up until the Eighties, I really didn't have any money. When we started the River tour, I had about twenty grand, I think. So, really, around 1983 was the first time I had some money in the bank. But I couldn't spend it, I couldn't have any fun. So a lot of things started to not feel logical. I realized there was some aberrational behavior going on here. And I didn't feel that good. Once out of the touring context, and out of the context of my work, I felt lost.

Did you ever go to a therapist or seek help like that?

Oh, yeah. I mean, I got really down. Really bad off for a while. And what happened was, all my rock & roll answers had fizzled out. I realized that my central idea—which, at a young age, was attacking music with a really religious type of intensity—was okay to a point. But there was a point where it turns in on itself. And you start to go down that dark path, and there is a distortion of even the best of things. And I reached a point where I felt my life was distorted. I love my music, and I wanted to just take it for what it was. I didn't want to try to distort it into being my entire life. Because that's a lie. It's not true. It's not your entire life. It never can be.

And I realized my real life is waiting to be lived. All the love and the hope and the sorrow and sadness—that's all over there, waiting to be lived. And I could ignore it and push it aside or I could say yes to it. But to say yes to part of it is to say yes to all of it. That's why people say no to all of it. Whether it's drugs or whatever. That's why people say no: I'll skip the happiness as long as I don't have to feel the pain.

So I decided to work on it. I worked hard on it. And basically, you have to start to open up to who you are. I certainly wasn't the person I thought I was. This was around the time of *Born in the U.S.A.* And I bought this big house in New Jersey, which was really quite a thing for me to do. It was a place I used to run by all the time. It was a big house, and I said, "Hey, this is a rich man's house." And I think the toughest thing was that it was in a town where I'd been spit on when I was a kid.

This was in Rumson?

Yeah. When I was sixteen or seventeen my band, from Freehold, was booked in a beach club. And we engendered some real hostile reaction. I guess we looked kind of—we had on phony snakeskin vests and had long hair. There's a picture of me in the Castiles, that's what it was. And I can remember being onstage, with guys literally spitting on it. This was before it was fashionable, when it kind of meant what it really meant.

So it was a funny decision, but I bought this house, and at first I really began to enjoy it, but then along came the Born in the U.S.A. Tour, and I was off down the road again. I had a good time, and I began to try to figure out things. I was trying to find out how to make some of these connections, but once again it was sort of abstract, like how to integrate the band into some idea of community in the places we passed through.

It was during this time that you met Julianne?

Yeah, we met about halfway through that tour. And we got married. And it was tough. I didn't really know how to be a husband. She was a terrific person, but I just didn't know how to do it.

Was the marriage part of your whole effort to make connections, to deal with that part of your life?

Yeah, yeah. I really needed something, and I was giving it a shot. Anybody who's been through a divorce can tell you what that's about. It's difficult, hard and painful for everybody involved. But I sort of went on.

Then Patti and I got together, on the Tunnel of Love Tour, and I began to find my way around again. But after we came off the road in 1988, I had a bad year right away. I got home, and I wasn't very helpful to anyone.

You were still living in Rumson?

Yeah, and then we lived in New York for a while. That wasn't for me, on account of growing up in a small town and being used to having cars and all that stuff.

I'd made a lot of plans, but when we got home, I just kind of spun off for a while. I just got lost. That lasted for about a year.

What kinds of things did you do?

The best way I can say it is that I wasn't doing what I said I was going to do. Somewhere between realization and actualization, I slipped in between the cracks. I was in a lot of fear. And I was just holding out. I made life generally unpleasant. And so at some point Patti and I just said, "Hell, let's go out to L.A."

I've always felt a little lighter out here. I've had a house in the Hollywood Hills since the early Eighties, and I'd come out here three, four months out of the year. I always remember feeling just a little lighter, like I was carrying less. So Patti and I came out here, and things started to get better. And then the baby came along, and that was fantastic. That was just the greatest thing.

Had you wanted to have a baby in the past?

I know there were a lot of things in the paper about Juli and me and that the issue of having a baby was what caused us to break up. Well, that just wasn't true. That's a lie.

But was it something you wanted to do—have a family—or was it something you were afraid of?

Well, yeah [*pause*], I was *afraid*. But I was afraid of this whole thing. That's what this was about. I had made my music everything. I was real *good* at music and real *bad* at everything else.

Was Patti the person who really helped you get through all of this?

Yeah. She had a very sure eye for all of my bullshit. She recognized it. She was able to call me on it. I had become a master manipulator. You know, "Oh, I'm going out of the house for a little while, and I'm going down . . ." I always had a way of moving off, moving away, moving back and creating distance. I avoided closeness, and I wouldn't lay my cards on the table. I had many ways of doing that particular dance, and I thought they were pretty sophisticated. But maybe they weren't. I was just doing what came naturally. And then when I hit the stage, it was just the opposite. I would throw myself forward, but it was okay because it was brief. Hey, that's why they call them one-night stands. It's like you're there, then *bang!* You're gone. I went out in '85 and talked a lot about community, but I wasn't a part of any community.

So when I got back to New York after the Amnesty tour in '88, I was kind of wandering and lost, and it was Patti's patience and her understanding that got me through. She's a real friend, and we have a real great friendship. And finally I said I've got to start dealing with this, I've got to take some baby steps.

What were some of those baby steps?

The best thing I did was I got into therapy. That was really valuable. I crashed into myself and saw a lot of myself as I really was. And I questioned all my motivations. Why am I writing what I'm writing? Why am I saying what I'm saying? Do I mean it? Am I bullshitting? Am I just trying to be the most popular guy in town? Do I need to be liked that much? I questioned everything I'd ever done, and it was good. You should do that. And then you realize there is no single motivation to anything. You're doing it for all of those reasons.

So I went through a real intense period of self-examination. I knew that I had to sit in my room for eight hours a day with a guitar to learn how to play it, and now I had to put in that kind of time just to find my place again.

Were you writing any songs during this period?

At first, I had nothing to say. Throughout '88 and '89, every time I sat down to write, I was just sort of rehashing. I didn't have a new song to sing. I just ended up rehashing *Tunnel of Love,* except not as good. And it was all just down and nihilistic. It's funny, because I think people probably associate my music with a lot of positives. But it's like I really drift into that other thing—I think there's been a lot of desperate fun in my songs.

Then I remembered that Roy [Bittan] had some tracks that he'd play to me on occasion. So I called him and said, "Come on over, maybe I'll try to write to some of your tracks." So he had the music to "Roll of the Dice," and I came up with the idea for that, and I went home and wrote the song. It was really about what I was trying to do: I was trying to get up the nerve to take a chance.

And then Roy and I started working together pretty steadily. I had a little studio in my garage, and I came up with "Real World." What I started to do were little writing exercises. I tried to write something that was soul oriented. Or I'd play around with existing pop structures. And that's kind of how I did the *Human Touch* record. A lot of it is generic, in a certain sense.

We worked for about a year, and at the end I tried to put it together. Some albums come out full-blown: *Tunnel of Love, Nebraska, Lucky Town*— they just came out all at once. *Human Touch* was definitely something that I struggled to put together. It was like a job. I'd work at it every day. But at the end, I felt like it was good, but it was about me trying to get to a place. It sort of chronicled the post–*Tunnel of Love* period. So when we finished it, I just sat on it for a couple of months.

Then I wrote the song "Living Proof," and when I wrote that, I said: "Yeah, that's what I'm trying to say. That's how I feel." And that was a big moment, because I landed hard in the present, and that was where I wanted to be. I'd spent a lot of my life writing about my past, real and imagined, in some fashion. But with *Lucky Town,* I felt like that's where I am. This is who I am. This is what I have to say. These are the stories I have to tell. This is what's important in my life right now. And I wrote and recorded that whole record in three weeks in my house.

Did you ever think about not releasing "Human Touch"?

Yeah, except that every time I listened to it, I liked it. Also, I wanted to put out a lot of music, because I didn't want to be dependent on my old songs when I went out to tour. I wanted to have a good body of work to draw from when I hit the stage.

And then I realized that the two albums together kind of tell one story. There's *Tunnel of Love,* then there's what happened in between, which is *Human Touch,* then there's *Lucky Town.* And basically I said: "Well, hey— Guns n' Roses! They put out two albums, maybe I'll try it!"

There's a perception out there—and a couple of the reviews of the albums mentioned it—that you've sealed yourself off from reality, living in a big house in L.A. and so forth. Yet based on what you're saying, I assume you'd say the truth is quite the opposite.

Those are the clichés, and people have come to buy the clichés in rock music. You know, like it's somehow much more acceptable to be addicted to heroin than to, say, hang out with jet-setters. But you know, it's the old story. People don't know what you're doing unless they're walking in your shoes a bit.

Some of your fans seem to think along the same lines, that by moving to L.A. and buying a $14 million house, you've let them down or betrayed them.

I kept my promises. I didn't get burned out. I didn't waste myself. I didn't die. I didn't throw away my musical values. Hey, I've dug in my heels on all those things. And my music has been, for the most part, a positive, liberating, living, uplifting thing. And along the way I've made a lot of money, and I bought a big house. And I love it. Love it. It's great. It's beautiful, really beautiful. And in some ways, it's my first real home. I have pictures of my family there. And there's a place where I make music, and a place for babies, and it's like a dream.

I still love New Jersey. We go back all the time. I've been looking at a farm there that I might buy. I'd like my kids to have that, too. But I came out here, and I just felt like the guy who was born in the U.S.A. had left the bandanna behind, you know?

I've struggled with a lot of things over the past two, three years, and it's been real rewarding. I've been very, very happy, truly the happiest I've ever been in my whole life. And it's not that one-dimensional idea of "happy."

It's accepting a lot of death and sorrow and mortality. It's putting the script down and letting the chips fall where they may.

What's been the toughest thing about being a father?

Engagement. Engagement. Engagement. You're afraid to love something so much, you're afraid to be that in love. Because a world of fear leaps upon you, particularly in the world that we live in. But then you realize: "Oh, I see, to love something so much, as much as I love Patti and my kids, you've got to be able to accept and live with that world of fear, that world of doubt, of the future. And you've got to give it all today and not hold back." And that was my specialty; my specialty was keeping my distance so that if I lost something, it wouldn't hurt that much. And you can do that, but you're never going to have anything.

It's funny, because the night my little boy was born, it was amazing. I've played onstage for hundreds of thousands of people, and I've felt my own spirit really rise some nights. But when he came out, I had this feeling of a kind of love that I hadn't experienced before. And the minute I felt it, it was terrifying. It was like "Wow, I see. This love is here to be had and to be felt and experienced? To everybody, on a daily basis?" And I knew why you run, because it's very frightening. But it's also a window into another world. And it's the world that I want to live in right now.

Has having kids changed the way you look at your own parents?

It was amazing, actually, how much it did change. I'm closer to my folks now, and I think they feel closer to me. My pa, particularly. There must have been something about my own impending fatherhood that made him feel moved to address our relationship. I was kind of surprised; it came out of the blue.

He was never a big verbalizer, and I kind of talked to him through my songs. Not the best way to do that, you know. But I knew he heard them. And then, before Evan was born, we ended up talking about a lot of things I wasn't sure that we'd ever actually address. It was probably one of the nicest gifts of my life. And it made my own impending fatherhood very rich and more resonant. It's funny, because children are very powerful, they affect everything. And the baby wasn't even born yet, but he was affecting the way people felt and the way they spoke to each other, the way they treated each other.

You said the song "Pony Boy" was one that your mother used to sing to you.

My grandmother sang it to me when I was young. I made up a lot of the words for the verses; I'm sure there are real words, but I'm not sure they're the ones I used. It was the song that I used to sing to my little boy when he was still inside of Patti. And when he came out, he knew it. It's funny. And it used to work like magic. He'd be crying, and I'd sing it, and he'd stop on a dime. Amazing.

You and Patti had a big wedding, didn't you?

It wasn't that big, about eighty or ninety people. It was at the house, and it was a great day. You get to say out loud all the things that bring you to that place. I'm now a believer in all the rituals and things. I think they're really valuable. And I know that getting married deepened our relationship. For a long time, I didn't put a lot of faith in those things, but I've come to feel that they are important. Like, I miss going to church. I'd like to, but I don't know where to go. I don't buy into all the dogmatic aspects, but I like the idea of people coming together for some sort of spiritual enrichment or enlightenment or even just to say hi once a week.

The fact that the country is spiritually bankrupt is something you've mentioned in connection with the riots in Los Angeles.

We're kind of reaping what's been sown, in a very sad fashion. I mean, the legacy we're leaving our kids right now is a legacy of dread. That's a big part of what growing up in America is about right now: dread, fear, mistrust, blind hatred. We're being worn down to the point where who you are, what you think, what you believe, where you stand, what you feel in your soul means nothing on a given day. Instead, it's "What do you look like? Where are you from?" That's frightening.

I remember in the early Eighties, I went back to the neighborhood where I put together my first band. It was always a mixed neighborhood, and I was with a friend of mine, and we got out of the car and were just walking around for about twenty minutes. And when I got back to the car, there were a bunch of older black men and younger guys, and they got all around the car and said, "What are you doing?" I said, "Well, I lived here for about four or five years," and I just basically said what we were doing there. And they said: "No, what are you doing in our neighborhood? When we go to your neighborhood, we get stopped for just walking down the streets. People want to know what we're doing in *your* neighborhood. So what are you doing in *our* neighborhood?" And it was pretty tense.

The riots broke out right after our second interview session. It was pretty frightening being in L.A. then.

It really felt like the wall was coming down. On Thursday [the day after the riots began], we were down in Hollywood rehearsing, and people were scared. People were really scared. And then you were just, like, sad or angry.

At the end of the Sixties, there was a famous commission that Lyndon Johnson put together, and they said it would take a massive, sustained effort by the government and by the people to make life better in the inner cities. And all the things they started back then were dismantled in the last decade. And a lot of brutal signals were sent, which created a real climate for intolerance. And people picked up on it and ran with the ball. The rise of the right and of the radical right-wing groups is not accidental. David Duke—it's embarrassing.

So we've been going backward. And we didn't just come up short in our efforts to do anything about this, we came up bankrupt.

We're selling our future away, and I don't think anybody really believes that whoever is elected in the coming election is going to seriously address the issues in some meaningful fashion.

On the one hand there seems to be a tremendous sense of disillusionment in this country. Yet on the other hand, it seems like George Bush could be reelected.

I think so, too—but not on my vote. People have been flirting with the outside candidates, but that's all I think it is. When they go put their money down, though, it always winds up being with someone in the mainstream. And the frustrating thing is, you know it's not going to work.

Do any of the candidates appeal to you?

What Jerry Brown is saying is true—all that stuff is true. And I liked Jesse Jackson when he ran last time around. But I guess there hasn't really been anyone who can bring these ideas to life, who can make people believe that there's some other way.

America is a conservative country, it really is. I think that's one thing the past ten years have shown. But I don't know if people are really organized, and I don't think there's a figure out there who's been able to embody the things that are eating away at the soul of the nation at large.

I mean, the political system has really broken down. We've abandoned a gigantic part of the population—we've just left them for dead. But we're gonna have to pay the piper some day. But you worry about the life of your own children, and people live in such a state of dread that it affects the overall spiritual life of the nation as a whole. I mean, I live great, and plenty of people do, but it affects you internally in some fashion, and it just eats away at whatever sort of spirituality you pursue.

Do you see any cause for optimism?

Well, somebody's going to have to address these issues. I don't think they can go unaddressed forever. I believe that the people won't stand for it, ultimately. Maybe we're not at that point yet. But at some point, the cost of not addressing these things is just going to be too high.

A lot of people have pointed out that rappers have addressed a lot of these issues. What kind of music do you listen to?

I like Sir Mix-a-Lot. I like Queen Latifah; I like her a lot. I also like Social Distortion. I think *Somewhere Between Heaven and Hell* is a great record, a great rock & roll album. "Born to Lose" is great stuff. I like Faith No More. I like Live; I think that guy [Edward Kowalczyk] is a really good singer. I like a song on the Peter Case record, "Beyond the Blues." Really good song.

How do you keep up with what's happening musically?

Every three or four months I'll just wander through Tower Records and buy, like, fifty things, and I get in my car and just pop things in and out. I'm a big curiosity buyer. Sometimes I get something just because of the cover. And then I also watch TV. On Sundays, I'll flick on *120 Minutes* and just see who's doing what.

Mike Appel, your former manager, has contributed to a new book ("Down Thunder Road: The Making of Bruce Springsteen") that essentially claims that your current manager, Jon Landau, stole you out from under him.

Well, that's a shame, you know, because what happened was Mike and I had kind of reached a place where our relationship had kind of bumped up against its limitations. We were a dead-end street. And Jon came in, and he had a pretty sophisticated point of view, and he had an idea how to solve some very fundamental problems, like how to record and where to record.

But Mike kind of turned Jon into his monster, maybe as a way of not turning me into one. It's a classic thing: Who wants to blame themselves for something that went wrong? Nobody does. It's tough to say, "Maybe I fucked it up." But the truth is, if it hadn't been Jon, it would have been somebody else—or nobody else, but I would have gone my own way. Jon didn't say, "Hey, let's do what I want to do." He said, "I'm here to help you do what you're going to do." And that's what he's done since the day we met.

Two other people who used to work with you, ex-roadies, sued a few years ago, charging that you hadn't paid them overtime, among other things. What was your reaction to that?

It was disappointing. I worked with these two people for a long time, and I thought I'd really done the right thing. And when they left, it was handshakes and hugs all around, you know. And then about a year later, *bang!*

I think that if you asked the majority of people who had worked with me how they felt about the experience, they'd say they'd been treated really well. But it only takes one disgruntled or unhappy person, and that's what everyone wants to hear; the drum starts getting beat. But outside of all that—the bullshit aspect of it—if you spend a long time with someone and there's a very fundamental misunderstanding, well, you feel bad about it.

You recently appeared on "Saturday Night Live." It was the first time you ever performed on TV. How did you like it?

It felt very intense. You rehearse two or three times before you go on, but when we actually did it, it was like "Okay, you've got three songs, you got to give it up." It was different, but I really enjoyed it. I mean, I must not have been on TV for all this time for some reason, but now that I've done it, it's like "Gee, why didn't I do this before?" There must have been some reason. And I certainly think that I'm going to begin using television more in some fashion. I think it's in the cards for me at this point, to find a way to reach people who might be interested in what I'm saying, what I'm singing about.

I believe in this music as much as anything I've ever written. I think it's the real deal. I feel like I'm at the peak of my creative powers right now. I think that in my work I'm presenting a complexity of ideas that I've been struggling to get to in the past. And it took me ten years of hard work outside of the music to get to this place. Real hard work. But when I got here, I didn't find bitterness and disillusionment. I found friendship and hope and faith in myself and a sense of purpose and passion. And it feels good. I feel like that great Sam and Dave song "Born Again." I feel like a new man.

■ **RANDOM NOTES** (September 17, 1992)

"I was in a blur for the first month," says Crystal Taliefero, the guitar and conga player cum saxophonist-singer who has been turning heads at Bruce Springsteen shows. "Bruce never does the same thing. We learn songs at sound check." And despite the accolades being lobbed at her, she oughta get used to staying on her toes when her boss designs the set list. "You have to keep it present and living," says Springsteen. "You can't let it get embalmed along the way."

■ **RANDOM NOTES** (November 26, 1992)

Bruce Springsteen jolted MTV execs, contest winners and audience dignitaries like Michael Stipe by delivering a fully amped, electric show for MTV's *Unplugged*. The ninety-minute performance also marked the eve of Springsteen's forty-third birthday.

■ **RANDOM NOTES** (February 18, 1993)

The new Stone Pony, in Asbury Park, New Jersey, was officially christened. In the middle of Southside Johnny and the Jukes' maiden set at the renovated club, Bruce Springsteen and Jon Bon Jovi joined in on a slew of Jukes standards. "Now that packed value for your buck," said Bon Jovi. "It felt great to let loose like in the old days."

THE 100 TOP MUSIC VIDEOS

VIDEO TRANSFORMED the making and marketing of popular music in the 1980s. ROLLING STONE examined the stars, the scripts and the stories of the very best music videos—Bruce Springsteen's "Atlantic City," "Brilliant Disguise" and "Rosalita (Come Out Tonight)" among the top 100.

#37 "Atlantic City"
Bruce Springsteen
1982

As if "Atlantic City" wasn't depressing enough already as a song, it had to be made into a video. Shot in hand-held black and white over a single day, it was directed by the head of Sony Music's creative services, Arnold Levine. "The whole idea was showing the disparity between the boardwalk and a block away from the boardwalk, after all those promises about how they were going to rebuild Atlantic City," Levine says. His drive-by documentary shows a day in the life of this town full of losers. The signs say it all: BALLY'S, SANDS, a bill featuring Paul Anka, Peter Allen and Dolly Parton and noble words about the public good inscribed on a building. Meanwhile, Springsteen wails his parable of "racket boys" and "sands turnin' to gold." He's not in this one, but every picture tells his story.   —*Rick Marin*

#64 "Brilliant Disguise"
Bruce Springsteen
1987

No babes, no cars, no band. Just one long close-up of Bruce Springsteen's angst-filled squint into the camera's unblinking eye. "Brilliant Disguise" is a song about lying and, says director Meiert Avis, "one of the things really good liars do is look you in the face." Shot with live vocals, it took twenty takes to get everything right. Springsteen subtly inflected his performance, Avis recalls, "from bitter to twisted to funny"—to truthful. Watch him sing, "Now you play the loving woman / I'll play the faithful man." If *Tunnel of Love* was his bummed-out wedding album, this is the wedding video: intimately emotional, starkly black-and-white. It's brilliant because of what it doesn't disguise.

—*Rick Marin*

#71 "Rosalita (Come Out Tonight)" Bruce Springsteen 1978

Filmed in the Phoenix Coliseum, this video, Springsteen's first, features one of rock's most legendary performers at a time when fans were still able to run onstage and kiss him. Performing "Rosalita (Come Out Tonight)," a song off his 1973 album *The Wild, the Innocent & the E Street Shuffle,* the twenty-something Bruce Springsteen is all goofy, giddy charm, leaping about the stage and making precious little effort to fend off the advances of female admirers emerging from the audience. Perhaps the most striking element of this performance clip, though, is the Boss' camaraderie with his E Street Band mates. "Bruce was the pivotal guy, the ringleader," says director Arnold Levine. "He created the energy between all the band members."

—*Elysa Gardner*

FRED GOODMAN

PRODIGAL SONGS

A TWO-CD SET OF EARLY STUDIO RECORDINGS by Bruce Springsteen is at the heart of a battle between the rocker and a new British record label.

A U.K. high court will soon decide the fate of *Prodigal Son,* a twenty-three-song collection slated for British and European release by Dare International. The album is billed as a mix of alternative versions of several songs that appeared on Springsteen's first two albums, plus numerous unreleased tracks. Originally set for a pre-Christmas debut, *Prodigal Son* was rescheduled for late January before the court granted Springsteen's request for an injunction staying the record's release. "These are not authorized recordings," says Steven Hayes, an attorney for Springsteen.

Gavin Dare, however, describes his release as "100 percent kosher" and says his company purchased the rights from a legitimate source and can demonstrate "a clear line of title." Although Dare would not name that source, several people involved in the court case identified it as Jim Cretecos, Springsteen's former co-manager. Cretecos, however, denies any involvement with the release. "I don't know about it," he says.

Among the well-known Springsteen songs slated for release are what Dare describes as studio demos of "4th of July, Asbury Park (Sandy)," "Growin' Up," "For You" and "Kitty's Back." Also included are sixteen previously unreleased songs, some of which have never even appeared on Springsteen bootlegs.

Dare International was formed solely to issue previously unreleased material by established artists. Dare says he has already acquired recordings for release by nine acts, which he would describe only as "known American performers."

One of those is the Grateful Dead. *Risen From the Vaults: 1970–'72* is slated as a future release and includes live and alternative studio recordings of such Dead classics as "Ripple" and "Sugar Magnolia." Like Springsteen, the Grateful Dead have asked Dare not to release the album. The group's attorney Hal Kant says he is waiting for Dare International to provide documentation of their rights to the recordings. Regardless of the validity of Dare's claims, the group—which, aside from being signed to Arista Records for new albums, releases historic live recordings on its own imprint—is expected to resist the album's release.

While Springsteen and his management have traditionally taken an aggressive stance against bootleggers and other record pirates, Dare represents something different: a legitimate and apparently well-financed company claiming legal title to the recordings it is releasing—albeit against the wishes of the artists.

"We represent an international music group spending millions to acquire intellectual-property rights," says Dare. "We own the property, and we have every right to put these albums out." The label has a distribution agreement in the U.K. with Total/BMG, a company co-owned by Bertelsmann Music Group.

Precisely when the Springsteen recordings were made may prove to be a key issue in determining whether *Prodigal Son* sees the light of day. Dare International maintains that the recordings predate Springsteen's 1972 signing to Columbia Records. A source close to Springsteen suggests the opposite, however, and Sony—which owns Columbia—is expected to join the suit against Dare.

■ **RANDOM NOTES** (March 24, 1994)

Bruce Springsteen's spare rendition of "Streets of Philadelphia" was a fitting overture to the annual benefit for AIDS Project Los Angeles, held at the Universal Amphitheater. The show, which raised $5 million, was crawling with Secret Service men (due to honoree Hillary Clinton) and divas (Liza, Whitney, Barbra).

PARKE PUTERBAUGH

GREATEST HITS ALBUM REVIEW

★ ★ ★

BRUCE SPRINGSTEEN is a peerless songwriter and consummate artist whose every painstakingly crafted album serves as an impassioned and literate pulse taking of a generation's fortunes. He is the foremost live performer in the history of rock & roll, a self-described prisoner of the music he loves, for whom every show is played as if it might be his last. Though some may argue the point, Springsteen single-handedly rescued rock & roll from its banal post-Sixties doldrums. Moreover, his music developed a conscience that didn't ignore the darkening of the runaway American dream as the country greedily blundered its way through the Eighties.

With the mighty exception of *Born in the U.S.A.,* however—a veritable greatest-hits album in itself—Springsteen's standing as a singles artist has seemed an incidental byproduct of his main focus: arraying his songs in theme-driven album-length statements. For this reason, *Greatest Hits* comes across as a collection of familiar songs, each stellar in its own right, that somehow adds up to something less than the sum of its parts—even with the grafted-on bonus of four new tracks recorded with the E Street Band.

First of all, this album is not even what it purports to be. A straightforward program of Springsteen's greatest hits would at least have had the virtue of a governing logic. Although some Bruce-smitten critic blessed with second sight will no doubt divine a wishful thesis about the "story" it tells, the simple fact is that *Greatest Hits* liberally violates its stated premise. Absent for reasons unfathomable are five Top Ten hits ("Cover Me," "I'm Goin' Down," "I'm on Fire," "War" and "Tunnel of Love"), as well as such essential charting singles as "Prove It All Night" (Number 33), "Fade Away" (Number 20) and "One Step Up" (Number 13). Also missing is anything preceding "Born to Run," which leaves out a big chunk of the Springsteen story. If the album's assemblers could find reason to include "Atlantic City," which failed to crack the Top 100, surely there was room for "Blinded by the Light" and "Rosalita (Come Out Tonight)." Those, too, rank among his greatest hits—ask anyone partial to FM radio or Springsteen concerts—despite the lack of corroboration from the charts.

In the early years of his career, a whole new palette of possibilities emerged from Springsteen's energetic vision—a playful, swinging landscape in which Bob Dylan met Roy Orbison at the Jersey Shore to a soundtrack produced by Phil Spector. All of that seemed to sour after *Born to Run* as Springsteen simultaneously fought a bruising legal battle with a former manager and tasted superstardom freighted with its share of hype. Thereafter, he began taking ever more penetrating and disillusioned looks into the troubled American psyche. His melancholy songs were often so intimate and personal (witness *Nebraska*) that the E Street Band eventually seemed an encumbrance, though he puffed out his chest for tours with them after the releases of *Born in the U.S.A.* and *Tunnel of Love*. In hindsight, *Greatest Hits* documents Springsteen's discomfort with the spotlight, the diminishing role of the E Street Band in his music and his rueful view of lives disintegrating against a backdrop of red, white and blues. After a certain point, he didn't want to be the Boss anymore.

By lining up a batch of Springsteen's biggest radio tracks, *Greatest Hits* unintentionally reveals a creaky, leaden quality that occasionally crept into the music he made in the post-*Born to Run* era. Plucked out of context, such popular hits as "Hungry Heart" and "Born in the U.S.A." sound stiff and muscle-bound now. The former is weighted by awkward lyrics ("Got a wife and kids in Baltimore, Jack") that sentimentalize abandonment, the latter grinds a ponderous riff into the ground, and both are stamped with a metronomic snare sound that's leagues removed from the natural swing of the band circa *The Wild, the Innocent & the E Street Shuffle*. The notion occurs that "Better Days," featuring one of Springsteen's most thoughtful lyrics, would have benefited from a subtler vocal treatment than the histrionic growl sustained throughout. And spanning twenty years, isolated from the albums that gave them meaning, these songs don't mix particularly well, nor do they portray a remarkable career in a flattering or accurate light. Every album Springsteen has made is best heard in toto; this vivisection is largely for dilettantes, come-latelies and radio programmers who wouldn't delve deeply anyway.

As for the four unreleased songs—three of them newly recorded with the E Street Band for this project—they sound more like a final coda than a new beginning. Two of them, "Secret Garden" and "Blood Brothers," are so restrained that the E Streeters' involvement adds nothing that session musicians couldn't have provided just as well with their competent anonymity. On "Blood Brothers," a barely electrified folk tune that recalls Dylan's *Blood on the Tracks,* Springsteen's harmonica is featured far more prominently than Clarence Clemons' sax or Nils Lofgren's guitar. The up-tempo songs—"Murder Incorporated" and "This Hard Land"—don't restore or redefine the band members' roles in any way that suggests they have a future together. "Murder Incorporated" (originally recorded in 1982 and remixed for this album) is broad and bombastic enough to be a hit, while "This Hard Land" repeats some of Springsteen's most pronounced tics—the use of rivers, seeds and rides as metaphors, the contrived device of addressing his words to some fictional "sir." Musically it begs comparison with Woody Guthrie's populist folk songs.

This may, in fact, be where Springsteen is headed. It wouldn't be surprising if, on his next travels, he walked alone with a guitar and harmonica for companions.

■ **RANDOM NOTES** (April 20, 1995)

When singer Dave Pirner announced, "We'd like to bring out a special guest," at Soul Asylum's surprise gig at Tramps, in New York, everyone expected Victoria Williams. Instead, plaid-shirt-about-town Bruce Springsteen jumped onstage for "Tracks of My Tears," then—pfft—he was gone. Soul Asylum, meanwhile, unveiled a ton of fresh material, including "Promises Broken," "Eyes of a Child" and "Just Like Anyone."

MIKAL GILMORE

THE GHOST OF TOM JOAD
YEAR-END ALBUM REVIEW

BRUCE SPRINGSTEEN'S BEST music has always been about the refusal to accept life's meanest fates or most painful limitations. Springsteen charges his audience to remain brave, despite all the disillusion, defeat, injustice and fear that invariably dog the pursuit of one's hopes. For more than twenty years now, Springsteen's music has worked as a cry of courage, an emboldening reassurance that life, no matter how closefisted it may seem, is worth keeping faith in.

The Ghost of Tom Joad tells a different story—or at least it looks at the story through different eyes. It's a record about people who do not abide life's ruins; it's a collection of dark tales about dark men who are cut off from the purposes of their own hearts and the prospects of their own lives. On this album almost none of the characters get out with both their bodies and spirits intact, and the few who do are usually left with only frightful, desolate prayers as their solace.

Plaintive, bitter epiphanies like these are far removed from the sort of anthemic cries that once filled Springsteen's music, but then these are not times for anthems. These are times for lamentations, for measuring how much of the American promise has been broken or abandoned and how much of our future is being transfigured into a vista of ruin. These are pitiless times.

The Ghost of Tom Joad is Springsteen's response to this state of affairs. Maybe it's even his return to arms. In any event, it's his first overtly social statement since Born in the U.S.A. The atmosphere created is as merciless in its own way as the world the lyrics describe, and you will have to meet or reject that atmosphere on your own terms. I'm convinced it's Springsteen's best album in ten years, and I also think it's among the bravest work that anyone has given us this decade.

Tom Joad bears an obvious kinship with Springsteen's 1982 masterwork,

Nebraska. The musical backing is largely acoustic, and the sense of language and storytelling owes much to the Depression-era sensibility of Woody Guthrie. The stories are told bluntly and sparsely, and the poetry is broken and colloquial—like the speech of a man telling the stories he feels compelled to tell if only to try to be free of them. On *Tom Joad,* there are few escapes and almost no musical relief from the numbing circumstances of the characters' lives. You could almost say that the music gets caught in meandering motions or drifts into circles that never break. The effect is brilliant and lovely; there's something almost lulling in the music's blends of acoustic arpeggios and moody keyboard textures, something that lures you into the melodies' dark dreaminess and loose mellifluence. But make no mistake— what you are being drawn into are scenarios of hell. American hell.

On the title track, a man sits by a campfire under a bridge, not far from the endless railroad tracks. He is waiting on the ghost of Tom Joad, the hero of John Steinbeck's *Grapes of Wrath.* But hopes of salvation in the mid-1990s aren't really much more palpable than ghosts, and you understand that the man sitting and praying by the fire will wait a long time before his deliverance comes. On "Straight Time," an ex-con takes a job, marries and tries to live the sanctioned life. But the world's judgments are never far off (even his wife watches him carefully with their children), and he waits for the time when he will slip back into the violent breach that he sees as his destiny and only hope.

The most affecting stories here, though, are the ones that Springsteen tells about a handful of undocumented immigrants and their passage into Southern California's promised land. On "The Line" (an achingly beautiful song with a melody reminiscent of Bob Dylan's "Love Minus Zero/No Limit"), "Sinaloa Cowboys" and "Balboa Park," Springsteen creates characters who come to their fates quickly without warning or drama. In one moment their "undocumented" lives are over, and the world takes no note of their passing or shot hopes.

By climbing into their hearts and minds, Springsteen has given voice to people who rarely have one in this culture. And giving voice to people who are typically denied expression in our other arts and media has always been one of rock & roll's most important virtues. As we move into the rough times and badlands that lie ahead, such acts will count for more than ever before.

PARKE PUTERBAUGH

DISCOGRAPHY

All releases are on Columbia Records, except where noted. Incidentally, every Bruce Springsteen album to date has been issued in LP, cassette and CD configurations.

ALBUMS

GREETINGS FROM ASBURY PARK, N.J.
(January 1973)

Tracks: Blinded by the Light; Growin' Up; Mary Queen of Arkansas; Does This Bus Stop at 82nd Street?; Lost in the Flood; The Angel; For You; Spirit in the Night; It's Hard to Be a Saint in the City

THE WILD, THE INNOCENT & THE E STREET SHUFFLE
(November 1973)

Tracks: The E Street Shuffle; 4th of July, Asbury Park (Sandy); Kitty's Back; Wild Billy's Circus Story; Incident on 57th Street; Rosalita (Come Out Tonight); New York City Serenade

BORN TO RUN
(September 1975)

Tracks: Thunder Road; Tenth Avenue Freeze-Out; Night; Backstreets; Born to Run; She's the One; Meeting Across the River; Jungleland

DARKNESS ON THE EDGE OF TOWN
(June 1978)

Tracks: Badlands; Adam Raised a Cain; Something in the Night; Candy's Room; Racing in the Street; The Promised Land; Factory; Streets of Fire; Prove It All Night; Darkness on the Edge of Town

THE RIVER
(October 1980)

Tracks: The Ties That Bind; Sherry Darling; Jackson Cage; Two Hearts; Independence Day; Hungry Heart; Out in the Street; Crush on You; You Can Look (But You Better Not Touch); I Wanna Marry You; The River; Point Blank; Cadillac Ranch; I'm a Rocker; Fade Away; Stolen Car; Ramrod; The Price You Pay; Drive All Night; Wreck on the Highway

NEBRASKA
(September 1982)

Tracks: Nebraska; Atlantic City; Mansion on the Hill; Johnny 99; Highway Patrolman; State Trooper; Used Cars; Open All Night; My Father's House; Reason to Believe

BORN IN THE U.S.A.
(June 1984)

Tracks: Born in the U.S.A.; Cover Me; Darlington County; Working on the Highway; Downbound Train; I'm on Fire; No Surrender; Bobby Jean; I'm Goin' Down; Glory Days; Dancing in the Dark; My Hometown

BRUCE SPRINGSTEEN & THE E STREET BAND LIVE/1975–85
(November 1986)

Tracks: Thunder Road; Adam Raised a Cain; Spirit in the Night; 4th of July, Asbury Park (Sandy); Paradise by the "C"; Fire; Growin' Up; It's Hard to Be a Saint in the City; Backstreets; Rosalita (Come Out Tonight); Raise Your Hand; Hungry Heart; Two Hearts; Cadillac Ranch; You Can Look (But You Better Not Touch); Independence Day; Badlands; Because the Night; Candy's Room; Darkness on the Edge of Town; Racing in the Street; This Land Is Your Land; Nebraska; Johnny 99; Reason to Believe; Born in the U.S.A.; Seeds; The River; War; Darlington County; Working on the Highway; The Promised Land; Cover Me; I'm on Fire; Bobby Jean; My Hometown; Born to Run; No Surrender; Tenth Avenue Freeze-Out; Jersey Girl

TUNNEL OF LOVE
(August 1987)

Tracks: Ain't Got You; Tougher Than the Rest; All That Heaven Will Allow; Spare Parts; Cautious Man; Walk Like a Man; Tunnel of Love; Two Faces; Brilliant Disguise; One Step Up; When You're Alone; Valentine's Day

HUMAN TOUCH
(April 1992)

Tracks: Human Touch; Soul Driver; 57 Channels (and Nothin' On); Cross My Heart; Gloria's Eyes; With Every Wish; Roll of the Dice; Real World; All or Nothin' at All; Man's Job; I Wish I Were Blind; The Long Goodbye; Real Man; Pony Boy

LUCKY TOWN
(April 1992)

Tracks: Better Days; Lucky Town; Local Hero; If I Should Fall Behind; Leap of Faith; The Big Muddy; Living Proof; Book of Dreams; Souls of the Departed; My Beautiful Reward

GREATEST HITS
(March 1995)

Tracks: Born to Run; Thunder Road; Badlands; The River; Hungry Heart; Atlantic City; Dancing in the Dark; Born in the U.S.A.; My Hometown; Glory Days; Brilliant Disguise; Human Touch; Better Days; Streets of Philadelphia; Secret Garden; Murder Incorporated; Blood Brothers; This Hard Land

THE GHOST OF TOM JOAD
(November 1995)

Tracks: The Ghost of Tom Joad; Straight Time; Highway 25; Youngstown; Sinaloa Cowboys; The Line; Balboa Park; Dry Lightning; The New Timer; Across the Border; Galveston Bay; My Best Was Never Good Enough

EPs

CHIMES OF FREEDOM
(September 1988)

Tracks: Tougher Than the Rest; Be True; Chimes of Freedom; Born to Run

SINGLES

Blinded by the Light/The Angel (1972)
Spirit in the Night/For You (1973)
Born to Run/Meeting Across the River (1975)
Tenth Avenue Freeze-Out/She's the One (1976)
Prove It All Night/Factory (1978)
Badlands/Streets of Fire (1978)
Hungry Heart/Held Up Without a Gun* (1980)
Fade Away/Be True* (1981)
Open All Night/The Big Payback* (1982, import only)
Dancing in the Dark/Pink Cadillac* (1984)
Cover Me/Jersey Girl (live) (1984)
Born in the U.S.A./Shut Out the Light* (1984)
I'm on Fire/Johnny Bye-Bye* (1985)
Glory Days/Stand on It* (1985)
I'm Goin' Down/Janey, Don't You Lose Heart* (1985)
My Hometown/Santa Claus Is Comin' to Town* (live) (1985)
War/Merry Christmas Baby (live)* (1986)
Fire/Incident on 57th Street (live)* (1987)
Brilliant Disguise/Lucky Man* (1987)
Tunnel of Love/Two for the Road* (1988)
One Step Up/Roulette* (1988)
Human Touch/Better Days (1992)
57 Channels (and Nothin' On)/Part Man, Part Monkey* (1992)
Streets of Philadelphia (1993) [Epic Records]
Murder Incorporated (1995)
Secret Garden (1995)

*Indicates songs or performances not found on any album

PROMOTIONAL AND AUDIOPHILE RELEASES (SELECTED)

"Circus Song" (live version of "Wild Billy's Circus Song" that appeared on *Playback*, a seven-inch promo-only EP also containing songs by Albert Hammond, Loudon Wainwright III and Taj Mahal; 1973)

"The Fever" (radio station promo-tape copy only, 1974)

"Spirit in the Night"/"Growin' Up"/"Rosalita (Come Out Tonight)" (seven-inch, 33 rpm promo-only disc, 1974)

Darkness on the Edge of Town (picture disc, 1978)

"Prove It All Night"/"Paradise by the 'C' " (live radio-only limited release, 1978)

"Devil With the Blue Dress Medley" (Asylum Records; released to radio stations as a twelve-inch single with a Jackson Browne B side in 1979)

Born to Run (half-speed mastered version, 1980)

Darkness on the Edge of Town (half-speed mastered version, 1981)

"Santa Claus Is Coming to Town" (released as a double-sided single in seven- and twelve-inch configurations to radio stations in 1981)

As Requested Around the World (Springsteen sampler album released to radio stations in 1981)

Born in the U.S.A. (five-song promotional mini-album, including the non-LP B sides "Shut Out the Light," "Pink Cadillac," "Jersey Girl" and "Santa Claus Is Comin' to Town," 1985)

REMIXES

Extended, revamped and remixed versions of Springsteen songs can be found on the twelve-inch singles for "Born in the U.S.A.," "Dancing in the Dark" and "Cover Me" and the CD single for "57 Channels (and Nothin' On)."

Appearances on Various-artist LPs

"Stay" and **"Devil With the Blue Dress Medley"** (These live tracks from the 1979 MUSE Concerts were included on *No Nukes*, a three-record set on Elektra/Asylum Records.)

"We Are the World" and **"Trapped"** (Springsteen is one of forty-five major artists who lent a hand to "We Are the World," a Number One single attributed to USA for Africa that appeared in 1985. The song, in which Springsteen was a featured soloist, appeared on both the single and album of the same name. The latter also included Springsteen and the E Street Band's searing version of reggae singer Jimmy Cliff's "Trapped.")

"I Ain't Got No Home" and **"Vigilante Man"** (Springsteen recorded these Woody Guthrie songs for the album *Folkways: A Vision Shared/A Tribute to Woody Guthrie and Lead Belly*, 1988.)

"Viva Las Vegas" (Springsteen recorded this for *The Last Temptation of Elvis*, a double album from 1990 comprising twenty-six versions of songs from Elvis Presley movies by various artists, including Paul McCartney and Robert Plant. It was issued in England by New Musical Express, with all proceeds going to charity.)

"Remember When the Music" (Springsteen contributed this version of a Harry Chapin song to the Harry Chapin Tribute album, Relativity Records, 1990.)

"Chicken Hips and Lizard Lips" (Springsteen's version of this children's song appeared on the benefit album *For Our Children*, Walt Disney Records, 1991.)

"Streets of Philadelphia" (From the soundtrack to *Philadelphia,* on Epic Records, 1993.)

"Dead Man Walkin'" (From *Music From and Inspired by the Motion Picture "Dead Man Walking,"* 1995)

GUEST APPEARANCES

Bruce Springsteen has contributed songs and/or vocals and/or guitar to recordings by a number of artists, most notably Southside Johnny & the Asbury Jukes. Nine songs written or cowritten by him have appeared on four Jukes albums: *I Don't Want to Go Home* (1976), *This Time It's for Real* (1977), *Hearts of Stone* (1978) and *Better Days* (1991). He also contributed lively reminiscences about the Jersey shore bar band scene in the liner notes on the jacket of the first Jukes album. He coproduced, played on and contributed songs to a pair of albums—*Dedication* (1981) and *On the Line* (1982)—by R&B survivor Gary "U.S." Bonds. Bonds has recorded ten otherwise unreleased Springsteen songs including "This Little Girl," "Your Love," "Dedication" and "Club Soul City." In addition, Springsteen sang with Graham Parker on the latter's "Endless Night" (from *The Up Escalator*, 1980) and played guitar on wife Patti Scialfa's *Rumble Doll* (1994). In September 1987, he was part of Roy Orbison's backup group at a memorable concert that was filmed for a Cinemax cable-TV special subsequently released as an album, entitled *A Black and White Night* (1989). Springsteen helped an old friend, Joe Grushecky, with his *American Babylon* album (1995), variously playing guitar, mandolin, keyboards, harmonica and percussion on eight of twelve tracks. He also produced the entire project and cowrote two songs, "Dark and Bloody Ground" and "Homestead."

Manfred Mann became the most successful interpreter of Springsteen's songs, recording "Blinded by the Light" (a Number One hit), "Spirit in the Night" and "For You" with his Earth Band. Other Springsteen songs that have been recorded by various artists include "Fire" (Robert Gordon; Pointer Sisters), "Because the Night" (Patti Smith Group), "From Small Things (Big Things One Day Come)" (Dave Edmunds), "For You" and "Rendezvous" (Greg Kihn), "Pink Cadillac" (Natalie Cole), "Protection" (Donna Summer), "4th of July, Asbury Park (Sandy)" (the Hollies), "Atlantic City" (the Reivers; the Band), "Reason to Believe" (Beat Farmers), "Johnny 99" (Johnny Cash) and "Born in the U.S.A." (Stanley Clarke). The last of these was parodied as "Born in East L.A.," by Cheech & Chong, and recast as "Banned in the U.S.A.," by Luke featuring 2 Live Crew. This is by no means an exhaustive list.

VIDEOGRAPHY

FULL-LENGTH VIDEOS

Video Anthology/1978–88
  (1989)
Songs: Rosalita; The River; Thunder Road; Atlantic City; Dancing in the Dark; Born in the U.S.A.; I'm On Fire; Glory Days; My Hometown; War; Fire; Born to Run; Brilliant Disguise; Tunnel of Love; One Step Up; Tougher Than the Rest; Spare Parts; Born to Run

Bruce Springsteen in Concert: MTV Plugged
  (1992)
Songs: Red Headed Woman; Better Days; Local Hero; Atlantic City; Darkness on the Edge of Town; Man's Job; Growin' Up; Human Touch; Lucky Town; I Wish I Were Blind; Thunder Road; Light of Day; Big Muddy; 57 Channels (and Nothin' On); My Beautiful Reward; Glory Days; Living Proof; If I Should Fall Behind ["Roll of the Dice" is additionally included on the 5MV laser-disc version.]

SINGLE-SONG VIDEOGRAPHY

"Rosalita (Come Out Tonight)"
  Date: 1978
  Director: Arnold Levine
  Location: Phoenix, AZ

"Atlantic City"
  Date: 1982
  Director: Arnold Levine
  Location: Atlantic City, NJ

"Dancing in the Dark"
  Date: 1984
  Director: Brian DePalma
  Location: Minneapolis, MN

"Born in the U.S.A."
  Date: 1984
  Director: John Sayles

"Glory Days"
    Date: 1984
    Director: John Sayles
    Location: Hoboken, NJ

"My Hometown"
    Date: 1985
    Director: Arthur Rosato

"War"
    Date: 1986
    Director: Arthur Rosato
    Location: Los Angeles, CA

"Brilliant Disguise"
    Date: 1987
    Director: Meiert Avis
    Location: New Jersey

"Human Touch"
    Date: 1992
    Director: Meiert Avis
    Location: New Orleans, LA

"Streets of Philadelphia"
    Date: 1993
    Directors: Jonathan Demme and Ted Demme
    Location: Philadelphia, PA

"Murder Incorporated"
    Date: 1995
    Director: Jonathan Demme
    Location: New York City, NY

"Secret Garden"
    Date: 1995
    Director: Peter Care
    Location: Los Angeles, CA

ABOUT THE CONTRIBUTORS

Lester Bangs was an editor at *Creem* for five years. He wrote about rock from 1969—when his first reviews appeared in ROLLING STONE—to his death in 1982, at the age of thirty-three. He is the author of *Blondie* and *Psychotic Reactions and Carburetor Dung,* a collection of essays.

Joe Breen wrote about rock & roll for *The Irish Times* from the late seventies to the late eighties. He is now the editor of electronic publishing at the newspaper but still contributes columns on world music and country music when not covertly listening to his son's grunge and Britpop CDs.

Debby Bull is a writer living in Montana.

Christopher Connelly, a former editor at ROLLING STONE, is the editor-in-chief of *Premiere* magazine.

Anthony DeCurtis is a contributing editor to ROLLING STONE. He is the editor of *Present Tense: Rock & Roll Culture* and coeditor of *The ROLLING STONE Illustrated History of Rock & Roll* and *The ROLLING STONE Album Guide.* He is the author of the introduction to *R.E.M.: The ROLLING STONE Files* and won a Grammy for his liner notes for the Eric Clapton retrospective *Crossroads.* He holds a Ph.D. in American literature from Indiana University.

Ken Emerson is writing a biography of Stephen Foster for Simon & Schuster.

Jim Farber is the pop music critic of the *New York Daily News.* His work has appeared in ROLLING STONE, the *Village Voice, Entertainment Weekly, New York* magazine and many other publications.

David Fricke is a senior editor of ROLLING STONE. He joined the magazine in 1985. He is also the American correspondent for the English music weekly *Melody Maker* and has written about music for *Musician, People* and the *New York Times*. He is the author of *Animal Instinct,* a biography of Def Leppard, and has written liner notes for major CD reissues of the Byrds, Moby Grape, John Prine, Led Zeppelin and the Velvet Underground.

Mikal Gilmore is a ROLLING STONE contributing editor and author of *Shot in the Heart.*

Merle Ginsberg is entertainment editor of *W* magazine and *Women's Wear Daily.* She has written about pop culture, from both coasts, for ROLLING STONE, *US, People,* the *Los Angeles Times, New York, TV Guide, McCall's, Newsday, Hollywood Reporter,* E! Entertainment Television, MTV, the *New York Daily News,* the *Village Voice* and the *Soho Weekly News.*

Michael Goldberg is a contributing editor at ROLLING STONE. He has also written about rock & roll, the music business and new technology for *Esquire, Wired, Mirabella, Musician* and other publications.

Fred Goodman is a freelance journalist and contributing editor to ROLLING STONE.

James Henke was on the editorial staff at ROLLING STONE from 1977 to 1992. During that time, he held a variety of positions, including managing editor, music editor and Los Angeles bureau chief. Coeditor of *The ROLLING STONE Illustrated History of Rock & Roll,* third edition, and *The ROLLING STONE Album Guide,* he is now chief curator of the Rock and Roll Hall of Fame and Museum.

Kurt Loder was an editor at ROLLING STONE from 1979 to 1988 and is still a contributing editor. He is the author of *I, Tina,* a best-selling biography of Tina Turner. He is currently an anchor of MTV News.

Greil Marcus is a contributing editor of ROLLING STONE. His books include *The Dustbin of History, Mystery Train, Lipstick Traces* and *Ranters & Crowd Pleasers,* which collects pieces following Bruce Springsteen through the Reagan era.

Dave Marsh edits *Rock & Roll Confidential* and has written and edited many books on popular music, including *Louie, Louie* and best-selling biographies of Bruce Springsteen and the Who. A *Playboy* music critic, he frequently lectures and writes about the relationship of music, politics and censorship.

David McGee is a regular contributor to ROLLING STONE and the co-author of *Go Cat Go!: The Life and Times of Carl Perkins, the King of Rockabilly.*

Jefferson Morley has been an editor for *Outlook,* the *Washington Post*'s weekly section of opinion and commentary, since 1992. An editor and reporter in the nation's capital since 1980, he has published investigative reporting, essays and interviews in the *New Republic,* the *New York Times,* the *New York Review of Books,* ROLLING STONE, *Spin,* the *Los Angeles Times,* and other national publications. He has written extensively about popular culture, racial issues, national security policy and Central America. He is the author of the introduction to *Rap: The Lyrics: The Words to Rap's Greatest Hits* (Penguin, 1992).

Paul Nelson has written about music for ROLLING STONE, the *Village Voice,* the *New York Times, Circus, Penthouse, Creem,* the *Real Paper* and the *Little Sandy Review,* which he cofounded in 1961.

Steve Pond is a ROLLING STONE contributing editor. His work also appears in the *New York Times, Premiere, Playboy, GQ* and the *Washington Post.*

Parke Puterbaugh is a longtime contributing editor and former senior editor for ROLLING STONE. He writes about music, travel and the environment for a number of other publications and is the coauthor of a series of travel books. He lives in Greensboro, North Carolina.

John Rockwell is a cultural correspondent, critic at large and principal recordings reviewer for the *New York Times;* from 1974 to 1980 he was also chief rock critic. Between early 1992 and mid-1994 he was based in Paris as European cultural correspondent. He has published two books, *All American Music,* a study of American composition from classical to experimental to Broadway to jazz to rock, and *Sinatra: An American Classic,* and has contributed widely to magazines, anthologies and encyclopedias.

Fred Schruers is a contributing editor at ROLLING STONE.

Rob Tannenbaum is a frequent contributor to ROLLING STONE, *GQ, Entertainment Weekly,* the *New York Times, Vogue,* the *Village Voice* and *Details,* among other publications.

READ THE BOOK THAT BRUCE SPRINGSTEEN REDISCOVERED . . .

JOURNEY TO NOWHERE
The Saga of the New Underclass
by Dale Maharidge, with photography by Michael Williamson
Introduction by Bruce Springsteen

Read the book that inspired Bruce Springsteen to write several of the songs that now appear on his 1995 album, *The Ghost of Tom Joad*. Through meaningful photographs and elegant prose, *Journey to Nowhere* takes a stunning look at the American underclass, and invites the reader to discover what it's like to suddenly be counted as one of the homeless. Also included in this edition are the lyrics to Springsteen's inspired songs.
[$17.95 (Canada $23.95); ISBN 0-7868-8204-2]

"It doesn't really tell you what to think, it just shows you things: This is what we found, this is what is out there. . . . It's a very powerful book, it should be out there, it should be read."
　　　　　—Bruce Springsteen, in an interview with the *Washington Post*

IN BOOKSTORES EVERYWHERE FROM HYPERION

OTHER BOOKS IN *THE ROLLING STONE FILES* SERIES

U2: The ROLLING STONE *Files*
By the Editors of ROLLING STONE
Introduction by Elysa Gardner
The ultimate compendium of articles, interviews and indispensable facts for
the die-hard U2 fan. This book covers everything about the band, from the
group's beginnings as a punk band in Dublin to susperstardom and the Zoo
TV Tour. From album reviews to fascinating snippets of trivia, learn all there
is to know about one of the hottest bands of the past two decades, from the
original rock & roll magazine.
[$12.95 (Canada $15.95); ISBN 0-7868-8001-5]

Neil Young: The ROLLING STONE *Files*
By the Editors of ROLLING STONE
Introduction by Holly George-Warren
Rock & roll will never die and neither will the amazing influence of Neil
Young. ROLLING STONE has chronicled this rock icon since its third issue
in 1967, covering his stint with Buffalo Springfield, his years of fame with
Crosby, Stills, Nash and Young, his early solo successes and later years of com-
mercial eclipse and his mainstream reemergence with songs like "Rockin'
in the Free World."
[$12.95 (Canada $15.95); ISBN 0-7868-8043-0]

R.E.M.: The ROLLING STONE *Files*
By the Editors of ROLLING STONE
Introduction by Anthony DeCurtis
Unmatched in depth and information, this compendium covers everything
from R.E.M.'s early days in Athens, Georgia, and years of nonstop touring
to the band's commercial breakthrough in 1991 with *Out of Time* and the
1994 release of the guitar-blasting *Monster*. Incisive Q & A interviews with
Michael Stipe and Peter Buck, in addition to news stories, album reviews
and performance critiques, make this a must-read for every true R.E.M. fan.
[$12.95 (Canada $16.95); ISBN 0-7868-8054-6]

IN BOOKSTORES EVERYWHERE FROM HYPERION